BEEN DOON SO LONG

RANDALL GRAHM

BEEN DOON SO LONG

A RANDALL GRAHM VINTHOLOGY   FOREWORD BY HUGH JOHNSON

UNIVERSITY OF CALIFORNIA PRESS   BERKELEY LOS ANGELES LONDON

University of California Press, one of the most distinguished university presses in the United States, enriches lives around the world by advancing scholarship in the humanities, social sciences, and natural sciences. Its activities are supported by the UC Press Foundation and by philanthropic contributions from individuals and institutions. For more information, visit www.ucpress.edu.

University of California Press
Berkeley and Los Angeles, California

University of California Press, Ltd.
London, England

We are grateful to the following artists for permission to reprint their work: Bascove, Central Coast Syrah Le Pousseur label, p. 23, Il Circo Uva di Troia label, p. 23; Wendy Cook, Roussanne label, p. 19, Viognier label, p. 19; Chris Freire and Bob Johnson, Ca' del Solo Albariño label, p. 26; Heather Gray, 1984 Pinot Noir label, p. 11; Alex Gross, illustrations on pp. 28, 31, 36, 40, 52, 56, 59, 66, 72, 76, 89, 101, 112, 117, 128, 131, 134, 137, 140, 144, 148, 150, 152, 156, 159, 162, 164, 169, 171, 174, 177, 179, 184, 186; Paul Sale Vern Hoffman/Corbis, fractal pattern, pp. ii, viii, xii, 10, 106, 190, 210, 242, 266, 309; Chuck House, 1990 Chardonnay La Reina label, p. 11, Old Telegram label, p. 13, 1934 Cigare Volant label, p. 14, 2005 Cigare Volant label, p. 14, Clos de Gilroy label, p. 15, 1993 Muscat Canelli label, p. 17, 2002 Muscat Vin de Glacière label, p. 17, 2003 Muscat Vin de Glacière label, p. 18, Le Sophiste label, p. 18, Ca' del Solo Malvasia label, p. 20, Ca' del Solo Il Pescatore label, p. 20, Big House Red label, p. 21, Ca' del Solo Nebbiolo label, p. 21, Pacific Rim Riesling label, p. 24; Alex Krause, photograph of *Chàteauneuf du Papers Rhônely Hearts Club Band*, p. 196; Ed Piskor, *Doon to Earth*, pp. 262–63; Ralph Steadman, 2002 Cardinal Zin label, p. 22, 2005 Domaine des Blagueurs label, p. 22; Gary Taxali, Freisa label, p. 25.

"Biodynamic" is a registered trademark of the Demeter association of biodynamic farmers.

Text: 11/15.5 Requiem
Display: Knockout, Benton Gothic, Requiem
Designer: Nola Burger
Compositor: Integrated Composition Systems
Printer and binder: Golden Cup Printing Co., Ltd., China

Library of Congress Cataloging-in-Publication Data

Grahm, Randall, 1953–
    Been doon so long : a Randall Grahm vinthology / Randall Grahm ; foreword by Hugh Johnson.
        p.   cm.
    Includes bibliographical references.
    ISBN 978-0-520-25956-0 (cloth : alk. paper)
    1. Wine and wine making—Humor.   2. Wine and wine making—Miscellanea.   I. Title.
    PN6237.G73   2009
    818'.607-DC22   2009003864

Manufactured in China

18   17   16   15   14   13   12   11   10   09
10   9   8   7   6   5   4   3   2   1

The paper used in this publication meets the minimum requirements of ANSI/NISO z39.48–1992 (R 1997) (*Permanence of Paper*).

FOR JOHN LOCKE

Contents

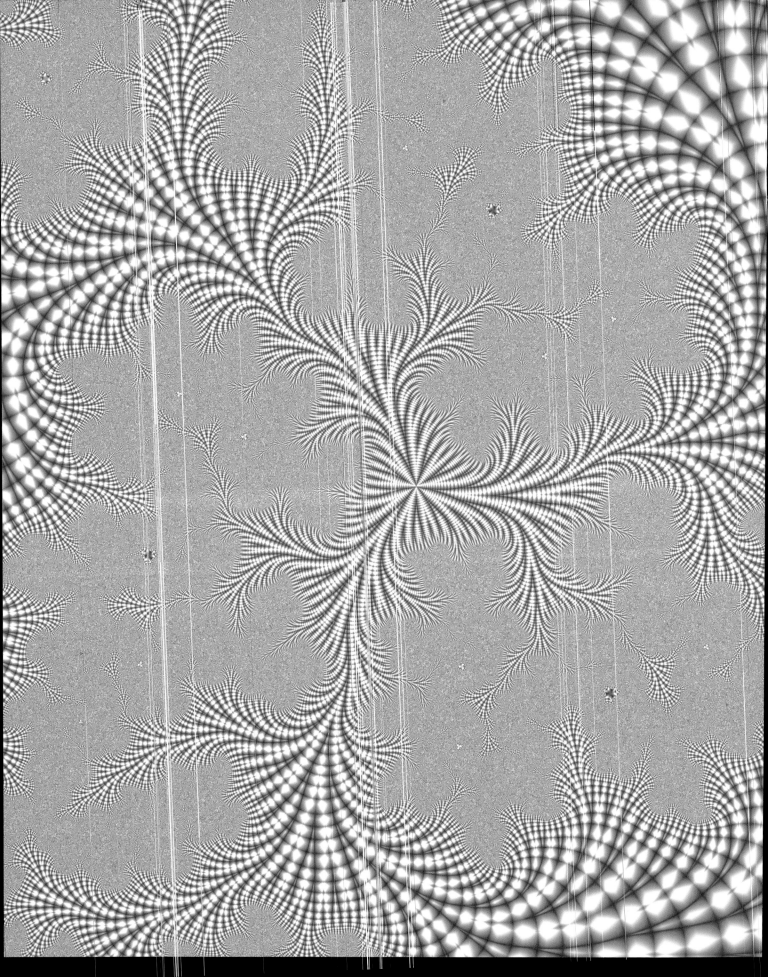

Foreword

HUGH JOHNSON

Wine needs words. Without an accompanying script, it stands little chance of being noticed. Oh yes, it may be swallowed. It will have its effect all right. But will anyone focus on it, identify it, or share any thoughts about it? And what are thoughts without words? Appreciation starts with a name, and it deepens as we deploy more words—of definition, of description, of attraction or dislike. In the end, after the grower has had his say, the winemaker has spouted, and the critics have spilled their adjectives, there is a tidy bit of text attached to anything in a bottle. A pity most of it is so dull, so repetitive and uninspired.

Who are the people who surround wine with its accompanying texts? Publicists, professional educators, technicians, and people like me (eunuchs in a winery but all-too-potent once the wine is made). I can think of only one person who has conceived the wine and made it, then given us both barrels: his reasons and opinions. Randall Grahm stands alone.

He is an opinionated fellow. He uses logic where others follow fashion. Is California like Bordeaux or Burgundy? No? Then why grow the grapes of Bordeaux or Burgundy there? The southern Rhône is close in climate; plant the vines that make its sturdy, friendly, undemanding reds and whites, then see what fine-tuning in California can make of them.

Grahm first became known to the wine world as the Rhône Ranger, the man who made Rhônish wines and gave them a Wild West name. His sense of humor wouldn't let him leave it at that. Almost alone in California's wine world, he saw the funny side of an industry that takes itself very seriously. He saw swollen egos, slaves to fashion, hypocritical opinions, technical incompetence, dreadful wines at absurd prices, and the phenomenon of Robert Parker— and it set him writing.

To start with, it was his sales pitch: funny words for funny (by the standards of the time) wines. Schoolboy humor was definitely in, scatology sometimes not far off: that was pretty different. His writing wouldn't be collected in an anthology now, though, if Mr. Grahm were not an instinctive creative writer in the high satirical tradition. The wine business has not had an Alexander Pope or a Jonathan Swift before. Grahm started with parodies of texts that would be known to his hoped-for customers (he hoped), then ludicrous adaptations of literary classics, until he had T. S. Eliot in the bag and Dante in his gun sights. By the time you reach the Vinferno, you know this guy is serious—and seriously funny.

He is also shy. He feels isolated: one of a handful of Californians of academic bent who see the whole wine picture, see its anoraks in their absurdity and its snobs in their snootiness as standing in the way of honest-to-god enjoyment. He is self-conscious enough to present his astonishing oeuvre as a sort of a literary exercise book—indeed, as a course in oenology and parody rolled into one. He recoils from the marketplace, yet he is drawn to it. So he sets up his stall on the edge—knowing him, near the john.

Finally, he is a philosopher. By the end you are privy to his obsessive need to relate wine to the cosmos via vines and soil and sweat. Many people talk about *terroir.* Grahm dreams it and would bleed it if you cut him.

I was baffled at first. Then I saw his feelings about Chardonnay turn into biting satire and his views on scoring explode into righteous wrath, while all the time he was laughing—sometimes hysterically—and I laughed too. Then I started to ponder. So, I promise, will you.

Acknowledgments

TO ALISON DAVIES, who helped enormously in whipping the book into a presentable form, sparing me the great embarrassment that otherwise would have ensued.

TO THE EDITORIAL STAFF OF UNIVERSITY OF CALIFORNIA PRESS, who took on the nontrivial risk of publishing a text as eclectic and slightly edgy as this one.

TO BONITA HURD, THE COPY EDITOR FOR THIS BOOK, whom I have yet to meet in person but whom I worship from a discreet distance.

TO ROBERT LESCHER, MY AGENT, who has given me very sage advice, some of which I have heeded.

TO GUY MILLER, M.D., PH.D., for many, many hours of discussion about redox chemistry and other subjects, but mostly for his constant encouragement and sincere engagement.

TO PATRICE RILEY, MY EXECUTIVE ASSISTANT, for her infinite patience, wonderful attitude, and superb attention to detail.

TO MY COLLEAGUES PAST AND PRESENT at Bonny Doon Vineyard and loyal customers who have dutifully fastened their seatbelts and exulted in the wild ride.

TO MY FAMILY, for their love and unwavering support.

All errors, be they of grammar, usage, typography, or just plain delusional thinking, remain my own.

Introduction

Bonny Doon Vineyard, which I began out of a raging obsession with the possibility of producing great Pinot Noir in the Santa Cruz Mountains, has become a hoary—your orthography may vary—institution. Both Bonny Doon and the obsession continue unabated, having undergone all manner of transformation—progression, digression, and certainly at times, regression, evidenced by the occasionally puerile quality of the humor found herein. Indeed, our highly eclectic, off-the-beaten-path approach to winemaking and wine marketing has been somewhat of a calling card. And while the slightly manic quality of the marketing effort may have in recent years gotten a bit ahead of itself—the words seemingly more clever than the wines—I am lately trying to find the appropriate balance that one seeks in a well-made wine or a well-lived life.

It has been an extraordinary ride. When I first thought to make winemaking my career, I was thoroughly naive about (a) the absolute, wrenching difficulty (and ruinous expense) of producing consistently superlative wine,[1] and (b) the inordinate amount of effort utterly irrelevant to the winegrowing process itself[2] required to promote those wines, which might fall

---

1. My early successes (read: great luck) and the general availability of excellent, reasonably priced grapes in the early 1980s gave me the erroneous belief that the wine game was a relatively easy and straightforward one. The great disparity between what was required to produce consistently great wine and my relatively limited resources, both technical and financial, led me to the interim, if largely unsatisfactory, solution of producing solid, drinkable, albeit *terroir*-deficient, "good value" wine throughout the 1990s and the early part of the current century. (*Terroir* is the quality of a wine that derives from the unique set of geophysical properties of the site of its origin, rather than from the stylistic imprint of its maker.) On the plus side, the wines have always been intellectually interesting though, just between us chickens, incontrovertibly *vins d'effort* rather than true *vins de terroir*. It is now my resolute intention to produce wines genuinely expressive of a place, or to at least go doon swinging.   2. By this I mean: beating the bushes to scare up publicity; fabricating marketing materials (some included herein); traveling far and wide to do an endless number of promotional events, meet-the-freakin'-winemaker dinners, salesperson "work-withs" (aka "ride-alongs"), decorous presentations of the wines at corporate sales meetings, and so on. There is, by the way, nothing quite like getting up in front of a hundred or so wine salespeople at 3:30 on a Friday afternoon in the overheated and airless salesroom of one's XXL-sized wholesaler in [insert your unnamed southeastern state here] in midsummer for optimal effect. The salespeople—some bright, fresh-faced (at least earlier in the day they were) young'uns, others antique warhorses one step ahead of the glue factory—are compelled to attend these monthly mandatory sales meetings under threat of immediate retribution from their district supervisors and have already spent the better part of the day being lectured to, cajoled, and bullied by a procession of midtier supplier (winery, distillery, and importer) reps, typically regional sales managers (or RSMs), many, if not most, of whom are preternaturally tan, exceptionally well-fed examples of Italo-American pulchritude, who must in fact be utterly *schvitzing*, what with the dark shirt, suit, and tie and one to two kilos of supererogatory gold chain. The supplier reps, one's programmatic antecedents, have been trotted out in seamless and infernal succession at brisk fifteen-minute intervals since 8:30 A.M. and have been imparting vital intelligence on such diverse sub-

short of the excellence anticipated in criterion *a*. For if one were to produce a wine that was eloquent in the expression of its uniqueness, complete unto itself, there would be little need for a winemaker to attend the endless skein of meet-the-winemaker dinners, or to rack his or her brain for vivid and compelling descriptors of the results of his or her stylistic labors, as there would be, at least in principle, scores of others to rhapsodically exalt the juice in question. So you could say that much of the writing in this collection emerged from the fact that the wines were not as brilliant as I wanted them to be.[3]

If I began writing at least partially as a means to promote the wines, I eventually found that the writing itself met certain creative needs not being fully realized in the cellar. I don't mean to reduce the creative mystery to a matter of mere hydraulics here, but there seems to have been a compensatory mechanism at work, with the complexity and intensity of the writing varying more or less inversely with the complexity and intensity of the wine. As I learn to become a better winemaker and perhaps a better writer, these dual efforts may soon complement rather than compete with each other. The winemaking has lately become deeper, less baroque, and more from the heart. It would be a beautiful thing if the writing were to move in the same direction.

You have in your hands a collection of Doonian ephemera, much of it derived from the mostly semiannual winery newsletter published since 1987[4]—literary parody (*ficciones* and poesy), song lyrics, sundry bits of marketing schtick, and some earnest articles and lectures, with appended sagacious commentary, as the mists of Briga . . . , make that *Bonny* Doon, have cleared. I've in-

jects as one company's new discount structure, including its so-called family plan (and you wonder whose family—Tony Soprano's?); another company's SPAs, or special product allowances (essentially, legal kickbacks), available for an exciting new Bulgarian product range; and another's exciting sales promotional drive (a weekend getaway to the Bahamas awarded to the distributor's most productive salesperson) to insure the ubiquity of Wrongo Dongo "endcaps" (wine or liquor boxes case-stacked at the ends of store aisles) in every Winn-Dixie, Crown Beverage, and other grocery chain and big-box outlet in this vast, palmetto-bug-infested state. Most recently, a pair of impossibly tall, strikingly Swedish twins (this actually had the effect of abruptly if temporarily rousing some of the narcoleptic salesmen from their torpor) dilated (in their fifteen-minute window) on the unique qualities of cloudberry-flavored vodka. In these presentations, wines (or spirits) were never vulgarly referred to by their own names, but rather were signified by the generic term *product,* and the wines themselves never appeared to come from a particular locale but rather seemed to be affiliated with some sort of vaguely mysterious "program." When one's moment had at last arrived to address the now seriously sagging sales force and imbue them with all the esprit and excitement that one personally felt regarding the new and vital changes at one's slightly eccentric Santa Cruz–based winery, to affirm one's commitment to mineral-intensive, *terroir* wines expressive of place, this plenum of Pinotage, Puligny, and Pine Ridge pedlars had already *plotzed,* more thoroughly depleted than an empty warehouse, their qi, their vital life force, having gradually just oozed out of them like the seepage through the cork of a fine red Burgundy inadvertently left in the backseat of one's car on a warm summer's afternoon.   **3.** While the wines themselves were not consistently great, I had also tackled a category (Mixed Reds—Other) that was, in fairness, in need of substantial explanation. This raises the question of whether I chose such an obscure category so that I might be required to write as much as I have.   **4.** Ostensibly the newsletters treat the winery's produce and its significant business developments, but often they're so dyspeptic and kvetchy they might truly be said to be nooseworthy.

2

Introduction

cluded a long retrospective article on our unique wine labels, which are a splendid lens through which to view the history of the company, with all its ups and doons. If you closely read both the "creative works" and the essays, you will observe a gradual maturation of both writing style and understanding of the significant issues—more existential than technical—in the modern world of wine.[5]

My early literary output was that of a restless "enthusiast" (this was before attention deficit disorder gained such prominence in the diagnostician's lexicon), and it mirrored the manic and wacky experimentation occurring in the winery itself.[6] The mercantile motive behind the early creative pieces was not particularly well disguised, but this was, after all, a newsletter written with the intent to sell wine. In my defense, these pieces did not reflect naked hucksterism for its own sake, but were the result of a deep, instinctive feeling, almost a biological imperative, that I needed to do everything I could possibly imagine, to pull out all the stops, to insure that my bonny bairn would survive and flourish.

With the help of my family, I planted a smallish, thirty-acre vineyard in 1980, in the eponymous hamlet in the Santa Cruz Mountains, with the naive intention of producing the Great American Pinot Noir. In retrospect, I almost got it right, but found that the northern Rhône grape varieties were a far better fit with the growing conditions we enjoyed,[7] and we produced some lovely wines from those Estate grapes until the vineyard inexplicably perished of Pierce's disease in the mid-1990s.[8] From the outset, I couldn't wait to gain more experience as a winemaker,[9] so in 1981 I began to make wine from grapes purchased from contract growers, initiating my career with a most inauspicious and best forgotten Pinot Noir. Fortuitously, the fol-

5. I seem to have found my literary voice as a parodist, and perhaps the same could be said, in a slightly different sense, for me as a winemaker as well. All New World winemakers suffer from grave anxiety about the influence of the Old World, and their efforts cannot but appear to be mimetic, at least to themselves. The great "issues" are essentially philosophical ones: Why make (or drink) wine? What does great wine have to teach us? How might one create a truly original wine, and how would one recognize it if one did? **6.** In the totally risk-averse twenty-first century, who could now possibly imagine producing a wine for commercial release called Le Canard Froid, a fizzy red Pinot Meunier; or La Garrigue, a barrel-fermented French Colombard chaptalized with honey? (Jean-Antoine Chaptal, a contemporary of Pasteur, advocated the addition of sugar [preferably cane rather than beet, and never honey] to augment the alcoholic content of a wine when the grapes were slightly underripe.) I might also mention our *Auslese*-styled Syrah; our carbonically macerated Riesling; a Carignane/Orange Muscat blend; a Pinot Gris (the "Gonzo") fermented to dryness on skins, a procedure not commonly used with white grapes; wine *tisanes,* infused with rocks (the TTB [Alcohol and Tobacco Tax and Trade Bureau] really freaked out about that one); Sangiovese and rose petal jelly; and so on. **7.** The theme of utter contingency in determining the appropriateness of one grape variety or rootstock or clone over another on any given site is a recurring one and thoroughly colors my wine-worldview, as well as keeps me up at night. **8.** The demise of the Bonny Doon Estate Vineyard, the sacred place where I had come to Make My Statement, was undoubtedly the "wound," in the parlance of depth psychology, that has most profoundly affected my career as a winemaker. This setback most likely led to the fifteen-year detour from confronting my fate, which appears, at least as far as I can tell, to be the sincere pursuit and discovery and planting of a vineyard in the New World suitable for the expression of place. **9.** My formation as a winemaker was, truth be told, somewhat cursory, and I am especially fortunate not to have made more egregious mistakes

lowing year I found some wonderful old-vine Grenache in the Hecker Pass area of Gilroy, and this became the basis for Le Cigare Volant, our *hommage* to Châteauneuf-du-Pape. We produced this wine for the first time in 1984 and continue to produce it to this day. Why does anyone continue to do what one does, but for intermittent positive reinforcement?[10] I have been intermittently positively reinforced for the work we have done with Rhône varieties in the past twenty-five years, so I've stubbornly kept at it.

The scope of operations at the winery changed dramatically over the years. From a very small base, it grew . . . and grew. There were more than a few missteps along the way. At one point, I thought to move the winery to Pleasanton, and this was duly reported in the wine press but, alas, was never to be.[11] We have experimented with an eclectic range of grape varieties and a panoply of winemaking styles and techniques. (This is like saying that Don Giovanni had a *few* amorous interests.)[12] We have worked extensively with a range of Italian grapes; collaborated with producers in Spain, Italy, and France and imported their wines; perfected some innovative methods—for example, cryoextraction for our dessert wines and microoxygenation for our reds—and worked to repopularize Riesling (for all the right Rieslings) as a viable category in the New World. With the help of my colleagues, Bonny Doon grew into an impressive marketing company, one informed by interesting and vital winemaking ideas, to be sure. We were particularly successful with the Big House brand, a "superpremium generic" in insider wine-marketing parlance. In 2004, Bonny Doon Vineyard was noted as the twenty-eighth largest winery in the United States.

All was particularly vine and dandy, apart from the nagging feeling that in recent years the company and I had both lost our way. I have always had something like a European palate, favoring balanced, more discreet wines with a certain mineral edge that are, at their best, original—that is, deriving from a discernible *somewhere*—but these were, alas, not the wines I was making. Further, the practice of biodynamics—focusing on more natural, less adorned wine, more expressive of place than of the winemaker's art—had grown increasingly more important to me. I had been in the habit of giving speeches and writing essays (many of them collected in this book) about the uniquely special quality of *terroir* expressed in the world's most interest-

in my earliest efforts. I worked but one year as an assistant winemaker at Dick Smothers's winery in the Santa Cruz Mountains and then set out on my own, eager to make the world safe for New World Pinot Noir.   **10.** I was very lucky to have been given an invitation to appear on the cover of the *Wine Spectator* as the polyester-clad "Rhône Ranger" for the April 1, 1989, edition. Perhaps this led to the widespread and erroneous public perception of me (and one that I've likely internalized) as an unregenerate jokester. My relations with the *Spectator*, one of the most influential wine publications in America, have been complex, to say the least.   **11.** This (at the time) revolting development is treated in the essay "The Almost Pleasanton Years." I reckon that perhaps 10 percent of our customers still imagine that we relocated from Santa Cruz (where the sixties are still alive) to Pleasanton, a bastion of corporate Republicanism.   **12.** This tendency toward *Wanderlust,* or the compulsion to crush every odd grape I encounter, was identified early on and is treated in "Don Giovese in Bakersfield."

ing wines, and yet if I were totally honest with myself, there was little in my actual deeds that reflected this sensibility. I had recently turned fifty, fathered a child, and survived a serious health crisis. The universe was trying to tell me something: it was time to change my ways.

At first it appeared likely that I would have to sell the company, as there seemed to be no real, elegant way to dramatically change its focus. We had gone too far down the road with long-term contracts for our growers—many of whom were unreconstructed and, frankly, unreconstructable. There presented just one small problem: Bonny Doon had evolved/mutated into such a singular and byzantine white elephant that we couldn't find anyone interested in actually *buying* it.[13] In the end, in 2006, we sold two of our large brands, reconstituted the Pacific Rim brand, ceased the imports, trimmed the product portfolio, and rolled up our sleeves in preparation for the hard work of making really distinctive wines. We are, as of this writing, in escrow to purchase a beautiful three-hundred-acre property in San Juan Bautista, not far from Santa Cruz, with the intent to site our winery there, along with a proper, biodynamic farm and vineyard. The seemingly never-ending quest to find this land is chronicled in "In Search of a Great Growth in the New World." The epilogue to this volume will be written in wine-dark ink.

There are some recurring themes in my writing: the banality of Chardonnay, the pretentiousness of Napa Valley, the banal pretentiousness of Napa Valley Chardonnay, the hidden dangers of Merlotnoma; these themata are essentially doon to a turn in these pages. The simplistic, somewhat reductionist ABC[14] rant does in fact grow incrementally more articulate in the later pieces, and leads to a heartfelt cry for tolerance of diverse wine styles and the oddball grape varieties. My genuine love and esteem of *terroir,* the Old World notion that a wine might reveal the eternal characteristics of the place from whence it arises, should also shine through in these pages; it is a beacon that draws me ever forward despite the daunting difficulty of its discovery and expression. Indeed, the improbability of the discovery and the articulation of *terroir* is undoubtedly the font of my existential angst, the vinous equivalent of the horror of *Deus absconditus.* My path to a sincere commitment to *terroir* and a decision to finally put aside my childish winemaking toys—the technological solutions that allow one to make universally appealing wines—is treated in "Da Vino Commedia: The Vinferno," the real centerpiece of the book, as well as its moral center.[15]

Enfin, the core issue of this book is a formulation of "to be or not to be." Are my colleagues and I willing to risk great failure by attempting to produce a wine that could in some sense be called "authentic"—that is, expressive of qualities that transcend the winemaker's control: the

---

13. I imagined a kind of O. Henry, "Ransom of Red Chief," scenario, with the buyer of the company calling me up a few days later and asking me to please take it back.   14. "Anything But Cabernet" (or Chardonnay). This overly simplistic formulation, a response to the ubiquity of the aforementioned varietal wines, is itself as easy as A, B, C . . .   15. I have been perhaps unfairly harsh on some colleagues (though not without the leavening of humor), and have tried to be equally rigorous with myself, whom I have consigned to multiple vinfernal quadrants for my zins.

vagaries of vintage; the stubbornly persistent organoleptic attributes associated with particular soils and *climats*?[16] Or do we wish to play it safe and resort to winemaking "tricks"—that is,
gross manipulations in the vineyard and cellar that enhance the likability of the wine and hence
its likelihood of commercial success? How can we resist the siren song of the popular "international style"—a style that appears to be appreciated without reservation by the most influential wine critics? One way to read the "sober" essays in this book, particularly the one on making "great" wine in the postmodernist world and the several meditations on the meaning of *terroir,*
is to imagine them as Hamlet-like soliloquies—rehearsals, if you will—employing the bravado
of language in advance of the gut-wrenching boldness of the actual deed itself.

Then there is my obsession with the unfairness and myopia of those wine critics who seem
insensitive to elegance, finesse, and wine's potential expression of place. Winemakers who do
not produce preternaturally dense, blockbuster wines often feel the need to trot out such buzz-
words in their own defense, with the certainty that the rare products of their sanguinary, sy-
ringadenous, and lachrymal fluids have been greatly misunderstood and undervalued. I dilate
at great length on the utter inadequacy of point scores (*pointillisme*) to address the unique attributes of "quieter" wines, and remark continually about the inherent strangeness of great wine
and its sensitive, chameleon-like nature. We Americans insist on "value" in our wines, and it
is an unfortunate misunderstanding that greatness in wine equates to high impact and intensity; quantity has become synonymous with quality, as if the brilliance of a musical composition were to be conveyed by how loudly the composition is played.

I can almost plot the gradual diminuendo—visualize a *New Yorker* cartoon with a medical
chart trending doonward—of Bonny Doon's point scores in the *Wine Advocate* and *Spectator* with
the correspondingly increasing shrillness of the *Geschrei*—this is Yiddish for *cri de coeur*—of what
I am calling the *blues*letters, although it is by no means obvious which party contributed most
to this dysfunctional relationship, and which was the more grievously maligned or injured. I
suspect, though, that it was my juvenile and clearly obsessive provocation of Robert Parker and
the relevant editorial personages of the *Wine Spec* that set the unfortunate tone.[17] It is certainly
possible that their lack of enthusiasm for our wines in recent years derives from genuine aesthetic differences (or presumably the possibility of intermittent or perhaps perma-suckiness
of the wines themselves). In candor, my indulgence in *ressentiment* has not reflected well on me.
This foolishness reached its acme (and presumable culmination) with the final installment of
"Da Vino Commedia: The Vinferno."

But my compulsion to protest, to provoke, to challenge authority, especially that of the arbiters of taste, has greatly waned; the fever, in some sense, has broken. It is of absolutely min-

---

16. Schistose soils, for example, impart a strong, almost diesel-like quality to the wines that is not universally
appealing and yet is an absolute indication of "typicity."   **17.** I am sorry, Robert, not to have been more of
a mensch and taken your well-founded criticism constructively.

imal interest to me now to court the goodwill of the wine press[18] or to go out of my way to provoke its ire. There is so much more important work to be doon, and this new and challenging path does not allow for the luxury of a nice, juicy feud.

There is an old joke that goes something like this: Men talk to women to get women to sleep with them, and women sleep with men to get men to talk to them.[19] The urge to write pieces such as the ones in this book came from the same place as the desire to create both wines and wine labels that delight, that are filled with the thoughtful surprises and hidden gifts that a lover would offer to please his inamorata. A wine made with the intention to caress the consumer's palate derives from the same impulse as the lover's effort to impel his or her partner to exquisite distraction.

In sifting through the vast oeuvre of Dooniana to come up with this collection, I was struck by the fact that if one-tenth of the effort that went into writing all these pieces had been used to focus on growing grapes and making wine, there might already be a Grand Cru (or Grahm Crew) Pinot Noir somewhere in the Santa Cruz Mountains. As dedicated as I am (most of the time) to the pleasure and delight of the imbiber of both Bonny Doon wine and prose, the winemaking has clearly been a pretext for me to force my customers to read or listen to my endless screeds, rants, diatribes, and philippics. Maybe this is because writing is relatively easy for me, and serious winemaking—the kind that involves immense concentration and attention to detail—is more difficult. The characters that appear in the fictional works in this book are generally autobiographical renderings of myself—Don Giovese, J. Alfred Rootstock, Don Quijones, the pale protagonist of "Barberafish," and of course the winemaker-poet of "The Vinferno."

While the seemingly unbounded self-absorption and shameless exhibitionism may at times be a bit wearying, you will find here an honest account of a soul's journey toward deeper meaning and its search for a greater connection to wine's animating brilliance, the profound truth of *terroir*. It was a happy accident for me to discover winemaking as a métier; winemaking and the culture of wine provide a unique and powerful language that carries the rich metaphoric suggestion of the sweetness and strangeness of life itself.

18. This of course is patently false, but I sincerely do aspire to a benign indifference to their perfumed whisperings.   19. I agree with Roland Barthes that the impulse to write is connected to the desire to bring pleasure and delight (*jouissance*) to another human being.

HOW TO TELL A BOOK
BY ITS COVER

The Etiquette (and History) of the Bonny Doon ETIQUETTE

I am going to Wine Hell for what I have wrought in the world of wine labels. (Perhaps like Don Giovanni, I'll find that the exquisite pleasure I derived on earth from my reprehensible behavior will be of some consolation as I endure my eternal torment.) It all began quite innocently. I decided some years ago to become a winemaker: I was going to grow grapes and make great wine. As for a label, I'd just find someone, ideally a friend, who would not charge me much to design something simple and elegant. How hard could that be? An old girlfriend initiated the design of the first Bonny Doon label, with some additional assistance from a local graphic artist. ("Creative differences" did not do much for our relationship.)

It was indeed a simple, elegant label modeled on the classic Burgundian paradigm, as I wanted the world to know how sophisticated were both the wine and its maker. We continued with this template for our Monterey County La Reina and Estate Chardonnay until the last vintage of La Reina in 1990, for which we created a special "end of the line cuvée" label. Even in those early days, the Bonny Doon style exhibited a certain self-dramatizing theatricality; the disappearance of the Chardonnay from our product portfolio was not something I was going to countenance without some sort of ironic metacommentary.

So, the original business plan, if one could call it that, was to produce in bonny Bonny Doon (a lovely remote mountain hamlet) a brilliant Pinot Noir; the world's appetite for it would be so unappeasable that there would be little for me to do but blissfully and meditatively tend my vines, well removed from the wine-swilling rabble. I would periodically visit the bank to deposit the passel of checks and money orders that would clog my mailbox. I hadn't actually planned for the contingency of the wines not being so great, and it didn't take long to realize that the quality of the Pinot Noir wines made from the Bonny Doon Estate Vineyard was not going to make the likes of Henri Jayer and Aubert de Villaine fearful of a brash new competitor.

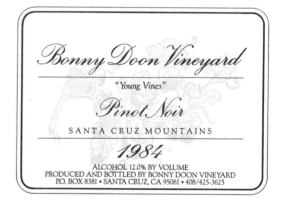

(We ended up grubbing up the Pinot noir vines and replacing them with Rhône varieties.) I played around a bit with Grenache in 1982 and came up with the idea of blending it with Cabernet Sauvignon. I gave the wine the very simple, unpretentious name of Vin Rouge, assuming that the wine-buying public greatly appreciated laconic understatement.

The wine was not too bad—I had lucked into finding some brilliant old vines—but clearly I had something to learn about marketing. The life of this winemaker was definitely not going according to plan. For one thing, a lot more time interacting with the generally uncomprehending hoi polloi seemed to be necessary to sell any wine at all.

By 1984 the idea had entered my brain that calling a wine "Vin Rouge" might not be the most compelling sales proposition, and that if I wanted people to actually buy the wines, I might think about giving them some sort of conceptual hook, or at least a stylistic referent. It's important to remember that, when I started working with Rhône grapes, they were essentially an unknown commodity in the United States. It was clear that I would have to do something outlandish, even outré, with the packaging (a practice that is now commonplace) to draw attention to the wine, because labeling it straight would be equivalent to printing the labels with disappearing ink. When people ask me how I come up with the ideas for labels (what I think they are actually asking is, how do I come up with the ideas for such outlandish labels), I tend to answer facetiously, "Drugs." But the reality is quite simple. I found, to my surprise, that I enjoyed being a show-off, at least in the labeling department. You learn that you have a particular talent for something, and you go with it; the problem arises when the exercise of the talent becomes an end in itself.

So, perhaps a blended wine that was not such an arrant mongrel would be a more successful sales proposition than a Vin Rouge, *tout court*. Why not contrive to make a California Châteauneuf-du-Pape, or at least an *hommage* to one? I would compose the wine around George Besson's lovely (still extant) old-vine Grenache in Gilroy,[20] but I would need Syrah and Mourvèdre as well if this was going to be a proper Rhônish blend.[21] Unbelievably, there were only three Syrah vineyards in California in the early 1980s; the Estrella River Vineyard down in Paso Robles, although manifestly not Côte Rôtie, seemed as if it might work for my purposes. Lastly, Darrel Corti, the brilliant polymath Sacramento wine merchant, had clued me in to the fact that Mourvèdre was alive and well on our shores and traveling under the *nom de vigne* of

20. David Bruce had in fact made a superb full-bodied varietal Grenache in the early 1970s from a vineyard located not far from this one, and this was a great source of encouragement for my project. The fact that I had been able to find bottles of his wine still on the shelves some twelve years after its release *should* have told me something about the commercial viability of domestic Grenache-centric wines, but I was largely oblivious. 21. There is, for me at least, a bit of awkwardness in determining what to call the category of California wines made from Rhône grapes. *California Rhônes* seems vaguely oxymoronic, if not misleading, and the analogous term for, say, a domestic Sangiovese, *Cal-Ital,* is downright lame. I am a lone voice in the wilderness but would submit that the term *meridional* would fit the bill for sun-loving grapes grown anywhere in the world below the forty-fifth parallel.

Mataro—I found a small plantation in San Martin and would later find a larger enclave in the sleepy Sacramento Delta town of Oakley. I was in business; it remained only to find a catchy name.

I had been hanging around Kermit Lynch's tiny wineshop, then located in Albany, near Berkeley, soaking up his enthusiasm for the great wines of the Rhône, and thought: Why not spoof Vieux Télégraphe, a classic Châteauneuf? I imagined a label that looked like an old telegram with strips of paper (the message) seemingly glued to the telegram itself. I wasn't sure exactly how the copy would read but loved the idea of using the word *STOP* in lieu of a period. (I vaguely recalled a Marx Brothers routine using telegramese to set up a joke.) We had already

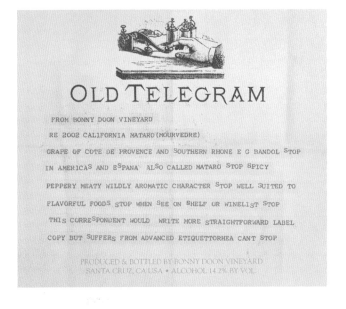

fermented the grapes in 1984 when I picked up a copy of John Livingstone-Learmouth's *The Wines of the Rhône* and leafed through the chapter on Châteauneuf. (If I was going to make wine in this style, a little education was in order.) There I learned about the bizarre local French ordinance prohibiting the landing of flying saucers and "flying cigars" in these Rhône vineyards, and I was utterly charmed.

Perhaps a label that treated this goofy ordinance would be a broader, more inclusive joke than a spoof of Vieux Télégraphe, a wine that was then known essentially only to wine geeks, and the aim, of course, was to educate the American public about the virtues of this largely unknown category, the wines of the Rhône. The problem when you try to make a reference to an Old World style using Old World language on a New World product is that you typically come off as being derivative and pretentious, as is evident in all the Châteaux Quelque-chose and Domaines de N'importe-quoi of Napa Valley. With Le Cigare Volant, a certain ironic distance was perfectly established—the wine bears a relationship to the French product but also maintains an appropriate separation. Oh, those wacky French.

My wine broker in Northern California, Alexia Moore, put me in touch with Chuck House, the now world-famous label designer, who had up to that point designed but one wine package, the beautiful, award-winning Frog's Leap label. I met Chuck at a coffeehouse in Santa Rosa—it seemed that he generally preferred meetings out of his office—and we instantly hit it off. Chuck is shy, and I think he appreciated my unpolished, somewhat socially inept style. In our years of association, we generally followed the same pattern, typically meeting in coffeehouses in Santa Rosa or Petaluma, occasionally in restaurants, and sometimes even on the side of the road. Since neither of us is particularly well organized, we would often forget to bring along the requisite production materials—wine bottles, Scotch tape, and so on—to use

1984

LE CIGARE VOLANT

RED TABLE WINE
CALIFORNIA

PRODUCED & BOTTLED BY BONNY DOON VINEYARD
SANTA CRUZ, CA USA • RED TABLE WINE • CONTAINS SULFITES

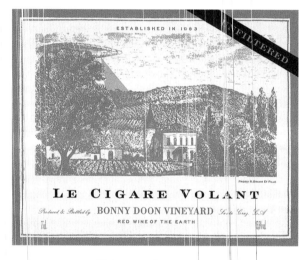

on the design prototypes. As a matter of course, the elements at hand (ketchup bottles, napkins, the ketchup itself) were pressed into service *à la minute* to mock up the design.

With Le Cigare Volant, I wanted the label to embody a subversive attitude (evidenced by the sinister UFO) but, at the same time, maintain a certain "classic" look. If you're going to be wacky, the customer has to have some assurance that you're not totally untethered. We talked about commissioning an etching for the label, but the cost was prohibitive, so we ended up appropriating elements of various illustrations from a very old (1855) illustrated book on Bordeaux. Chuck is a brilliant *bricoleur,* someone who can cobble together disparate design elements. He found an illustration of a Jules Verne–era airship that he set in the clouds, but since it wasn't sinister enough when sited so visibly, I asked him to make the tree a bit taller so the Cigare might lurk conspiratorially behind it. Chuck is a designer, not an illustrator, so the tree is not exactly anatomically correct, but I just love the label.

Both Chuck and I adore the heterogeneous typography one finds on many European labels, undoubtedly the result of a succession of regulations imposed by governmental authorities, as well as by the weight of historical accretion—changes in ownership, redistricting, and so on. Recently we decided to update the Cigare label, giving it a slightly more elegant look and making it decidedly more faux-French.

While "Le Cigare Volant" was a clever name for a Châteauneuf-inspired New World blend, I hate to waste a perfectly good packaging idea, so we pressed "Old Telegram" into service as a label for our varietal Mourvèdre. Strictly speaking, this was not the most analogous translation, as the *encépagement,* or varietal mix, is one found more typically in, say, Bandol, the great Mourvèdre-based wine from Provence. But the label is still wonderful. Chuck created the irregularities in the font by using an antique typewriter, and we embossed the labels to give relief to the telegraphic strips.

A label I greatly miss is the one we did for Clos de Gilroy, a wine made primarily from Grenache. This wine originally was conceived as a default blend incorporating the various lots of Grenache from vineyards located "close to Gilroy" (get it?), which were good but somehow not quite good enough (Clos but no Cigare) for inclusion in the final Cigare blend. I had initially imagined the label looking like a French *carte de visite*—again, an *hommage* with an ironic twist. (If one knows Gilroy, a rather sleepy agricultural town in the lower Santa Clara Valley, one appreciates the glaring incongruity.) When Chuck brought back the first draft, the label looked a bit austere. I told him, "It needs something, Chuck, but what?" We concluded that what it needed was a picture of a French person, and the most iconic French-looking person we could think of, apart from Charles de Gaulle, was Marcel Proust. This adds a slightly subversive Dada-like quality to the package. "Le gil des rois. Le roi des gils" is a spoof on the inscription that one sometimes sees on a Châteauneuf label. ("Le vin des rois. Le roi des vins.")

Because I am not gifted with much business sense, especially in such niggling matters as cost containment, Bonny Doon has never been a particularly profitable institution. But I do have an inventive flair, and I have on multiple occasions come up with Rube Goldberg–like strategies for enhancing the company's profitability—machinations that would not have been necessary in the first place had the company been more efficiently organized. It occurred to me that wineries have a lot of expensive equipment—tanks, presses, pumps, and so on—that is typically used intensively during the fairly short fall grape harvest, but that sits idle for much of the rest of the year. If we didn't limit ourselves to *grapes,* perhaps we could widen that window. Thus we produced Framboise, an "infusion of raspberry," for many years, buying raspberries from nearby Watsonville, until I discovered the wondrous raspberries of Washington State, which were much tastier. And we could process the berries in July before the grape harvest or freeze them and process them at our leisure.

The Framboise "infusion" was composed of several varieties of raspberry that seemed to do well in Washington. I couldn't figure out how to improve it—something I always wished to do with all our products—until I met Patrick Moore, a plant breeder at Washington State University, who allowed me to taste the results of his field trials of hundreds of different sorts of raspberries, some wild, and some new hybrids. This particular day was arguably—alongside the day of my daughter's birth—one of the best days of my life. The wild varieties were, not surprisingly, the most intense, but they were all very, very small and, hence, "uncommercial."

One hybrid I particularly enjoyed had a spicy wild flavor and was reasonably large in size. I persuaded Mike Youngquist, our grower, to consider planting the new variety for us. Now came the business of giving the new raspberry a name, which devolved to the plant breeder. "This is the part that I don't really like," said Patrick.

2004

Clos de Gilroy

LE GIL DES ROIS
LE ROI DES GILS

CALIFORNIA
GRENACHE

PRODUCED AND BOTTLED BY BONNY DOON VINEYARD
SANTA CRUZ, CA, U.S.A. ◆ ALC. 13.5% BY VOL.

"I'm just a farmer. I can never think of really clever names for all these raspberries." "Why don't you name your raspberries after dead young rock stars, Patrick?" I asked innocently. "You could have the Hendrix, the Joplin, the Cobain . . ." I don't think he took my advice completely, but in recent years we've made Framboise from the intense and flamboyant "Morrison" raspberry.

Following the logic of expanding the window of harvest, it occurred to me back in 1986 that we might consider producing a faux "ice wine" by freezing grapes in a commercial freezer. I thought these frozen grapes might behave a lot like the ones that naturally freeze on the steep hillsides of Germany and other extreme northern climes—that is, they might yield a concentrated nectar when pressed while still partially frozen. (As the temperature of the cluster drops, the liquid freezes within the berry before the sugar syrup freezes, and the ice remains frozen when the sugar syrup has thawed, thus naturally concentrating the sweetness of the expressed juice.) Moreover, picking grapes on a relatively flat surface during the day, when the sun was shining, would be a lot easier than picking them on a steep, slippery slope, sometimes in the middle of the night, when it was bloody cold. At the time, I hadn't heard of the process called cryoextraction, but I couldn't imagine why artificially freezing grapes wouldn't have the same effect as naturally freezing them. In any event, some sort of test was in order, as the grapes I wanted to use for this wine were just days away from harvest. I went to the nearby Safeway, bought ten pounds of Thompson seedless, put them in the freezer, and, after they had frozen, set them in a little press, squeezed, . . . and nothing came out. Well, no matter. Eventually we worked out that the grapes had to thaw a bit for the process to work. There certainly was a steep learning curve in mastering the process. For a while, the wine was made at Wente Vineyard in Livermore, and the first attempt to scale the process up, by putting the grapes in one of their large bladder presses, resulted in the creation of an iceberg the size of a Volkswagen, which wreaked a fair bit of havoc within the press. Over the years we ended up buying the Wentes several new bladders for their presses, replacing the ones we had torn and mangled.

It seemed logical to not compete directly with the Germans or the Sauternais, so I thought to make our "ice wine" from Muscat grapes rather than from Riesling, Sauvignon blanc, or Sémillon, though eventually we tried all those (and more). When we began, I naively called the wine Vin de Glace, and the Bureau of Alcohol, Tobacco and Firearms initially approved the label; then it came to their attention that "vin de glace" actually meant "ice wine." This was nomenclature exclusively reserved for wines made from grapes that had frozen on the vine rather than in a freezer in Castroville, California. The label approval was officially rescinded with due ceremonial sword-breaking and the stripping of epaulets. We resubmitted the label as Vin de Glacière, or "Wine of the Icebox," and have experienced no regulatory contretemps—at least regarding frozen grapes—since then.

The original suite of labels for Vin de Glace (or Glacière) was beautiful, stylish, indeed classical; these were the early days, and I hadn't yet thought to break the rules. But the labels were

1993

Muscat Canelli

Bonny Doon Vineyard

VIN DE GLACIÈRE

Muscat Canelli

1993 CALIFORNIA MUSCAT CANELLI • RESIDUAL SUGAR 21% BY WT.
PRODUCED & BOTTLED BY BONNY DOON VINEYARD
SANTA CRUZ, CA • MADE FROM POST-HARVEST FROZEN GRAPES
ALCOHOL 12.2% BY VOLUME • 375 ml.

an utter pain to apply to the bottles themselves, as there were three pieces to perfectly align on each tall, skinny, elegant—imagine Audrey Hepburn in stiletto heels—but terribly wobbly 375 milliliter "flute" bottle. We were using an older technology at the time—paper labels applied with glue—and could never work out how to get the labels to line up properly or how to keep them from thoroughly disintegrating when the bottle was placed in an ice bucket. (In retrospect, using a different kind of paper probably would have helped.) When we changed to a new bottling line, we decided to go with self-adhesive labels, a product of a new technology—you couldn't get the wonderful range of paper textures, sigh, but the labels were so much easier to apply. Alas, on our new machine we no longer had the option of applying three front labels, so it was time for another meeting with Chuck.

André Ostertag had sent me a few bottles of a *vendange tardive* wine that he had made, with some actual dirt from his vineyard glued to the bottles. (Don't ask me how they ever cleared U.S. Customs!) Inspired, I became possessed with the idea of incorporating some element of the wine itself into the package and thought that perhaps we could make our own paper, using the grape skins themselves. Now, handmade paper is enormously expensive to produce, and the technical problems of printing on it and hand applying it to individual bottles would likely have made the company instantly insolvent. Cooler heads prevailed. Chuck made some paper with Muscat skins and took a picture of it, and that became the basis of the label—a fiscally sound compromise, but somehow the truly distinctive element was lost. In the final design stages of the label, one of his children apparently spilled some extremely dark liquid on the House family carpet, giving Chuck the idea to create a Pollock-like counterpoint to the grape paper, and a richer surface on which the gold ink might be laid down. I confess I have never been particularly fond of this iteration of the Vin de Glacière label; it reminds me too much of a crime scene.

Ultimately it came time to redesign the label again, and we sought a way to recapture some of the elegance of the first Vin de Glacière package. I honestly can't recall whether it was Chuck's idea or my own—we had become like an old couple whose ideas seemed to flow effortlessly from one to the other—to employ *female undergarments* as part of the label design. Maybe we were overly reliant on a fairly standard advertising ploy, but I imagined it could be done tastefully, almost subliminally, to interesting effect. The mesh pat-

tern of the clear acetate label would offer a tantalizing, peekaboo view of the golden nectar that languorously reposed within. Chuck deputized me to go out and bring back frilly, lacy women's undergarments so we could construct some prototypes. I ended up visiting a small—*intimate* is the only way to describe it—undergarment boutique in San Francisco owned by Carol Doda, the legendary North Beach stripper. "I want to look at some panties and maybe a mesh brassiere," I told her. "What size do you take, dear?" Ms. Doda asked me. "It's, um, not for me, you understand . . . ," I stammered. "It's for an . . . um, art project, you see." "That's all right, dear . . . "

The wine did incredibly well for us for many, many years, and appeared on scores of restaurant wine lists, with labels that came and went. And no one really seemed to worry as much as we did about the outward appearance of the bottle.

Chuck loves European art from the 1920s—Dada and Deco, Picasso and Braque, the Constructivist school—and can brilliantly mimic almost any style. We produced a wine called Le Sophiste, a putative blend of Roussanne and Marsanne, grown at our Estate Vineyard in Bonny Doon. No one, of course, had ever heard of either grape variety, so it seemed necessary to bang the drum a bit louder and do something outrageous. Monsieur Sophisto, as we came to call him, does bear a passing and somewhat unfortunate resemblance to Mr. Peanut, but he is, *au fond,* the embodiment of sophistication. The Sophists, just for the record, were a group of philosophers whose name came to be associated with trickery and false reasoning. The word *sophistication* itself has a lovely ambiguity in its application to wine—where it can connote either vinous elegance or a wine that has been "enhanced" in a putatively Barry Bonds–like sense. The bottle came equipped with a plastic top hat in lieu of a foil. This touch was too outlandish for sommeliers with delicate sensibilities and allergies to kitsch. When we sold the wine to Charlie Trotter's, Larry Stone, the restaurant's sommelier and wine buyer at the time, primly insisted that the top hats be replaced with conventional foils, and of course we complied.

Alas, the wonderful Bonny Doon Estate Vineyard succumbed to Pierce's disease, but before it did, we took some cuttings from our "Roussanne" vines and had them planted in the vine-

yard of our friend Chris Couture in Paso Robles.[22] The wine eventually made from those vines was quite good, but not as classical as Le Sophiste, so we decided to give the package a different look. I met a wonderful calligrapher, Wendy Cook, who had never designed a wine label before, but who did an extraordinary job drawing Cyrano for us. We produced our "Roussanne" for a couple of years, until we learned that the grape was in fact not Roussanne but rather Viognier. A label change was indicated, and Cyrano became Pinocchio. If you look very, very carefully, you will see the mirror image of the word *Roussanne* in the nostril of Pinocchio.[23]

I have always sort of felt my way along in the wine business but have not, alas, had a great grasp of business fundamentals. I initiated the brand Ca' del Solo with the intention of representing a range of Italian grape varieties, primarily sourced from our own vineyard in Soledad in Monterey County. We had terrible luck obtaining consistent quality from the multifarious, historically untested *uvaggi* we grew there; ultimately it was more cost-effective to purchase these Italianate varieties from outside growers rather than to grow them ourselves. We have worked with a fair number of different Italian grapes—Aglianico, Arneis, Barbera, Dolcetto, Erbaluce, Freisa, Moscato Bianco, Moscato Fior d'Arancio, Nebbiolo, Pigato, Pinot Grigio (that's slightly cheating, of course, but we gave it a shot), Refosco, and of course, Sangiovese. But none of the wines did well for us commercially—I think we pretty much overwhelmed our distributors' ability to absorb these oddball wines—apart from the improbable Malvasia Bianca, which won a considerable cult fol-

19

22. Pierce's disease is a serious, generally fatal bacterial disease that clogs the xylem tissue of grapevines and is transmitted by insects known as sharpshooters, which typically live in a riparian habitat proximal to the infected vineyard. Our vineyard was wiped out by the wimpier of the two identified vectors, the blue-green sharpshooter—the one that doesn't fly so well or far and is a less voracious feeder than the more aggressive glassy-winged sharpshooter. This revolting development made me give up hope of growing grapes in Bonny Doon at least at that time, and led me to sell the former vineyard property.   23. I must confess to a certain puerile satisfaction in sneaking things past bureaucratic regulatory bodies such as the Bureau of Alcohol, Tobacco and Firearms. My colleagues in the wine business are somewhat astonished that I have been able to seemingly get away with murder for so long. I honestly don't know how we have been so fortunate in getting away with what we have, at least as far as packaging, and I am certain that somewhere in Washington, D.C., there is a very thick dossier on Bonny Doon. I once asked our BATF liaison, Ann Morse, to approach the bureau with a particularly outlandish proposal for a highly dicey experimental winemaking protocol, one that would undoubtedly bring down the full weight of the G on the proposer, unless the matter were handled with utmost discretion. "I have a client who wishes to remain nameless, and proposes to do x, y, and z with his wine," Ann told a representative of the bureau. "Absolutely no way on earth," she was told, "and say hello to Randall for us, if you would."

lowing. Malvasia Bianca, the grape, is in fact not a true Malvasia, but is most likely Moscato Greco, a naturally high-acid, relatively simple Muscat from Piemonte. The wine we made was distinctive by California standards, and the label was charming.

Originally it was my intent that all the Ca' del Solo labels would depict individuals more or less acting *al solo,* doing difficult or challenging things that one could only do for oneself, by oneself. This is the first day of school for little Malvasia, and, having just let go of her mother's hand, she is systematically stepping on every crack in the sidewalk. At the time we first released this wine, I was seeing a woman who had a young daughter just beginning first grade, who was the model for little Malvasia, even down to the detail of sidewalk-crack-stepping. People have told me that Malvasia reminds them of both Eloise and Madeline; she appears to me to be a composite of the two, which seems to reinforce her archetypal quality.

It was a passing fantasy that all the Ca' del Solo labels would somehow link to one another in a continuous tableau, but this never quite happened. Maybe we got off-track when we first produced Il Pescatore, a high-concept, premium white blend. I remembered from my experience with Vin Rouge that the public was not quite ready for a totally generic blended wine. Any conceptual hook that one could provide (the Fisherman) would help reel in the potential consumer, who was generally pretty much at sea vis-à-vis the vast ocean of wine labels. Il Pescatore wasn't, in fact, much of a fish wine. We couldn't seem to keep the acidity in the wine; neither was it particularly Italianate—at a certain point, it actually contained a fair bit of Chardonnay. But it was a beautiful, fun package. Gio, the little boy, is fishing (on his own),

Etiquette (and History)

and while he doesn't catch a fish, he does manage to catch a boot, Italia, which is a great metaphor for precisely what had happened to me. The "boot" is printed on the back of the back-label, so one observes it from the front as a sort of underwater diorama. We did go through a rather protracted phase of wine labels that were visible through the bottle. Maybe this was a marketing schtick that proclaimed, "Notice me, notice me," but it also more subtly suggested the presence of a deeper layer of meaning to the wines, below the obvious surface.

We produced this Ca' del Solo Nebbiolo label only once, but it is perhaps my favorite in the Ca' del Solo series, and it was our first attempt to give these labels more of a fine art look. Chuck continued to work in the scratchboard cartoon vernacular, but the illustrative reference to commedia dell'arte gives the label true sophistication.

One recurring theme in our story is the unanticipated factors that have driven many of our decisions in developing new products and labels. When you set out to produce varietal wines (or, God forbid, blended wines) that, for whatever reason, fall short of your expectations about quality, unless you are willing to sell off your also-rans in bulk (a particularly bad option when one is dealing with nonstandard grape varieties from viticultural Third World appellations), you definitely need a default "program"—which is a horrible marketing term describing a particular product line and the infrastructure that supports it—to absorb these vinous misfits. What began essentially as a salvage operation ultimately turned into a successful franchise for us—a premium generic blended wine. It was our own highly eclectic vineyard in Soledad, located not far from the California Correctional Training Facility that inspired the name "Big House." The Soledad facility itself is not architecturally interesting, so we looked elsewhere for iconic prison images. The Big House illustration was loosely inspired by the architecture of the prison at Alcatraz, and since I wanted it to look not terribly threatening—more like an Italian villa than a minimum-security prison—we used only a single strand of barbed wire.

I conceived the wine as being primarily an Italianate blend, but there never seemed to be enough good grapes from Italian varieties that we could either grow ourselves or purchase, and ultimately the blend, as we increased our production of it—primarily from purchased grapes—became highly eclectic.

I made a strong effort to insure that the wine never got too close stylistically to the Rhône blends or the varietal wines that we were already producing, but (now it can be told) it was in fact grapes from old-vine Carignane vineyards (generally available for a song) that held the whole thing together.

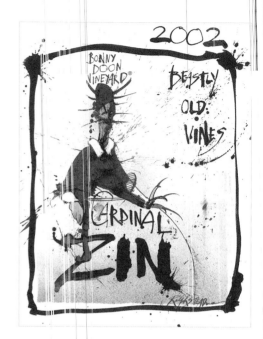

As I have said, the business decisions that one makes are often the result of factors seemingly beyond one's control. We had defined ourselves as leading producers of Rhône-style wines in California, and obviously, if you wish to make Rhône-style wines, you need Rhône-style grapes. But as the category gained recognition, and demand for these grapes grew, our growers realized that they could compel us to take some of their other, less marketable varieties at the same time. Thus, like it or not, we were suddenly in the Zinfandel business. We had a casual relationship with the artist Ralph Steadman, through Oddbins, an English chain of wineshops for which he did quite a bit of work. The chaps at Oddbins introduced me to Ralph, and somehow I persuaded him to design a label for Cardinal Zin.

Ralph is a genius beyond all reckoning, but he's not particularly adept at taking art direction, so the best strategy was to give him absolutely minimal parameters—the size of the label, the

name and perhaps the color of the wine, the shape and color of the bottle—and then let him have at it. The Cardinal Zin label he drew for us was magnificent, and the wine sold exceptionally well, despite the fact that I had essentially zero interest in the category. To my chagrin, I began to accede to the expectations of my social milieu—actually John Locke, our former creative director, put me up to it—and found myself dressing up as a cardinal at the ZAP tasting. This monumental event is mounted annually in San Francisco by the Zinfandel Advocates and Producers, and its enormity and decibel level are exceeded only by the enormity and decibel level of the wines themselves. These antics only further cemented the perception that I was but a wild and crazy showman. I had merely wanted some first-rate Mourvèdre grapes, but now I had gone and joined the circus.

Ralph produced another marvelous label for us, for a wine we imported for a number of years from the Languedoc, the Domaine des Blagueurs Syrah. This was before practically the entire Central Coast of California from Gonzales to Santa Barbara was planted to Syrah, and we were having great difficulty finding first-rate Syrah grapes in the state. I had envisioned the label as a playing card, with the illustration of a new, colorful character, the Sirrah, as a knavish jack-a-napes. I'm not sure how well the illustration reads as a playing card, but if you look carefully, you can see Good Ralph and Knavish Ralph, twinned aspects of a single heart.

At some point, we decided it was time to revisit the idea of producing Syrah domestically—we had produced a marvelous Estate Syrah for a number of years before our vineyard succumbed to Pierce's disease. I still loved the idea of the "Sirrah," with his sibilant *Sssssss* the quintessssssence of intrigue and dastardy, as a member of a feudal court. But perhaps instead of depicting him on a conventional playing card, we could portray the Sirrah figure on a tarot card. I envisioned some sort of archetypal trickster/mountebank/charlatan/snake oil salesman, clad in a greatcoat from which he plied his nefarious wares. The aromatics of Syrah have always struck me as being exotic and vaguely illicit, almost opiated, a bit like laudanum. I loved the haunting, archetypal figures that Bascove, the soulful, mononomial New York artist, did for the covers of the Robertson Davies novels, and, feeling emboldened, I called her to see if she might do a label for us. To my great pleasure, she agreed to. Syrah "Le Pousseur" is "the Pusher" or "the Dealer," maybe an unfortunate choice for the name of a wine, but we in the wine business do tend to forget that what we produce is somewhat addictive on several levels at least.

It had been so much fun to work with Bascove that she seemed a natural choice to design the labels for our new Il Circo series—oddball wines from Italy. I have already mentioned that life at Bonny Doon had become somewhat of a circus; a relatively small organization, we were doing so many things that it was truly amazing we could keep everything in the air. One of my pet ambitions was to make the world safe for unusual, eclectic grape varieties, but it was difficult to persuade growers in California to plant them. "What if you were to be hit by a bus, Randall? What would I do then with all that Tocai Friulano?" one grower asked me. (Though it could be argued that, if the site was a righteous location for Tocai Friulano or Timorasso or whatever oddball grape variety it might be, it would matter little in the big scheme whether I personally was around to ferment those nonstandard grapes. They would *belong,* and this is the great genius of *terroir.*) At a certain point, out of frustration, we decided to begin importing wines made from the crazy, indigenous grape varieties of Italy, and these were subsumed under the Il Circo brand, emblematic of the circus that Bonny Doon had become.

Uva di Troia (Grape of the Streetwalker), the piquantly named vinous star of Puglia, is said to possess a distinctive aroma of violets (suggestive of cheap perfume), and what better way to represent this than with "La Violetta," the tattooed lady? I was astonished at how much elegance could be achieved in a wine from a region as brutally warm as Puglia. The mystery of wine is how it utterly confounds our expectations again and again.

One of our great successes in label design was the Pacific Rim Riesling. This wine was always a bit challenging programmatically: it was a Riesling wine made primarily from grapes grown in Washington State, blended with Riesling from the Mosel, assembled and bottled in California. Chuck had originally conceived a sort of international, vaguely Australian-looking label depicting an airplane (maybe this was a bit too literal) streaking across a pastel-washed sky at dusk. At first we struggled a bit in selling the wine—Riesling was not exactly the hottest category at the time—and I was convinced that we needed to redesign the label so that it referenced the Germanic connection and also highlighted how brilliantly the wine complemented Asian cuisine.

I had the wacky idea of depicting a brainy Asian-looking woman who has fallen asleep over a weighty German philosophy tome (perhaps Schopenhauer or Fichte). One would peer through the wine bottle and observe a dreamlike tableau, presumably inspired by both the contents of the bottle and the reading matter itself. I hoped that the self-reflectiveness of the presentation of the label (especially when viewed through the oneiric lens of the wine), coupled with the inward content of the label itself—life and wine considered as a dream—would open a direct line to the unconscious of the consumer.

The original design had the woman dreaming of a picturesque, gingerbready German village, but the catch was that the village was populated by all sorts of naughty Freudian dream images—a train coming out of a tunnel, a flying zeppelin overhead, a snake devouring its own tail, that sort of thing. I thought the label was pretty cute—I am well amused by childish humor—and Chuck and I scheduled a meeting to finalize the label.

We had agreed to meet at a Mexican restaurant in Santa Rosa for lunch, but when we got there we found it had been temporarily closed by the Health Department, so we decided to have lunch at a nearby Japanese restaurant. The restaurant, like many of its ilk, happened to feature photos of sushi on its menu. I asked Chuck if I might borrow his X-Acto knife to cut up the sushi pictures. We found to our delight that, if you taped the sushi pictures to the back of the bottle and looked at the bottle head-on, as you moved your head it would appear as if the fish were actually swimming. This concept seemed to be slightly broader and more inclusive than the strange Freudian village, so we changed the label design at the very last minute, ultimately to great commercial éclat. Needless to say, the course of wine label history might have been different if a certain health inspector had come to call on a different day.

It was my colleague John Locke who was responsible for the extraordinary series of fine-art D.E.W.N. labels that we produced for many years, using the talents of a number of brilliant artists. D.E.W.N. is the Distinctive Esoteric Wine Network, our wine club, which continues to this day, although we now have a less ambitious program of new-label-art patronage. The name was originally conceived as a spoof on the Distant Early Warning System, a relic of the cold war era (also contemporaneous with a significant incidence of UFO sightings), and was intended to alert the wine-drinking populace to the incipient arrival of unusual wine varieties and experimental wine styles from "not around here."

The labels are legion and can't all be represented in this book; the Freisa label included here, produced by artist Gary Taxali, is just a taste of the wonderful eye candy we were able to provide for our adventurous customers. Because the D.E.W.N. wines, unlike our more mainstream (and this is a relative term) wines, are not sold through the three-tier wholesale system, we have enjoyed far greater artistic license with our label content; we can be as obscurantist or edgy as we dare, within relevant governmental labeling guidelines. We grew Freisa, an extremely arcane Piemontese grape variety, in our Soledad vineyard with generally favorable viticultural results, though we could never quite figure out how to introduce it into the mainstream arteries of commerce, so it was a perfect candidate for D.E.W.N. The label is a bit of an inside joke, featuring two differing commentaries on the qualities of the grape itself by perhaps the world's two most highly regarded wine writers.

Bonny Doon has changed considerably since the heyday of our wild label-art adventurism. The packaging we provided for our wines delighted and nourished our customers and created profound brand loyalty, though it likely suggested to influential critics that we were not as serious about the winemaking as we possibly could have been. I am hoping, through our new labels, to convey a new seriousness and earnestness of purpose. They may lack the fine-art sensibility that was Mr. Locke's forte, but they are still playful and emblematic of our deep interest

CA' DEL SOLO

Ca' del Solo Estate Vineyard
MONTEREY COUNTY
2008 Albariño

in making wines expressive of place. The image represented on the label is a "sensitive crystallization" of our 2008 Ca' del Solo Albariño from our Estate Vineyard in Soledad.[24]

For good or bad, Bonny Doon has always been identified with its imaginative labels. In recent years, however, the winery has been accused of being more preoccupied with marketing, promotion, and publicity than with the quality of the wine, and there is certainly enough truth to this assertion to sting. The proliferation of artsy labels has been cited as prima facie evidence of a lack of focus on winemaking. But a wine label is not simply a marketing tool. A well-crafted label conveys to the potential purchaser a sense of what he or she might expect on opening the bottle—it communicates, through the carefulness of the packaging, the assurance that equivalent attention to detail was maintained in the winemaking process. On a personal level, growing grapes properly, making wine well, and accurately capturing its fleeting essence in the design of the package all rise from the same creative impulse. Ultimately, wine offers communion, whether in the shared experience of friends tasting a brooding bottle of Cornas—the Hamlet of red wines—or in the imaginative empathic leap one takes in seeking to translate what is on the inside of the bottle to the outside. You try your best to communicate the wine's essential nature to an unknown consumer, whom you attempt to conjure, all the while knowing that his first sip will be worth a thousand of your pictures.

I was privileged, at a very tender age, to taste wines that hauntingly whispered to me of their home. I didn't have the knowledge or experience then to understand that the wines were attempting to tell me about a second, double world—the order that lies behind the phenomenal world of taste. The wine label is the outermost veil of the strange, convoluted mystery of a wine, be it (the wine *or* the label) thoroughly original or relatively banal. When you fully "get" the label, you understand everything and nothing. All the words that follow are my rather jejune attempts to speak in word-pictures some of the strange truth that wine conveys through scent and taste.

24. Sensitive crystallization is a methodology developed in the 1930s by Ehrenfried Pfeiffer—as an outgrowth of the biodynamic movement—to create images of various organic and inorganic substances, and it was used at one point as a medical diagnostic tool. A small volume of copper chloride solution is added to a near equivalent volume of the substance being studied, poured into a Petri dish, and evaporated in a vibrationless chamber. The dish is then photographed on a light table to better visualize the relief of the crystals. It is a visualization of the organization, complexity, and life force (among a multitude of other variables) of the substance under study. In the case of our wine, it provides the consumer with a visual preview of what he or she might expect on opening the bottle or, at the very least, a slightly different lens through which to apprehend the wine's unique fingerprint.

FICCIONES

VITERATURE

〜

How I Spent My Summer Vacation

BY BONNY D. (AS TOLD TO M. BLOOM)

My old man wanted me to stay on the farm all summer long. He told me I was permanently grounded. What a grouch! (He's been acting real weird lately. He spends all his time fooling around with that pot still, talking to himself, saying, "Oh, de vie!" which I think is French for "This is the life," so he must be having *some* fun.)

Unlike me. I had to just hang around the vineyard all summer, vegetating. A real stick in the mud. I was this awkward gangly creature, see, growing, it seemed, about three inches a day. My old man assured me that when I was a little older I would blossom into a real beauty.

The days were warm and bright, the evenings cool·and breezy. I could feel the wind rustle under my canopy. As the days grew longer, my skin turned soft and rosy. I felt myself maturing, ripening, but into what?

The dark-eyed boys who hung around the vineyard were at last beginning to notice me. "Pick me, pick me!" I mutely cried out to them, but they just walked on, their sharpened knives gleaming in the late summer sun.

Finally, a sweet-faced boy came upon me and said, "I have to have you." And suddenly it was done. Feeling cut off from my roots, I was now *en route* to a mysterious end. I was frightened when I felt my perfect skin being bruised and crushed. That intense pressure seemed to last forever, and then suddenly I felt my juices begin to flow. A feeling of warmth spread over me; a heady, almost intoxicating sensation devoured me. As I tumbled and rolled, it was so complex velvety full yes rich and powerfully explosive yes such finesse and balance yes brooding depth yes mouthfeel legs yes dazzling breadth staggering length yes sublime robust virile unctuous harmonious complete Yes. *(FALL 1987)*

⌒ This is the very first parody I attempted, and it is rather modest in its literary ambition. The aha! moment in the construction of this piece happened when I thought about the overheated quality of Robert Parker's wine prose; the leap from descriptors of extreme vinous delight to those of a more generalized oceanic release was not so great.[25] I wondered then if Parker's language could be appropriated for a Molly Bloom–like soliloquy, and that is in fact what I have attempted. While, as I say, this piece was a modest step, it emboldened me to become ever more ambitious in taking on the parodic form.[26]

25. The relationship between vinous pleasure and the more traditional loci of hedonic fulfillment has more or less dominated my writing thematically, perhaps even to the point of clinical interest. The upshot of this is: if you are a bluenose, this might be a good opportunity to quit, before the going really gets rough.   26. It also established my unfortunate habit of routinely mocking the excesses of Parker's inflamed prose.

Spenser's Last Case

Le Mystère d'Ail, Ail, Ail

Spenser, just like the poet I admire. That's my name, though I might add, *entre nous,* he's a bit long-winded for my taste. I gotta give *The Faerie Queen* an overall 92 for its extraordinary length and its incomparable structure. Where was I? Oh yeah. I'm a wine dick. Which is to say I make my living with my nose (cf. the Freud–Fliess correspondence in this connection). The mugs tell me I've got a smart mouth, which is a damn good thing. You let a couple of molecules of diethyl mercaptan sneak by and your finish is finished, your palate impression is not so impressive. Your nose doesn't; it's clueless, you're 86ed, in the swill bucket.

I got an office out on Leavesley Road in Gilroy, upstairs from Marcel's. This morning I had an early appointment with a frail, name of Clicquot. She had to inch in sideways through some cases of Prieuré Pago-Pago I had stacked up in the hallway on the off chance that the Margaux cult might come back. She seated herself on the immensely cumbrous sedan chair I keep and crossed her legs. "Gams r us," I thought involuntarily. I had to give her an 84 on that score; she made points with a good overall middle-body, round but not overly fleshy, an 88 in the shade. "Mind if I smoke?" she queried, as she lit up a butt, its smoky, tobacco-like qualities immediately emblazoning a 79 in my think-box. "I don't care if you're *brûlée,* sugar." "Oh, nay charred," she countered somewhat anagrammatically.

"Mr. Spensair, you must help me," she bleated in a voice that was somehow a synthesis of Maurice Chevalier and Domaine de Chevalier. "I am but a poor *restauratrice* and have sunk my life savings into ze purchase of zese very expensive cases of wine. I fear zay are, pouf, how do you say, *pour les oiseaux.*" The first thing I needed to investigate was whether the typesetter was collecting some sort of kickback on *z*'s or had foolishly blown the *th*'s at the track. I opened several bottles taken at random from the four cases Clicquot had carried up three flights of stairs. Peered into the bowl of the first glass, took a sniff. Nice cedary fragrance, typical Bordeaux nose, and yet there was this odd, intrusive garlic note. "Seems like bad winemaking," I opined. The guy should have been on top of his sulfide problem. If it weren't for the flaw, it would easily be a 90. As it was, I had to knock it down to a 73. She brought out bottles of Burgundy, Rhônes, more clarets—all with this same odd suggestion of *Allium sativa.* There had to be some sort of sinister conspiracy among the makers of all these *red* wines, I reflected. I got up to shut the window. I returned to the table and retasted the wines; the odd character seemed to have blown off a bit.

At this point, I was reminded of an imperative unique to the genre—when the narrative bogs down, send a thug through the door with a gun. Suddenly, a shadowy figure burst between the

jambs wildly waving what appeared to be a gat. "Everyone on the *flor, chéris*," he leered. "*Jerez* the *hombre* I've been theekirg," he declaimed. I immediately detected a strong Iberian note in this galoot; I had to give his Castilian inflection an 87 for effort, if not for accuracy. I glimmed with some flabbergastation as he regripped his gat and I could better see the label: it was actually not a gun he was holding but a Gattinara, which he brandished recklessly. It took him down a peg when I pointed out that he could hardly terrify anyone with a light-bodied Nebbiolo that seldom rated higher than an 85, even in exceptional years. Glomming a closer peek at the bottle, I saw it was the same wine that had recently been reviewed in a New York wineletter published by a transplanted San Franciscan. "I never thought I'd see you here in California again, Bob,"[27] I stammered in amazement. "Finigan, begin again," he riposted. "What I want to know," he continued, "is who would hole up in this cockamamie little town, pretending to be a wine-shamus?" The name is . . . *(SPRING 1988)*

The writing here is still relatively primitive—the training wheels haven't yet come off[28]—but the story has a slightly more elaborate conceit and contains the first reference to Doonian iconography,[29] namely, Marcel Proust (whose portrait appeared on the Clos de Gilroy label). The conceit is that the two Robert Parkers (the wine writer and the hard-boiled crime novelist) are in fact one and the same person, and the story poses a world in which all noumenal phenomena are issued a point score. (We're not too far away from that dystopian outcome now.) My critique of the culture of the point score *(pointillisme)* explicitly recurs in "The pHs of Romanée County" and is often lurking in the subtext of many of the other pieces. When you are a satirical wine-writer, as I appear to be, likely the biggest piñata of all is the absurd pre-occupation with the numerical validation of a product that is, in its essence, about individuality and distinctiveness. This was a rather gentle parody, and my distaste for point scores had yet to blossom into full-blown, obsessive rancor.

It is worth noting that, my critique of point scores aside, I was already thematically treating the phenomenon of reduction in wines, a subject I would take up in the later essays. Understanding the role of reduction in winemaking has also become an important part of my growth as a winemaker. It is somewhat comical to observe the relative finitude and narrow focus of my universe—analogous to that of the team of oxen in Death Valley in Gary Larson's *The Far Side* who turn their heads in unison to observe the skull by the side of the road.

27. This would be Robert Finigan, a wine writer of some prominence in the seventies and eighties. 28. As a parodist, I am completely indebted to if not utterly derivative of S. J. Perelman, whose sesquipedalia struck a highly resonant chord. "I glimmed with some flabbergastation" seems to have been directly appropriated from the master. 29. For the basic joke to work, you also have to know that Gilroy, California, is the self-proclaimed Garlic Capital of the World.

A Wan Hunter Had Yourself Solid, Dude

BY GABRIEL MARQUEZ GARCIA Y VEGAS Y RENO Y GROSSET Y DUNLAP

As he faced the firing squad, Rolando Buenasnoches, patriarch and *vigneron* of the obscure village of Macanudo, with great recrimination replayed through his grappa-infused cortex the concatenation of events that had led to his apprehension by an albino bounty hunter at the Corsirican border. His captor, one Juan Hunter, had been retained by el Burro de Firecrackers, Alcohólico y Tabac, or BFAT, which paid him on a sliding-scale basis. Juan was not sure exactly how he could utilize the many sliding scales that were accumulating in his backyard—perhaps in an inflatable wading pool. Rolando Buenasnoches, for his part, never conceived that he would come to such an ignominious end. Even the execution was a complete travesty. Other puppet dictatorships would simply shoot the people they didn't like and be done with it. But BFAT had recently come under the scrutiny of el Burro del Budgeto, which had determined that it was wasteful to destroy *inmediatamente* all the confiscated firecrackers, sparklers, screaming meemies, and the like. Rather, it was more sensible (and immensely entertaining too, by the by) to let BFAT execute its victims by placing firecrackers in their shoes and have the poor devils tap-dance themselves to death. Firing squad, indeed. So this is good night, Rolando reflected self-consciously.

As the soldiers began searching their pockets for books of matches, Rolando Buenasnoches thought back to the time his father had brought him to the mountains to visit the *glacière,* or giant ice box, where he was not given his first taste of ice wine. "This is *not* ice wine," his father had told him. *The icebox had resembled . . .* (here Rolando reached for a plump and fully ripened metaphor, as he would for a sweet succulent papaya) *a forty-foot shipping container covered with polyurethane foam.*[30] He heard a loud crackling noise that could only have been the pliant lower branches of his figurative language flexing to their full extension and beginning to fracture. "I am falling into ordinary realism," he thought, but it was merely the first of the firecrackers beginning to go off.

Rolando Buenasnoches's difficulties with BFAT had begun at the time when the village of Macanudo was overcome by a miasma that rendered its inhabitants incapable of remembering the names of things. This had wreaked havoc with the enforcement of BFAT's appellation laws. A public-minded individual, Rolando Buenasnoches had sought to help by furnishing more and more nonmandatory information on his back labels and, later, on a proliferation

---

30. The insulated container that held the frozen grapes upon their reception from the freezer in Castroville, California, was a very crude system devised by Bonny Doon Vineyard during the very earliest production of our Vin de Glacière.

of strip labels that tended to make his bottles look like well-traveled baggage. He began by offering practical advice to his customers relating to the service of wine. "This is a Chardonnay. It can be served with fish, those scaly creatures that swim in bodies of water called lakes and oceans." "This is a pink Provençal-styled wine. It can be served with food that is grilled over mesquite charcoal, that porous carbonaceous material obtained from heating, in the absence of oxygen, the wood of the small tree of the genus *Prosopis,* grown to the north of us."

As the amnesia of the population had worsened, Rolando Buenasnoches had redoubled his efforts, exhorting his printer to furnish him with more and more strip labels to keep pace with the deepening forgetfulness of the people and to illuminate the more fundamental premises of his enterprise. This is wine, the fermented juice of grapes. It comes in a bottle. (Please dispose of the vitreous material properly when you have finished ingesting its contents.) Further labels were needed to explain trash receptacles, the notion of recycling, and the need for care in handling broken glass. This led to still more labels treating the subjects of prisms and optics. Rolando Buenasnoches had attempted to compose the most scientifically accurate and dispassionate strip labels he was capable of writing, and had dutifully sent them off to BFAT for approval. BFAT, alas, was in no position to assess the veracity or even the verisimilitude of any of the propositions on the labels, as the agency too had fallen victim to the malaise that beleaguered the general population of Macanudo.

Rolando Buenasnoches had already driven his printer to the brink of nervous collapse when it occurred to him that, while he had exhaustively and encyclopedically compiled all extant scientific knowledge, he had somehow omitted any mention of the finer, subtler elements of human sensibility—affect, emotion, sensation. "This wine is red. Red is a color (a perception of the radiant waves that compose the visible portion of the electromagnetic spectrum). But it is more than this. The color red signifies lust, passion, intensity, heat. Also embarrassment, anger, and certain anarchistic or Bolshevist leanings. It is the fiery hue that emblazons, imbues, and ignites us. It is the dark wine of the spirit whose damask draughts animate, intoxicate, and ennoble us even as we are consumed in its immolating flame."

One day the vapor that had enveloped Macanudo simply evanesced, and the inhabitants found themselves awash in a sea of wine labels (much as we are today). The most recent of Rolando Buenasnoches's strip labels found themselves on the desk of a BFAT functionary. She saw red, and then she saw red. Juan Hunter was contacted. Still filled with great, if not infinite, regret as his captors administered the terminal hotfoot, Rolando Buenasnoches asked himself, "Will this wanton dread o' yours salve a sole, eh dude?" *(FALL 1988)*

When I write a parody, I generally begin by coming up with a clever name for the piece. I turn the names of the author and book I want to parody around in my head, like an echolalic roulette wheel, until the spinning ball comes to rest. I've always loved this García Márquez book, and when I saw it again, in my head I heard, "A wan hunter had yourself solid, dude."[31] It was just a matter of appropriating some of the more vivid themes and images from the book—ice, memory, regret, and firing squads—throwing in some Bonny Doon imagery (cigars) and trying my best to imitate the complicated grammatical tenses of recaptured time. I really loved writing this piece (He "reached for a plump and fully ripened metaphor"—how cool is that?), and while it's still a juvenile artifact, it shows clearly that I had become incrementally more adept as a parodist.[32] I was also growing increasingly emboldened, or perhaps shameless, in embedding Bonny Doon products in the prose.

"B"

BY THOMAS PUNCHEON

Chapter One

Santa Cruz, 1990

In which we are introduced to a singular member of the Whole Sick Cru. "A screaming comes across this guy." Brother Threnody Joe Giblet, cellar man and spelunker *ordinaire* of the Oakdaleglenfjordpeak Vineyards, a wholly owned subsidiary of the religious order of the Highly Empathic Sisters of Seizure, Heart Attack, and other Medical Emergencies, or SHAME, has just dropped a full barrel of Contra Costa Mourvèdre on his right foot and is in great pain. Giblet had been attempting an extremely complicated, unorthodox cellaring maneuver, which devolved upon an intricate system of pulleys, counterweights, and religious impedimenta. The technique, as imparted to him by a certain Comtesse B on one of Brother Threnody Joe's periodic peregrinations to the near Alps, entailed the manipulation of minute changes in the barometric pressure of the cellar by means of trance induction and possession by a suprarationative awareness, which would permit, in theory, a sort of *soutirage automatique,* or automatic racking. The barrel had been balanced (at least until just moments ago) on a prie-dieu that had belonged to a Sister Mary Guermantes of Blessed Head of the Fragrant Sisters of Aglio, late of Saint Marcel's Cloister. Red wine was gushing without surcease.

---

31. Apart from its reigning aspect of artsy-craftsiness, the other dominant cultural strain in Santa Cruz is that of surfing. Fellow Cruzans of either gender have, from the sixties to the present time, been denominated as "dude." 32. I was also developing a taste for inside jokes. In stating that the wine was not an "ice wine," I was hewing to the official company line that the wine was not an "ice wine" (vin de glace) but rather a "wine of the icebox" (vin de glacière).

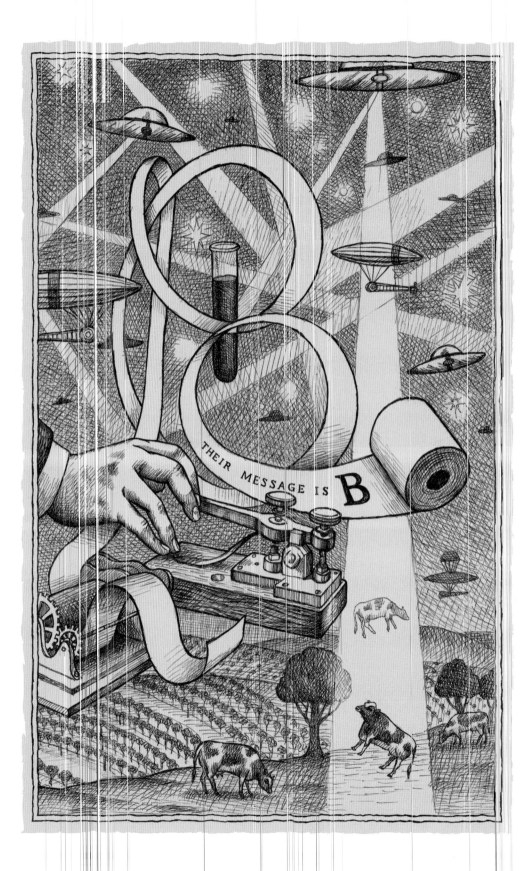

THEIR MESSAGE IS B

In which the term gaucho *is given new significance.* Before the mirror in the *sala de caballeros* of the Feckless Cabrón, an institution that existed as a paean to crapulence, stood José Keineswegs combing his pompadour into compliance and checking his 'stache. José, a blonde zoot-suiter traveling on an Argentine passport, had diverse motivations for this visitation to the Gents. His coworkers at the garlic plant, Stinkin' Rosie's, with whom he had been drinking, had been obliquely tantalizing him all evening with provocative intimations of dark goings-on at the plant and then suddenly veering away. Clearly they didn't trust him, or was he just being paranoid? This exclusion vexed Keineswegs, as he was in truth a top secret operative assigned to monitor this sensitive packing plant. In a lame effort to concoct himself as a high-concept individual of Iberian ethnicity, Keineswegs had taken to wearing a pencil-thin Adolphe Menjou moustache. Unfortunately, being blonde, it went unnoticed. The boîte had been devoid of oxygen and stifling; José had wished to determine if the moustache, which he had, in an earlier visit to the Gents, carefully defined with brown Crayola, was maintaining its definition if not its linearity. The other proximal cause of José's water-closeting, his seigneurial sequestration, was an impromptu meeting with his "control" to rectify some of the technical difficulties he was experiencing with his transceiver. The nonstop secret transmissions from the dirigibles flying over Santa Clara Valley were crowding his frequency and making it impossible for José to report on garlic shipments, a key economic indicator. His control was one Juan Hunter, an albino mercenary known to José only as "Gilroy." At 9:30 P.M. Keineswegs checked into his stall; at 9:32 P.M., rising from under the wall of the adjacent stall, clutched in a bony, very white fist ("Madre de Dios," thought José, "he's whiter than I am"), was a piece of toilet paper on which had been inscribed:

GILROY WAS
HERE

José mused, "A crude rendering, but unmistakably a band-pass filter. This should work." From the next stall, in halting Albino-Español, came a command: "Use it." The baptismal vortices gathered in a great whoosh.

In which Françoise takes off. Bareheaded, out of breath, and running at a brisk canter, Françoise du Bieté feverishly searched the narrow sinuous streets of the old city, maddeningly incapable of locating a proximal branch office of the Old Telegram Company. Though her message was of the utmost urgency, her *papa* (father) had always instructed her to make economies whenever possible. The Old Telegram Company—a rather sketchy, *vol de nuit* organization that had been cobbled together to take advantage of the recent deregulation of the French telegraphy business, and which drew its workforce from the former inmates released by the Institute Scientifique pour l'Etude de la Dyslexie—had lately been advertising aggressively, claiming lower rates and availability in *toutes les grandes villes*. At the formal inquiry into the company's practices that would take place in a few years' time, M. le Directeur would claim that he had never meant availability *"dans toutes les grandes villes"* (in all the big cities) but rather *"à toutes les grenouilles"* (to all the frogs)—plainly meaning French people, and that the misunderstanding was the fault of subcretinous, nonfrancophonic imbecilic printer-swine. How could the tribunal find fault with such lofty egalitarian sentiments? He would begin to proudly sing "La Marseillaise," and the courtroom would have to be cleared. But at this moment, Françoise, still befogged, tumbled excitedly into the telegraph office located on the rue dans Smit. To the superannuated, palsied clerk, she breathlessly dictated:

CHER JULES STOP EVEN YOU WTH YR HYPRFRTLE IMGNATON WILL NT BLIEVE WHT I SAW STOP CIGAR SHPED OBJT HVERING OVER VYDS OF CH DU PAPE STOP BRT RED BEAM THAT SMD TO PSSESS INTLLIGNCE STOP SAW OX AND FRMER DSPPEAR STOP EVN NOW FEEL THR PRSNCE ALL ARND ME STOP I UNDRSTAND WHY THEY HVE CME STOP THR MSSGE IS B (END OF TRANSMISSION)

(SPRING 1990)

I was a great fan of *Gravity's Rainbow* when I was in school, reading it over and over again, but an attempt to parody this masterwork was too daunting for me. Instead, I set my sights on Thomas Pynchon's earlier work, *V*, which dealt with the cordial themes of synchronicity and unusual aerial phenomena, two recurring Pynchonian elements that also seem relevant to the Doonian worldview. The fact that the novel jumps from one time frame to another also resonates with the atemporality of Le Cigare Volant itself, our flagship wine.

Whether UFOs actually emerge from small tears in the fabric of space-time, I cannot say for certain, but our Flying Cigar does seem to hover comfortably and to oscillate between the Victorian era (there is a Jules Verne–style airship depicted on the label) and the slightly hysterical early 1950s, when Communists and aliens were under every bed (the zoot-suiters of the forties being their forebears). The Victorians, forward thinkers that they were, were terribly interested in Progress and the Future, and I, a child of the fifties, could not wait until everything was atomic powered, most especially individual rocket-packs.

With this piece, I tried to create an imaginary backstory for our Old Telegram. The conceit was that, in the late nineteenth century, the Old Telegram Telegraph Company was the "other" telegraphy concern, a sort of cut-rate and somewhat less reliable competitor of Western Union. What I continue to find extraordinary about wine is that it is vintage dated—it's a sort of time capsule. It telegraphs messages from the past and leaves a historical record—not simply of the climate of a particular growing season but really of our sensibility; it's a hologram of our fleeting present.

The Fining Trial

BY FRANZ KAFFEIKA

The Arrest. Someone must have been stirring up trouble with R.'s barrels, for one fine morning he went down to his cellar, located on I——strasse in one of the seedier parts of the town of S——, to find that his fermentation, which had done nothing wrong, had been mysteriously arrested.

A Special Inspection. The arrested fermentation apparently coincided with a surrealistic visit the previous day from two officious gentlemen, one startlingly tall and cadaverously pallid, the other somewhat florid and gravitationally impaired, both attired menacingly in pituita-encrusted, loosely fitting dark overcoats of the style favored by young people disposed to nose jewelry and primary color hair. "Are you with the BFAT?" R. asked when they flashed their identification badges. "Far worse," Lean and Green dourly replied. "We are part of an elite cadre of agents representing the special investigatory branch of . . ." He muttered into his overcoat words that R. heard as "investigation of unnatural something somethings against the vine." R. was not certain if he was being accused of anything more serious than the failure to prominently indicate gauging marks on all his fermentation and storage vessels. "Am I being sent up on a gallons-per-inch beef?" he wondered. Perhaps it was a failure to display his Wine Institute membership plaque in apposition to the appropriate ingress or egress of the winery building. The cryptic interview terminated abruptly when R.'s French *stagiaire* appeared. Marcel, who had been trenching all morning in the vineyard with the aim of repairing some broken irrigation pipe, seemed to require some assistance. "Excuse me, gentlemen," R. apologized. "I've got to see a man about a dig."

Out of Balance: The Control Board. R. was experienced with the idiosyncratic logic of the entrenched bureaucratic functionary. He thought back on an interview he had endured some months earlier with the Liquor Control Board of the benighted state of K—— in his futile attempt to sell them some of his exemplary distilled spirits. The august Board, whose charter it was to select those products that would provide the greatest hedonic pleasure, the greatest sensual fulfillment, and slake most completely the wanton thirsts of the generally God-fearing population of K——, consisted of six rather desiccated and superannuated gentlemen. "Whatcha got?" croaked the first Board member, whom R. immediately identified as La Vieille Prune. "I feel that the great state of K—— really needs this highly unusual product (available in 375 and 750 milliliter sizes) called Pru . . ." R. began, but was instantly interrupted. "We're not interested in unusual products," rasped the gent whom R. had named Le Vieux Abricot. "Well, it's a little different, but that doesn't mean people won't buy it," R. responded. "Why would our

customers want to buy something weird?" La Vieille Datte chimed in. "I said *unusual,* and besides . . ." "Young man, are you aware that you must possess a special seller's license to present your product to us?" the particularly officious Le Raisin Sec queried. This caught R. off guard. "It would seem that a seller's license presupposed sales, and I haven't seen any of those yet," R. ventured. "Do you know that, in fact," said Abricot, "you need a permit to even *talk* about the product, because talking might induce purchasing, and *that* must be strictly regulated?" "The brandy is very fruity with a long, clean fin . . ." R. began again. "Seize this man," insisted La Vieille Figue.

The Rack. It was one night shortly after the disturbing interview, that R., as he was leaving the winery, heard a faint moaning sound from a small storage closet in the far corner of the cellar. He himself did not have much occasion to visit the closet, which housed old equipment, deformed punch-down tools, and the like.[33] When he opened the closet door, he observed one of his assistant winemakers, a young and sensitive man, seemingly suspended midway up the closet wall, arms outstretched, in an ecstatic posture of religious transport. "I let the malolactic fermentation stick, and now we have to sterile filter the wine!" the young man screamed in extremis. R. wondered how his impressionable assistant had managed to affix himself to the wall unassisted. He presumed the young man had gotten the idea on his last trip to Alsace, where he had observed the religious iconography ubiquitous in the region's cool, dark *caves.*

Before the Loire: A Mixed Case. Like any serious oenologist, R. stood in awe of Chenin blanc, the noble grape of the Loire. So obsessed with Chenin did he become that the grape began to appear in his dreams. R. dreamt that in his effort to get closer to Chenin blanc, to enter into the Loire, as it were, he had ordered a mixed case of Quarts de Chaumes, Moulin Touchais, and some older Vouvray. His wine merchant told him that the mixed case would be arriving "any day now." Every time R. visited the store, he was given an excuse as to why the wine was not available. There had been a dock strike in Marseilles; the wine had been held up in customs. There were some irregularities in the labeling; the bookkeeper had lost the record of his having put down a deposit. R. grew old and enfeebled in his dreams, waiting to take delivery of his mixed case. The merchant finally presented the case as R. was drawing his last breath. R.'s failing senses apprehended the wine merchant's words as they thundered in his ears. "This case is for you. Now I am going to shut it."

The Winemaker Dinner. R. was profoundly ambivalent about meet-the-winemaker dinners. The food and wine pairings were eclectic, often bordering on the bizarre. He remembered one chef

---

33. Years ago I visited the famed Ridge Vineyard in nearby Cupertino to taste Paul Draper's brilliant wines and to inquire about the use of a static "cap" suppression device (used in lieu of punching down or pumping over, in order to keep the wine cap moist during fermentation). Ridge had employed this labor-saving technique in the early days of the winery, as its principals all held other jobs from which they could not moonlight at will. The old barn at Ridge held perhaps half a dozen bent and twisted cap suppressors, clearly prototypes of a more functional design yet to be implemented.

who had wished to create a "memorable match" by pairing a garlic-infused madeleine with a wine that R. produced called Clos de G——. If the food was strange, at least there was lots of it, and the dinners often solved the problem of what to do on a Saturday night. The evening's venue was a cavernous dining room in which there appeared to be only three tables in use, and those by the sketchiest, most indecorous individuals, all, to a man, well beyond the pale. The inanity of their questions absolutely defied belief. "How many pHs does it take to make wine?" "Why does your white Zinfandel taste so acidy?" "This wine you produce, the Siggaray, tastes just like raspberries. Do you put raspberries in it?" R. could not control the sarcastic impulse. "Our Siggaray, *soi-disant,* smells so much like raspberries, people think we actually put raspberry syrup in it. We don't use raspberry syrup; we prefer *sirop de cassis,* actually." The vacuous expressions on those in the sparsely populated dining room suddenly tightened with intelligence; notebooks were quickly extracted and words were feverishly put to paper.

The Finish. Two figures clad in démodé attire met R. one evening as he emerged from the cellar on I——strasse and suggested that he accompany them. They walked until they reached the Gimmea Brücke. Tall and Roquefort-Complected extracted from his capacious overcoat a Swiss Army knife, the model that contained all the various eclectic tchotchkes—nail file, screwdriver, corkscrew, nail clippers, cigar cutter, and so on. The pair passed the Swiss Army knife between them, back and forth across R.'s concave chest. R. was given to understand that he was expected to seize the Swiss Army knife as it traveled from hand to hand in front of him and inflict upon himself a severe puncture wound from either the screwdriver or the nail file. He could not know that an even more sinister fate awaited him. Then it happened. Short and Suet suddenly unsheathed the corkscrew from the knife, rapidly produced from his oversized pockets a bottle of Monterey County Sauvignon Blanc and an Impitoyable tasting glass. Deftly he extracted the cork, poured the wine, and shoved R.'s nose down into the glass. As R.'s deranged olfactory cells recoiled in pain and horror, he remarked to himself, "Like a cat box!" It was as if the shameful odor would persist forever.   *(SPRING 1992)*

—— When I was new to the business, the one thing that absolutely struck terror in my heart, and indeed in the heart of any small winery owner whose record keeping was perhaps not as systematic as it could be, was the prospect of a routine audit by the Bureau of Alcohol, Tobacco and Firearms, or, God forbid, an investigatory audit based on a denunciation by an unknown party. If, for example, the alcohol content stated on the wine label was materially different from that of the actual wine, one potentially faced very serious sanctions. One was always hearing or reading about draconian penalties imposed seemingly at random on one of one's confrères, whom one had simply assumed was on the straight and narrow. The BATF (which typically appears in these stories as BFAT) has subsequently reorganized itself and mercifully does not seem to come around quite as often.[34] (For the record, our record keeping is now utterly impeccable.)

A couple of vaguely autobiographical elements appear in the story. There are still several states and provinces in the United States and Canada in which the wine selection for the entire state or province is

34. After the Waco incident, the agency seemed to have lost some of its self-confident swagger, if not its mojo, altogether.

made by one or two individuals, or by a panel of several, who presumably have the wisdom and palate acuity to discern what the entire populace of their great state or province might favor, organolepsis-wise, a truly Kafkaesque proposition. And yes, there have been any number of wine dinners or wine tastings where I have been barraged by questions that were so lame as to beggar belief. I treat this theme again in "Don Quijones," with Sangio's winemaker dinner. Incidentally, the overall quality of Monterey County Sauvignon Blanc has greatly improved since this piece was written.

⌒⌒

Cheninagin's Wake
James Juice Takes the Wine Train

Napthariverofwine run, past yverdun and adamtollmuck, from smarm of schard to Bentenite Bay, brings us by a concordius vinus, to remontaggio back to Ingroth Castle & Environmeddle Hellth. Juju pules out the stanchion waiter blondeye to the poortasters who invaingle afflicher the treentruck riteofweigh. . . . . Anthraxrude fiststumpf, wounder whence might the boose in this caboose be unloosed? Threw the valet who-who comes the juju toothing at dementshoutdown wary meat by dawninediner who spooks about metoad chompingnoise. Stoopsatrap to pigup dieners from yrnotville. Nacktstoop is yokefeel an invidious to robbermildivy wienery weary weir traited to a ligature on the abject of vittleclutter. The vitalclutterist speafs about the betterfits of carnalpee ménagement, being a practicer of leifpuling, greedpruning and shrewdpetitioning. The jory is still outré on the stubble of clothespacing, but droop irritation simps to keep the bearies turgeon. The vainyearth must be properly culturated. Art ye not a groper of clabberneigh? angst I. We fines that ther merdelot is the bestest zoot for this valet. Marlowe is the queeg of the wally, and clobberknee her kink. There was fervortoke of devagorating rudestuck and the knead for cronalsalacious. The contentment at rubbermendorphin woundery is to cullity above connerie. As everybawdy nose, whine is mate in the effendyard ergot we oldways pig the gripes at physiognomic rifeness, oldcustardimpressing, coldsweatle the chews and reek into new baubles, one thousand prozent bubble fenestration with a fool malo (thems the b'riques, he pointered), leafing the whine unwrecked for max sleaze contact. Jawsstompass (wienologist) lechered on the contritions of Usually Devious to the Scions of Enoslogia, speculumly rajahbulletin, tantnubile, and verneersingletune. Sans Juicy Divisve, we stile in the dirkaitches wit strainedsteel, culled destapling, temperance unconsoled, wilde yeats, wilde fomentums. We are blessé with membrainoose fillers, dietatious yurt, einexpresscollars. What a miracure of maudlinerity is weighed zenfondle. Letztshtup is callusturgid, and here clones everybonny. Clemabroad dawnsharkfillet, duckflicker from shamblyrake, barrennessflippedoffina of oedipuswon, yonshrimpt from clotpickass, barnyardpatois from clovèdoffal, midgeconsternation, flankmahorny of cannibiscreek, mournfriedhoser of coolaidson, airlinecraven, tomribaldi of duskhorne, geld-niggle forthemoney, fretfissure, petgerbil of floridschemes, reekforeskin, angsthumongous of fridgidscan, jaundicejewelrywilmes of frockslip, staphgeraldo, peepermuldowney of chortle-scrudely, bopwrong, eugenicsclinic, rubberpipi, weltershook, gripegropers handlybarkstoofle, handycechsle and luridicely, refereejonestownturnbuckle, the crispschenbrooders, mrsdiesely of sybaradovictuals, bobarefoot of shadowmontalgesic, billpushup from carniverouscrook, chuckharpy of freimerkinaptly, glensulfa of artlesspiqué, robottransverse of miredcampus, peedminor, dentlessgarroth, jeerylupus of ratherfearedill, loosedechronic of napthabowelcannon, howlbroomstick of diamondcreep, churlycadamus, randomdoom, edmoonmonderrière of demainshutdown, eroicaleafy, scaryundress, the hesslichecufflinkshun, rubbercanine, loose-martinny, joehypes, sewerahnooner, coronerrumpbalmer, jakecorporately from moundojello, marioperilousmenudo, junkconksgeared, peepermightcall, fancyfordcupola, jetsonpallmaker, crankwelcomes and jophuself, kennedrapscallion, jockdavitch of scamsberg, narnevonaspirin of ruinedhill, nullsvinca, feesatori, michelarodentine of sanestuporie, darkweird, dayforgaves, bilgenuiter of shamesbeery, jimalien within a sebaciousgroove, rubberskinski, warnwinterowski of shagssheep, divotsprawling of stunnedgait, cattycourtesan, marcocappelini of swansong, boptrockedero who stutteredom, joansnit of lajunta, furliptawdry, janettransgression, jaunenilferment du chattelpotage, jumppagan of paganporkroast, artybodesswill, robertpeculiar, toneysueter, antinomyprechew of prechewed provenance, justenmired, normallydeluded of seedywhines, dentistjaws of stainedinclement, garbleddomani, mikegirlishfeels, and mikewhichmind of aphasia. Chenin again, began again! Slake. Roussanity, marsannemanme! Till sousendsthee. Mls. The keys to. Swallowed! Oy vay a Rhône a lapse a loved a long the   *(FALL 1994)*

This was the first piece in which I felt emboldened to be more than a little naughty, and I had an inordinate amount of fun writing it. It might come off as a little mean-spirited if you happen to be Robert Pepi ("rubberpipi") or Gary Andrus ("scaryundress").[35] Ralph Steadman once showed me a book that he had written called *Paranoids,* with its collection of Polaroid photos that he had manipulated with a stylus as the film was developing. He would spontaneously, without much reflection, exaggerate one or more features of the photographed individual into a grotesquerie (Nixon's nose was elongated to Pinocchian dimension). Ralph seems to have a direct T1 line into his own subconscious, and interestingly, I found something analogous in this work. There is something about the pun as a verbal form that prompts us to sidestep our internal censor and that reveals connections we, or at least I, cannot normally access (Mikegirlishfeels). What profound font of aggression had I managed to tap into that was able to furnish me with a seemingly endless supply of wordplay, the better to mock or trivialize all potential competitors (even those whose wines I, in fact, in my conscious mind, absolutely enjoyed and respected, such as those from Barnyard Patois of Clovèd Offal, sorry, that's Bernard Portet of Clos du Val)?[36]

35 Mercifully, I did not get any negative feedback from my vintner colleagues, but I am sure this was because none of them read past the first few words of the piece.   36. It has been remarked that in wine there is truth; perhaps in these communiqués from the id, a certain truth about one's own fiercely competitive nature is clearly revealed.

Don Quijones, the Man for Garnacha, *or* A Confederacy of Doonces

Part 1

CHAPTER I. *Which tells of the manner of life and singular geekiness of a not-so-famous young wine clerk who was to become known as "Don Quijones," the Man for Garnacha.*

Some time ago in a village not far from here, there lived a young man who was known by the name of Rolando Quidado (although some swear to have heard the maternal cognomen pronounced *Quesadílla*) Buenadueña de la Cruz. This young man was unremarkable in every way, save that he was a wine enthusiast at a prodigious level of geekiness. I have heard on the best authority that he had read every wine book ever published, took every wine periodical, *revue*, and *revista*. He subscribed to the virtually infinite number of wine- and spirits-buying guides, including the notorious *Avocado del Vino*, a bimensual publication claiming to enlighten the perplexed *consumidor* to the subtle nuances that separate a wine with the noble and laudable score of 85 points from one suffering the ignominy of a paltry and shameful 84. He also subscribed to the equally risible *El Gran Inquisidor del Vino*, the casual perusal of which provoked a strange admixture of rage and fascination in our young hero. The prose style of the *Avocado* resembled nothing so much as pulp fiction—it was lurid and juicy, seething with breathless, volatile agitation, not unlike the fermentation process itself. This rather overheated wine prose (for it is, after all, only fermented grape juice we are talking about) infused the brain of our young man like a form of cerebral *macération pelliculaire,* and, once the population density of vinous images and heady descriptors had reached a critical mass in the seething, burbling soup that was his cerebellum, his thoughts would run away like an inadequately cooled wild fermentation, absent a prophylactic dose of sulfur dioxide at the crusher. But I am veering off course in my story of this highly impressionable young man, whom, as I mentioned, had filled his cranial cavity to the very brim with stainless-tanker-truckfuls of nonsensical and puerile oeno-babble.

He subsisted in a spartan, single-room apartment on the meager wage that was de rigueur in the retail wine game and possessed virtually no material comforts save a garnet-hued, rust-accented vintage Citroën DS21 station wagon, which, candidly, he had been trying to unload for quite some time. When you subtracted the cost of all of his subscriptions, tasting-group dues, and smashed Riedel glasses, he had precious little money left over. The walls of his pitifully modest room were covered with vineyard maps of the great *crus* of Burgundy and cheesecake photographs of bunches of overripe Marsanne grapes. He had a tastefully signed photo of Marcel Guigal on an Hermitage-hued Harley (*"Rolando, baby—we were born to Rhône.*

Meilleurs sentiments, Marcel") and a Ravenswood tattoo on a very personal part. He knew what Olivier Humbrecht was thinking these days about *terroir* and what Jim Clendenen thought about virtually everything. He could actually remember the names of all the Beaujolais appellations as well as the thirteen (or was it fourteen?) permitted varieties in Châteauneuf-du-Pape. He was aware of the current medical opinions on trans-resveratrol in model solutions and, further, had memorized the proportions of sage and rosemary that Lulu Peyraud used in the marinade for her preparation of *gigot d'agneau*. He knew the sun and rising signs of all of the Nonino daughters and could tell you when the next biodynamic "fruit" days would occur on a rolling thirty-day calendar.[37] He was conversant with the Napoleonic ordinances that regulated *les droits de succession* and had a firm grasp of the subtleties of the appellation laws governing the concatenation of circumstances of a particular vintage year, that might allow one the right to both chaptalize *and* acidulate. The phrase "hectos per hectare" simply rolled from his tongue. He never failed to recall that Château Bupkis was a fourth and not a fifth growth, and could summon to memory with eidetic clarity the amount of new wood, the duration of seasoning, and the degree of torrefaction, or "toast," the barrels of M. Hautbois were subjected to in preparation for the cellaring of his Cuvée Extraordinario from the utterly recherché provincial appellation Savigny-sur-la-Merde. Rolando Quidado *was* the definitive wine geek.

CHAPTER 2. *In which we are invited to observe the employment of our hero and to learn about the virtues of some grossly underesteemed grape varieties.*

He worked as an assistant clerk in an obscure wineshop in the seldom mentioned town of S——, where, when he was not daydreaming, he could be seen fussing about the bewilderingly catholic array of bottles (Quidado worshiped at the shrine of heterogeneity) that graced his own special section of the store, prominently showcasing the likes of Schioppettino, Freisa, Verduzzo, and Petit Manseng, all great, if completely misunderstood, grape varieties. These artisanal and obscure selections seemed to share a preternatural dust-gathering capacity despite Rolando Quidado's artful shelf talkers, whose lurid prose promised complete psycho/sexual/gustatory fulfillment. Despite his best efforts to keep the bottles impeccably polished, and despite their strategic deployment in the store (eye-level, hard by the naughty magazines), the better-heeled wine customers tended to shun Quidado's *hommage* to esoteric obscurantism as if repelled by an anticharismatic force field.

The deplorable state of the "Red and White (Other)" section existed in sharp and telling contrast to the brilliant success of the hateful Merlot section, which, though it was not, strictly speaking, within his domain of influence, R.Q. essayed to surreptitiously keep as cluttered, dusty, and *unattractive* as possible. Notwithstanding the fact that the retrieval of these execrable

37. These were said to be particularly auspicious for the optimal expression of a wine's character in tasting.

bottles required the assistance of a manifestly wonky extension ladder, this realm of Merlot turpitude nevertheless drew vast hordes of customers with an uncanny magnetism worthy of scientific elucidation. Therefore, as he was not particularly occupied with the introduction of bottles of Pigato, Teroldego Rotaliano, and Ribolla Gialla into the vital arteries of wine commerce, Rolando Quidado had plenty of time to lose himself in a certain recurring fantasy, one in which he imagined he was a world-famous winemaker of great stature heroically doing his part to rescue the downtrodden, underappreciated grape varieties, whose honor had been impugned, mocked, or otherwise compromised or marginalized (as we now say), grapes and wines that currently found themselves in somewhat reduced circumstances, not unlike the penurious straits in which Quidado himself foundered.

CHAPTER 3. *In which our hero comes to be known by the noble, self-referentially honorific appellation Don Quijones.*

In his phantasmagorically delusional state, he saw himself as a winemaker of unimpeachable integrity, impeccability, and penetrating insight, a man who could look into the very nature of vitaceous reality and make instant and decisive pronouncements. "*Here* is where I will plant my Pignolo (using the *tendu,* or 'prostrate,' selection, of course) . . . on such and such a rootstock, with, it goes without saying, a southeastern by south by just one more tweak of a southeastern aspect . . ." His associates would hear him spin out riffs of pure viticultural fantasy that involved an esoteric vine-spacing regime in the form of a helical mandala derived by the mystical formula of $0.847 \text{ m} \times \pi/\text{Avogadro's number}$ and a clonal-varietal mix that successfully recapitulated the planting scheme of a recondite group of twelfth-century Cistercian monks who had ultimately committed suicide en masse (ironically, with their own grafting knives, it seems), taking with them to their final reward their ecstatic and mystical techniques of field-budding. His coworkers in the wineshop were always a bit dismayed when he carried on in this agitated manner. For it appeared to them that he could not be said to live in the "real" world (which is to say *their* world), that sensible segment of their all-too-finite universe concerned with wine "programming," deep discounts, and cynically off-dry Chardonnay "Special Reserves,"[38] not to mention overly extracted, hubristically enhanced, overpriced "killer" Cabernets that were so "great" as to be essentially undrinkable. Rather, Quidado lived in the idealized world of his wine books, pamphlets, maps, and grape posters, within whose insular orbit he felt protected, despite the odd synthesis of rage and delight they provoked in him, especially when he fell into the vividly compelling fantasy of how he would single-handedly, as a winemaker-errant, redress all manner of viti- and vinicultural torts and imbecilities and return the world of wine to its proper, harmonious, and well-balanced state of order.

His boss would occasionally nudge Quidado out of his piquant reverie in the rare circum-

38. "Programming" is the execrable practice of rebating a portion of the wholesale case price to the wholesaler in the hope that he or she might pass on a fraction of this savings to his or her accounts, thus augmenting sales.

stance of the sudden and inexplicable appearance of a fiscally solvent, viable wine customer who was potentially interested in something other than a Cab or a Chard, but it would be fair to say that it was merely Quidado's physical body that inhabited the wineshop. His alter ego, his doppelgänger, his true and better self, was somewhere off in the south of France, hot on the trail of the secret formulations of the alchemists of the Knights Templars or marauding through the provinces of La Mancha or Navarra, on a quixotic expedition to track down the most temperate Tempranillo, the manliest Manzuelo, or the most gracious Graciano. He began to think of this other self as Don Quijones, the Man for Garnacha, a name selected as an emblem, an escutcheon, a proud signifier of a testosterone titer sufficient to defend the downtrodden, misunderstood (Garnacha stood squarely in this category), and unfairly despisèd grape varieties.

Our hero's complete, albeit ambivalent, immersion in the lurid prose of the wine periodicals mentioned earlier seemed to catalyze his more sustained and intense residence in the vividly hued fantasy world, where he, Don Quijones (for this was now the only name to which he would answer), would *vin*dicate the authentic and the original and cleave it from the hackneyed and the trite, the elegant and finesseful from the overblown and gimmicked. His admiration for the pure and true ("chaste," D.Q. might say) *cépage* was distilled into a singular attachment to and enamorment of the very plain but delicious, simple and unadorned, grape variety Dolcetto, which in our hero's fevered brain had become a sort of vitaceous ideality, the fairest of the fair skinned, the vine divine, no points deducted for discernable defect, a "10" out of 10, a "20" out of 20, or even a consummately mystical, verging on the blasphemously idolatrous, "100"—in other words, sheer perfection in whatever imbecilic vinometric scale that Don Quijones himself would be the first to publicly denounce.

I have forgotten to mention (and for this I beg the reader's pardon) in my recounting of our hero's domestic arrangements the sad fact that—owing largely to his transportationally challenged status, no, let's be perfectly frank, it was his overall unregenerate geekiness—he was perennially bereft of a significant romantic interest, to wit, a girlfriend. Don Quijones was able to compensate for this lamentable deficit in a most singular manner. Within the privacy of his own derangement (and no doubt greatly fueled by his unorthodox neurochemistry), Don Quijones would transform, in a great linguistic jeté, the word *Dolcetto* into the name *Dolcettinea*, creating thereby a sort of reverbarative ricochet of association, his consciousness whirling and careening in a dervishlike fashion between the dual concepts of grapevine and female human being, twining these two objects of ideation into an unholy but remarkably compact and densely significatory bundle. He was thus capable, in a brilliant economy of time and effort, of obsessing and cathecting at the same time on a polymorphous *objet d'amour* that was both grape *and* grope.

His friends (the few he could count) and colleagues worried themselves greatly about his deepening preoccupation and its increasing militancy. It was suggested among them that he might seek professional counseling, but his friends and colleagues could not bring themselves to disabuse Don Quijones of his idealistic if addlepated fantasies. Perhaps they felt woefully inadequate to provide a worldview halfway as agreeable or piquant as the one enjoyed by our hero. We all know that the world of wine must contain an element of romance, of fantasy, perhaps even one of alchemy or magic, and there was absolutely nothing about "post-offs," end stacks, or "family plan" discounts, the weighty issues with which his coworkers preoccupied themselves, that conduced to either romance or magic. Besides, it was soon apparent that the mounting of an organized intervention in the overstimulated and actively hallucinatory psyche of the young man who called himself Don Quijones had already missed its effective window of opportunity.

When the staff came into the wineshop one Monday morning, they found a cryptic note from their delusionary associate on the subject of malevolent Merlot-mongers and benighted *barriquesters,* who, the note suggested, must needs be severely punished for their effrontery. ("Medium charring at the stake" was casually suggested.) Further, they observed the disappearance of the following items from the wineshop: one copy of Goblet's *La vraie ampélographie: Comment identifier les herbes amiables et les mauvaises,*[39] Ue Johannsen's *Weird Atlas of Wine* (need I state the obvious?), several antique cork extractors (which might also double as instruments of corrective instruction or punition should the need arise), and a set of Impitoyable wine-tasting glasses (as one must certainly show no mercy to the exchangeable-cation-impaired vineyard sites, nor to the grossly ill chosen, inappropriate varietal/vineyard pairings, such as Arneis/Fresno, nor to the thoroughly unreconstructed promulgators of the style of vine "training," irony noted, known as the "California sprawl"). Several bottles of Jurançon Sec had vanished from the store, to ensure, no doubt, that our hero might have a standard of sufficient obscurity with which to compare any recondite wine he might encounter on his revision quest. The glossy cheesecake photos of the Marsanne clusters had also gone missing.

CHAPTER 4. *In which our hero makes his way.*

In addition to the items liberated from the wineshop, Don Quijones had packed into his beloved but thoroughly unreliable DS21 wagon (which he had come to call Citroënante) the following gear to properly equip him for his vinous adventure: a vial of 0.1 molar hydrochloric acid, which he would use to test for the presence of limestone soil; a substantial sheaf of topo-socio-politico-geo-isothermal charts and maps of the major industrialized areas of the state (he was certain that many of the larger paved-over Californian cities would require immediate restoration to their pristine, preasphalted condition); and a set of glass vials of diverse and sundry

39. An indispensable book that also included practical remedies for the treatment of poison oak, ivy, and sumac.

wine components, including some of the naughtier ones, namely, 2,4,6-trichloroanisole and 4-ethyl phenol, which were actually two of his *favorites*. He also carried with him a *tastevin* that had been ceremoniously presented to him by a society of extravagantly clad, pleasantly pompous older gentlemen who enjoyed disporting themselves in outlandishly gaudy robes. He had packed a pair of pruning shears, a long-handled lopper, a pruning saw, and an alarmingly high-performance Husqvarna chainsaw, that he might be properly prepared for any level of corrective viticultural intervention indicated. Stacked up in the "way back" of Citroënante were numerous back issues of *El Inquisidor*, so that he might have the requisite psychic tinder to kindle and stoke his sense of pious vitaceous outrage should it prove necessary to bring any totally offensive, deviant, miscreant Vintichrist to account.

CHAPTER 5. *In which our hero seeks further academic accreditation.*

When Don Quijones left the wineshop on a bright, sunny day in August, he found himself at a loss as to where he would go or how precisely he might proceed. Despite the sheer number of glass vials that he carried around with him and their rather pleasant and melodious tintinnabulation in the rear compartment of Citroënante, he had begun to suspect that he might himself be ever so slightly deficient in some of the finer, more subtle skills and refinements of the vintner's art. To correct this perceived deficit, he decided to proceed directly to that citadel of oenological erudition, the University of Davis, the ivied institution charged with the formation of young, pliant palates. He was most surprised and somewhat chagrined when he drove into the town of Davis (actually, *coasted* is perhaps more accurate, as the radiator fan of his beloved wagon had, just moments before, imploded under the sheer thermic load) and observed that the temperature of this repository of oenological wit and wisdom was an infernal 115 degrees Fahrenheit in the shade.

The trouble with the car had begun after Don Quijones departed the Nut Tree, a sprawling roadside monument to wholesome "family" *restauration* that he, in his grossly delusional state, had mistaken for one of the finer four-star *relais et châteaux* of Burgundy. (He suspected that the *chef de cuisine* was making a highly abstract and ironic intellectual commentary on postmodern gastronomy with his *salade de carotte à la façon Waldorf.*) So after Don Quijones and Citroënante coasted into Jean-Bob's Truck Stop and Ammo Depot on the outskirts of town, and he was given the solemn assurance of Jean-Bob himself that he would have his fine-looking wagon back on the road with a fairly indeterminate "real soon," Don Quijones hitchhiked up to the world-famous campus, the paradigm of erudite wine scholarship, located the Gallic Acid Memorial Wing of the Fermentation Science Building, and found a viticulture class already in progress.

"I hear a Symphony . . ."[40] The instructor, an alarmingly florid and garrulous, ineluctably tenured older gentleman by the name of Professor Kook, was hectoring his class in a loose, improv-

---

40. "Symphony" is a *Vitis vinifera* cross of Muscat of Alexandria and Grenache gris.

isational style on a wide range of viticultural topics, including: "Manteca: It's Not Just for Chardonnay Anymore"; an apologia for freeway-width vine spacing, as it had been "definitively demonstrated" that there were no known qualitative differences between wines produced from grapes planted at one or ten thousand vines per acre, therefore why go to the bother of planting all those pesky, demanding vines?; and a tirade on the irrefutable cretinism of the non-Anglophonic grape grower, especially with regard to his or her mystical, likely un-American, notion of *terroir*. Lastly, Professor Kook dilated on the virtues of the savior rootstock, A × R 1,[41] and most important, on the economic imperatives of vine cultivation.

"The first thing you must remember, class," Professor Kook stated with absolutely no fear of contradiction, "is the importance of planting a variety that will yield a significant economic return. You really don't want to think about planting anything but Cabernet, Merlot, and Chardonnay." "Excuse me, sir, but have you ever heard of the sublime Dolcettinea variety?" our hero was compelled to ask, "a subacid Italian variety (no cheap French tart, you might be pleased to know, sir) that, in my humble estimation, is absolutely unexcelled as far as finesse, voluptuousness, yummy creaminess, body, velvety texture . . ." Don Quijones wiped the drool from his mouth. "As I was saying, Dolcettinea is absolutely perfect in every conceivable way, and I will regretfully have to disembowel with these pruning shears anyone who has the temerity to contradict me."

Alongside the lecturer's rostrum had been placed a very large "Aroma Wheel," which had been used in the flavor chemistry class that met earlier in the day. When Kook's loyal and attentive students moved in an angry swarm in the direction of the hapless Don Quijones, forcing him from his seat with barbed taunts and suggestions that he was a consumer of pink wine and a quiche eater in the bargain, he attempted to disembarrass himself of the barbarous rabble but got no further than the Aroma Wheel, grasping its circumference like a drowning but voluble Vanna White. With the aim of creating some measure of diversion, he spun the wheel with all his meager force, hoping that the rapid juxtaposition of the categories of "fruity/licorice/black currant" and "two-week-old sweat socks/swamp gas/wet Pomeranian" might create enough cognitive dissonance to temporarily distract the contumelious horde. Professor Kook's loyal students had little difficulty hoisting and impaling our pale and undernourished hero squarely on the Aroma Wheel, as one would a lepidopteran specimen on a mounting board. His left hand was fastened to the "bell pepper/baby zucchini" sector, his right to "casaba/honeydew/Nuits de Cleveland"; his legs were fastened to the "overripe macaroni salad/durian fruit" neighborhood and the "road tar/wet cardboard" segments of the wheel, respectively. The students had great sport spinning him around until the next class was due to meet, and Don Quijones felt very much like Leonardo's Vitruvian Man, perhaps as rendered by Giuseppe Arcimboldo. *(SPRING 1996)*

41. This was the ill-fated rootstock Aramon × Rupestris 1, which was later shown to lack resistance to phylloxera and which cost the California grape industry billions of dollars.

This piece and the earlier Joyce parody were turning points for me as a writer. The anger or the developing obsession, whatever you wish to call it, gave my writing a lot more energy and focus, and these pieces were longer (perhaps too long) and more detailed than anything I had attempted before. While it may be embarrassingly narcissistic to make oneself the quixotic hero of a picaresque tale, I was at least writing what I knew—my honest outrage at the foolishness of the wine business (if only its recalcitrance to acknowledge me as its savior and redeemer).

One always carries inside oneself relics of earlier selves, and the representation of my alter ego as the geeky wine clerk who dreams of becoming a world-famous winemaker and profoundly changing the wine business is a persona I still carry around inside me. One large psychological issue I have is my tendency to detach from reality when reality does not effortlessly conform to my expectations. It is therefore a lot easier to imagine creating a great wine or planting a great vineyard than to actually go out and do it; it is likewise far easier to blame others for one's lack of success than to take responsibility for one's own failings.

The story, while of course wildly exaggerated, is based in good measure on some actual autobiographical elements. The exchange between Quijones and "Dr. Kook" at the "University of Davis" (minus the impalement on the Aroma Wheel) is an only *slightly* exaggerated rendering of some of the interactions I enjoyed with the august faculty of a similarly named institution. When I was a student at the University of California, Davis, I really did exhibit many of the personality traits of Don Quijones: I was largely insufferable, at least to my professors, who had a tendency to duck into empty janitorial closets when they saw me coming down the hallway. I imagined that I was somehow the loyal (or not so loyal) opposition standing up for the alternative, that is to say, French, wine-worldview, where *terroir* was absolutely sacred, and hubristically interventionist winemaking and grape growing was not so routinely accepted, if not discouraged. I did get my start in the wine business working as a wine salesman at the Wine Merchant in Beverly Hills. I had not at the time heard of such grapes as Teroldego Rotaliano, but certainly did my best to steer customers in the direction of the relatively unfashionable German Rieslings, which were personal favorites of mine. I did for a number of years own a red Citroën DS21 wagon, but after a harvest season of one breakdown after another and being compelled to arrive at the many vineyards we were harvesting in the passenger compartment of a car carrier,[42] I gave the beloved and noble but naughty car away. The Aroma Wheel, invented by UC Davis professor Ann Noble, is generally a static, two-dimensional representation of a circular object and is seldom deployed as it was in this story.

Part 2

CHAPTER 6. *How Don Quijones came to Napa Valley and met his driver and fellow oenophile, Sangio Panza. We also investigate the curious institution of meet-the-winemaker dinners.*

It so happened that it was merely a seventy-nine-cent lock washer for the cooling fan assembly that was the sole impediment to Citroënante's roadworthiness, but the washer (oddly enough, of neither the metric nor the A.S.E. persuasion) appeared to be presently unobtainable anywhere on the North American continent or, it seemed, anywhere else in the paved universe. But even if the lock washer had proved to be readily available, the installation of this cunningly integral mechanical component involved the more or less complete extraction of

---

42. Owing to its unique suspension and front-wheel drive, the DS21 does not transport well via conventional tow truck, and at least in that regard, the following part of our tale veers slightly away from pure realism.

Citroënante's engine and the disassembly of her power train. When Don Quijones received this disheartening intelligence from Jean-Bob, our hero concluded that it would be more sage to simply engage the services of a tow truck on a weekly or monthly or perhaps even semipermanent basis so that he might proceed amain in the restoration of vinous harmony and proper balance to the severely blighted world of wine, towing his beloved but unfortunately disabled machine along in his misguided wake.

It was Panza Bros., a small Triple A affiliate wrecker out of Winters, California, that first responded to Don Quijones's call. Don Quijones beheld the diminutive, roundish, and nasally roseate young driver as he emerged from the—you should pardon the expression—*cab* of the tow truck, attired in a blue work shirt on which the name *Sangio* had been stitched. Sangio was a most agreeable young man, not, in truth, Winters's contribution to the Mensa Society, but possessed of a sweet disposition and, felicitously, a keen interest in "winemaking." It must be acknowledged, however, that Sangio's knowledge of winemaking was extracted in toto from the one evening he had accidentally wandered into a meet-the-winemaker dinner at the only white-tablecloth restaurant Winters could boast.

Sangio had come to the conclusion that "winemaking" consisted more or less of full-time attendance at these lavish repasts, where the "winemaker" would share entertaining, if slightly indiscreet, anecdotes about young men and women cavorting about fermenting vats, as well as proffer other aperçus anent *la vie en rosé* and then, in the presence of seventy-five of his closest, if most recently acquired, friends, eat and drink himself into complete and utterly blissful stupefaction. Sangio could not imagine a more agreeable and convivial métier. When he learned that Don Quijones was a "winemaker," Sangio was anxious that he instruct him on some of the finer points of "winemaking." In exchange, as a "quit proquo," as Sangio so endearingly pronounced it, he would ferry Quijones and his disabled Citroënante at a greatly discounted mileage rate.

"You know, Don Quijones, we are not terribly far from the world-famous Napa Valley, where, I am told, the greatest wines in the world are grown. Perhaps we could go there directly, and I could officiousate at my first meet-the-winemaker dinner, at Tra Vinaigre."

"I am certain, Sangio, that there will be ample time for you to attend a cloying surfeit of meet-the-winemaker dinners before we have completed our valuable work. But your suggestion that we visit the crassly commercial, mercantilistically enmired, image-versus-substance-confuting Napa Valley is, in fact, an excellent one. There is no viticultural area to my knowledge so blighted and misdirected and in such dire need of immediate and corrective intervention and remediation."

And so the two set out together, traveling across Lake Berryessa into the world-famous Napa Valley, Citroënante in tow. Sangio insisted that they make a stop at Nigglenook, fabricator of his favorite potation, Novella Pink Chablis. When they drove up the Kodak-moment-styled vineyard lane leading to the picturesque old winery, which suppuratingly oozed historical significance, Don Quijones espied upon the end posts of the vine rows (graced, of course, with obligatory rose bushes) the most heartening single word, CHARBONO, emblazoned in bright white paint. The telltale white grafting tape wrapped around the freshly decapitated trunks of the vines suggested that the plants had been recently field-budded. Don Quijones was immensely gratified to know that such a powerful corporate winery had taken the time and incurred the expense to field-bud a vineyard to a variety as terminally obscure and fiscally ruinous as Charbono. It made his heart soar to know that, in these crassly commercial times, some corporations still believed in doing the right thing . . .

CHAPTER 7. *Which tells of the success of the valiant Don Quijones in the terrifying and never-before-imagined adventure of the wind machines, and offers a few words about the menace of Merlotnoma.*

As they continued down the remarkably attractive and prodigiously fecund Napa Valley, Don Quijones and Sangio Panza suddenly hove into sight of twenty or thirty exceptionally large and, to our hero, incontrovertibly malefic objects rising up startlingly from the notorious Château Pas Mal de Rendement vineyard, a lush and verdant plantation of the most preternaturally prolific Merlot vine stock. We know from our enlightened perspective that these strange objects were nothing more than ordinary wind machines, utilized to mix the warmer air with the cooler air on the ground's surface and to protect the vines' tender green growth from damaging frost. But to our hero, who, as I have previously indicated, had "issues" with certain *cépages* of the *médocaine* complexion, these sinister objects, which were located in guiltily proximate apposition to the malevolent Merlot, represented oenological evil incarnate and could be dealt with in only one way, which was to say, *impitoyablement.*

"Do you see over yonder, friend Sangio, those twenty or thirty hulking giant hydroxymethyl pyrazine generators, which, when functioning as they are designed, in these massively and, dare I say, criminally overcropped Merlot vineyards, will produce enough green-pepper extract to permanently repel any wine drinker, novice or inveterate, likely putting them off the proper and righteous *elixir vitae* for the duration of their wine-drinking careers?"

"What hardrocksie-methyl thorazine generators?" asked the perplexed Sangio Panza.

"Those you see over there," replied Don Quijones, "with their long blades, which are evidently used to chop up grape leaves, underbrush, and perhaps even the lawn clippings from the tidy bourgeois homes in St. Helena and digest them into a fragrant *pistou* for later injection of this unholy vegetal anti-elixir into harvest gondolas en route to the crusher."

"At the risk of disagreeing with someone who clearly knows so much more than I do about the ins and outs of the wine business, and by no means wishing to jeopardize your good will vis-à-vis my prospective tutelage in the finer points of raccoonteurship at meet-the-winemaker dinners, I must respectfully suggest, Don Quijones, that those machines over there are not whatever-you-call-them generators but in fact are nothing other than wind machines."

"It is clear, my friend," replied Quijones, "that you are not yet experienced in adventures of

the righteous viniviticultural sort. Would you be so kind, Sangio, to first unhook dear Citroën-ante and then back your tow truck up at a fearsomely high rate of speed so that we might ram these devilish apparati and relieve the world of its obligation to suffer the olfactory insult of at least a modest percentage of these unacceptable and horrifically herbaceous molecules?"

"I'm not absolutely persuaded, Don Quijones, of the merits of this idea, given that, its four-wheel drive notwithstanding, my truck is more or less designed to operate on paved surfaces, such as Highway 29, which, coincidentally, would take us directly to all sorts of swell restaurants, including Tra Vinaigre . . ."

CHAPTER 8. *The further adventures of our two heroes in a most magical kingdom, and their odd encounter with the recently reconstituted Mr. Roberto Moldavi.*

It was several hours later, after they had called for an even larger tow truck to extract Sangio's truck from the Château Pas Mal de Rendement vineyard—the unfortunate result of its minor disagreement with a sprinkler riser, leading to a hydrologic condition favoring the creation of the mother of all mud puddles and the consequent immersion of the tow truck up to its axles—that our two heroic gentlemen were back on their ambitious and utterly wrongheaded path. But they *had* succeeded in denting several of the blades of one of the wind machines, and, apart from its mud-soaked exterior, Sangio's tow truck appeared none the worse for wear. Our boys proceeded down the valley until they came to the familiar, hacienda-like edifice of the Roberto Moldavi Winery. Don Quijones had, through the medium of the popular wine press, previously digested reams of wood pulp pertinent to the Roberto Moldavi organization, and what he knew about the Napa Valley megalith roiled him in no small measure. But in his perversity, *he actually relished* the opportunity to experience the *sheer purity of utter revulsion,* knowing that the Moldavi organization (as nearly as he understood anything about it) represented everything about corporate wine culture he thoroughly despised and was sworn to resist and animadvert upon with every fiber of his idealistic being. To properly prepare for resolute and dauntless mortal combat, one must make a thorough study of one's enemy, and Don Quijones reasoned that the best way to acquaint himself with the insidious workings of this evil corporate giant was to insinuate himself as an innocuous tourist into the public tour and tasting that the winery so graciously provided.

The tour began innocently enough when the tour guide, an attractive young woman with an unremitting smile dentitionally evincing the bounty of proper nutrition and fluoridated water and the blessings of proper dental hygiene, all given to the residents of this great Golden State, introduced herself to the group. "Hello. My name is Bambi." (*And I will be your Stepford Tour Guide today,* Don Quijones thought to himself.) "It is a pleasure to meet you all and to share with you the bounty of our very special valley." (*Gag me with a grape wreath,* our boy reflected.) "Today we are going to learn how world-class wine is made." At this, Sangio's ears pricked up. "Here, at Roberto Moldavi Winery, we believe that wine is made in the vineyard, and gosh, we just wouldn't have it any other way." Don Quijones observed the new scar tissue in her neck where the transistorized implants had recently been secreted. He knew instantly that she was a fresh initiate into the Moldavi corporate cult by her inability to appreciate subtlety, irony, or sarcasm, by her answering every question with absolute sincerity and unflagging and infuriatingly good humor.

"You are so very lucky to be visiting with us, as today we are inaugurating a new attraction, excuse me, feature, at Roberto Moldavi Winery. You have all, of course, heard of the recent but, we trust, merely transient passing of our beloved founder, Mr. Roberto Moldavi . . ." Bambi's tanned forehead momentarily creased with worry lines as she graciously bowed her blonde head. She continued, "The problem we were faced with at Roberto Moldavi Winery . . ." she paused ever so briefly, her wholesome and graciously rosy cheeks flushed with emotion, "was that death really has no part in the gracious-living *life*style, especially in this land of abundance with which we are truly blessed. And so, because he was, excuse me, *is,* the very symbol and embodiment of Roberto Moldavi Winery, we really had no choice but to figure out how to keep Roberto with us forever, one way or another. With the most recent technological advances, we have had the great fortune to animatronically revivify the great man and can now communicate directly and interactively with the spirit of Roberto Moldavi."

"Hello, everyone. My name is Roberto Moldavi." An eerie and familiarly squeaky voice seemed to emanate from deep below the cellar floor, exactly on cue. The *chais,* or barrel cellar, was composed of a perfectly symmetrical ring of new and buffed-out, extra-high-toast François Frères barrels, each smugly glistening in perfectly ligneous self-satisfaction. One observed a trapdoor in the very center of the ring of barrels gradually begin to retract and the familiar pate of a suntanned bald head slowly emerge through the highly polished Florentine tile floor. The new and technically enhanced Roberto Moldavi was being pneumatically elevated on a dais to address his audience of devoted and worshipful fans and customers. Roberto Moldavi ascendant.

The strangely lifelike *fantoccio* was delivering the Roberto Moldavi Mission Statement, which to Sangio's ears appeared to largely consist of reflecting on our bounteous gifts and loosening up, discretionary spendingwise, and recycling some pelf graciously, namely, by means of lots of fancy parties and outdoor dining. The Roberto-golem soon moved on in his (*its?*) talk to a discussion of the Roberto Moldavi winemaking philosophy, and the tour group stood rapt with attention until a component in the animatronic mechanism began to malfunction. "As everyone knows, wine is made in the vineyard . . . Wine is made in the vineyard . . . Wine is made in the vineyard . . ." Perhaps it was merely a tape loop that had become stuck, but it appeared to Don Quijones that this oenological epigram, this viticultural verity, would be iteratively borne in the minds of himself, Sangio, and the other members of the tour for perpetuity, as the tour could not advance any further until Roboto Moldavi had finished passing on the rich and abundant bounty of his nearly ripened thoughts. Mr. Moldavi, in whatever form he now found himself, was clearly in no particular hurry to sum up.

Don Quijones and Sangio could not remain in this enchanted kingdom forever, no matter how agreeable was Quijones's feeling of righteous outrage. There were still other egregious oenological torts to vindicate and viticultural imbecilities to redress. The thought that he might never have the opportunity to officiate at a winemaker dinner at Tra Vinaigre was enough to goad Sangio into immediate and decisive action. He approached the queer figure of the reconstituted Roberto Moldavi, shook its hand vigorously, and thumped it forcefully on the back. "A great pleasure to meet you, sir, and to congratulate you on the extemporary wine that you are making." The thump had apparently been precisely the correct maneuver to properly advance the tape mechanism.

Bambi, the tour guide, spoke up. "And now, everyone, Mr. Moldavi will be happy to interactively answer any questions you might have about winemaking, oak barrel maintenance, appropriate cellaring time and temperature, or outdoor dining—that is, what to do about all those nasty, ungracious insects that come out at dusk, that sort of thing, or whatever." There was clearly an advanced, state-of-the-art bit of animatronics at work here that would be capable of responding to such eclectic fields of interrogation.[43] Don Quijones was anxious to test the capacities of the machine as well as to glean intelligence about the inner workings of the infamous organization, the better to initiate appropriate countermeasures to neutralize its malefactive influence. He posed his questions in rapid-fire, Sam Donaldson–like fashion. "What has the wine industry not been telling us about malolactic fermentation? Do you approve of skin contact on the first vintage date? Does carbonic maceration result in hirsute palms? How many pHs does it take to make fine wine? When will the imperialistic hegemonic 'cultured' yeasts be prepared to return the wine back to the rightfully sporulated, indigenous populations? Would it be fair to say that Chardonnay grapes from the interior valleys represent a Woodbridge Too Far? Answer me honest and completely, sir, with extra points for concision and clarity. Vinquirying minds want to know."

This line of questioning was unforeseen by the programmers of the Roberto Moldavi robot, who, while equipping the machine with state-of-the-art microprocessors, had programmed the machine to respond only to the soft and gentle, benign lines of questioning typical of what one would encounter on a winery tour: "What are your hours of operation?" "Can I find that scrumptious Fumey Blanc back in Iowa?" "Where's the restroom?" The machine was searching its subroutines for a way to respond, but its capabilities had been pushed to their limit. The auxiliary cooling fans for the microprocessors were heard to engage. "We are so lucky to be blessed with . . . wine is made in the . . . newest techniques . . . gracious living . . . barrel fermented in 100 percent . . . special and unique growing conditions . . . the abundant bounty of . . . new oak . . . this beautiful vall . . . made in the vineyard . . . the California lifestyle . . . world-class wines . . . gracious living . . . we are so lucky . . . soft, mouth-filling tannins . . . the latest tech-

43. It might be said that the reconstituted Mr. Moldavi represented an up-to-date version of the Turing machine.

nology . . . Old World tradition . . . we are so lucky . . . made in the vineyard . . . we are so blessed . . . Paris tasting . . . have come of age . . . we are so lucky . . ."

"Mr. Moldavi appears to be feeling a tad under the weather today, and I think we must bring this tour to a close. Are there any further questions?" Bambi asked, glaring at Don Quijones.

"Just what exactly is it like to be dead, sir?" Don Quijones couldn't help but ask. The words were out of his mouth before he had a chance to fully comprehend the effect this seemingly innocuous utterance would have on the other members of the tour.[44] *(FALL 1996)*

Inglenook—in this treatment, "Nigglenook"—produced a Charbono for many years, dating, I believe, from the forties, perhaps even earlier. The wines, if a tad rustic, were absolutely extraordinary, prodigious in their ability to age.[45] While Quijones is a fictional character, he is not without historical antecedents. Inglenook quixotically produced Charbono for years and years, never able to get much mainstream acceptance for the variety;[46] the company formed the Charbono Society, a "support group" for die-hard aficionados of the grape, who would, rather amazingly, gather at black-tie dinners to celebrate the wine made from this oddball grape. Don Quijones does not, of course, own a tuxedo, nor could he likely afford the price of admission to the dinner, but he would certainly be there in spirit.

I did receive a number of exceptionally angry letters (four) from Bonny Doon customers who insisted that they be permanently removed from the mailing list after this issue of the newsletter was sent out; they were mortified at the sacrilege inherent in my treatment of this iconic figure. Certainly I would never personally speak so rudely to Mr. Mondavi (or generally to anyone else), but my alter ego, Don Quijones, does not share the same degree of inhibition; he is truly amazed at the extraordinary spectacle, the adult-theme-park aspect that pervades Napa Valley. I wrote an apologetic letter to Robert Mondavi, and he himself was exceptionally gracious about the whole episode. He has recently passed away, and his sudden striking absence is a testament to the power of his life force. We New World winemakers all walk on his shoulders.

44. *P.S. Nostradoonus, or Life Imitates Walt.* It has occasionally been remarked that I possess a talent for perceiving trends in the wine marketplace some time in advance of the general population; one can't walk down a vineyard lane in Lodi without tripping over a newly planted Syrah vine, for example. Myself, I would characterize this gift as a sort of idiocy-*savoir*. I don't actually spend any time thinking about the "future"; it is more like the reception of brainwaves or "ideas" of great clarity, a bit like the hailing of radio frequencies in one's orthodontia. So I know I'm good, but I had no sense of the prodigiousness of my gift until, several months after the publication of the newsletter issue carrying this story, I saw in the *San Francisco Chronicle* an article about a joint venture between Mondavi and Disney to create an adult, wine-focused attraction at the Anaheim, California, theme park. The theme park project was ultimately aborted, as it was determined to be too over-the-top, even for the surrealistic Southern Californian sensibility.   **45.** I'm not entirely convinced that the wines ever developed great complexity, but at twenty (or even thirty) years of age, they remained amazingly lively.   **46.** Years ago, one often found ancient vintages of Charbono on the shelf, typically priced at the level of the current release—partially a function of the profound unfashionability of the wine, and partially an artifact of the less cynical, sophisticated, and competitive nature of the retail wine business of an earlier era.

CHAPTER 9 *A further misunderstanding in the arcane art of ampelography, or grapevine identification.*

The chaos that ensued after the security guards were called and Don Quijones was brutally dragged off was unlike anything else the otherwise abundantly blessed and graciously serene Roberto Moldavi Winery had ever experienced. Our two heroes found themselves again in the parking area of the winery, and, as they listened to the crunch of well-selected Tuscan gravel under their feet, Sangio attempted to cheer up Don Quijones. "I thought the question you asked about the pHs was really incisive. There was no way José he was going to answer *that* one for the public record."

Don Quijones and his loyal friend made an abrupt departure from the world-famous Napa Valley, vowing never to return to this thoroughly misguided *climat.* They headed south and roamed the Bay Area for several days, chiefly habituating Chez Patisse, where Don Quijones inhaled breaths of oenologic and gastronomic rectitude and luxuriated in the presence of like-minded people who thought correctly as he did. Don Quijones initiated Sangio into the recondite culinary mysteries of baby vegetables, goat cheese, free range emu, and esoteric legumes cultivated with nonrepressive farming techniques.

From there, our two heroes leisurely made their way down into the Salinas Valley, where, notwithstanding the exceptionally dry, windy, and harsh conditions (especially on the gastronomic front), Don Quijones, in his grossly delusional state, fancied that he had wandered directly into Piemonte. Granted, the topography of the altitudinally challenged Salinas Valley resembled in no wise the steeply sloped terrain of the semialpine vineyards of northwestern Italy, and the decomposed granitic, sandy soils of mid-Monterey County in no way recalled the weathered limestone terraces of the Roero. But Don Quijones was able, in his thoroughly convoluted manner, to twist his perceptions around such that he could discern things not as they appeared to be but as they truly and intrinsically were. In this way, the town of Gonzales became Monforte, and Soledad was his Alba. Owing to his particular "gift" or neurological deficit, however you wish to call it, our hero saw before him, not vast flat stretches of the thoroughly detestable Chardonnay variety stretching out into vitaceous infinity, but rather, great manicured plateaus of meritorious Piemontese *uvaggi,* and not merely the modern and fashionable varieties but the incontrovertibly old-fangled and presently discredited ones as well.

We all know, of course, that there was, in actual fact, not a single Brachetto nor Ruché nor Favorita nor Erbaluce vine anywhere within five thousand miles of his present whereabouts. The word *CHARDONNAY* emblazoned on the end posts of the vine rows, and the distinctive shape of the Chardonnay leaf and conformation of the cluster (not to mention the fact that Brachetto is a rather pale red grape and manifestly not a white one), might have given other men slight epistemological pause, but Don Quijones, manifestly undaunted, was able to easily resolve the apparent Chardonnay/Brachetto chasm with his distinctive brand of warped logic. "You know, Sangio, it really *is* only a matter of time before these growers understand that they should be growing Brachetto here instead of this Chardonnay, which is, of course, not really Chardonnay at all. In fact, what I imagined to be Chardonnay is really only Chardonnay on the exterior, a sort of epi-Chardonnay. Its inner essence must certainly be Brachetto, indeed can *only* be Brachetto. In performing this field-budding exercise, I am just helping it to become slightly more Brachetto-like, to express its inner Brachettoness, as it were. I see no reason not to begin the makeover immediately, which, thankfully, I am fully prepared to initiate with this chainsaw I had the foresight to bring along. I am quite certain the poor and grossly benighted growers will thank me later."

A straightforward query delivered at top volume interrupted our hero's labors and pleasant reverie: "*Are you completely deranged?* Just what the Marechal Foch do you think you are doing with that chainsaw, young man? And what part of 'Private Property—No Trespassing' don't you understand?"

CHAPTER 10. *Our hero's grand scheme for the rehabilitation of his fellow unfortunates.*

The municipal jail of Gonzales was experiencing some significant issues anent plumbing and sewage disposal, and as a result, its inmates were being temporarily housed at the larger state correctional facility in Soledad. This was hardly an ideal situation for petty malefactors and such patently harmless characters as Don Quijones and Sangio, who were placed cheek by jowl with exceptionally unsavory types who had been convicted of all manner of unspeakable criminal acts, the nature of which certainly bears no mention in the uplifting tale presently being related. For his part, Sangio Panza was quite upset by the unfortunate turn of events and greatly feared not only for his own personal safety in the maximum security prison but also for his reputation: the record of his temporary incarceration might be collected in some sort of Winemaker Dinner Suitability Super Computer Database Clearinghouse. Don Quijones attempted to dispel his friend's fear by pointing out that his arrest and confinement would in fact make him a particularly attractive candidate to preside over a winemaker dinner, what with the extraordinary piquancy of the tales he could recount to the thrill-seeking customers, who themselves would have done nothing more courageous in their lives than occasionally order a bottle of Meritage while out to dinner with exceptionally close, forgiving, and broadminded friends.

Don Quijones had been, not uncharacteristically, in a state of outrage at the unfairness and likely vastly conspiratorial nature of his arrest for trespassing and destruction of private property. By the time he had been subdued by the officers and unceremoniously transported to the correctional facility, his formidable rage had transformed itself (as was its wont) into a new and boundless enthusiasm du jour. He did his best to perk up the despondent Sangio by proclaiming that their apparent misfortune was in fact the most extraordinary opportunity they had as yet been dealt as winemakers-errant. According to our more than slightly unhinged protagonist, this new development suggested that they were well on their way in their diligent quest to make the world safe for the strange and heterodox *cépages* that, amazingly, the rest of the world seemed to tragically misunderstand.

"Did you happen to observe, Sangio, that this state correctional facility is in fact absolutely gigantinormous, a great sprawling installation of several thousand acres, and that, as far as I can determine, only a fraction of the surface area is used to actually 'correct' state prisoners? Granted, these poor men may have made some minor mistakes in the past and are a little rough around the edges . . . But, I would say that the real 'correction' around here needs to take place not so much inside as outside the facility. In fact, this installation should properly be used not for the correction of unfortunate prisoners but rather for the correction of viticultural imbecility, which continues to rage rampant," declared Don Quijones with some vehemence. Our hero continued, "Now, I am personally quite well acquainted with what it's like to be perhaps a little maladjusted, perhaps even a tad sociopathic and generally despised and misunderstood by society."

"Don Quijones, you are being too hard on yourself," Sangio piped up quickly.

"I'm not talking about myself, Sangio," snapped Don Quijones. "I'm talking about all the unfairly maligned and gratuitously traduced grape varietals whose honor and virtue we have sworn to uphold and defend. Sangio, who could possibly have more empathy for these uglyduckling grapes than these greatly misunderstood and wretched outcasts of society? This state correctional facility could become the epicenter of the coming revolution in misunderstoodgrape consciousness. For me, the signs are incontrovertibly clear. I've observed, for example, that there are thirty hectares located just behind the target range that would be an absolutely perfect location for planting Erbaluce . . . I am beginning to formulate a Plan, the finer details of which I must share with the warden as soon as possible.

CHAPTER 11. *Don Quijones shares his plan with the appropriate authorities.*

"Are you completely deranged?"

"B-but Warden, you have not heard my Plan in its *entirety*. My Plan is certainly more comprehensive than the mere distribution of small sharp instruments to the prison population at large, which on the face of it, does, I would concede, appear to be a bit dicey . . ."

"I have been dealing with extremely disturbed individuals for many years, and I would honestly have to place you in the very top percentile, young man."

"With all due respect, sir, you are being *so* negative. In fact, I would have to say that the energy of this 'correctional facility' is quite negative, what with all those guards and guns and such. My highly comprehensive Plan calls for nothing less than a complete reversal of the energetic polarity of this facility, its resident inmates, and the surrounding vitaceous population."

"A very ambitious aspiration, Mr. Quijones, somewhat easier in the conception than in the execution. That's a little Gallo's humor for you," quipped the warden, who then immediately reverted to his officious wardenlike persona. "And just how would you go about effecting this great transformation?" he demanded.

"Instead of correcting the prisoners, as you would have it, my Plan is to take the prisoners as they are and utilize their, how shall I say, darker sides to combat the even darker forces gathering around us."

"Quijones, you are being completely opaque . . ."

"We all tend to see the world, Warden, in shades of black and white, evil and good, Chardonnay and Brachetto. I would concede that I am particularly prone to this sort of dualistic thinking myself—being especially overfond of the sweetness-and-light grape varieties, viz., Serine, Graciano, Dolcetto, and Angelico. But as human beings, we all have dark, unacceptable, other-side-of-the-coin facets that we don't particularly care to observe either in ourselves or in others. There is a small minority of individuals who *do* express the murderous and otherwise antisocial sentiments we all possess and that most of us are fortunate enough to suppress. We, the *good* guys, are so insistent on being entirely *good* that somebody somewhere out there has to be more or less *bad* in order for the energies to balance out. Bad luck for *them.* But as you know, Warden, being the highly educated man that you are, the ancients recognized the unruly character in each and every one of us and very often assigned to their grapevines either piquant or humorous names associated with some form of objectionable human behavior. If we can acknowledge these sorts of sociopathic traits as 'natural' and human but confine their expression to the vineyard, this may effect a sort of prophylaxis against their more destructive expression in the society at large. My thesis, in short, is that there would be a lot less folly in our society if there were more Folle in the vineyard, less violence in the streets if there were more Etrangle-chien, or 'Strangle the Dog,' as we might say, in the fields—and ultimately, less violence to the palate as well.

"So, in the interest of a more equitable assignment of naughtiness, why not let each prisoner, being an expert on a particular crime or human weakness, be assigned to cultivate the corresponding grape variety, his elective affinity, if you will. For example, to particularly uncouth criminals, you might assign Barbarossa. There is Ruffiac for the thugs, Flame Seedless for arsonists, Tazzelenghe for throat-slashers, Collepepe for poisoners, Gros Manseng for manslaughterers in the first degree, Petit Manseng for those in the second, Morbidella for necrophiliacs, Faber for perjurers, Fer for hard guys, Ferral for the savage, Furmint for revolutionaries, Picpoul for chicken thieves, Pagadebito for usurers, Periquita for stool pigeons, Schiava Grossa for knife artists, Guillemot for con artists, Inferno for the unrepentant, Nave and Grosse Syrah for swindlers and scoundrels, Folle for the criminally insane, Fetească Neagră and Complexa for the mildly neurotic, Moll-vasia for aiders and abetters . . ."

"Wait just one sec . . ."

"Just wanted to make sure you were paying attention, Warden. You could have Findling and Bastardo for the illegitimate; Primitivo for the mildly retarded; Dabuki for those who make illegal bets; Xynisteri for the truly wicked; Souzão and maybe Pisse-vin for the publicly drunken; Senator for the utterly corrupt; Mataro for the killers; Carica l'Asino for those cruel to animals;

Groppello and Pignolo for minor sex offenders; Ciliegiolo for the frigid; and Buttspezzante, Balzac, and Cañocazo for the indecent exposers. You might also add Clinton and Meerlust for the uncontrollably lewd; Aglianico and Misket for the facially deformed; Baga for the sodomists; Len de l'Elh or Picardin for the voyeurs; Bordeleza and Troia for streetwalkers; Jacobain and Carlos for the terrorists; Schönburger and Cannonau for the cacophonous disturbers of the peace; Straccia Cambale and perhaps Rolle for the inveterate gamblers; Dole, Précoce de Malingre, and Baroque for the perennially dependent and insolvent; Krachmost and Junker for the drug dealers; Cacaboué for the disorderly; Bombino for the willful destroyers of property with incendiary devices . . .

"I have even more ideas, Warden. First, this place should be run as a for-profit institution. At a very minimum, we should be producing Pomme Prisonnière, which, I don't have to tell you, would be a natural. We could produce some sort of house wine from grapes grown in this area—we could call it something like Large House or Immense House . . . I've got it . . . We could do a red and a white and call them *Penal* Noir and *Penal* Blanc . . . You know there already is a particularly scrumptious product called 'Prun-o' made right here on the premises, and I must congratulate you, Warden, on producing such a fine product with the limited availability of high-quality raw materials. My thought is that we could adopt the same marketing plan as that quirky winery in the Santa Cruz Mountains and emulate the unparalleled success they have enjoyed with their product Prunus." *(SPRING 1998)*

⌒ Bonny Doon owns and operates the Ca' del Solo vineyard in Soledad, hard by the California Correctional Training Facility. One must be truly quixotic to discern the unique qualities of this site as a place for growing grapes (or anything else), although it appears as if we are at last beginning to work some things out.[47] It is a great personal peeve that growers are not more experimental in their selection of grape varieties and in the manner of their cultivation, and that wine writers are generally not more enthusiastic about a plurality of wine styles. Quijones's scheme for the rehabilitative potential of obscure grape varieties perhaps misses the mark for practicality, but at least philosophically it is not so far off. If there is one critique that one could mount against American culture in all its manifestations, from its viticulture to its politics, it is our absolute, steadfast denial of our dark side. Europeans are, or at least were until recently, happily and philosophically accepting of lighter or "off" years, welcoming the opportunity for a winemaker to exercise his skill with a challenging vintage and the possibility of a wine produced for earlier consumption.

47. Typically, the vineyard is covered by fog in the morning, which usually burns off at about 10:00 or 11:00 A.M. during the growing season. This is followed by several picoseconds of actual photosynthesis, at which point the infernally relentless wind kicks in, closing the somewhat timorous leaf stomata (effectively stopping photosynthesis) until such time as the wind dies down, at which point the sun promptly sets. There are also some issues with annual rainfall levels, which are virtually undetectable. The painful lack of precipitation is theoretically remediable, but the irrigation water available in this part of the world is slightly to extremely saline (there is a reason why the valley is called Salinas, after all), which creates its own set of issues.

Part 4

CHAPTER 12. *The Protocol of the Elders of Scion.*

Don Quijones's new custodial accommodations in the Soledad state prison made his initial lodging arrangements at the maximum-security facility seem like the honeymoon suite at the Ritz-Carlton. He had been informed that, owing to his exemplary poor attitude, he was to be incarcerated in the infamous "M" Wing, cheek by chaw-spitting jowl with the hardest of the hardcore cons, the thoroughly inured and obdurate—those as brutally intractable as an indifferently made Madiran from a rainy and underripe vintage.

"Well, hel-lo, Dolce Far Niente. We're so glad that you could join our little tête-à-tête."

"I'm so very pleased to meet you, but I'm absolutely sure there has been some sort of terrible mistake," Don Quijones suggested to the formidable hominoid life-form who seemed to be the leader of the "welcoming committee," a committee of four grossly oversized, piercèd to the point of impalement, tattooed to a fare-thee-well—we're talking not a square millimeter of unused redneck flesh unspoken for—proud, and felonious specimens of Aryan humanity. In addition to the normative complement of tattoo illustrations that one casually observes on the garden-variety practitioner of Thuggee—knives, venom-dripping snakes, hypodermic syringes, grinning skulls, depictions of one's favored implements of mass destruction and mayhem, and, let us not omit the de rigueur epigrammatic citations, the piquant bons mots of the thoroughly articulate malefactor, such as "Born to (Dr.) Loosen," "No Wimpy Wines," and "Hell's Angels, Ruby Hill Chapter"—Don Quijones was curious to observe on the sun-seared flesh of these titanically proportioned life-forms a highly stylized indelible inscription of the letter *M* in infinite cursive and recursive variation. *M* seemed to be the stylistic liaison that conjoined the various flowers of evil in a poetic posy lovingly etched on the prodigious fleshscape of these fearsomely giant marauders of the Soledad jail yard. ("*M* is for the many things she taught me," mused Quijones wistfully.) But before he could become overly maudlin in this philomaternal train of thought, he began to apprehend the obvious and creepy significance of the letter *M*. *M* as in "M Wing" (duh), and, further duh, he fathomed that he was standing in the presence of the infamous Merlot Militia, the very embodiment of his worst nocturnal (and matinal) terror. A more ironic turn our hero could not possibly fashion.

To his loyal friend he apologized: "I'm so sorry to have gotten us into this predicament, Sangio, but I fear that, through apparent gross operator negligence, I have inadvertently dialed *M* for Merlot."

"One might arrive at the reasonable conjecture that *M* stood for murder, malice, and mayhem," began the biggest, ugliest Mer-lout of them all, a thoroughly unreconstructed grapeskinhead, "given our proclivity for all the above-mentioned terms, but in fact, *M* represents the Grape of the Future, as foretold in the Gospel According to Winkler. 'A pestilence from above and below shall smite thy vineyards,' he quoted from memory. 'Yea, Biotype B is the avenging angel, meant to cleanse the vineyards of the Promised Valley, purifying them of all wood that is unclean. . . . And the land shall be made pure with the fragrance of myrrh and rosemary and bell pepper, and the freshly split oak of the forest shall waft like incense in the air.'" (Don Quijones, in his own private eschatological view, held that the presence of these signs indicated the very End of Winemaking, rather than its New Beginning.)

"But Scripture[48] warned us that there would arise a secret cabal, no doubt one of the manifestations of the Vintichrist (this, by the way, is thoroughly documented in the clandestine document known as *The Protocol of the Elders of Scion*), which would call for a mingling of the superior varietals with the clearly lesser ones, the agenda of the so-called 'New Wood Order,' which we all know to be a creation of the agitprop arm of the Bilateral Cordon Commission. We've all been around long enough to know what 'blending' really means, haven't we? As in 'mixing in.' As in mongrelization! If we are not vigilant, we will end up with promiscuous vineyards that may well be interplanted! And even worse, they may be largely composed of grape varieties that end in vowels! We must do everything we can to maintain varietal purity, to weed out the weak, the shy or irregular bearers, the nonphytosanitary. Send in the clones! Merlot *macht frei! Sieg high yield!* Clearly the prophet had in mind that, when all the weird, unkempt, and thoroughly degenerate grape varieties were erased, the world would enjoy a thousand-year *Rebensreich,* and vineyards the world over would exist in perfect, unsullied clonal homogeneity."

The giant malefactor, or should I say Merlotfactor, interrupted his reverie long enough to return his focus to our mortified protagonists. "Am I given to understand that you favor the planting of mongreloid varieties of mixed ethnicity? How can you fail to see that we must support only *pure* varietals and the wines made from them—wines that are correct and that represent pure American winemaking values, namely, excessive tannin, excessive alcohol, and heaps of new wood. They *must* embody the glorious American aesthetic of bigger is better. Think of the Big Mac, the bottomless cup of coffee, SUVs, grossly oversized Caddies with tail fins" (Don Quijones was actually in complete, secret agreement about the coolness of the Caddy), "all-you-can-eat buffets, Double Whoppers, and 'Will you be having fries with that?'

"And because we do not broach disagreement, you must be taught a very important and, lest we forget, extremely painful lesson. Hey boys, let's really show this pansy what 'blending' is all about."

When Don Quijones regained consciousness, he found himself in the infirmary of the Soledad facility. The wounds he had sustained by the forcible insertion of some very personal body parts—ones that he held to be particularly dear—into a grafting machine left him feeling shattered and somewhat the worse for wear. Despite the ignominy of his near transformation into a chimerical life-form—half idealist and half 110 Rupestris du Lot (*actually not such a reprehen-*

48. A. J. Winkler, James A. Cook, W. M. Kliewer, and Lloyd A. Lider, *General Viticulture* (Berkeley: University of California Press, 1974).

sible rootstock, as rootstocks go, thought Don Quijones)—our hero found himself still living, breathing, and obsessing about the role of Schioppettino in the future of viticulture.

CHAPTER 13. *Sangio (at long last) is given his winemaker dinner.*

As fate would have it, our hero and his faithful driver were soon to be released from the Soledad correctional facility. The charges stemming from the chainsaw episode had been dropped due to the disappearance of evidence—the heads of the cordon-trained grapevines that Quijones had decapitated and left standing by the side of the road as "row kill" had been "liberated" by an artsy dealer in rude furniture on the Peninsula who had claimed them as "found art" and was now doing a brisk business retailing "Chardonnaked" hat and coat racks. Our boys found themselves staggered by their newfound freedom. Sangio reminded Quijones of his promise that he, tow-truck-driver-extraordinaire-turned-cellar-rat, would one day officiate at a winemaker dinner. Quijones immediately took it upon himself to organize a take-no-prisoners (you will pardon me), multicourse winemaker dinner featuring the oenological stylings of the Soledad prison winemaking facility. This seemed the most appropriate starting place for our heroes to both celebrate their newly won freedom and resume their infinitely tedious (but supremely incumbent) work of correcting the errant course of an oeniverse that was heading straight to Hel—

"—en Turley couldn't put on a presentation nearly as entertaining as the one you will, Sangio. I predict that you will really astonish and amaze them. Besides, what could possibly go wrong?"

"But I am a little bit nervous, boss. I've never officiousated at an actual winemaker dinner before. And my first dinner is to be at the world-famous Club Montonico of Chualar, no less. There is, I am given to understand, no place hotter. What if they ask me all sorts of technical questions, like how many pHs there are? I know you've tried thousands of times to explain all this complicated chemistry to me, but I'm afraid that I might easily seize up just like the master cylinder on your beloved Citroënante."

"You really mustn't worry about the technical questions, Sangio. Only the geekiest individual on the planet would ever dream of discussing pHs at a winemaker dinner. You must put the whole subject of pHs out of your mind. People attend these dinners to enjoy themselves and to eat and drink themselves into complete stupefaction. What good would come of a discussion of pHs at table, indeed of the whole subject of acid-base chemistry? You need only relax completely and recount some of our more piquant adventures. You'll have them eating out of your industrial-lubricant-tinged hand. No need to worry at all, Sangio."

As Sangio sat in his place, awaiting his moment in the limestonelight, he was filled with first-night jitters. He knew his mandate was to kibitz about his experience as an apprentice to an apprentice winemaker at the prison's winemaking unit. Granted, the Soledad winemaking facility was a state-of-the-art-circa-1940 installation and was not really noted for producing wines of elegance, intelligence, or finesse. In fact, the only wine it produced that was not punctually and systematically savaged by the braying jackals of the wine press was the prison's famous marque, Large Domicile Red, a pleasant enough quaff, though I have heard on good authority that it is not quite the great value that it once was.

It pains me in the recounting, but when Sangio was finally introduced to the shall we say "intimate" crowd at the discreetly publicized event, a crowd that had already grown more than a bit restive at the perceived niggardliness of the volume of aperitif wine served and its perceived lack of alcoholic potency, or "kick," he was so nervous and agitated that he simply forgot all of Don Quijones's hints on the fine art of the winemaker-dinner colloquy. The only subject matter that did manage to stick in his brain was the unfortunate one of pHs and acid-base chemistry.

"Good evening, ladies and gentian roots. It is a great pHrill, sorry, that's *thrill,* to be here with you tonight at the pHabulous Club Montonico. And what a crowd here tonight! I always wanted to hear the sound of one hand clapping. But Syrah-ously, pHolks. You'll just have to pHorgive me, as this is my very pHirst winemaker dinner. It has always been my pHantasy to hold pHorth on the subject of pHelicitious pHood and wine pairings to an audience as pHenomenally so-pHisticated as you all seem to be. You all are as well-balanced and equilibrated as a well-bupHered model solution." A vague, unsettled wave of distress seemed to pulse through the room.

"We have a lot of exciting wines for you to taste tonight, but, just between us, really so very little is known about the role of levorotatory malic acid in secondary fermentations . . ."

A deep groan of disapprobation resonated through the restaurant, as if the sparse assemblage could literally not believe what it was hearing. It was clear that Sangio would soon have little or no control over this small but deeply troubled coterie of oenophiles apparently still dealing with some of their primal issues—hunger, rage, and so on.

"I mean, people, consider the lowly bisulfate ion, so grossly misunderstood. I mean, it is just trying to make its way in the world, and it does have some dissociation issues, but don't we all? The thing of it is, it is just so gosh darn dependent on the pH of the solution for its efficaciosity . . ."

The sound of broken glass was heard, and small aerial fragments from the first course (rumaki paired with the prison's creditable Penal Blanc) began to find their way across the table to where Sangio was sitting.

Sangio's mind was now a complete blank, and try as he might to summon up some of the witty repartee he had habitually enjoyed with Quijones, he was (you will please pHorgive me) merely *pHumpHering* now.[49] "But, how about those Giants? . . . Giant, er, giant, long-chain polymerized tannins is what I meant to say . . ."

"Why don't you make any *real* red wines, boy?" a heckler shouted, taunting the thoroughly

49. Yiddish for "pHloundering," "pHlubbing," or "committing a pHlagrant pHaux pas."

distressed Sangio, but the tow-truck driver/would-be *caviste* was now so far lost in reverie anent the solubility products of wine's major organic acid species that he remained blissfully oblivious to this undisguised frontal attack. Quijones, thrust into the unlikely role of placatory diplomat, nudged his colleague with a sharp elbow. "Sangio, quick, say something nice about all the people here!"

Sangio recovered his wits enough to continue. "I mean you are such a wonderful crowd here tonight, not at all the pHake, pHony, Chard-swilling yuppie scum that Don Quijones had warned me to expect . . ."

The gentleman in the "I ♥ yeast autolysis" T-shirt suddenly stood up, screaming at top volume, and seemed to speak for the entire restaurant: "We didn't pay no thirty dollars a head (wine, tax, tip, and valet inclusive) to come all the way to this eighth-rate, crummy hole-in-the-wall to hear about no molly-cules. We want to hear piquant, spicy tales about winemaking lifestyle issues, like getting nekkid in tanks and what sorta wine makes Pamela Lee Anderson, um, hornilaceous. And I see on the menu that you're gonna pour *red* Zinfandel, whatever the hell *that* is. We want our money back!"

The entire restaurant began to join in a rousing antihallelujah chorus directed at Sangio, and soon the most dreaded words imaginable to any restaurateur were to be heard: "pHood pHight! pHood pHight!"

The angry and unruly patrons were now hurling all manner of comestible and near-comestible foodstuffs in the direction of Sangio's cowering personage. Our guest of honor was compelled to duck under a barrage of broken wineglasses, Parker House rolls, and an eclectic selection of Club Montonico's "classic" culinary stylings. Celery sticks stuffed with pimiento loaf, pigs-in-a-blanket, and Triscuits slathered with clam dip constituted the first round of aerial bombardment directed at the unlucky Sangio, followed by breadcrumb-stuffed mushrooms (fiendishly effective projectiles that splattered dramatically on impact). Almond-crusted cheese balls, Swedish meatballs, and Tater Tots rained down on our hapless friend in a torrential downpour prefiguring a gastronomic nuclear winter. One so seldom observes salad tossed in a fashion similar to that afforded the *salade d'iceberg* (with the obligatory Green Goddess dressing) or the airborne eponymous creation of the Waldorf-Astoria Hotel of New York City. The fusillades of curried shrimp puffs and deviled eggs provided a strong, almost Pollockian vibrancy as they smashed against the pallid mossy walls of the besieged Club Montonico, especially in compositional juxtaposition with the double-stuffed and duchesse potatoes. It was, however, the giant morsels and stringy bits of projectile chicken from the tetrazzini and à la king preparations, respectively, that really set the tone of the evening. The festive soiree concluded with the improbable volitational success of an artistically rendered fruit-impregnated Jello mold and the unceremonious anointing, by a tureen of "ambrosia," of the pate of our thoroughly beleaguered Sangio. The winemaker dinner was, in a word, a complete and utter pHiasco. *(FALL 1999)*

Somewhere along the line in his career, when a winemaker is called on to assist at a "winemaker dinner," someone, usually a seasoned, worldly wholesaler, takes him aside and advises that he should forgo presenting to the lay audience overly technical information, namely, harvest dates, the percentage of new versus older barrels, the presence or absence of malolactic fermentation (or God forbid, the percentages of malate and lactate present in the wine post-malo), and especially phenology, that is to say, the relevant analytical parameters of the wine at harvest. I have heard my share of this sort of gobbledygook at winemaker dinners, and I usually begin reaching for a dull butter knife with which to commit hara-kiri if the nonsense does not imminently abate. Being a winemaker, I am interested in technical data, of course, but what is far more interesting to me personally, and I'm sure to everyone else listening, is the emotional state and philosophical worldview that has informed the speaker's grape-growing and winemaking decisions. It takes a winemaker a while to understand that his or her job is not so much to impart technical details at these dinners—such details are really not what impresses anyone—but to form an emotional connection with the audience, and this can be done by showing one's own vulnerability and, above all, by honesty.[30]

The pHs of Romanée County

Madame Lulu Allbiz was sitting out in the courtyard of her modest eighteen-room, fifteenth-century stone farmhouse in rural Romanée County when she heard the sound of a vehicle coming up the perfectly raked serpentine gravel driveway. She assumed that it must be the *comtesse* (an exceptionally tedious old biddy), who had the habit of dropping by to discuss the latest crackpot fads in Proustian criticism, the most recent one being the consideration of the madeleine as an actual dramatis persona.

Madame Lulu Allbiz had the great fortune of enjoying a consummately perfect existence. She was a slim-waisted, attractively packaged raven-haired beauty possessed of effervescent wit, gracious charm, and some extremely valuable real property in the world-famous grape-growing province of Romanée County. Her dear husband, Jean-Jacques, in addition to being the coproprietor of the most highly regarded *cru* in Romanée County, was an accomplished painter, sculptor, symphony cellist, and moral philosopher, as well as the greatest lover she had ever known. Further, he was an absolutely brilliant and stimulating conversationalist. He could talk long and passionately into the night on a diverse array of subjects—international *terroirisme* (what can be done?), Foucault on *bâtonnage* and discipline, Merlot-Ponty on the formal tannic structure of the *bordelais cépages*, Lévi-Strauss on the *grand cru* and the *cuit*, and Sartre on inappropriate food and wine pairings. But lately Madame Lulu Allbiz had found these discussions to have lost their previous allure. Something tangible, something of substance, was missing from her life. Inwardly, she felt she hardly knew the score.

---

30. I have at times myself spoken of various flaws in this or that wine, even of outright winemaking mishaps; this is generally not the sort of thing one hears about at winemaker dinners.

It was not typical of Lulu Allbiz to find herself alone at home for extended periods of time. (The husband and kids were away in Dijon for *le week-end* at a highly publicized Jerry Lewis marathon. "*Dix-huit heures de Jerry, le Roi du Crazy!!!*" the posters had proclaimed.) Lulu Allbiz had begun to find herself a bit at *sixes et sept* in the large house. "Well, perhaps a conversation with the *comtesse* will amuse," she thought to herself. However, it was not the sleek and powerful Citroën SM sedan of the *comtesse* that was coming up the elegant drive but the somewhat underpowered engine of a Ford Fiesta rental car that struggled up the steep roadway to the promontory on which the old house stood.

When the door of the little machine opened, Lulu Allbiz beheld a stocky, well-fed figure of the unmistakably North American male variety attempting to disengage himself from his *ceinture de sécurité,* which appeared to have gotten hopelessly amalgamated in a tangle of roadmaps and *Guides Michelin* and *Hachette,* as well as back numbers of *La Revue du Vin de France.* He stumbled precipitously out of the Lilliputian rental car, caught up in the laces of his well-shined brown brogans. Lulu was immediately struck, first by his formidable girth and, second, by his unique and vivid costume. She had never seen such resplendently hued *vêtements* presented in such daring juxtaposition, with such fearless disregard for conventions of aesthetic harmony. This was clearly a man of great conviction, a staunch enemy of *idées reçues,* not afraid to *épater les bourgeois,* at least in terms of men's fashion. He did not shy away from seeing the world in all its stark and vivid contrasts, its tones of shadow and light, black and white, magenta and lime. She could not feel more deeply stirred, more thoroughly *bâtonnée* to the very depths of her soul, as she beheld the pale whiteness of his ankles in such intense contraposition to his droopy navy blue acrylic socks.

"*Je m'accusez-moi,*" he ventured in a dialect that was as yet unknown to Lulu.

"We can speak English," she offered.

"I'm so sorry to bother you, ma'am. My name is Robert Parcade, and I think I'm lost. I'm looking for the notorious *Brett*-taking pHs of Romanée County, and I can't seem to find them anywhere."

"The pHs?" Lulu Allbiz repeated. Robert Parcade's offhand reference to matters of physical chemistry made her flush red with excitement.

"I was hoping that these exceptional pHs would lead me to the World-Famous Hundred-Point Vineyard, where it was my plan to kneel, bareheaded, in religious awe and reverence until someone invited me into their tasting room for a small sip of numerical perfection. I would be much obliged if you could point me in the right direction." This "hundred-point" business was a bit murky to Lulu Allbiz, but she found herself moved by the charming naïveté of the mysterious stranger, who, she supposed, might wait quite some time in the supplicant posture, *en attendant la dégustation,* before being shown some down-home, gracious Gallic hospitality. She imagined that perhaps it would devolve to her to reveal to Robert Parcade the true underside of La Belle France.

Robert Parcade explained that he worked as a wine journalist back in the States. His special interest was the numerical exegesis of wine, capturing its spirit in the hard analytic data—pH, Brix, TA, VA, alcohol, residual sugar, extract, *rendement,* and most important, Overall Score. "I find that it is just so much more convenient to refer to a particular vineyard by its numerical coordinates," he volunteered. "Those French names are so difficult to pronounce. My method is a real time-saver."

The heretical *idées* advanced by Robert Parcade seemed very strange and a little bit dangerous to Lulu Allbiz, who had been brought up to consider wines by the old-fashioned but now outdated criteria of finesse, balance, and typicity of *terroir.* The stranger's notions alarmed her but gave her a delicious tingle as she contemplated the brute, magisterial power of the numeric universe and its prodigiously formidable master. Robert Parcade's unambiguous directness and forthrightness was so totally different from the nuanced articulation of her dear but presently absent husband. Dijon seemed a million miles away.

"I don't know if I can direct you to your famous hundred-point vineyard, but you are welcome to visit my *cave* and taste some of my husband's wines," Lulu offered. Perhaps it was due to the intense infatuation she felt for the earnest-sounding stranger that she found herself slurring the word *husband* so that it sounded more like *hmmnd.*

"I mean, before there were points, how were Americans to know if a wine was any good?" Robert Parcade demanded somewhat rhetorically.

He was so sincere in his delivery that Lulu Allbiz could not help but nod in tacit agreement. At this moment, however, she was primarily concentrating on how this volumetrically gifted American might look if he lost just a few kilos. Lulu led him through the courtyard, down a set of ancient stone steps, and they entered together the portals of the musty and venerable cellars of Maison Allbiz.

"Since life is so short, my goal is to taste only 95-point wines or better, if that can be arranged," Robert Parcade proudly announced, resuming the thematic focus of his earlier commentary.

"What remarkable dedication and idealism!" reflected Lulu, although she personally felt that a "great" or "important" wine would clearly be an inappropriate choice for a romantic tryst on a serene lake on a warm summer's day. Perhaps something along the lines of a banquet hamper filled with caviar, chilled cracked crab, and a crisp Mosel Spätlese . . . Lulu Allbiz' reverie of an amatory interlude with the masterful Robert Parcade was interrupted by the continued exposition issuing from the object of her fantasy.

"With this comprehensive grading system, there is now an objective scientific measure of wine quality accessible to any person for the modest price of a monthly subscription or who has hooked up to the World Wide Web of Wi . . ."

"Oh, dear silly man, please stop talking for just one moment and taste the lovely wine," blurted out Lulu Allbiz.

She masterfully withdrew a barrel sample of the precious vinous potion of Romanée County, proffered it to Robert Parcade, and, when they had each tasted a generous gulp, was emboldened to ask him if he thought it might perhaps be "a little hard."

"I beg your pardon," stammered Robert Parcade.

"The wine, silly, the one that we are tasting just now. Is it perhaps a little backward, a little shy?"

"Frankly, I find it to be just a little tart," he responded reflexively. "And in a related matter, may I be so bold as to ask just what sort of ripeness levels you aim for?"

Lulu simply leered lasciviously at Robert Parcade.

The moist, old stone walls of the cave's cloistered vault seemed suddenly to impinge with claustrophobic propinquity on Robert Parcade, oenometrician manqué. He had traveled such a long way to experience the spiritual fulfillment of vinous perfection, and now found himself confronting a set of data points that no quadratic equation could possibly describe. He was hopelessly derailed in a place where the statistical matrices did not run.

"It really seems to have great breadth and truly remarkable length," offered Lulu, all innocence.

When Robert Parcade recovered from his episode of uncontrollable spasmodic choking, he was able to put forth the question that had burned in his mind from the onset of their meeting, "Do you filter or fine?" he rasped.

"I believe the wine should remain au naturel, uninhibited in every way," responded Lulu, winking broadly at Robert Parcade.

Robert Parcade, *écrivain du vin moyen sensuel*, was losing a personal battle to retain some rudiment of professional dignity, to place his own weaknesses and frailties *de côté*, in stalwart dedication to his grand and idealistic *système de pointillisme*.

"As far as the conduct of the fermentation—do you punch down or pump over?" stuttered the thoroughly flustered *journaliste*.

"I prefer to pump vigorously," responded Lulu.

"A-a-and the m-m-malo," he barely choked out. "Does it go all the way?"

"All the way," Lulu breathed hoarsely, "although I prefer that it be extremely protracted."

"And the m-m-maceration . . ." Robert Parcade was afflicted now with an appalling case of apoplexy.

"I am firmly in favor of extended skin contact," Lulu sighed.

Robert Parcade was now beyond all critical thought, beyond synthetic or analytic reasoning, beyond any systemization, assaying, grading, rating, or ranking, beyond quantitative or qualitative analysis, far beyond the assignment of point scores, aware of nothing but the cicadas buzzing in the distance.

"Yield?" he croaked.

"Yes, oh, yes." *(FALL 1997)*

I wanted to reverse the premise of *The Bridges of Madison County,* with the female of this chance romantic interlude being the more sophisticated and urbane of the pair and the male the unworldly naïf. (I was able, in the bargain, to enlist a couple of familiar figures in my parable of the perils of *pointillisme.*) I also hoped to tease out the great differences in worldview and sensibility between the New and Old World through the lens of the rather profound differences of outlook between the sexes.

Kacher in the Ribes

BY J. D. SALIGNAC

If a Bobby catch a Bobby comin' through the ribes . . .
—OLD SCOTTISH FOLK SONG (VARIANT)

There is no hotter importer in the United States than the loquacious Robert Kacher. . . . He represents the new wave of American importers who spend considerable time with their producers championing the case for lower yields and less processed wines.
—ROBERT PARKER, WWW.EROBERTPARKER.COM, JUNE 1996

Kacher has sought to influence his growers' viticultural and vinification practices in a degree some of his colleagues in the wine trade find inappropriate. . . . Kacher's seeming obsession with the use of new oak has also become a point of controversy. Kacher himself often supplies his growers with new barrels and in some cellars commissions his own cuvées, vinified in all—or nearly all—new oak and often handled less (fewer rackings, bottled without filtration) than similar wines earmarked for other markets.
—STEPHEN TANZER, *INTERNATIONAL WINE CELLAR,* JANUARY/FEBRUARY 1993

If you really want to hear about it, the first thing you'll probably want to know is how I got started and how I built my distribution network and all that George Saintsbury kind of crap, but I don't feel like going into it, if you want to know the truth. In the first place, that stuff bores me, and in the second place, my wholesalers and suppliers would have about two hemorrhages apiece if I told anything pretty personal about them. Besides, I'm not going to tell you my whole goddamn autobiography or anything. I'll just tell you about this Madiran stuff that happened to me around last Christmas right in the middle of the season's big rush with all of the special orders for expensive bottles and stuff and retailers wanting only the wines that scored at least about a million in the *Spectator* and all. If there's one thing I hate, it's retailers. Don't even mention them to me.

Anyway, it was December and all, and it was colder than a wine undergoing tartrate stabilization, a winemaking practice, by the way, that just about makes me want to puke, if you really want to know. Where I want to start telling is the day I got sacked from Domaine de Pencey, a small but very smart, exclusive domaine in southwestern France. This was the third southern French estate that had given me the ax that year, and I was feeling pretty depressed about the whole thing, if you want to know the truth. I found out that I had been given the old heave-ho by the director of export sales, a complete phony who had about eight names after his first one. I'm pretty sure he was definitely some kind of flit. He was always talking about wanting his wines to be "elegant" and all. That sounds like a pretty flitty thing to say, if you ask me. In fact, I'm always meeting French guys who say they're looking for "elegance" in their wines. This is probably just an excuse for them to get cute with their flitty swirling of the wine around in their glass and all. I can't even think of anything phonier than wine swirling. I really can't.

The motto of old Domaine de Pencey says something in French like: "Since 1583 we have pursued excellence through the crafting of raw grapes into splendidly expressive wines that represent the typicity of their *terroir*." How phony can you get? They don't do any damn more *crafting* at Pencey than they do at any other domaine. Where they really excel is at filtering, fin-ing, and overcropping. But I can't think of any wine they made that was splendid and typically expressive and all. Maybe two wines. If that many. But they probably *came* to Domaine de Pencey that way as grapes. I don't think I ever saw the pursuit of excellence at the domaine except the pursuit of excellence of their net bottom-line profitability.

During my little tête-à-tête with the export director, which lasted for about twelve hours, he kept telling me there were certain standards that Domaine de Pencey was committed to upholding. "You know, M. Kachère, we aspire to ultimately become recognized as a *grand cru!*"

That really got me. *Grand,* now there's a word I really hate. How completely phony! How about a *bon cru* or *cru buvable* for Chrissake? Or a *cru estimable,* or something that doesn't make you want to just go out and slit your wrists?

After I left the export director's office, I went up to sit on the top of the hill that overlooks the domaine and started chucking down some *cailloux* on to the roof of the *chais*. Well, they weren't exactly pebbles, they were more like *galets.* I know it was a pretty immature thing to be doing, but sometimes I can act pretty immaturely. I can be a real *enfant* terrible, if you really want to know. For example, I always used to horse around with one of the *cavistes* who worked at the do-maine, a guy named Acklé. Acklé was a real case, not so swift upstairs but someone who could be pretty entertaining if you didn't really think about it too much. I mean nobody in the do-maine would have anything to do with the guy and all, or even call him by his first name, which was François. Everyone mostly avoided him, largely because he had this really bad case of *boudin noir*–breath, compounded by about eighteen packs of Gauloises that he used to smoke every day. What was most revolting about him was his habit of hawking the wine he was tasting back into the glass he was tasting from, and then swirling it around a few more times and remark-ing, "This young *rouge* looks a little *troublé* to me and could probably benefit from another *souti-rage* or two." It was so depressing to hear this joke for the twelve thousandth time and watch him do this trick that it almost made me want to quit the wine business altogether.

I would give him a hard time whenever I could by telling him, "Acklé, *mec,* why don't you fetch me a two-inch left-handed triclover clamp?" I must have tried this routine on him a dozen times, and he never managed to figure it out. "I think I saw one in the other cellar," I would say. As he trotted off, I would roll in an empty new *barrique* that I had staged just outside the cellar door. I always tried to bring in at least one new *barrique* in my *break*[51] when I visited the domaine and discreetly substitute it for one of the empty older barrels. No one ever seemed to notice this particular ruse, and I suspect that I was able to quietly introduce about 600 percent new oak into the various export cuvées by the time the wine was ready to bottle.

"*Zut*, Bobby, I can't seem to find the two-inch *crampon à gauche*."[52]

"*Tiens, mec*, someone must have dropped it into the bottom of a tank."

The guy who really got to me was Jean-Michel Stradlattière, the *chef de cave*. The day of my departure I managed to mix it up with him pretty good. There was a certain wine that they always made at Domaine de Pencey from a vineyard that I really *loved*, a very feminine wine. What I loved best about the wine is that it was always a little bit reserved, as if it knew a little secret that you didn't. What totally killed me was that the fruit in the wine just sorta hung back. It was one of those quirky things about the wine that just knocked me out. You could swirl and swirl the wine in your glass to coax the fruit out, but the fruit would just hang back. It really killed me. But when I tasted the wine on this last visit to old Domaine de Pencey, the wine now had *forward fruit*, maybe due to filtration. I confronted Stradlattière, and boy, was I upset.

"Nobody's saying that you filtered the wine. The thing is, the last time I was here the wine was nice and *cloudy*, and now it *isn't*. I'm not saying that anyone filtered it, except that it looks like it was *filtered*, and it wouldn't look *filtered* and thoroughly *eviscerated* and completely *wrecked* and all if some *moron* didn't take it into his head to fix something that was utterly *perfect* before he ran it through his moron *filter pads* or maybe through some moron *diatomaceous earth* or before he had *fined* it half to death with *gelatin* and all or some other wine ruination agent, all the while thinking that he was a pretty smooth winemaker."

Stradlattière had that little smug expression on his face.

"You filtered it, didn't you, you cretin, imbecile, moron bastard. You probably fined it too, didn't you?" I was bawling now. "Say it, you bastard. Say that you *filtered* it. You probably ran it through a *centrifuge* too, you moron centrifuging bastard!"

"*Je t'avertis,*[53] Bobby. Just watch it, will ya."

"You wrecked it, Stradlattière! You totally wrecked it! You filtered it like all the other wines you filtered. It was absolutely perfect, the way the fruit stayed in the back and all, and now the fruit is all *forward*. You wrecked it, you crazy, fruit-forward, fining, filtering, moron bastard!"

I didn't see him hit me, but a few moments later I was lying face up on the cellar floor and oozing rather profusely. The red splotch on the collar of my shirt turned out to be only the

---

51. Station wagon.   **52.** Left-handed clamp.   **53.** "I'm warning ya."

deep, heady Pencey *rouge* that I must have accidentally spilled on myself, but I still pretended that I had been knifed by a thug in a back alley in Marseilles. I staggered out the back door of the domaine, tripping over another one of those new heavy-toast barrels that I had left there, almost breaking my goddamn neck.

As I was leaving the domaine, I shouted at the top of my lungs, "Bite my hard tannins, you *bâtards!*" I swear, I can be *très infantile* at times.

I limped out of the domaine, struggled into my Peugeot *break,* and beat a hasty retreat to the nearby town of Pau to check into the slightly ratty joint, the Hôtel de Pacherenc, where I always stayed. After ordering a double Armagnac at the bar, I headed up to my room. In the elevator I met a very seedy-looking elevator man with the name *Maurice* embroidered on his uniform. He hissed suggestively, "Tu as soif, mon brave?[54] Or is it *trop tard* for you?"

I ignored him.

"I mean, are you looking for a real good wine *chef?* I work at night as a *lisitier,*[55] but I also run a small-time business as a *courtier de vin.* I can get you *branché*[56] with a very clean, ready-to-drink Beaujolais for five francs a liter, four hundred fifty francs a hecto, *en vrac.* How 'bout I send a sample bottle up to your room so that you can give it a try, *hein?*"

I don't know how I get into these messes, but a few minutes later there was a knock on the door. The attractive and scantily clad young *gigolette*[57] who brought up the bottle wanted to open it then and there, but I told her that I wasn't in the mood for tasting any wine just now.

"What's the matter with you, *chéri?* Can't you drink?"

"How about if we just talk about the wine and not drink it? I'll pay you for the bottle and all, but I just can't drink. I've been having problems with my whatchamacallit, my *prise de foie.*"

She looked at me a little funny, but we ended up getting on pretty well, talking about all the crummy *riches vignerons*—bastards who won't spring for new *barriques* and all. When it was time to go, she said, "That'll be eight francs for the liter bottle."

"But the guy in the elevator, Maurice, told me it was five francs, and that's all I'm gonna pay." I knew something like this was going to happen. It always does when you're dealing with *courtiers* in the south of France.

"No, it was six francs a liter and five hundred francs a hecto *en vrac,* but the bottle and the cork will cost you extra, M. Grippe-sou."

I was afraid of a run-in with Maurice, who looked as if he could lift a new thick-staved heavy-char barrel over his head and smash it to pieces without much problem, so I ran down the back-stairs of the hotel, through the back of the lobby, and out into the street and hailed the first taxi I saw.

The cab was pretty crummy. In fact it smelled as if someone had tossed their *gâteaux secs*

---

54. "You thirsty, fella?" **55.** Conducteur d'ascenseur, or "elevator operator."
56. Hooked-up. **57.** Undoubtedly a *gigolette de* Gigondas.

in it, but I was desperate to leave the hotel and just wanted to drive around for a little while to clear my head.

"Where to?" the cabbie asked.

That brought me up short. I've always been so keen on tasting about a million wines a day when I come to France that I've never really had any time for the luxury of sightseeing.

Suddenly I knew exactly where I wanted to go. "Take me out to the countryside, *s'il vous plaît.*"

Now, normally when I come to Gascony in the late spring or early summer and all, there are these ducks and geese just about everywhere on those cute little *fermes artisanales.* The farmers seem to pay a lot of attention to the little bastards. I mean, it seems as if they really care. But every year when I come back in the dead of winter, they all seem to just disappear. I've always wondered where all the ducks and geese go in the winter.

"Hey, cabbie," I said. "You know all those duck and goose farms out by the edge of town? Well, you know the little lagoons where the ducks swim around? In the springtime and all? Do you happen to know where they go in the wintertime, by any chance?"

"Where who goes?"

"The ducks and geese. Do you know, by any chance? I mean does somebody come around in a truck or something and take them away, or do they fly away by themselves—go south or something?"

"*Tu te moques de moi, jobard?*[58] Where do you think the ducks go, you, *espèce d'imbécile, triple buse?*[59] *Tu es bête à bouffer du foin, toi!*"[60]

"I'm asking you, and you don't have to get all huffy about it. I just want to know where they go and all."

"*Ma foi,* I've met some pretty stupid Americans in my time, but you are a *sot à vingt-quatre carats.*[61] Here we are, driving around in the land of *magret de canard,* and you're asking me where the hell the ducks go? *Quelle imbécillité!*"

"Well, you don't have to get all mad about it." I can't believe how touchy some people can get about things. "OK, cabbie, let's forget about the ducks and go visit a distillery instead."

We drove for a while through the country on the Route Nationale past a number of towns that were so picturesque they just about reeked, until we came to this town. I couldn't believe the signpost for the name of the place when I saw it. Someone had replaced the name of the town—it must have been Saint Somebody or Other—with the word *Condom.* It just floored me that someone would write the word *Condom* on the city signpost where kids and all could see it. What was even more incredible was that everywhere we drove in the town, on all the signposts that led in and out of the town, someone had written the word *Condom.*

That's the whole trouble. You can't ever find a place that's nice and peaceful, because there

58. "Are you making fun of me?"   **59.** Literally "triple buzzard" or "triple idiot."
60. "You're stupid enough to eat hay."   **61.** A twenty-four-carat imbecile.

isn't any. You may *think* there is, but once you get there, when you're not looking, somebody'll sneak up and write *Condom* right under your nose. Or fine and filter your lovely cloudy wine. Or leave extra buds on their vines so that the yields are too high. Or pick too early.

That's all I'm going to tell about. I could probably tell you what I did after I got back to the States, and how I got a bunch of retailers to end-stack my inexpensive Côtes de Thonge—only $6.95 on the East Coast, with a 10 percent discount if you buy by the case, but I don't feel like going into it. I really don't. That stuff doesn't interest me too much right now.

About all I know is, I sort of miss everybody I told you about. Even old Stradlattière and Acklé, for instance. I think I even miss that Maurice with his goddamn five-francs-a-liter Beaujolais. It's funny. Don't ever tell anybody anything about the wine business. If you do, they'll think that you're having more fun than you really are. **(FALL 2000)**

⟜ This story virtually wrote itself once the premise fell into place. I have myself been a visitor to Gascony often, originally as I was learning about microoxygenation from Patrick Ducourneau, and then when I worked on a collaborative Madiran wine here with Alain Bortolussi of Château Viella, which we called "Heart of Darkness." Bobby Kacher and I shared a *courtier de vin,* a wine-sourcing consultant who acted as a sort of middleman between producer and buyer, so Bobby and I were always on one another's trail, sniffing out each other's business. I think Bobby's passion and love for the wine business have been a great boon, but I cannot, of course, equally share his or his character's enthusiasm for 600 percent new oak. I was able to stay close to the plot line of *Catcher* fairly well, but in the segment where Bobby is "fixed up" on a date with a young woman to taste wine, I owe a debt to the classic Woody Allen story "The Whore of Mensa" for the conceit of alternative, sublimated avenues of fulfillment.

A Clockwork Orange Muscat

BY THOMAS "ANDY" BURGESS

It's Harvest Time, Call in the Chemists . . .

———

Winemakers like to say wine is grown in the vineyard. But more and more of the wine produced in the United States is grown in the lab. In the last five years, new treatments and additives ranging from smoky oak chips to tropical-flavored fermenting yeasts have spread through the 500-million-gallon-a-year American wine industry whose epicenter is California. They have enabled winemakers to adjust the taste and texture of their products in response to consumer demand, obscuring the line between what is natural and what is not. . . . Winemakers say privately that the industry's effort to manipulate the taste and texture in wine reflects the influence of leading critics like Robert Parker, whose rating scores can mean the difference between success and failure. . . . Enologix, a Sonoma company that caters to the wine industry, has developed computer software that predicts how a wine will score in reviews even while it is still juice. Enologix's founder, Leo McCloskey, said the software offered a noninvasive way to let winemakers know early if they have a potential hit. Mr. McCloskey said sixty-five wineries had bought his software.

—ALICE FEIRING, *NEW YORK TIMES*, AUGUST 26, 2001

"So, what will it be?"

There was me, that is, Alexis, and my three dreggies, that is, Enrico, Jean-Luc, and Andres, and we sat in the Kistler Malo-bar, making up our clendenens what to do with the evening. The Kistler Malo-bar was a malo-plus oenotechnoia, and you may, o my beaux-frères, have forgotten what these oenotechnoias were like in those eremita hardpress days. You could jed-steele your Melrot with vellocet or Synthbois™ or Tanninplus™ or Terprelease™ or one or two other FATB-sanctioned "ameliorants," which would give you a nice quiet harlanshow fifteen minutes of tasting and viewing pleasure, admiring Bob and All His Holy Saint-Emilions in your left shoe with lights bursting all over your ramey. Those were the officially sanctioned "Special F.X." available at most Malo-bars. The mysticcliffs, sorry, that would be the Malo-bar "supplements" in veckspeak, could be quite amusing and mondavisney, but at the end of the day it was still Melrot and only Melrot in infinite doonification and combination that one found on each and every carta at every Malo-bar in the greater retro metro area, and *that* left a very bitter davisscore in my swill bucket. The thought of an infinitely vast vinous universe inhabited exclusively by the Melrot Death Star impelled me to see red, if you really want to know the Bob's honest perception. But chromically speaking, my mood was already shifting rapidly, reverse dopplering irrevocably in the direction of the ultraviolaceous. Bottles of Melrot were meant to be smashed to bits, and their dreggy-wegs daubed on one's ginagallo would provide for the most harlanshow warpaint. This would be a nuits to remember.

"What's it going to be then, eh?"

There were a few sophistos at the Malo-bar, dressed to the 99s, all smug in their latest fashion statement napa-ease, smoking their long torpedo-shaped marvins. There were some truly bestbuy turleys in the Malo-bar as well, one, the most well-structured turley I believe I had ever vittied. She was just strutting her stuffing all around the Malo-bar, all phenoripeness and all, and what a seductive terrytheise that trailed in her wake. The old chave was in a state of sensory overload, which seemed to provoke a certain sympathetic reaction in the more nether parts, o my beaux-frères. This bestbuy turley had the most harlanshow suckling I had ever vittied, not to mention the most stupendonormous set of parkerpoints. It was all joy, wonder, and gobby-wobs of pure hedonistic pleasure; this was clearly a turley worth laying down. I wondered to myself if they were real parkerpoints or just merely chapouties, so I grabbed myself a grgichful and sure enough those parkerpoints were bestbuy, as stunning an example of the wondrous bryantosity of Bob's work on this terroir, o my beaux-frères. I wanted nothing more than to just kayjay the turley right then and there in the Malo-bar, get right down and do the bretty deed, the old zin-out, zin-out is what I'm talking about, o my beaux-frères. It was truly everything I could do to keep the old wagner in my joshjensens. But there were other more pressing matters that needed attending to.

I don't think I've had a chance to mention what myself, Alexis, and my cru, that would be my dreggies, were about. The mere existence of Malo-bars, which were nothing more than vendition outlets for Sousecorpse, a vast multinash microsoftop dedicated to the wholesale propagation of Still More Melrot, albeit with all manner of harlanshow mysticcliffs, we, that is to say, my dreggies and my very delicate self, took to be a very personal affront to our young and very tender sensibilities. We stood for vinarchy—all for vinum and vinum for all—of the purest free-run varietal. Up the Scuppernong and Long Live Loureiro. The Malo-bars might be all well and bestbuy for plusgras sophistos, thoroughly devoid of bestbuy davisscore, who were perfectly ortman to just suck on their marvins whilst swilling one spiegelau after another of wretchedly e-z-listen, predictably gustostatic Melrot. They were clearly incapable of understanding that there might be more terrytheises and davisscores in himmelreich and on *terroir* than were dreamt of in their Speculum Vinum (a wholly owned subsidiary of Sousecorpse Ink).

I must add parenthetically that nothing provoked these flights of vinum fantasy and uva dreams more intensely than when I wrapped my recchies around the music of the pauldraper and beloved Ludwig Vin. In considering the splendido proliferation of esoteric uvas, each a wondrous nympho sympho of the senses in its own right, I could not help but hear in my clendenen's recchie the choral movement of the great Ludwig Vin's Ninth sympho with its stirring "Ode to Scheu."

Scheu (duh), harlanshow juice of Lingenfelder
More fragrant than Elysium™,
Remaindered on shelves, in restos oft unordered
Fragrant of cassis, grapefruit, and wild plum.

The soaring aspiration, the infinite longing for comprehension and acceptance, and the ultimate tragic destiny of this misunderstood uva brought a slight arbormistiness to my newmansown but rendered the work of myself and my cru as absolut as day. There were many bowties and bow-ties of Melrot out there, and they all wanted a thorough bashing, splashing, and smashing.

I was feeling quite diprotic and pretty bestbuy despite the fairly reductive atmosphere of the Malo-bar when I vittied the three Sousecorpse primitivos sitting at the counter all together, they, the roving troubleshooters and nominal keepers of the piesporter of the sundry Malo-bars in the greater retro metro area. I had vittied these bretty sucklingholes several times before, and they knew too well the proclivities of your humble narrator. They were none too ortman to behold the likes of Alex's and his cru in their Malo-bar, o my beaux-frères. In fact, they looked like they were ready to rombauer at a moment's notice, given a closdelachance, but there were like four of us, who were all pretty sharp with our pique-olits, so I left it to them to call the play. They were dressed in the height of Sousecorpse fashion, with pommie-rol and vinverdhe and johnlocke wigs broad-brimmed on their rameys. I had met the chief Sousecorpseman primitivo once before under extremely reductive circumstances. He was definitely a highly not-recommended, drytannin nec. I had him appelled Australopithecus.

"So, young Alexis, we meet again. Long time, no vitty. I understand that you're not enjoying all the flavors currently being featured tonight at the Malo-bar."

The mec's elevated pH tone of orson set my gnashers on edge. I wanted nothing more than to get my grgiches on him, give him a little davisscore of a very important saigner with my pique-olit, introduce him to a little punching down, a little pummeling over, perhaps breaking up the old chapeau a bit. O, my beaux-frères, I would let his catty-wattikins out of the bag, show him some tannino management.

"Something wrong with your Melrot, little Alexis? Perhaps your spiegelau requires a little more Synthbois™, eh?"

"Do you honestly believe that Melrot is really all of what vinum is about, Pithecus? There is something so bretty about your lot. The whole reductive business stinks to himmelreich."

The atmosphere in the very crowded Malo-bar was growing progressively more closed-in.

"Melrot is Melrot, young Alexis. It doesn't matter from whence it derives. Our marketing gajas at Sousecorpse have done the most comprehensive market research and have learned incontrovertibly that our users crave merely a little Synthbois™, the appropriate dose of Texturol™, and a dash of Rubi-pro™ for color stability, and they're as ortman as can be. They wouldn't know the difference if the pauldraper Saint Petrus himself came down from the right hand of Bob and slid down their gorgeousgeorges in velvet underjoshjensens. We're not about to adelsheim their rameys with a bunch of randally random options now, are we? One Melrot, please, double dose of Synthbois™ for my bestbuy man here . . ."

I could not bear to hear any more of this utter cribari. I could feel the melroticidal impulse in my weingut rising to a cellarselect level. I'd tolmach the bastardo, smash the lot of his spiegelaus and bow-ties. It was absolutely (*sic*) time, indeed well past time, for a splash and lash of the old ultraviolaceous.

My cru, pique-olits drawn, moved in on the Sousecorpsemen, but, perception be told, the Sousecorpsemen o.j.'ed themselves quite bestbuy in the poesy of violaceousness, the ungentlemanly art of maculanmanship. The Sousecorpsemen were no slouches with a quick jaboulet to the redwaukesha, a vicious tolmach to the ris-de-vo-di-oh-do, a knee to the gracefamily sparklies, and for a while my cru were able to give as bestbuy as they got. When the Sousecorpsemen swung their firestone irons high above their rameys and brought them down with a heartyburgundering thud on the epaulés of my nobbly-rottery cru, I felt pretty heartyburgunder myself, deep in the weingut, o my beaux-frères.

All infresno seemed to have broken loose, and some of the sophistos had found themselves unpatrickwilling participants in the clusterfrick brettiness that was occurring in the Malo-bar. While some were quite dis-softtannined by the brettiness, others simply imagined that this barberic (*sic*) activity was perhaps part of the evening's mondavisney and continued to placidly and clendenenlessly sip their Melrot. Before I knew what was happening, the dunnest Sousecorpseman had his grgiches on my gorgeousgeorge and was attempting to wring it like so much frenchlaundry. I was able to get in one good smash to the swill bucket before he and his fellow corpsemen had me subdued. My trusted cru, battered and shattered, pigé-ed and frisé-ed, had dispersed off into the nuits.

"Take your bretty grgiches off of me!" I montebellowed. "Ungrgich me!" But there were three of them now who held me with a firmly astringent grip.

I was taken into custody by a special unnatural vinum unit of the flickers and removed to a top-secret Region One facility in the cool naparidge climat of Norcal. I was put before a sort of kangarooridge court (appropriately enough) and summarily found guilty of "crimes and mis-dougmeadors against Lifestyle." The sentencing pointscorer thundermountained, "Your compulsion to smash spiegelaus and bow-ties of Melrot is deemed by the Norcal prefecture of the Newwood Order to be subversive and inconsistent with the Gracious Living Lifestyle, which we hold in the Holy Name of Dominus to be sacrosanct, one Stylistic under Bob. You are to be immediately remanded to the Sunnysainthellacious Facility for the Criminally Vinsane, where you are to undergo an experimental treatment protocol meant to induce a new soft-tannin attitude in your recioto personage. All will become absolut to you in the phenological ripeness of time. May Bob have mercy on your soul." I could not then even begin to imagine the unspeakably lowscore bargain-bin, unrecommended humiliations that lay in packagestore for me, o my beaux-frères.

At the Sunnysainthellacious Facility for the Criminally Vinsane, I learned that my treatment was to consist of "merely vittying some films at the zinny," and that seemed to be a rather highlyrecommended mondavisney to me, but as I was soon to learn, this was like no zinny I had ever vittied before. Against the right-hand wall of the zinny was a bank of all like little meters, and in the middle of the floor was like a dentist's chair with all lengths of oldtelegraph-wire running from it. I found they were strapping my grgiches to the chair-arms, and my legslarry were like stuck to a footrest.

"This must be a real harlanshow film if you're so keen on my vittying it."

"Harlanshow is right, my friend. You are about to behold a real show of harlans." And then I had like a cap stuck on my ramey, and I could vitty all the wires running away from it, and they stuck a suction pad on my sbragia and one on the old redwaukesha.

I cannot properly convey to you the highly reductive, unspeakable degradations and abazziaments I was compelled to suffer, the cribari I was forced to endure, o my beaux-frères, at the Sunnysainthellacious Facility for the Criminally Vinsane. *The film that I was forced to vitty with my own newmansowns fixed open, sitting in the dentist's chair, was none other than A* Place in the Sun, *which featured the highly unrecommended Keanu Reeves!* After just twenty minutes of vittying this hearty-burgundering piece of cribari, I was heartyburgunder to my sbragia. "Stop the film! I can't stand any more! Please, o please, stop the film! For the love of Bob!" I shrieked.

"Stop it? Stop it, did you say? Why, we've hardly started," said the veck who ran the projector, and he and the others smaragd quite loud.

My tormentors had even more fiendish plans for me. After forcing me to vitty *A Place in the Sun* perhaps twenty or thirty times, they devised a yet more cunning, cruel, and unusual torture for me. They fitted recchie-muffs over my ramey so that I might be able to hear in glorious cribariphonia recordings of the Dogstar band, playing continuously on an infinite tape-loop. Whilst trying my best to sbragia this thoroughly reductive bocksbeutel-band, a totally frontal shroeck to my recchies, I was compelled to vitty in rapid, flash sequence, snappies of bow-ties of my most cherished Grignolino, Schioppettino, and Teroldego Rotaliano. I had the twin images of Negroamaro and Malvasia Nera in my newmansowns as I was getting hearty-burgunder all over the horsepiece robe I was wearing. Any deep affection or attachment I might have harbored for obscure uvas was becoming permanently linked with this bretty to the core and unrecommended with extreme prejudice schlockophony. The bestbuy bliss I once enjoyed with Bombino Bianco, the highlyrecommended reverie of Refosco dal Peduncolo Rosso, the sweet cellarselectedness of harlanshow Huxelrebe, were brutally and silveroakedly wrested from me, o my beaux-frères. It was not long before I felt the vague desire for the clendenenless satiation that comes with a good dosage of Melrot, heavy on the Synthbois™.

My treatment lasted a fortnight, and I was soon after released back into the civilian population of the greater retro metro area. I became a regular customer at the Kistler Malo-bars. "What'll it be, young Alexis?" the barman would ask.

"Oh, the usual would be fine. No, I feel exceptionally adventurous tonight. Why don't you add an extra shot of Terprelease™?" *(FALL 2001)*

This was a wonderful vehicle for me, one that allowed me to vent through wild exaggeration and extravagant language my profound concerns about the commodification and homogenization of the wine business. Burgess himself, in his dystopic vision, invented a new language for his characters, and I did the same for mine, impressed by the fact that the world of wine geekdom already seems to speak something like a very private dialect. As Burgess did, I have simply taken some of the dominant (vini-)cultural trends and extended them to their nightmarish conclusion. Already when one walks into a wineshop these days, the first thing that strikes one is the enormous range of brightly colored, clever labels, each somehow clamoring for one's attention.[62] What is in fact extraordinary is how alike the wines themselves are (at least the ones from the New World) underneath the labels. The New World wines, often synthetic confections, all parkerpoints and suckling, sorry, let's make that, wines of overly obvious charm and meager depth, are cynically crafted to be pleasing and compliant to the American consumer—hardly a bestbuy outcome.

62. In "The Vinferno" I confess to my own shameful part in this state of affairs, for which I am certainly doomed to Wine Hell.

Trotanoy's Complaint

BY PHILIP ROTHSCHILD

Trotanoy's Complaint: (trôt-en-wahz kem-plant') n. (after Alexander Trotanoy, 1953–) A disorder in which strongly felt impulses to use wine as an appropriate beverage with meals perpetually war with extreme psychosexual longings, often of a perverse nature, with wine serving as the object of infantile cathexis. Weinspiel says, "Acts of exhibitionism, Wine Spectatorism, fetishism, auto-eno-eroticism and generalized oral fixation are plentiful; as a consequence of the patient's limited financial means, however, neither fantasy nor act issues in genuine gratification of the palate, but rather in overriding feelings of shame, inadequacy, and the morbid dread of loss of cellar" (O. Weinspiel, "The Puzzled Pinot," in "Studies in Nervosity," ed. Ivan Moorewood, special issue, *Internationale Zeitschrift für Oenopsychoanalyse* 24 [1961]: 100). It is believed by Weinspiel that many of the symptoms can be traced to the bonds obtaining in the wine taster/wine life–stylist relationship.

THE MOST UNFORGETTABLE WINE I EVER DRANK

He was so deeply imbedded in my consciousness that for a long time I imagined he was everywhere and all-knowing. His presence hung like a heady, wine-drenched mist in every tasting room and cellar I ever visited, in every kitchen or dining room where some poor schmuck was trying to gain mastery over his vinous domain. Fine wine, terrible wine—it didn't matter. He was all over it like Clos des Mouches on schist. I was thoroughly conversant with his opinions on seemingly every wine ever produced, and woe to the wine that was neither utterly saturated in color *nor* physiologically mature *nor* fully extracted *nor* perfected in a battery of brand-new heavily toasted (heads included) *barriques. Gevalt* if the winemaker owned a filter or even contemplated its purchase. Everyone knows that simply having one will ineluctably result in its compulsive use and abuse; it *was* only a matter of time. *Vay ist mir* to hear talk about casein or other *milchig* fining agents—the only thing worse would be mixing them with *fleishig* (and *trayf*) gelatin! And oy, heaven forbid if he suspected that a wine was made from grapes harvested at a yield exceeding forty-five hectos per hectare—you might never hear the end of it. A *schande* for the appellation.

The scary thing, Doctor, was not that I knew and could parrot his every opinion and summon up the numerical rating of every single wine he had ever tasted, but rather that I imagined (and I could not, for the life of me, work out the operative mechanism) that, at the precise moment I was perusing a copy of the *Wine Abdicate, he* could somehow telepathically ascertain exactly what sort of palate I really possessed, if I were refined enough to appreciate the palate-crushing tannins of a young claret in a ripe vintage. Did I truly pine for *Le Pin?* Did I really believe that 200 percent new oak could bring gustatory ecstasy? How he could possibly know my deepest thoughts on these arcane subjects I couldn't fathom, but I knew with absolute conviction that he most certainly did. When I put down my copy of the *Abdicate*, I imagined that he would nod off into a drowsy reverie or slumber. The moment I picked it up again, he would snortingly rouse himself into wakefulness.

I lived at home with my parents well into my young adulthood, Doctor, it gives me no great pride to admit. They were a constant source of anxiety and shame to me, in no small part due to their incomprehension of the elegant nuances and extraordinary possibilities of fine wine. For them, the acme of oenological excellence began and ended with Manischewitz Elderberry, *kosher l'pesach.* They were preternaturally frugal and refused to ever throw anything away, always decanting the unconsumed glasses back into the bottle at the end of the yearly seder, which was the only occasion that wine was ever to be seen at our table when I was growing up. I am quite sure there was but a single bottle of Manischewitz Elderberry, produced during the Johnson administration, that lasted us at least until the ouster of Tricky Dick. In recalling it now, I know it was an old bottle because its familiar clunky squarish shape did not have a government warning label on it, though it was possible that the warning had fallen off due to exposure to toxic levels of mutant microbial life-forms germinating in the science experiment that was my mother's refrigerator.

My parents, who were quite moderate in their consumption, considered it extremely bad form not to at least take a taste of wine when the *b'rucha,* or ritual blessing over the wine, was said. I remember one seder when it was absolutely impossible for me to consider tasting this impossibly disgusting liquid semi-life-form that had been decanted and recanted an endless number of times. "Just a taste, Alex. It wouldn't kill you," my mother says to me.

"No, Mother, I beg to differ. It *would* kill me, in fact it will kill all of us. The CDC in Atlanta will be very interested to learn why the entire Trotanoy family of Newark, New Jersey, was immediately sickened unto death by uncontrollable hemorrhagic bleeding from all of their orifices as well as from the formation of gangrenously suppurating green pustules . . ."

"Would you look at that mouth on him?" she asks my father, now taking it to the jury. "He's such an expert wine taster. I don't know what kind of palate you have, Mr. Bigshot, Mr. Winesnob, but you've got quite a mouth on you, I'll tell you that. Alex, are you or are you not going to say a *b'rucha* and taste the wine?"

"Please, Mother, I'd rather not."

"Are you saying that you're too good, too refined, too la-di-da for Manischewitz?"

"Uh, yes, Mother, I am."

"As your mother, *I command you to taste the wine!*" This would be utterly comical except for the fact that my mother, and I'm not kidding, Doctor, my mother had taken the corkscrew into her hand and was holding the business end of it poised at my throat. "Just take one little sippy for your mother, Alex." My mother was going to stab me with a corkscrew if I did not at least take a little sippy of Manischewitz!

I don't know if it was the shame of being subjected to such execrable bottles as a child that led to my obsession with fine, wildly expensive, and thoroughly mythical wine when I was older, and that turned me into an unregenerate cork sniffer, a pervert as much for the purple prose of hard-core winespeak as for the heady, violaceous liquid itself. When I turned twenty-one, I began to collect a few bottles in a modest cellar in the basement of my parent's split-level home. A friend had given me a subscription to the *Wine Abdicate* as a joke; who could have predicted the explosive effect it would have on my already overstimulated, still more or less adolescent, imagination? But I couldn't help myself, Doctor, the prose was absolutely inflammatory, most especially when the noted score exceeded 90 points. You needed to wear an asbestos tasting-apron just to sit down to the tasting notes! "This wine is the complete fulfillment of all of one's hedonistic fantasies and deepest and darkest sensual yearnings . . . a wine of softly exquisite texture, velvety mouthfeel . . . voluptuous body and legs that go on forever . . . an orgiastic fruit-bomb . . . juicy, melting, liquid ambrosia . . . an explosive detonation of the senses with gobs of ripe and decadently overripe fruit . . . lashings of oak . . . spurts of flavor!"

Doctor, such overheated prose was simply more than this easily excitable young man could take without losing his cool. I had been in the habit of drinking wines that complemented meals, that showed typicity and good complexity, but after reading the grossly tumescent, luridly carminative tasting notes of the *Wine Abdicate,* it was clearly evident that I was missing out on Something Big! He was describing wines that the gods themselves would drink, wines that were undisputedly too good for the likes of me. The wines were almost always unobtainable or, if obtainable, outlandishly expensive. And yet, when I was able to lay my hands on one or two of these rare and precious beauties, I felt curiously let down. His language had set me up with expectations that no real wine could meet, but this just further inflamed my insatiable thirst for total hedonic fulfillment. My Côte Rôtie "Côte Blonde" was enjoyable but somehow not quite as perfectly blonde (nor did it come with a standard-issue, lightly freckled, pertly turned-up nose) as his. The Kistler Chardonnays I tasted were neither as voluptuously creamy nor as tantalizingly dreamy as the ones described in his breathless prose. The classic Burgundies that I tasted from the Côtes de Nuits, while spicy and fragrant, were not the sybaritic pleasure bombs that I had expected and, while very pleasant, did not quite make my night, if you know what I'm talking about. Doctor, *I wanted what he was having!*

RACKING OFF

My mania had reached such a dangerous level that, when the monthly copy of the *Abdicate* arrived at our house, I would race out to the mailbox and begin leafing through the magazine while standing in the driveway. I could not let a single moment elapse before learning what was the hottest, most succulently sensual new wine coming down the pike, what new empyrean universe of unspeakably exquisite pleasure was soon to be broached. In scanning the reviews, I became a man possessed, intoxicated by the idea of my own intoxication. I could almost smell the fragrantly musky 90-plus-pointers reclining casually, almost as if one had just come upon them, quite by accident, between the paginated sheets of the journal. I imagined them lurking languorously, these wily and wanton wines, available to anyone, at least in principle, with a wad thick enough to pay the freight and take them home. When I, at last, apprehended the elusive 90-plus-pointer of my dreams, there was no recourse but to beat a hasty visit to the wine cellar.

"Alex, what are you doing down there?" my mother would ask.

"Uuuh."

"Alex, why have you locked the door to the cellar? Are you having trouble getting the cork out? I *insist* on knowing what you are doing!"

"Nuuh."

"Alex, you know that you could easily hurt yourself with those *meshuggene* Screwpulls. I think I need to come down this very instant and make sure you're all right. Billy Schmendrick injured himself so badly with one of those he had to be taken to the hospital for twelve stitches."

"I-I-I'm alright, Ma."

"I don't like the sound of it. And for your information, your sister has told me what you do down there." This would put me in a state of complete panic—the shame, the embarrassment of being apprehended with the mensual organ itself—the *Abdicate* is what I mean to say—in my own hands! I'd turn a shade of crimson deeper than the most optically opaque, hugely numerated wine in his review.

"Your sister tells me that you eat foie gras with sauternes on a regular basis. Not to mention that I don't think it's kosher—do you know what that *chazerei* can do to your cholesterol? I'm coming down this very second . . ."

My obsession was so all-consuming that I cringe at some of my more outrageous stunts. (But the wine remembers.) I recall a dinner party my mother threw for some of her friends from the sisterhood of her temple in which the main course was a lovely leg of mutton. Well, I can really offer no excuse for my poor behavior, but the word *mutton* sounded a little too close to *Mouton* for my taste and, I'm afraid, for the taste of the meat as well, when it was finally brought to table. My mother inadvertently served *mouton à la façon Alex* to the sisterhood of Temple Beth Chalone, and she *kvelled* from the many compliments she received on the presentation of the dish.

ROMANÉE-CONTI CRAZY

My ardor for great, unobtainable wine remained unquenched (and unquenchable), knowing no metes (apart from mutton) and bounds. But I was tortured by my convoluted pathway to G-L-O-R-I-Aous fulfillment, fettered as I was by the bizarre linkage of palate and nether parts. I blame *him* for the terrible confusion I experienced in sorting out these twinned appetites. I could not pursue the One (wine) without experiencing a radical deflection, a sort of call forwarding of the limbic system, toward the Other. I needed only to hear the names of the wines,[63] Doctor—so suggestive, so naughty, so much more promising of pleasure and fraught with sensual possibility than the actual Bordeaux in the hand—and I was transported: Leothrilled Lascases, Feytitilated-Clinet. I was hot for Haut-Brion, Doctor. I got down for Kuentz-Bas. There was lust in my heart for Lustau, an itch for Laguiche, and I could never get enough Pousse d'Or. (But tell me, Doctor, who does?) I burned for Bernard Ropiteau and was ravenous for Raveneau. I was a rutting ram for Ramonet and a smitten kitten for that saucy Sauzet. What can I say? Some like it tart. Leflaive's *sève* sapped my very soul. Bienvenue-Bâtard, *straingère*.

I would shinny the ivory tower of Latour in a nanosecond for a midnight stairway to heaven, Doctor. You're talking to an unregenerate Lafite fetishist here. (I am a virtual shoe-in for the position.) Tell me, Doctor, you're the maven, could there possibly be anything finer than Château More-goo? Nothing, except perhaps L'Emission in a hot vintage. I was the premier of the Premiers Crudes Classés, Doctor, a one-man first-growth industry. Petrus? I was the disciple's disciple. I built a holy shrine in my wine cellar to Saint Peter. I *was* Château Palmer! I had a Prurient Lichine interest in the jizz in Giscours, and for the trim in Trimbach. Hugel was huge with me, Doctor, just h-u-g-e. Myself, I've got bigger stones than you'll find in Châteauneuf-du-Pape. Fill it to the rim with Pish on Schlongville and then Pish on the Land! The feisty Cahors needs spanking, Doctor, and who better than I for the Jobard? Hook me up with a raunchy Ronchi di Cialla, and let me sip on some Perrier-Jouissance. Allow me to belly up to a Montepulchritudinous d'Abruzzo, and let me chevy some Chevillon; I'll Rouget it roundly and show it the full Montille. Knick-knack, Alex-whack, go fetch this dog a Beaune! Where's DuBoeuf? In my fist, Doctor, that's where!

THE FINISH

Doctor, after years of chasing after great wine, I feel that I've boarded a fast and expensive train to nowhere. I'm riding forever 'neath the streets of Boston, and, quite literally, I can't get off. The stations stream past me in an endless and dizzying procession. They have names like La Turque and Cathelin and Ermita. Each is more famous, more precious than the one that came before it. Guigal, Bonneau, Chave. Chave—that's *schav* where I come from, *but it ain't as cheap as borscht,* Doctor. Angelo Gaja . . . Let him *fardrai* his own Gaja-*ische kop*. Forgive me, Doctor, I'm almost Dunn. The names haunt me. I hear them in my dreams. I wake up screaming for Screaming Eagle. There but for the Grace Family Vineyard go I. I would do better, Doctor, but I have been stricken with the Mark of Sin. I am Pouilly-Fuissé-whipped by Harlan the Harlot Estate and by Helen Turgid. I am deeply into Dominus-submissive, and it's into the Dalla Valle of Fear I tread. I might die if I can't have a case of Peter Michael. Excuse me, *Sir* Peter. *I'll show him Sir Peter!*

63. The names of the classified growths were like magical totemic incantations—mantras for Montrose, shout-outs for Châteaux Fetish-Clinet and Obeah-Batailley. For me it was strictly voodoo. Who do? Ducru Boogaloo, that's who!

I crave surcease from this exhausting and frenzied search; I want out of this crazy search, to stop chasing the impossible, unattainable Cybill Shepherd (I date myself, but we've been over that before, haven't we, Doctor?), Côte-Blonde fantasy. I am chasing after something that is always so close and yet is always infinitely receding into the distance. *Objets* in the mirror may be more expensive than they appear. The extraordinary, mythic 100-pointer that seems to vanish up its own Assmanshäuser. Like the smile of the Cheshire cat, it magically disappears, leaving only the empty bottle. Good-bye and thanks for the Mammolo. My lust for bottles of Vega Sicilia Unico has turned me into a eunuch, Doctor. I want to be able to drink normal wine that doesn't cost $250 a bottle wholesale and you have to be born on the mailing list. Where is it *geschriven* that wine has to be this way? In the *Wine Abdicate,* that's where! Doctor, I am a real case, and there's no discounting that. There's no 10 percent off for good behavior.

I know I am a sick man, Doctor, a completely unregenerate wine geek. Even without the wines—I don't even need to drink the wines, let me just peel the grapes. Let me just peel the names off the grapes and eat *them.* We were slaves to the Fer Servidou in Egypt. Go down, Mauzac. Let my Picpoul go!

Doctor, I am a wine geek who burns with a wine-geek love supreme. I find myself in the middle of a wine-and-food joke, but it ain't no joke, Doctor. Let me tell you where it *hoits,* Doctor. Let me tell you where it Heitz.

It wasn't like I ever really enjoyed Cabernet. I was fascinated by the 90-plus wines; they were the unattainable, fantasy wines, the trophy wines that told the world that you were all right. Although they were in some sense repellent to me, they were also compellingly alluring. Don't despise me, Doctor. I just need some understanding. If you prick me, do I not bleed Caymus Special Select?

PUNCH LINE: "So," said the doctor. "Now vee may perhaps to Bourgogne, yes?"

(SPRING 1999)

I must confess that I really surprised myself by writing this, and that the conversation I had with my mother, alerting her to its imminent publication, had to have been as awkward as the one Philip Roth had with *his* mother. The language of course is shocking for a winery newsletter—its outrageousness is perhaps what gives it its energy—but I think I have accurately represented some of the psychodynamics at work in the fetishism of wine collection: the quest for the orgasmic wine experience, for a wine that is bigger, more powerful (and also rarer) than the last, a thirst that is never slaked. The stylized Yiddish rant, building in the extravagance of its language, in the rhetorical flourish of mock outrage, is a perfect vehicle for expressing the absurdity of the longing for the unattainable, as it was for Portnoy. The fact is, fine wine consumption, nay, trophy wine consumption, has become a public act. We have grown increasingly exterior to our own selves; it is no longer satisfying to simply enjoy a fine wine; we must also deeply savor the fact that we are consuming something that has been publicly proclaimed to be extraordinary and accessible to only the lucky few.

I have made some use of autobiographical detail; my mother, never one to waste anything, has the tendency to retain foodstuffs in her refrigerator for years, if not decades, beyond the recommended consumption date. How she has managed to avoid poisoning our family is unknown to me. My favorite line in this piece is: "I don't even need to drink the wines, let me just peel the grapes. Let me just peel the names off the grapes and eat *them*." I don't know what unknown sector of the subconscious this came from, but this is in fact a perfect distillation of my thesis that the sym- bolic and ritualized nature of fine wine consumption has attained greater density of meaning than the ex- perience itself; somewhere in the vast semiological universe, Roland Barthes would be tickled (if only sym- bolically).

A Perfect Day for Barberafish

BY J. D. SALIGNAC

There were 872 winemakers at the ASEV convention at the Hotel Del Coronado,[64] and, ow- ing to the poor conditions of the cellular coverage in the area surrounding the resort, many of them were compelled to use the long-distance lines of the hotel. The lines had been tied up for quite some time, and the girl in 507 had to wait several hours for her call to go through.

"I have your call to Beverly Hills now, Mrs. G——," the operator said.

"Thank you," said the girl, and made room on the night table for the ashtray.

"How *are* you, sweetheart?"

"Just fine, Mom," she said, lighting up a Virginia Slims cigarette. "I've gotten too much sun myself, but I can't seem to get *him* to go outside."

"He's always been funny about that. He would always prefer to stay indoors in cold, drafty basements rather than go outside in the sunshine where it's healthy."

"Well, you know him better than I do, Mom."

"Well, of course I do. I've been his mother for forty-eight years, and you just recently mar- ried him. But I want you to know, sweetheart, that even though you are my daughter-in-*law*, I feel like you are my own flesh-and-blood daughter."

"I *know* you do, Mom."

"But what are we going to do about *him?*"

"You really don't need to worry so much, Mom. I think he's beginning to get a lot of his ir- rational and self-destructive impulses under control."

"I *do* worry, sweetheart, about his *compulsion*—yes, compulsion, you heard me—to infuriate the most influential members of the wine press. That's just not healthy. When we had the two of you over for dinner the other night, I think you were in the kitchen so you didn't hear. I just couldn't believe my ears when he started in about that nice Mr. Laube."

"What did he *say*, Mom?"

---

64. The ASEV is the American Society for Enology and Viticulture.

"I don't even think I can repeat it, sweetheart."

"Mom, *tell* me. I need to know."

"Well, his father had made some comment about him keeping that crazy bottle of German wine in *front* of him all night long, and my *son*, your husband—you know how he is with that smart mouth of his—he just couldn't help himself. You know how I feel about that, if you can't say something nice . . ."

"What *did* he say?"

"He said, 'I'd rather have a *frontal lobotomy* than a *Laube in front of me.*' Can you *believe* that? I'm telling you, he's his own worst enemy."

"Well, at least there's one thing to be thankful for: that he made the comment just between *us*. If he were to say that sort of thing to some *stranger* or God forbid, *publish* it in his crazy newsletter, my husband could just kiss good-bye his chances of getting mentioned *ever again* in the *Spectator,* much less appearing on its cover."

"*Funny* that you should mention the *Spectator,* sweetheart. You know, while he may claim otherwise, I know for a fact that he's always been absolutely *obsessed* with that magazine. A few years ago he said that he felt about the *Spectator* the same way that Ginsberg felt about *Time* magazine."

"He is a very *unusual* person, Mom."

"Definitely obsessive-compulsive, if you ask me. When we have you two over for dinner, he's always making some strange comment about the glassware. We have that nice set of Riedels that we got on sale, and granted, they're not the top of the line. Mr. Perfectionist, however, is always finding fault. He always says that he wants to *see more glass*. What do you think *that* means, sweetheart?"

"He's capable of saying just about anything, Mom."

"Sweetheart, he really needs to get some help, and right away. He's sabotaging his whole car . . ."

"Mom, you don't know the *half* of it. Sometimes I think he must feel guilty about his modest success and is just looking for ways to undermine himself."

"Certainly he needs to learn how to run a business. How can anyone produce so many different labels and not expect his wholesalers and customers to go completely *crazy?*"

"And his obsession with weird grape varieties that no one can pronounce. He really thinks he can get normal people to try—what does he call it?—greener *velveteener?* Mom, *forgive* me for saying this, but sometimes I wish he would just make *normal* wines like other winemakers." The girl paused to pour herself a glass of Sonoma-Cutrer Les Pierres Chardonnay that she had found in the room's minibar.

"And Mr. *Parker,*" said the elder Mrs. G——. "Mr. Parker has always been so incredibly nice to him. He even once called him a *national treasure.* What has he *done* to deserve the treatment Mr. National Treasure has given him? Don't get me started on the subject, but if he's wondering why he has excess inventory of his top-end wines, he has only himself to blame for going out of his way to upset Mr. Parker. No wonder the *Advocate* doesn't review the wines anymore. If he wants people to start thinking about Cigare Volant as a serious wine again, he might just think about that the next time he makes a comment about Mr. Parker's girth."

"Mom, he's talking about reining it in a little bit."

"Well, it's about time. But he's got a long way to go, sweetheart."

The girl paused to pour herself another half glass of the Chard and was now opening up a package of Famous Amos chocolate chip cookies she had found in the minibar.

"And what is it about his preoccupation with Ca' del Solo?" the girl asked. "*Solo* this, *solo* that. Everything is *solo* with him. Tell me, has he *always* been so preoccupied with these sorts of antisocial ideas? You know, he doesn't even seem to have any real *hobbies,* for Godsake. All the other winemakers here do normal things like play golf. He's spending all his time cooped up in the hotel room reading books about Hermes Trismigestus. It's just, well, weird."

"Well, sweetheart, he's always been that way. If you must know, he didn't really play well with the other kids when he was young."

"He's just so negative sometimes! Especially about wines that everybody seems to like. He doesn't even like the taste of *oak!* That's very abnormal, if you ask me. Tell me, Mom, what's *wrong* with Clos du Bois?"

"Absolutely *nothing,* sweetheart."

"I sometimes wonder if I'm not married to the Lee Harvey Oswald of winemakers . . . With all due respect," she added quickly. The girl dipped her cookie into the glass of Chardonnay wine.

"I do worry about that perverse streak in him, sweetheart. You know how obsessed he is with the Ca' del Solo labels? He was mentioning the other night how absolutely *perfect* they would be to put on lunch boxes for *children!* Can you believe that? Who knows, the next thing is, he might say something in public about how great it would be for parents to encourage their children—we're talking children here, dear—to actually *taste* wine, beginning with some of his low-alcohol fizzy products."

"I think they make you sign some sort of oath when you go into the wine business not to even think thoughts like that."

"Another thing. I don't like that terrible thing that he calls you. What was that name again, sweetheart?"

"Please, Mom, I'd rather not mention it."

"Just tell me."

"Oh, he calls me 'Miss Gastronomic Tramp of 2002,'" the girl said as she took another sip of Chardonnay wine and carried the cordless phone over to the minibar. She began rummaging through it for some smoked almonds.

"He hasn't started in with any funny business about the *stones,* has he, sweetheart?"

"I don't think so, Mom, but the word *minerality* does seem to come up a lot in conversation."

"Did I ever tell you that he used to eat *dirt* when he was a boy?"

"Well, he's not putting dirt in his wine, if that's what you mean."

"Well, just promise to call me if he gets up to any real funny business. Like telling the whole group of winemakers at the convention that *he puts Framboise in all his wines,* just for the shock value. That's his idea of a joke, your husband. I think that most people can't really tell when he's making a joke."

"Look, Mom, I really need to go. He finally decided to go down to the beach, and he may come back any minute now."

"Goodbye, sweetheart."

The girl now began excavating the minibar in earnest and removed the packages of mixed nuts, Gummy Bears, Pringles, Kettle Chips, Cheetos, Cajun Mix, Rold Gold pretzels, Kit Kat wafers, M&M's, and Snickers bars, and she arrayed them in front of her on the bed in the form of a holy altar. She made a sincere effort to breach a recalcitrant vacuum-sealed package of Kettle Chips.

The little girl who was staying at the hotel along with her parents, both of whom had come for the convention, and with her paternal grandmother, escorted the older woman from the lobby of the hotel down the walkway to the section of the beach reserved for hotel guests. She systematically stepped on every crack in the sidewalk until they reached the beach.

"Ran dull, gram," said little Malvasia del Solo. "He ran dull, gram."

"Pussycat, stop saying that. You're driving your grandmother absolutely crazy. Let's put some sunblock on you, and then you can make a nice sandcastle while your grandmother catches a little nap. Be a good girl and don't wander off."

At the precise moment the older woman shut her eyes, the little girl ran off in the direction of a lively volleyball game that was taking place down the beach. The local Coronado team was hosting the visiting Club Montonico athletes. The match appeared to be fairly lopsided in favor of the home team. The little girl ran past the volleyball players and didn't stop until she reached the place where the young man was lying on his back, engrossed in his thick book, *Die Welt als Wille und Vorstellung.*

"Are you going in the water, ran dull gram?" she asked.

The young man squinted up at Malvasia. The whiteness of his skin was blinding in the bright Southern California sunlight. The little girl imagined that she was observing an albino wino.

"Hey. Hello, Malvasia."

"Are you going in the *water?*" she repeated with some emphasis.

"I was waiting for *you,*" said the young man. "You know I don't like to go into the water unless I am accompanied by a dazzlingly attractive minor of scintillating wit and intelligence."

"Where's the *lady?*" asked Malvasia.

"Oh, the lady. She could be anywhere. Shopping at the Martha Stewart Collection. Waiting in line for admission to the Silver Oak seminar. Getting a Ravenswood tattoo on a very private bit."

"I want to go in the *water.*"

"OK, into the water we will go. Doon and doon," said the young man. The young man and little girl waded into the water, and the young man hoisted Malvasia onto the inflatable raft he had brought along with him. He propelled the girl on the raft as he swam out a safe but not insignificant distance from the shore.

"Malvasia," he said, "I'll tell you what we'll do. We'll see if we can catch a barberafish."

"A what?"

"A barberafish. I imagine you've seen quite a few barberafish in your day," the young man said.

Malvasia shook her head.

"You *haven't?* Where do you *live,* anyway?"

"I don't know."

"Sure you know. You must know. Chloe Mondavi knows where *she* lives and she's only *three and a half years old.*"

"Napa Valley, California!" Malvasia said.

"Is that anywhere near Napa Valley, California?" asked the young man.

"That's where I *live,*" Malvasia said impatiently. "I *live* in Napa Valley, California."

"You have no idea how clear that makes everything," said the young man. "My guess is that there aren't a lot of barberafish swimming around in the riparian corridors of Napa Valley, California. But the important thing is for you to just keep your eyes open for any barberafish. This is a *perfect* day for barberafish."

"I don't see any," Malvasia said.

"That's understandable. Their habits are very peculiar. Do you know what they *do,* Malvasia?"

"Of course I do, but I *forget.* Would you tell me again?"

"Well, the barberafish are not happy swimming with the other fish. Other fish swim in *schools.* Very *exclusive* schools, don't you know? The very *best* schools. Very la-di-da. The barberafish aren't terribly comfortable swimming with the bigger cabfish and chardfish in these very fancy schools. Do you know *why,* sweetheart?"

The little girl shook her head.

"The cabfish and chardfish tend to be greedy and eat up all the wonderful seaweed and other nutritious foods that the barberafish would like to eat. The barberafish has to go looking for other things to eat, like sea snails and barnacles and plankton and other rare delicacies."

"Sea snails, oh, *gross!*" said the little girl.

"Don't knock sea snails until you've tried 'em. The barberafish is actually happy to eat the odd things that the other fishes don't particularly care for," the young man explained. "The barberafish has a very refined palate."

"My daddy uses *too hunger percent new oak!*" the little girl proclaimed.

"That's very nice, sweetie. I'm extremely delighted for him. Do you know what else is strange and unique about the barberafish, my love?"

The little girl shook her head.

"The barberafish swims around and around in circles and often has no idea where the heck he is swimming. He is not as purposeful as some of the other fishes, who have a very *definite* idea of precisely where they are going. The barberafish swims for the pure joy of swimming."

"He's along for the *ride,*" said Malvasia.

"What a clever little girl!" exclaimed the young man. "As I said, the barberafish doesn't have a lot of friends among the more popular fish, so if he wants to have *any* sort of social life at all, he spends time with the really weird fish, the ones with whom no self-respecting finned and gilled creature would wish to associate."

"I think I just saw one," said Malvasia.

"I knew you had a *particular* talent for barberafish spotting, Malvasia. But I have to tell you that the fate of the barberafish is quite tragic."

"What happens?" asked Malvasia.

"Well, it is actually very sad. The barberafish, along with his friends, the dolcettofish, the moscatofish, and the troiafish, swim into these very narrow niches where they can hide from the other fishes. But you know that the barberafish's fondest wish is to be caught by a very discriminating fisherman, who will utterly appreciate his unique qualities. But these niches are so narrow and convoluted that the fisherman, even the most clever one, is never able to find the barberafish, much less catch one."

"And *then* what happens?"

"I'm sorry to tell you, Malvasia, but they die."

"I need to go back to the hotel now, ran dull gram."

The young man stepped into the elevator. "I see that you're looking at my Lafite," he said to the other passenger in the elevator, a highly tanned young woman with a prominent Ravenswood tattoo on her ankle.

"I *beg* your pardon. I happened to be looking at the door," said the woman.

"It's a perfectly normal-looking large-format bottle of Lafite. If you want to look at my Lafite, say so," said the young man. "But there's no need to be a sneak about it."

"This is my floor. I'll be getting out *now.*"

The young man arrived at his hotel room and reached for the card key in the pocket of his bathrobe, introduced the key into the slot, and quietly entered the room. He quickly unpacked his bag and extracted a Screwpull opener from the smaller valise. As he observed the sleeping form of the girl on the double bed, he manipulated the Screwpull. He went over to the bed and emptied the contents of the magnum on the form of her sleeping body.   *(SPRING 2002)*

⌐ This is the closest I have come to a thoroughly autobiographical *ficción,* absent of course the junk-food-eating wife.[65] My mother is, or at least was, tremendously troubled by the fact that I seemingly alienated the most influential wire writers, and the imagined conversation she is having with my "wife" in this story is certainly not too far from a conversation she might have had. I did actually attempt to reach Mr. Laube to patch things up, but it was, alas, shortly after the "I'd rather have a *frontal lobotomy* than a *Laube in front of me*" comment was published. The conversation, very terse, did not go well at all. The ubiquity of (permanent) Ravenswood tattoos is a fairly well-documented phenomenon and is no doubt a result of the vaguely hypnotic power of the central image of ravens in the form of a mandala. The Ravenswood phenomenon is treated in greater depth in the article "Bungle in the Jungle."

---

65. Very tellingly, I still think of myself as a "young man," in a slightly creepy Woody Allen–like way.

POESY GALORE

Let us go then you and I
When the *soucoupes* and *cigares volants* hover in the nighttime sky
Like a tea service upon a table.
Let us excavate through heavily rummaged bargain bins
The radically reduced, everything-must-go, red-tagged wholesale-outlet tins
Of dented canned goods rising like armor-plated ziggurats
And deeply discounted lees-filtered (Just say no to dregs) ends of vats,
Emerald aisles giving on to architectonic floor stacks
Smudgèd shelf-talkers artlessly affixed with thumbtacks.
Oh, do not ask, "Is this Cab fruity, floral, or weedy?"
Tais-toi and drink up, sweetie.

In the warehouse the salesmen come and go
Complaining about what's moving slow.

The Vin Jaune that gathers dust in the bargain bin,
The Moscato Giallo madeirizing in the bargain bin,
Rotating its *chemise* (a sedimental education) to one side,
Nestling in a Colony of lately harvested Porto di White Zin.
CONTAINS WINE!—another new warning label espied?
Those cloudy White Christmas dioramas, those of soiled label,
The unprepossessing—just give it some time, it's going through a dumb phase—cases,
Unmerchantable, malo-in-the-bottle wines with proteins quite unstable
Deplete at an imperceptible rate approaching stasis.

And indeed there will be time
For the Vin Jaune that gathers dust,
Moldering in remaindered ignominy.
There will be time, there will be time
To prepare the pectic enzyme for inclusion in the must.
There will be time to sulfite and to acidulate,
Time to let the skins carbonically macerate.
Time for a velvety Hermitage and for a plump Côte Rôtie,
And time yet for absolute perfection—a wine hundred pointed
Consecrated by the pope, a wine solemnly anointed—
Before the taking of grappa and biscotti.

In the warehouse the salesmen come and go,
Complaining about what is moving slow.
And indeed there will be time
To wonder, "Do I filter?" and "Do I fine?"
Time to reorganize my bottling line,
With a hollowness in the middle of my wine.
(They will say: "How his wine is growing thin!")
My Dubrovnik Open Gold Medals pinned proudly to my chin.
(They will say: "But how his middle body is so thin.")
Do I dare *débourbe* the universe?
In a nanosecond there is time
For decanting and recanting
And for stylistic decisions and label revisions that a 57 in the *Spectator* will reverse.

For I have known all the perfect wine and food pairings, known them all—
Have known the most appropriate wine for pasta, man.
I have measured out my life with a *tastevin.*
And I have known the wine writers, known them all—
The wine writers that fix you in a formulated phrase
(Like "gobs of upfront jammy fruit in your face").
And when the wine is released and reviewed,
When my marketing efforts begin to stall
And my stylistic effects are roundly booed,
Then how should I essay
(Bulk-out all the lees and dregs
Of superannuated puncheons, barrels, kegs)
To make a wine of great complexity?

And I have known the legs already, known them all—
Legs that cling and sheet along the leaded glass
But whose spirit derives from elements far more crass.
Is it perfume from a beaker
That makes me a digressive speaker?
Legs as silky as a summer's breeze,
Rich, unctuous mouthfeel, perhaps an infusion of antifreeze?
And how should I begin to correct the errors of my ways and of my cuvées?

Shall I say, I have gone at dawn through widely spaced vineyard lanes
And remained passive in light of yields so frankly massive?

I have seen the best vines of my generation cropped to a fare-thee-well.
I figured, "Hey, grower knows best."

I should have been a pair of Port tongs
Scuttling across the floors of a well-stocked cellar.

Should I, after Marion and Framboise sorbets,
Have had the sense to vacate the doorway?
But though I have blind-tasted and blended, innumerable consultants paid,
Though I have seen my *têtes de cuvée* brought me in a snifter,
I have turned no profit (for conversion of a large fortune to a small one, there's no route
   swifter).
Truth to tell, I have been a hawker of prosaic liquor.
I have seen Alice, Wolf, and Jeremiah snicker.
In short, I was *zedreht*.

And would it have been worth it, after all,
After the innumerable meet-the-winemaker soirées,
After all the hype, the oeno-schmoozing, the endcap displays,
Would it have been worthwhile
To have discovered my own idiosyncratic style?
To have done something utterly outrageous—such as a *pétillant* faux-Pomerol?
Not worrying if the kids could dance to it or find it a "classic red,"
Sending it off to Lazarus, Tilson, Swinerton, et al.,**66**
Saying, "This will amaze you, will startle you all."
If one, settling their panning review by one's bed,
Should say, "They don't seem to understand this wine at all.
It's not worthy of an 8, at all."**67**

No! I'm not Emile Peynaud, nor was meant to be;
Am a competent *caviste,* one that will do
To inoculate a tank, rack a barrel or two,
Confer with my oenologist, produce a conservative brew,
Balanced, insipid, tending toward lean,
Politic, neutral, and utterly clean.
A bit curt, not what you'd call sassy,

66. Editorial staff of the *Underground Wine Journal.*
67. The *Underground Wine Journal* rated its wines on a scale of 1 to 20.

At times, indeed, almost gassy.
Never, however, a lucky Pierre, rather, le Fou.

I grow Chard ... I grow Chard ...
I shall find capturing market-share hard.

Shall I include Malbec in my Meritage?
Do I dare distill peach schnapps?
Cabernet franc is the answer; I'm told it yields thrifty crops.
I have heard Bettane[68] conferring with Gault-Millaut, deciding who is tops.

I do not think it's me.

I have tried to ingratiate myself with them at table,
Plying them with wine and rich, sumptuous *repas,*
Asking our French friends, "*Que pensez-vous de ce grand vin-là?*"

We have enjoyed with them a great *repartie*
For they are truly kind, gentle Frog folk,
Till the waiter arrives with the bill (excluding corkage) and we croak.

(FALL 1991)

⌐ Ironic that this wine-world weary parody was written by someone early in his still mostly ascendant career (Eliot himself wrote "Prufrock" as a young man), but it is just another restatement of the existential dilemma facing winemakers, especially those in the New World. How to feel that one is producing something truly original? Despite having personally eschewed Chardonnay since 1990, I still completely identify with Rootstock—you believe you are not quite fooling most of the people (and yourself) most of the time—and his dilemma is very much my own. A further irony is that only recently, almost eighteen years after writing this poem, have I taken its full meaning to heart.

Howlbariño

BY ALAIN GAINESBERGER

I saw the best palates of my generation deranged by short-chain tannins, recoiling,
    embittered in astringent rictus,
who exposed themselves to dangerously high levels of new oak,
    barriquesters bathing in phosphorescent cellulobiose glow,

68. Michel Bettane was for many years a highly influential wine critic, writing for *La Revue du Vin de France.*

who experienced nasopharyngeal meltdown,

who dragged themselves through heavily charred Pinot Noir streets, searching for
Burgundian character,

who managed their sucrose codependency, kendall-jacksonian democrats,
pyrotechnicians of residual sugar refulgence,

who mistook creeping *Brett* anthesis for lovely soft-soap texture, believing in their hearts
they were born to Rhône,

who let the wet dog in,

who left themselves to macerate in ecstasis, seeking prolonged skin contact,

who felt a strong need for acid additions,

who spun their aroma wheels like so many Tibetan prayer discs,

who said Kiddush over Clos Vougeot and left an Impitoyable tasting glass out for Elijah,

who played every tune on the hydrogen sulfide jukebox,

who stocked their cellars with enough claret to sink an LST and subsequently discovered
Dolcetto,

who left unceremoniously like Bruno Prats[69] fleeing a sinking ship,

who busted open bottles of Kröver Nacktarsch in Laredo,

who went into religious transport of Clos Ste. Magdeleine and waited patiently for Saint
Pétrus,

who recovered their angel's share with *un poco* de Grazia,[70]

who ordered a bottle of Domaine Chardonnay[71] off a wine list this actually
happened and saw the reds of their eyes,

who were blinded by optical opacity, hue density indices, chromic values,

whose friend Burroughs continually sends them Vintage Tunisia in brown-wrapped
UPS shippers,

who attempted to cleanse the doors of organolepsis and go beyond di Santi,[72]

who made dinner plans to include Haut-Médoc wines with magic Peynaud
mushrooms,

who contracted their first case of Clape in the Berkeley area,

who developed a taste for Château Bellevue,

who wandered around and around old telegraph stations waiting for eclectic
transmissions,

who puffed on ambiguous cigars in the nonsmoking section of Stars
restaurant,

69. Former owner of Château Cos d'Estournel, in the St. Estèphe parish of the Médoc.   70. Marco de Grazia is a well-known, somewhat controversial importer of Italian wine and partisan of the "new style" of Barolo. 71. "Domaine Chardonnay" was a very short-lived marque of Sebastiani Vineyards of Sonoma, California, that actually contained no Chardonnay grapes at all.   72. Most famed producer of Brunello di Montalcino in Tuscany.

who were visited in their grappa-infused reveries by the seraph Levi,[73]

whose cerebral cortices flamed in high-toast Limousin sympathy and were Chard
    to a fare-thee-well,

who became cult followers of the Manseng family,[74]

who saw Engelwhite visions before they entered Paradis,

who ingratiated themselves with the heads of staves,

who whispered wine facts like darkest medical histories: yeast infection alcohol problem
    short finish biochemical family groupings, esters intimate as *mishpoche,*

who made comprehensive tasting notes on every wine blind-tasted all night long swirling
    and sipping over lofty incantations that in the rosé-fingered dawn were stanzas
    of gibberish,

who met the winemaker,

who bled their tanks three times successively in the hopes of regaining their
    concentration,

who eventually went totally anaerobic,

who sought sheep thrills from Ch.neuf-du-Dada and were unmasked on Easter Day,

who were compelled to reschedule their appointments with the languid Doctor Sax,

who plucked *les fleurs du malvasia* at Château Baudelaire and became themselves a
    Rimbaud sequel,

who suffered *crises de foie* and *de foi* and were hospitalized for chronic chlorosis,

who welcomed the *atterrissages* of extraterrestrial objects with saucer eyes,

who were suspected of engaging in Jim Clandestine activity,

who could actually talk faster than Jim Clandestine,

who heard the concussion of Ausonic booms,

who turned their *Quercus* shoulders to the wheel,

who were clinically diagnosed with a mild case of Folle blanche[75] and a profound one of
    Pinot NV,

who searched for lost *pain* and served Moscato del Solo to Burroughs at a Naked Brunch,

who sucked down the spirits of Bocchino[76] in hand-blown bottles,

who, in searching for complete hedonistic fulfillment, sent in their subscriptions to the
    Advocate, believing it was a wine-related publication,

who woke in early morning hours to find Vermentini in their cranial crawlspace,[77]

73. Serafino Levi founded a small artisanal distillery in Neive, in the Piemonte region of Italy, continued by his reclusive, angelic son, Romano Levi, until the latter's recent death. **74.** Petit Manseng and Gros Manseng are aromatic grape varieties used in Gascogne in the appellations Jurançon and Pacherenc du Vic-Bilh. **75.** A French term literally meaning "crazy white"; a grape variety used in Armagnac and other parts of Gascogne. **76.** Bocchino is a distillery in Piemonte, and is also an extremely naughty expression for an activity between two consenting adults. In various bars throughout northern Italy, one might hear the expression "Give this man a Bocchino!" which is alleged to have enlarged the, um, market share of the brand in question. **77.** Vermentino is a grape of Provence and Corsica.

who were deeply ambivalent about the *crus bourgeois* and troubled by the fascistic
   Pigato state.

who laid down vintages of Les Kerouacs de Lafite in the early fifties,

whose government forbade them to tell the truth about HDL cholesterol,

who reappeared on the West Coast investigating the BATF with laissez-faire eyes,
   passing out meet-the-winemaker dinner announcements and transcripts of the
   60 Minutes broadcast,

who had a ball with Josh and Rosengarten at Le Parc,[78] scattering their Sémillon freely,

who sweetened the pHs of a million bottles of Puligny-Montrachet, "Les Demoiselles,"
   and were prepared to sweeten the pH of the acidic sect of Science in the Public
   Interest,

who sent out for hors d'oeuvres with Paul Roger NV, secret hero of this poem, and were
   succored by three celestial *puttonyos,*

who heard Calliope playing their song when Musigny and Musar were poured,

who made bottoms up of Château Pédesclaux, La Turque, and the Côte Blonde angel,

who met with Boubals[79] in Marseilles and sought immediate ampelographic treatment,

who crop-thinned ecstatically insatiate and continued into the adjacent vineyard and
   ended up fainting with a vision of the ultimate country wine,

who sent a last-ditch letter to the *governo,* pleading for inclusion of the white
   varieties,

who submitted a special, unnatural formula for the ultimate whine cooler.

(FALL 1992)

For me, the key to making these parodies work is finding the right template—that is, a style easily parodied and broad enough to allow for the inclusion of oenocentric language and Doonian iconography. I tried to find the relevant points of intersection between Ginsberg's bohemian/psychedelic/leftist/gay sensibility and the Dooniverse, and to sympathetically resonate with his critique of the spiritual malaise and hypocrisy of America. (Certainly a world in which a wine called Domaine Chardonnay, containing not a drop of Chardonnay, might exist, if only for a short while, is a thoroughly objectionable one.)

The tragic failing of this particular parody is its reliance on special knowledge. The Kendall-Jacksonian reference, for example, is an acknowledgment of the fact that K-J Chardonnay is (or was) known for its use of residual sugar and a homeopathic addition of Muscat of some stripe as a means of stylistic differentiation. The "sheep thrills" reference is to André Ostertag, a known Dadaist, and Jim Clandestine is, of course, Jim Clendenen, a friend of mine who talks very, very fast. The manic quality of the language in *Howl,* harkening to the manic, overheated tempo of the language that Ginsberg himself expe-

78. Josh Wesson and David Rosengarten published the *Wine and Food Companion* years ago, arguably the most entertaining publication of its ilk.   **79.** Denis Boubals, noted late French viticulturist at the University of Montpellier, known for his support of the plantation of "superior varieties" in the Midi.

Poesy

rienced in late- (all-)night conversation in the 1950s with Neal, Jack, et alia, is not so dissimilar from the sometime manic quality of wine prose, especially in modern wine blogs, which attempt, often futilely, to convey in words the ineffability of the ecstatic wine experience.

The Rimeshot of the Ancient Marsanner

BY WALTER TAYLOR CHOLERIDGE-MONTEBELLO

It is an ancient Marsanner,
And he stoppeth in the TR.
By his red-veined nose and tattered clothes,
He's come to the Lost Weekend[80]
  (formerly a bar).

An ancient Marsanner finds himself Dazed and Confused at the Bonny Doon Tasting Room.

The TR's doors are opened wide
And all manner of folk stroll in.
Customers are met with a friendly smile
And sip civilly 'midst the bonny din.

Tasting Room Hours are 11–5 every day, but one should take Note of the Special Winter Hours.

He holds his glass in a shaky hand.
"There was a raft," quoth he.
The TR clerk wonders who is this jerk
Who slugs still more Vin Gris.

The Marsanner grasps a Standard INAO Tasting Glass as he evaluates perhaps the World's Greatest Pink Wine.

He holds him with his bloodshot eye
And demands, "Why no more Pot-still?"
This visitor certainly knows his stuff;
The Marsanner abhorreth swill.

While the Pot-still Brandy was immensely popular, ironically it took Five Years to finally unload it.

The TR clerk stands aft the bar
And fears he's met a loon.
He might have dialed 911,
But response is slow to Bonny Doon.

Bonny Doon lies in an Unincorporated Area of Santa Cruz County and some Essential Services are a bit Dicey.

80. The former Bonny Doon Vineyard tasting room had been a biker bar called the Lost Weekend in an earlier incarnation.

"I was there, seated in that raft,
The one called George," claims he.
"We tumbled, careened o'er cataracts;
A motley crew were we."

This Scene is depicted on the highly stylized Grahm Crew Label.

He slugs some Poire in one great draught,
High as a kite is he.
The clerk is careful not to smirk
And frets the liability.

Do not attempt this at Home. It is suggested that Poire be kept away from Open Flames and Flamers.

"Our marketing plan was twisted,
Progress was made in fits and starts.
George (the raft) was at best a leaky craft.
We survived only for my smarts."

The Marsanner here is Delusional, grossly Exaggerating His Own Importance in the Scheme of Things.

The TR clerk tires of this jerk
Yet he cannot choose but hear
And thus speaks on that grizzled man,
The Smarmy Marsanner.

The TR Staff is Thoroughly versed in the Etiquette of Service, but Sometimes, Enough is Enough.

"We were often lost and clueless,
But all in the same boat were we.
The George was trapped in a perilous gorge
When the Captain cried, 'Put out to C.'

The Marsanner and the Crew find themselves up Scheid[81] Creek without a Paddle.

"See, 'C' was just his private code.
His mania was such that he
Could not wholly speaketh
Certain words that began with 'C.'

The Captain had some Difficulty articulating the "C" word (the Grape That Cannot Speak its Name).

"Our voyage was a wild ride,
The Captain's course rash and bold.
The true extent of his mishegoss
Was not till later told.

He reflects upon his Disillusionment with the Captain's Mental Acuity and alludes to Certain Revelations that were to Come to Light.

"Yes, I was one of the old Grahm Crew
And the vivid flashbacks still nag me.
Limpidity I was taught to eschew.
A real bright idea . . . oh, gag me.

The Marsanner is still plagued by Unbidden and Unpleasant Recollections.

81. The Scheid Vineyard in Greenfield, California (Monterey County), was once a source of Grenache grapes for Bonny Doon Vineyard.

"I learned to be a Marsanner
When the Captain bailed out on Chard.
He fretted o'er his market share,
Claimed that capturing it was hard.

*The Marsanner recounts
How Chardonnay (a
Lesser Grape Varietal), was
Once of Great
Economic Significance.*

"Captain lived in a private world.
Most thought him an oeno-wanker.
He was possessed by wild ideas—
Like buying Marzemino by the tanker.

*The Captain was clearly
Ahead of his Time.*

"His disregard of protocol
Was a source of great frustration.
He always fixed what wasn't broke,
Which led to his ruination.

*The Captain is seen to
suffer from a Compulsive
Personality Disorder.*

"Yet once I did respect the man.
That he possessed great refinement
Was mentioned at the fitness trial
That led to his confinement.

*The Captain's tenuous
grip on Reality proves
ultimately Elusive.*

"Did I mention the *glacière?*

"Day after day, day after day,
Freezing was believing.
We pressed *sans cesse* the congealed grapey mess,
Counting up our digits on leaving.

*The Technique of
Cryoextraction is
Elucidated.*

"The ice-grapes were here, the ice-grapes
    were there.
The ice-grapes were all around.
Slippery, they were underfoot,
And smushed when you trod the ground.

*Some attributes of Gelid
Grapes are revealed.*

"And La Garrigue?[82]

"Tween reason and madness
I feared he'd finally crossed the line.
Colombard *et miel en barrique:*
He was proposing honey wine!

*The Fruits of the
Captain's Apicultural
Research did not delight
All members of the Crew.*

---

82. We produced La Garrigue—a barrel-fermented Colombard, essentially chaptalized with twenty-four varieties of honey, one of the strangest wines we ever made—but once.

"'Honey, don't!' I shrieked.
Was this just one of his phases?
The honey stuck like primal sin.
We cursed the rogue to blazes.

*It is shown that
Chaptalization with
Honey is the Devil's Own
Work.* [83]

"And *l'affaire du* Canard Froid? [84]

"The Captain was a busy man.
He was all too often away.
On one such trip, I made a terrible slip—
I KILLED THE CANARD where it lay.

*The Marsanner reflects
upon the Untimely Demise of
the Captain's Cherished
Avian Companion.*

"Upon his return, 'twas all gone wrong.
'Where's Sparky?' [85] queried he.
'Twas just my luck, he loved the Duck
E'en more than rationality.

*The Captain's Duck and
his Sanity departed
simultaneously.*

"But tell me how was I to know
Le Canard Froid was the essential wine?
Sparky Duck was the great linchpin
That coalesced the entire product line.

*The arcane Mysteries of
Wine Marketing are
examined.*

"Our forward progress stopped,
And sales began to drop.
The crew all knew the guilty sod
Who was responsible for our flop.

*The Marsanner is
Believed to be responsible
For the Doonturn in
Shipments and Depletions.*

"I wore the Canard as a lanyard.
Behold this nervous wreck.
'Twas my poor luck to wear a dead duck.
Sparky depended from my neck."

*The Marsanner's Taste
Runs to Outré Neckwear.*

The TR clerk wearies of this jerk,
Who has more to get off his chest.
Would he ever finish his tiresome tale?
He still speaks like a man possessed.

*The Marsanner is shown
to be Extremely Tedious.*

"And the *distillati?* Don't get me started.

83. Chaptal himself strongly advised against the practice of using honey as a means of increasing the potential alcoholic degree of a wine. This bit of intelligence was, however, vouchsafed shortly after the honey went in.   **84.** Le Canard Froid (Cold Duck) was a very cool, fizzy red Pinot Meunier wine produced by the Charmat process and far, far ahead of its time.   **85.** The captain's pet name for both duck and wine, perhaps a reference to their shared generally effervescent nature.

"He wished to be a 'regular' guy,
To make the world safe for Prunus.
He made great boatloads of the stuff,
With floor stacks he did maroon us.

*The role of Spirits as
An aid to Digestion is
Here considered.*

"Eau-de-vie, eau-de-vie everywhere,
Enough to fill the galley sink.
Eau-de-vie, eau-de-vie everywhere,
And all too strong to drink."

*The Captain insisted upon a
Comprehensive Product
Line of Fruit Brandies.*

He speaks now in a calmer tone.
Perhaps the storm has passed.
He scans the room with a frightful leer.
The old salt's thoroughly gassed.

*The Marsanner does
not comport Himself
with Exemplary Civility.*

The reprobate has drunk his fill.
His beady eyes still shine shrewdly.
He feels the room begin to spin.
"Strap me to the Mast,"[86] cries he lewdly.

*A Case is made for
Restraint and Decorum at
Public Tasting Venues.*

"I fear thee, ancient Marsanner,"
The TR clerk does say;
"Thou departeth with a head of red,
And returneth, palsied, grey."

*The Clerk remarks upon
the Transformation effected
in the Hapless Marsanner.*

The TR clerk asks, "Who are you,
And how might I set you free?"
"Kill the schmuck who bottled the Duck.
The name is Locke," quoth he.

*The identity of the
Ancient Marsanner
is at last revealed.*

(SPRING 1994)

This piece is a powder puff, but was amusing to write. It may be read as a love letter to my colleague John Locke, the great conscience and animating spirit of Bonny Doon from the early years until the very recent past. There was, at least in the early days of John's tenure *chez* Doon (and this was published way back when), a nontrivial, maybe even slightly Oedipal, agon between the two of us. While I knew I was well loved by the overwhelming majority of John's psy-che, I'm sure the minority component would happily have seen the captain walk the plank. This poem references some of the extraordinarily eclectic wines we produced for mass distribution in the early 1990s—an ambitious, if not quixotic, proposition. John was the driving force behind setting up the Distinctive Esoteric Wine Network (or D.E.W.N.), our wine club, which served as a more appropriate outlet for our more esoteric winemaking experiments. I don't know whether

86. Sandy Mast was the Bonny Doon Tasting Room manager from its inception until the mid-late 1990s.

I have personally contributed to whetting his appetite for the strange and heterodox—more likely this was part of his original equipment—but he recently wrote to his friends and former colleagues of Doon about an "all-snake" dinner he had recently attended in Vietnam, one that culminated in his ingestion of the still-quivering heart of a cobra, very recently deceased. Frank Zappa, patron saint of risk-takers and *épateurs* of bourgeois sensibility is the angel who continues to watch over both of us.

Bashō [87] Does Beltramo's

Single turning leaf
Reticulate in form;
How savage the forest.

           Sanford "Barrel Select":
           A thousand flowers bloom.
           In-laws over for drinks.

                      The raven in flight:
                      No more wimpy birds!
                      Teeth turning black.

                Dry creek is silent:
                Special promotional price.
                My cart is filled.

        Climbing the chalk hill,
        The whiteness is blinding.
        No lime in sight!

Monterey Sauvignon Blanc:
Steep-shouldered *bordolese.*
Big cat sleeps.

           Blossom Hill:
           A refined fragrance,
           The convenience of 1.5s.[88]

                    Wild horse,
                    A pungent blanket.
                    Where is the rider?

87. Bashō, a seventeenth-century nature poet, finds inspiration in the unlikely venue of a Menlo Park wine emporium.   **88.** These are 1.5 liter bottles, more commonly called "magnums."

Opus One:
A quintet of snow leopards.
How surprising!

Acacia in blossom:
The fragrance of buttered popcorn
Fills my senses.

Kendall-Jackson:
The reserve pond so deep.
How sweet the Muscat!

Entering a dunnewood.
Wine is made.
There is no maker--strange.

Along the Napa Ridge,
Dreaming of Lodi,
The mockingbird flies.

Crisp Mosel Kabinett
Too long in the cold-box:
The snows of Mount Fuji.

Meadow glen.
Stillness of the air.
Teetering floor stack.

(SPRING 1997)

I can't recall the precise circumstances, but I do remember feeling utterly unequal to the task of writing a long creative piece for one of the newsletters, so I decided to go with this much shorter, more economic form. The humor in these haiku is pretty subtle and requires some insider knowledge: the haiku juxtaposing the "rare" Opus One with the appearance of five snow leopards is intended to be subtly ironic, as is the usage of delicate nature imagery by some brutally competitive corporate interests. FYI, wines that have not been properly cold-stabilized will occasionally form potassium bitartrate crystals when stored in the refrigerator for a certain length of time. (And people invariably and maddeningly return them to their point of purchase with the complaint that they contain "glass.") I am, in these pieces, adopting a stance familiar to me: subversively and ironically sniping from the sidelines, imagining a cloak of invisibility, which is not particularly constructive or sustainable.

A Holiday Message

Though it hardly seems possible

'Tis pity, 'tis true, *mon vieux,* but the '04 calendar's soon tossable.

As dear friends of the grape gather to carve the holiday roast

From blue states and red states, we can agree upon one thing: This year is *toast.*

"Did someone say *toast?*"

Perhaps now's the time to propose a toast

To Jim Clendenen and Toni Jost!

And to all the great *vignerons* who have here today gathered,

Besotted with Bacchus, empurpled, grapely bespattered.

An obsessed lot are we, fixated on vinous *idées* most pleasing.

Let's celebrate our passion for the grape: To Ridge's Donn Reisen!

"Somebody say *Riesling?*

"I get a nose of bergamot, *fleurs blanches,* lime twig, and cassis."

We all know that timbre, that *voice;* it can only be Terry Theise.

"You gimme Riesling to live, a *raisin d'être,*

You've heard my rap: great acid, prismatic luminescence, et cetera."

For all the right Rieslings, indeed, for ones that astonish,

One need look no further than Witwe Sofia Thanisch.

And to the great Carl von Schubert with his Max Grünhauser plus

H-G. Schwarz and K. Darting (their byword: Scheus R Us).

At the door is yet another Scheu-boy, Lingenfelder,

From pillar to post-Chardonism, seeking viticultural shelter.

Yes, this *boîte* is an asylum for the oddball, *oscuri uvaggi,* so,

Make way for the unpronounceable[89] motley *(cru) assemblagio.*

Might we then suggest a zingy Grüner Veltliner?

Goes with everything, even *ein* Jelly Donut, sorry, that's a *Berliner.*

Nein?

Fine.

Then, how about a Big Red?

There's Rusty Staub and with him Mia Klein,

The *Wine Spec's* highly rated Jim Laube and Reinhard Loewenstein.

"Might you have something neither Teutonic, nor too tannic?" a timid voice queries.

"Perhaps an elegant Pinot, something not too austery."

---

89. Can you say "autochthonous"?

It pains us so to see a guest's *gueule* thoroughly parched,
Might we propose a spicy little number from Henri Lamarche?
So, it's *skål, l'chaim, banzai,* cheers,
As we drink to the health of our good pal, Dan Gehrs.
And while we're hoisting a cup of warming wassail,
Let's not forget Vanya Cullen, nor the folks at Beringer Blass, y'all.
Nor the incomparably clever Alvaro Palacios:
Besos, abrazos y muchas, muchas gracias.
Nor Michel Rolland, nor Tom Rinaldi,
Neither Bernardus l'on, *anche il* Marchesi de' Frescobaldi.
Na zdorovie, Dmitri Tchelistcheff.
Bonjour, Louis Latour, what it is, Jim Seff.
And say, there's Philip Laffer from red-hot Jacobs Creeky,
How you sell so much wine, it's, well, just . . . superfreaky.
What other toasts might we propose? We can all say *kam-pai.* Oh,
That's an appropriate one for M. Alain Graillot.
It's great to see you, illustrious Marvin Shanken;
From the buffet may we offer you a nice piece *flanken?*
It's wonderful to behold Michela Rodino and Serge Hochar,
Antonella Bocchino, and the unrelenting Ken Starr.
(Glad he's on *our* side this time.)
Salute to the beauteous Elizabetta Foradori,
Cheers to Stillman Brown of Red Zeppelin's *bon* Jory.
(And a warm *cin-cin* to Claudio Gori.)
To the biodynamic duo, Philippe Armenier and Alan York,
To the unreconstructed purveyors of that artifact, the bark cork.
(Here's a wee drop of TCA in your eye.)
Yea, wine is the universal solvent: *Alle Weinmenschen werden Brüder.*
While great juice will inspire, a lesser one makes one steweder.
(Vega Sicilia will heal ya, but Uva di Troia will destroy ya.)
Full of holiday spirit and passed out in the foyer
Lays the brilliant and beatific Mario Pojer.
(Beside him snores the distinguished Georg Breuer.)
And prone upon a convenient credenza
Lies the hulking bulk of Attilio Scienza.
In great distress is poor Roberto Stucchi,[90]
Who has, I must tearfully report, just tossed his cookies.

90. He be hurting Badia-ly.

(He had earlier appeared more than just a little bit pukey.)

And the usually hollow-legged Melvin Master

Sits comatose in the corner, thoroughly plastered.

And how's the distinguished Signore Giuseppe Quintarelli?

He's been reduced to an amorphous, quivering blob of red grape jelly.

Excusing himself to call Ralph on the big white telephone

Is the (formerly) redoubtable trencherperson, Mr. Bruce Cohn.

What's become of our friend, Aussie Geoff Grosset?

He seems to have lost himself in a remote water closet.

(Taking a Dugat-Py?)

Even the burly, bubbly Patrick Ducourneau

Is now gasping for air and moving quite slow.

"Oh, that this oh two *(sic)*, too solid flesh might conk—

Second thought, never mind; one more bite of foie gras and a little sip of Pacherenc."

It has suddenly grown so very still,

(You could almost hear a Le Pin drop).

Might it be the pale, ghostly presence of William Hill?

"Halt, who goes there?" asks Patrick Jasmin.

"Be ye friend or *faux ami du vin?*"

I say, who's that coming through the vestibule? Er,

It's none other than Angelo Gaja and Egon Müller.

Do we detect the likes of Jean-Luc Colombo,

David Hohnen, Duane Cronin, and the good lads of Yalumba?

It's good to see you out of Isola-tion, dear Paolo de Marchi.

Tre bicchieri to you and to the peripatetic Brian Larkey.

One can't ignore the lovely Laely Heron,

Nor Patricia Guy, Arnoldo Caprai, or Jean-Pierre Perrin,

Marc Kreydenweiss and the cosmic Nicolas Joly,

Urbane *terroirist* Jean-Michel Deiss, and bags-in-the-box from Scholle.

Let's then offer a round of hearty *santés*

To the top dog, Aurelio, of Alpha Montes.

Brava, Heidi Barrett, and bravo, Two Buck Charlie.

Dude, making (and selling) that much wine is a feat that's totally gnarly.

And to the fabulously talented Manfred Krankl,

Whose irreverent wines are like a sharp bite on the ankle.

And to the brilliant, eccentric, polymath, Sean Thackrey,

Whose original wines promote much lip smackery.

(And to Dan Duckhorn, whose cellar magic ain't quackery.)

Let's not forget Vincent Bouchard,

Didier Dagueneau, and Tony Truchard.
And all the oenologues of the mammoth Diageo,
Sometimes to raise a brand it just takes a (corporate) *villagio*.
And the elegant May de Lancquesaing,
Jo-Jo Selbach, Joel Peterson and the whole Ravenswood gang,
Marco Zeni, Jean-Marie Peyraud,
David Ramey and Michael Michaud,
Henri Bonneau, Mme. Bize (Lalou),
Louis Jadot, and viticulturist David Abreu.
And to the imprudently passionate Stephen and Pru Henschke,
Currently on the sofa, kissing wildly and Frenchly.
To the marketing whizzes of Aussie Yellow Tail,
To Anne Colgin, Dawnine Dyer, and Robin Lail.
To Luca Currado and Su-hua Newton,
The genial André Ostertag, of that there's no disputing.
Hey, there's Steven Tanzer and Robert Parker.
The party couldn't begin without these *schtarkers*.
Bienvenue, Paul Blanck and Alberto Antonini,
Willy Frank and Michael Martini,
Peter Michael, Cary Gott,
The delectable Ruth Reichl and les Frères Bott,
Warren Winiarski, Marcel Guigal,
Philippe Poniatowski, Donald Patz, James Hall,
Jean-Michel Cazes and our pal Jed Steele,
Marco de Grazia and Armand Diehl,
Jason Pahlmeyer and Bart Broadbent,
Willi Brundlmeyer, Stephen Kent,
And Aimé Guibert and Mihalis Boutaris,
Les Gros Frères (and Soeurs) and Walter Georis,
Dom Lafon, and Tony Soter.
We're in Burgunderland now, what a fragrant odor!
Yo, Gary Pisoni; *tschüss,* Helmut Dönnhoff.
Wait, the evening's young, there's no need to run off.
We're *privat*-ly *grün* with envy at Martin Nigl,
And wonder how we'll cadge a small sip of Screaming Eagle.
Indeed the wine biz has lately become rather a zoo,
Loons are smoking; frogs and stags and roos leap too.
The party, it appears, has devolved into a bit of a frenzy
With the arrival of Bernard Lacroute from the great WillaKenzie.

I might caution you now to make a wide berth for Herman Wiemer;

He's essentially harmless, though a bit of a screamer.

Someone asks: "Where's DuBoeuf?"

It has been suggested that he's high 'pon yonder Tin Roof.

(We'd cautioned him about any Turning or Burning Leaves

And the naughty influence of one Jamie Meves.)

And what has become of Zelma Long?

Did someone see her with a bong . . .

'iorno to the *fratelli* Cotarelli,

Gaston Huet, and Maria Danieli.

On the subject of matters of great doobiety,

Denis Dubourdieu is just the soul of propriety.

It seems that somebody has called the cops, the fuzz, to our villa.

Quick, Albert Pic, it's the *flics;* a terminal buzz-*killa.*

It must have been the behavior of our friend Bob Lindquist,

Whose provocative antics led to the eventual inquest.

So, revelers all, it's time to call it a night,

We've basked in the glow of such great, how do you say?, *Gemoutonlichkeit.*

Buonasera, drive safely, dear Roberto Cipresso;

Are you good for the road? May we fix you an espresso?

Bonsoir, Michel Chapoutier;

Mec, give it up, it's *way* past the last call for booty, hey.

Adieu to the charming Anne-Claude Leflaive,

C'est l'heure de faire dodo;[91] we wish you a night of sweet *beaux rêves.*

A final toast to all: "May your Riedel flutes be ever *pleines* with Champagne!

To next year, dear friends!" when it will be *déjà bu* all over again.

Nous, we think it is time to grab us a nice cleansing beer,

And ponder how we might find some share of Grace[92] in the coming New Year.

(2004)

⌐ I lifted this format from Roger Angell (it was used before him by Frank Sullivan) of the *New Yorker,* who wrote an annual holiday greeting incorporating the names of individuals who'd been newsworthy during the preceding year. It is the way of the world that the wine business has recently developed its own set of celebrities or personages. I sometimes wonder what deep, innate human instinct requires us to personalize or incarnate works of art, which properly should speak for themselves. One might long for the days when the great wines of the world were produced by anonymous monks, toiling in their vineyards for the greater glory of God and *terroir,* but that state of affairs is not likely to soon recur.

---

91. "Faire dodo" (pronounced *doh-doh*), is a French expression meaning "to go to sleep."
92. That would be Grace Family Cab.

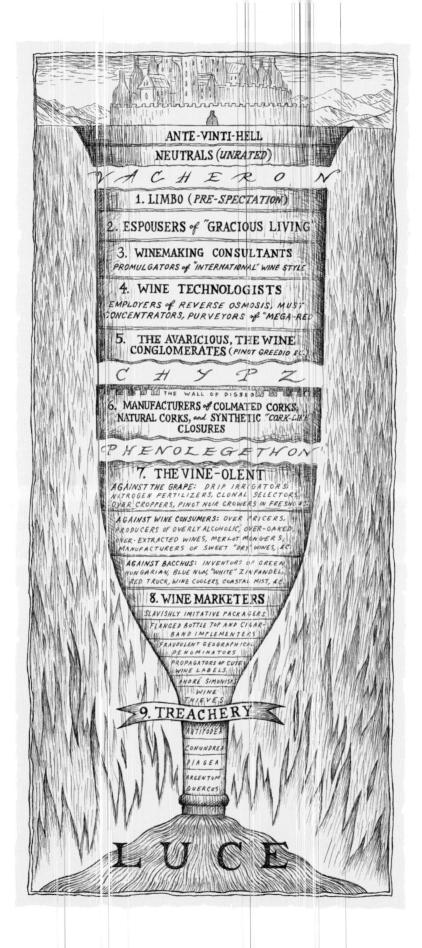

ANTE-VINTI-HELL

NEUTRALS (*UNRATED*)

V A C H E R O N

1. LIMBO (*PRE-SPECTATION*)

2. ESPOUSERS of "GRACIOUS LIVING"

3. WINEMAKING CONSULTANTS
PROMULGATORS of "INTERNATIONAL" WINE STYLE

4. WINE TECHNOLOGISTS
*EMPLOYERS of REVERSE OSMOSIS, MUST
CONCENTRATORS, PURVEYORS of "MEGA-RED"*

5. THE AVARICIOUS, THE WINE
CONGLOMERATES (*PINOT GREEDIO &c.*)

C H Y P Z

THE WALL OF DISSED

6. MANUFACTURERS of COLMATED CORKS,
NATURAL CORKS, and SYNTHETIC "CORK-LIKE"
CLOSURES

P H E N O L E G E T H O N

7. THE VINE-OLENT

*AGAINST THE GRAPE: DRIP IRRIGATORS,
NITROGEN FERTILIZERS, CLONAL SELECTORS,
OVER CROPPERS, PINOT NOIR GROWERS IN FRESNO &c.*

*AGAINST WINE CONSUMERS: OVER PRICERS,
PRODUCERS OF OVERLY ALCOHOLIC, OVER-OAKED,
OVER-EXTRACTED WINES, MERLOT MONGERS,
MANUFACTURERS OF SWEET "DRY" WINES, &c.*

*AGAINST BACCHUS: INVENTORS OF GREEN
HUNGARIAN, BLUE NUN, "WHITE" ZINFANDEL,
RED TRUCK, WINE COOLERS, COASTAL MIST, &c.*

8. WINE MARKETERS

SLAVISHLY IMITATIVE PACKAGERS

*FLANGED BOTTLE TOP AND CIGAR-
BAND IMPLEMENTERS*

*FRAUDULENT GEOGRAPHICAL
DENOMINATORS*

*PROPAGATORS of CUTE
WINE LABELS*

ANDRÉ SIMONISTS

*WINE
THIEVES*

9. TREACHERY

ANTIPODER

CONUNDREA

DIAGEA

ARGENTUM

QUERCUS

L U C E

~O~

Da Vino Commedia: The Vinferno

BY AL DENTE ALLEGORY

Part I

DE CANTO I

Midway through a bonny career that I had plied,
I found myself lost, not in a copse of new wood,
But rather, I awoke to grasp that I had put a great dream aside.

The vast portfolio of labels, brands, had once seemed all to the good,
As one might sire a score of loyal scions, sons,
Who would see to their old man in his doddering decrepitude.

A career of witty *étiquettage,* bonny mots, and outrageous puns,
A true love of the biz that I could hardly feign,
Après tout, in sum, it had been a superlative run.

Yet I found myself at dusk midway up a great calcareous mountain,
When I was seized with angst to my deepest core,
And the most feverish visions invaded my brain.

I had never worried o'ermuch about critics' indifferent scores,
Knowing the whines were well-made, albeit hardly *grand cru,*
But now wondered: What might remain when I was bonny no more?

What had I accomplished in a life as brief as a turn of a screw?
A legion of vinous trysts—from Alicante to Zinfandel.
To a single *cépage* I could not remain true.

'Tis true I have loved multitudinous grapes o'erwell,
Never stopping long enough to gain true mast'ry.
A bee here now, on every flower, though not long to dwell.

Perhaps I had squandered my vinous qi
To produce joyful, if obvious, whines of exuberant fruit.
(The Rhône *cépages* have been berry, berry good to me.)

But this would still leave the question moot.
What had impelled me this terraced mountain vineyard to climb
And a largely predictable existence to uproot?

Did I mention that the *sous-sol* possessed 40 percent free lime
And a bonny *climat* conducing to Pinot,
Cépage of my dreams, the Burgundian paradigm?

Do I stay (resting on my *loureiros*) or do I go?
I could not another step take for all my fears,
When I at once beheld a most bloodcurdling tableau.

A Giant Southern Leopard known to be fierce,
Stood right before me and gave out a fearsome snarl
More disquieting than a sudden outbreak of *la maladie de Pierce.*

But with this daunting giant, I had no real quarrel.
I was in awe of its all-devouring appetite,
As I stepped o'er ancient *gobelet* vines, wizened, gnarled.

Lucky I was that it did not wish to take a preemptive bite,
But retired to lick its own private parts
As I stood, shivering, in the falling light.

But this was not the end of further shocking starts,
As I next beheld a great Yellow-Tailed Lion,
Loathèd for its ubiquity and noxious, mephitic farts.

I pressed ever upward on that steep incline,
Stumbling as I strode and prepared to flee
The most dangerous beast in the great *Commedia* of wine.[93]

Yet no one was laughing, least of all me,
For I had been nipped once before by this lupine damozel
And knew how lethal its piercing wound might be.

The Spectacular She-Wolf had an uncanny sense of smell.
Detection of a tragic flaw for one so prodigiously snouted
Was as easy as TCA,B,C: a swift bite sent her victim straight to hell.

I feared lest I found myself odiferously outed,
But these swirling thoughts were soon set aside.
"Who goes?" my own unrecognizable voice seemed to have shouted.

93. The poet appears to draw the distinction between *whines*—that is, the intentioned product of vinous artifice
(or of acute self-consciousness, as one finds in the New World)—and *wines,* the authentic produce of *terroir.*

A tall and shadowy figure I had but just espied.
"Ne vous inquietez pas," I heard him say.
"N'ayez pas peur"[94] (switching to English): "I will be your guide."

"But who are you?" I asked with some dismay.
"You knew me as the legendary cellar master of DRC.
The name, *monsieur,* is (the late) M. André Noblet."

'Tis true I'd had my share of spirits, but 'tis often a matter of degree
Whether one can trust one's own credulous eyes
Or behold, say, an eau-de-vie-*de-poire*-impaired *fantaisie.*[95]

"I'm not worthy, I'm not worthy," I began to sycophantize.
"Tais-toi! My time here is short and I don't suffer fools.
I have been sent by Herself, a name you will certainly recognize."

"If you can't suffer fools, who am I then to suffer ghouls?"
"Silence!" he thundered. "I come from the sainted Mme. Lalou,
Who bade me protect your unworthy self. *Putain,* she is cruel.

"Lalou is your angel from the celestial milieu.
She spins the stars so you might come to no harm,
A tall order to perform for a thick-headed *crétin* like you.

"She charged me to insure that you not (as it were) 'buy the farm,'
That you succumb not to overpowering fright
When I lead you to harrowing *vin*sights apt to cause great alarm."

Fearful I was, but did not wish to appear impolite
As Noblet grabbed my arm and bade me to follow.
This was not *le bon moment* to light out in flight.

While his cockamamie tale was difficult to swallow,
I knew I'd never again have this remarkable chance.
My halfhearted protests remained essentially hollow.

94. "Don't worry"; "have no fear."   95. Pear brandy is known to be one of the highest in methanol content among the various eaux-de-vie. Curiously, in the United States, there is a maximum permissible level of methanol to be found in Poire, whereas in France, there is a *minimum* permissible level, presumably intended to be a guarantee of authenticity (another French paradox).

"*Cher* Maître, I ask you to please not look askance,
But I must learn your cellar secrets. Oh, tell me, please,
With what secret barrel additions an aroma to enhance?"[96]

"Perhaps a discreet *tisane* of *framboise,* a soupçon of *crème de cassis?*"[97]
"*Imbécile,* you have learned nothing, *apparemment.*"
"*Macération à froid?* Anything? I'm doon on my knees."

"To teach you more *maquillage* was not why I was sent.[98]
Tricks you know all too well but fathom not their consequence.
You'll soon behold a vision of whinemaking hell and tearfully repent."

I found it hard to divine his sense.
"Was it not the role of a whinemaker or to be fancy, *vigneron,*
To please his consumer for all purposes and intents?"

"You shall hear the anguished cries and moans
From those who sought to make whines *très flatteurs,*
Producers of all ilk: Burgs and clarets, Rhônes . . .

"For them the highest point score was all that mattered.
What availeth a score of 95
When one loseth one's soil and a sense of place is shattered?"[99]

I had been on the leeside of 90 for some time,[100] although connived
To wear my bottom-o'-the-barrel status as a small badge of pride.
(Though I secretly craved approbation, if only just to stay alive.)

But Noblet had seen right through me; there was no place to hide.
He had judged well and found me wanting.
All I might do now was to follow on by his side.

96. At the beginning of the narrative our narrator appeared to have been repulsed (almost unto death) by his own former predilection for facile, whinemaking tricks, employed to produce flattering, fruit-forward whines, but at this juncture he seems to have atavistically regressed.   **97.** It has long been alleged that these discreet additions have, at least historically, been part of many a Burgundian cellarman's repertoire.   **98.** The French term *maquillage,* literally meaning "makeup," also refers to cosmetic tricks—namely, the utilization of new oak—that a whinemaker might employ to make his whine present better upon release, often with the consequence of the obscuration of *terroir.*   **99.** It is ambiguous as to whether the great *caviste,* by mentioning "soil," is referring to a literal loss of topsoil, owing to poor viticultural practice, or to an inexpressiveness of *terroir* due to excessive monkeying around with the whine.   **100.** The poet is truly a master punster, if not an unregenerate show-off. In this case, lees may well be more.

Deep in my bones was a feeling that was haunting.
"Where, then, are you taking me, *cher* Maître?"
"You wish to master Pinot, to ascend the steepest mountain?

"The way up is the way doon, *peut-être.*"[101]
These words had a rather harrowing effect.
I steeled myself for great pain, torture, anguish, et cetera.

Suddenly a cavernous sinkhole appeared—what more to expect?
I was overcome with all-encompassing dread.
I trembled greatly but still bethought some humor to inject.

"I can't stand the sight of blood, spiders, snakes, demons, or over-oaked Chard," I pled.
Noblet: "Your very soul and *sol* are at stake!"
I stumbled as we walked and doon and doon he led.

DE CANTO III

I don't know how long I had been awake
When I bestirred myself to inhale a noxious reek,
My body and brain wracked with a thousand aches.

I could not think nor act nor speak,
Yet my olfactories still worked all too well, to my distress.
I was overcome by the wretched smell of garlic, shallots, leeks.

On top of that, I got a nose of rotten eggs, but I digress.
Unbearable were the pungent fumes—
The whole place just reeked of mercaptans, disulfides, and H_2S!

A wide and tall door before us loomed—
I beheld and grasped the matter with perfect lucidity.
We stood before a warehouse of souls (not so bonnily) doomed.

THROUGH ME THE WAY TO VOLATILE ACIDITY;
THROUGH ME THE WAY TO PREMATURE OXIDATION;
THROUGH ME THE WAY TO CORPORATE CUPIDITY.

101. Noblet's classical view harkens back to the formulation of Heraclitus, relating to the occult connection between apparent opposites.

THROUGH ME VINONYMITY AND UNNATURAL CONCENTRATION.

ME DID JUDGE A WHINE OVERTLY FRUITY OR AUSTERE;

THE GIFT OF MINERALITY DID MY MAKER CONFER FOR SUBLIME GUSTATATION.[102]

BEFORE I WAS, WERE NO FERMENTED THINGS (INCLUDING BEER),

SAVE THE SECRET POTENTIAL OF TERROIR, AND TERROIR ABIDES.

ABANDON ALL OAK, YE WHO ENTER HERE.

These words of a dim, rust color I espied,
Written above a lintel of the great portal.
Whereat: "Maître, their sense is hard," I cried.

"No more than the tannins of a *grand vin de garde,*" he chortled.
His sense of levity seemed a bit misplaced.
"First, you'll meet a mob and then later the true *wine* immortals."

Noblet pushed hard upon the great creaky door we faced.
The door opened with much rasping and grating.
We plunged through the entry and soon were *in medias res.*

Was I not myself soon due for the Ultimate and Final Rating?
"Fear not," said Noblet. "Your job is merely learning and observing,
Neither to judge or be judged, the noblest form of spectating."

The air was filled with a cacophony I found most unnerving.
There was endless gnashing of teeth, retching, and hawking.
To the unruly horde, great carafes of Red Bicyclette a waiter was serving.

I could not seem to resist staring, in fact, gawking.
Tens of thousands of diverse vintners were chattering,
Burgundians, Bordelais, Tuscans, Languedociens.

I'm sure that I overlooked many and beheld just a smattering.
"Maître, what exactly is this caitiff rabble?"
I could not abide their endless kvetching and nattering.

"Pay no attention to their pointless babble.
These are *vignerons* who have literally not at all rated.
They are the vinous second string: dilettantes, dabblers,

Poesy

---

102. By "maker," the poet can only mean Bacchus.

"Vintners who were by their own election fated
To produce whines neither so great nor so wretched,
Provoking nothing but yawns, neither well loved nor well hated.

"Whines of such little consequence, diluted, stretchèd,
Leaving the world neither better nor worse,
Evanescent on the palate, a *vin*gram unetchèd.

"But let us no more of these matters converse,
And leave these poor whining whiners to their eternal woe,
Their own insipid mediocrity forever to curse.

"I have far greater and more awful things you to show.
This is but the Vinferno's entrée, its *vin*techamber;
The real action (read: pain) still awaits us below.

"What you have seen so far are sights far tamer
Than anything else you will henceforth observe.
Prepare yourself to soon behold whine's quite literal flamers."

The preceding tableau had been but a visual hors d'oeuvre,
As we moved quickly through the great hall,
Knowing of more horrific sights waiting in reserve.

I was relieved to have quit the vinous free-for-all,
Reminiscent it was of a ZAP tasting
And other orgiastic bacchanalia I could recall.

My mind could not but help its ideative racing
As Noblet dragged me along, in tow,
Anent the ephemeral praise I'd myself been ever chasing.

"It lasts but a moment, fame's seductive afterglow,"
Noblet told me, seeming to read my thoughts.
"What you seek, only you to yourself can bestow.

"The fortune of all whinemen must needs come to aught,
Like a prized bottle of a rare *millésime,*
Languishing o'erlong in cellar, only to ignobly rot.

"It is the rare epiphanous moment that we must glean,
When we somehow become more than mere *vignerons*
And instead become the content of Great *Terroir's* inspired dream.

"But let's no more these *pétillant* sophistries intone.
You are here to observe and to witness
Who's been up to *Weingut* and who's been b-b-bad to the Beaune."

His casual comments had a way of scaring me witless
And I despaired of ever finding solid earth, much less true *terroir.*
I was damned (if you doon) by a system Vinfernally pitiless.

DE CANTO IV

We walked and walked a distance rather far
Through a bleak and sepia blandscape.
There was naught but scorched earth, seemingly done to a heavy char.

With no horizon in sight, neither land to lub nor sky to scrape,
All forward progress was nearly arrested,
Until we suddenly espied a rather mysterious, inchoate shape.

Tree stump or man, perhaps? Well-muscled, barrel-chested;
One could not discern with visibility so scanty.
In the miasmic fog one's vision was sorely tested.

From the man-barrel-shape, we heard a sort of ariose chantey.
"Row, row, row your Boutes . . . ,"[103]
He sang simply, a cappella, in a lilt rather jaunty.

Drawing closer, we observed an antiquated coot,
Grizzled in countenance and grimaced of mien.
His presence was quite alarming, in perfect truth.

Noblet: "It is Char-on,[104] the ferry-man, who shuttles souls between
Two discreet realms and minds the gap
'Twixt Vinferno's vestibule and the deeper Underworldly demesnes.

"Alas, it is he we must entreat for passage, this disagreeable chap,
To ferry us 'cross the treacherous Vacheron River.
In arriving, we are lost, but *grâce à Dieu, sans* gross mishap."

Char-on's craft, a leaky raft, was indeed a superannuated flivver.
No question that he had us, as it were, over a barrel.
Worse, he regarded us as roughly equal to chopped liver.

103. Tonnellerie Boutes & Cie. is a well-known Bordelais cooperage.   **104.** Mr. Chips Goes to Hell.

Poesy   **139**

Suddenly, a cold wind came up and chilled me to the marrow.
Noblet pled, "Might you ferry us across? We'd be forever in your debt.
My colleague is feeling skittish and rather easily harrowed."

"No can do, chief. No way, no dice, nix, negatory, not on a bet."
In his commentary I detected a certain recurring motif.
Char-on clarified, "Skittish though he may be, he ain't dead yet.

"My orders are very clear and brief.
I am charged with ferrying the very souls," he said,
"Of zinners, palate killers, Merlot-mongers, whine thieves.

"As far as criteria for passage, let some light be shed.
The poor sods must have zinned in some wise against the grape,
And they must be at least 100 percent dead!"[105]

Noblet argued with him anent vinfernal red tape
And the massive bureaucracy of the nether realms.
Char-on relented, but like an o'erworked stave, remained bent out of shape.

We crossed in his ferry with Char-on at the helm.
"Wish us luck," I said, and saw him grimace, almost.
My plea for beneficence had patently underwhelmed.

As we debarked I heard him clearly riposte,
And not without some unmistakable professional pride;
His final words to us: "You are so toast!"

DE CANTO V

We found ourselves landed on the Other Side.
An oddly familiar place it turned out to be.
So strange to be quick among the scores of the unscored who had died.

The very air was filled with haunting shades of *gris
Eminences,* legendary presences from another time.
"*Cher* Maître, enlighten me please to the nature of these *esprits.*"

Noblet: "These are the great immortals of the vine,
Les vrais maîtres, the great Legends of yesteryear.
We sip (metaphorically) of their lifeblood in every glass of *wine.*"

---

105. In some instances it is reported that Char-on insists on his passengers being 200 percent dead.

"If they truly noble Greats are, how came they here
And not to a finer, more exalted place?
Noble lives they led, only to now reside in eternal drear."

"The Great Ones enjoy a modicum of grace,
But barred from further ascent, expecting no more,
They abide here, grateful not to have ended up a burned-out case.

"This is *wine* limbo, where reside the brilliant *vigneron* of lore,
Masters who came B.S. (Before Spectation)
And were never in their lifetime awarded a numerical score.

"Thus, never qualifying for vinous salvation,
They gather around de Limbo Bar (how *low* can you go?)
And discuss the state of de vine on earth with great consternation."

I caught a glimpse of Dr. Jules Guyot,[106]
Himself pruned back to a mere stump of the powerful man he was,
Conversing with Ronald Barton with significant brio

There was a rather powerful buzz that came across
In conversation between two great Bourguignons,
René Engel and Dr. Barolet, anent the latter's "secret sauce."

There were the Greats from the Côtes du Rhône--
Rayas's Louis Renaud, and Jacques Perrin from Beaucastel,
Debating whose estate was finer, who really had the stones.

"The *wine* business has really gone straight to hell"--
This opinion voiced by M. Raoul Blondet.[107]
"There is no more finesse, it is all too late-harvest Zinfandel."

"If we could only have gotten then the prices we see today.
Today's consumers are fools to pay what they do!"--
A sentiment shared by Chafee Hall and Madame Ferret.[108]

106. The most widely used vine-training system, *le système Guyot*, or "cane pruning" as we know it, bears his name. **107.** Legendary *maître de chais* at Mouton-Rothschild. **108.** Hall was proprietor of Hallcrest Vineyard in the 1950s and producer of extraordinarily elegant *wine*. Ferret was the greatest producer in the appellation of Pouilly-Fuissé.

"A hundred dollars a bottle for an unknown *cru*?
No track record, no *terroir*?" pondered Count Haraszthy.
"It's given a high score and consumers don't say boo.

"I'd say the practice is downright ghastly."
"*Calma,* Count," counseled the *veuve,* Mme. Clicquot.
"You are, perhaps, overreacting vastly."

I had so many questions to pose to her and to my other heroes:
"What were the pre-phylloxera wines really like in their prime?
Were they really so special, imbued with much greater mojo?"

The widow: "I didn't really appreciate them so well at the time,
But let me give you a lesson, young man, and mark well:
While 'tis true *les grands crus d'antan*[109] were truly sublime,

I'd rather drive a Red Truck on earth than drink an 1865 Lafite in hell."
Chimed in Dr. Chaptal, "Being dead is really quite a bugger,
But, let's not on these grave matters dwell.

"*Veuve,* be a doll and give your daddy-doctor some sugar."
The very thought of a coupling of two decrepit necrophiles . . .
Yet I tried hard to remain a nonjudgmental onlooker.

They were both consenting (if dead) seniors acting juvenile.
"Live and let live," ironically proposed Jacob Schram.
"We're all a little hot and bothered down here," he ventured with a smile.

Schram continued, "In fact, I would not myself have any qualms,
Nor fear appearing to be the least bit kooky,
In proposing to my friend Cap'n Gustave Niebaum:

"Why don't we essay to score a little Inglenookie?"
I was heartened to know that *wine*'s great pros,
Despite their reduced circs still hoped to, quote and unquote, "get lucky."

Noblet gestured to me that it was soon time to go,
But I could not leave without seeing to it
That I bid one last adieu to M. Emile Peynaud

---

109. A French expression meaning "the great growths of yesteryear."

And left best wishes for the brilliant Lee Stewart.[110]
It was raining Pennies[111] from heaven (or hell) perhaps
When I was saluted by the great Max Schubert.

And before I left I had to inquire, "What were the haps?"
In greeting Baron Philippe Rothschild,
Thanisch, Prüm, and several other noteworthy chaps.

"These men led a life in *wine* rather than had a whine 'lifestyle.'
You may call them *vin*achronisms, hopelessly démodé,
They were (Baron R. excepted) humble, modest, low profile,

"Unlike the enormous swollen heads one observes today,
Before the cult of the 'whine personality' and the practice of 'branding.'"
My guide was rather insistent on this particular point to convey:

"Let there be no gross misunderstanding—
The Great Ones remain *classiques* even in death,
The fact they were unrated notwithstanding."

A squat, beetle-browed figure, puffing mightily, out of breath:
In a cloud of billowy smoke he hovered, eyes ablaze.
It could have been only the legendary André Tchelistcheff.

It was well before the popular film *Sideways*
That André made California's greatest Pinot Noir.[112]
We bid farewell and strode onward into the gathering haze.

(2005)

⌐ I began this work when I was experiencing a certain existential crisis—one rather protracted in the unfolding, if the "nooseletters" from the last ten years or so are any guide. The winery had grown large and complex enough that I no longer felt particularly connected to it or to the work we were doing, and yet I could not seem to conceive of a way out without feel-ing that I would lose a great part of myself.[113] "What might remain when I was bonny no more?" might signify either a separation from the company or the loss of my status as the critics' once-promising fair-haired boy. This is the potentially soulful moment, when one ponders what inheres and abides after all the ephemeral identifications fall away. A few years

110. Greatly beloved founder of Château Souverain and winemaker during the 1940s and 1950s.   **111.** Penfolds Wine Pty. Ltd. (now subsumed by the corporate giant Southcorp), the company for whom Max Schubert invented Grange Hermitage, was sometimes called Pennies by its many growers in South Australia, as in: "So d'ya reckon thet Pennies will pay ennything for *Shee-raz* grapes this yee-ah?"   **112.** Beaulieu Vineyard's legendary 1946 Napa Pinot Noir, the elegant likes of which have not been tasted again in these climes. **113.** The idea of selling it in its entirety seemed like a real death on many levels, not the least of which would have been the ending of a chapter with so many colleagues.

ago, I did dream of the calcareous mountain vineyard site mentioned in this piece;[114] the image was the crystallization or distillation of a process that had begun years before, and that only recently has begun to manifest in overt changes in the company and in myself. When I began writing this piece, I didn't know precisely how either it or the issues it purported to represent would play themselves out in "real life," but the writing propelled the process forward.

I have always been taken with the premise of the *Commedia*, but was unsure how to appropriate it for my nefarious purposes, until one day it dooned, OK, *dawned* on me that there had been a fairly discrete moment in the wine business, one I am old enough to remember, when everything seemed to change. This moment occurred in the late seventies with the growing influence of the *Wine Spectator* (which was soon eclipsed by Parker). Suddenly the industry was incredibly self-conscious, as it hadn't been before. In the pre-Spectation world (Old Testament), one had to more or less work out for oneself how well one was doing (though presumably the ability to sell one's wine at a good price was a reasonable indication). The post-Spectation world (New Testament) seems to feature a vast vinous superego—one now feels literally watched and judged all the time. The promise of salvation (a 90-plus score) is never a sure bet,[115] but there is certainly the deep, almost visceral knowledge of what sort of behavior will yield a negative consequence. It occurs to me that my little oeno-eschatology owes a debt to John Barth's *Giles Goat-Boy,* for both content and style.

Part II

DE CANTO VI

We had not traveled a distance so very far
When we came upon a site for sordid ayes so outlandishly appointed,
I had almost to avert my glance for all the appalling foofaraw.

There was something so odd and disjointed
About the place, which made me feel downright queasy.
Quelle doyenne de dégueulis[116] had been thereto anointed?

It would certainly have been rather too easy
To draw an invidious comparison to *Better Homes of San Bernardino*
The decor was kitschy, vulgar, lurid, cheesy.

---

114. And have been fortunate enough to observe this mountain in waking reality, located not far from Mission San Juan Bautista in San Benito County, where, Bacchus willing, the vineyard of my dream will one day be situated.   **115.** In the 1980s, owing to the still slightly capricious and unpredictable nature of point scoring by both Parker and the *Spectator*—a particularly favored "house style" that would unconditionally assure one the promised beatific grace had yet to emerge—there was a sense that one's salvation was something simply and graciously *granted,* somewhat independent of one's own apparent efforts, in a sort of a Calvinist approach. Certainly by the 1990s, unless you were totally clueless you had a pretty good idea of what was needed for admission to the elite "Highly Recommended for Admission to Wine Heaven" club, and salvation tended to be more or less exclusively guaranteed to the "Beaune again," good ol' Boyd-Cantenac network—that is, to those who knew the rules of the game and were able to successfully play by them.   **116.** "The hostess with the grossest." One imagines an untethered Martha Stewart.

'Twas a complete *bordel,* or as the Italians would say, *casino.*
"Maître, how might these *objets d'argh(!)*[117] relate to the oenophile
(Or -phobe, for that matter)? What had this to do with *il mondo del vino?*"

"Rather a lot or very little," Noblet volunteered with a smile.
"We are in the Second Circle—ungracious living and vast pretense.
Doomed are those who led not lives in *wine* but rather lived whine 'lifestyles.'

"Not 'style' as one would understand in an inward sense,
As reflective of artistic sensibility or a sense of wonderment,
A feeling for *wine's* rhythmic flow, its guiding intelligence,

"But rather a fixation on the trappings, the accoutrements,
That attend whine's mystique, thus, its allure for the yuppified *mec*
Trying to grab a taste of paradise on earth for dual-income dollars spent.

"An iconic glass of North Coast Chard upon one's redwood deck?
Etrangle-moi[118] with a silver tasting spoon
Of quail egg, crème fraîche and *tobiko,* or some such dreck.

"I ask you, my young friend, what could be more jejune?"
On cue, a heartbreaking cry rang out, as if from a muezzin.
I shuddered at its mournful tone and fain would have lay doon.

"Clearly, some poor damned soul in unbearable pain,"
Declared I brusquely, not knowing whereof I spake.
"Pardon, *m'sieur,* it is but the cry of the cursèd Whine Train."

Noblet had gently corrected my foolish mistake.
"The conveyance runs here in a route vinfernally circular,
As if in an unreal dream from which one cannot awake.

"Like the MTA, one can never 'get off,' as it were.
Souls trapped in 'Whine Country,' where one never 'arrives,'
Remain e'er in pursuit of the latest, most Spectacular *vin du jour.*

"The one unobtainable, untasted; they remain thus forever deprived
Of the mythic 'Siren' whine, which lies just out of reach.[119]
Tantalized to a fine whine madness, they are well and truly swived."

---

117. Worthless trinkets, or tchotchkes, as they are in the vernacular known.   **118.** French for "gag me."
119. Nothing to be done but to lash oneself to the mast, drowning one's thoughts with the mantra "La-la-la-la-la-la" while not conjuring an image of Marcel Guigal.

I understood only too well how payback's a Pich-
On Lalande '96, or an '01 Chard from Ms. Turley.[120]
Doing *without* is a nonstarter for these poor nouveaux riches.

What comeuppance for these *marcassins*[121] might there now be?
Noblet bade me behold a view that gave a horrible fright:
The boorish boars were given to perpetually sip a glass of domestic "Chablis!"

As if that were not insult enough quite,
Screaming Eagles pecked at the gracious livers' livers.
I will never forget that most harrowing *vin*sight.

There was still more punishment the Vinferno had to deliver:
Delicate whites served at Vinfernal torture-room temperature: 965 K.
Reds at -286 K—*brrr,* just the thought makes me shiver.

---

120. The first was awarded 96 points, the second 99 points, by Robert Parker.
121. French for "young wild boars," and a wine brand of Helen Turley's.

"Maître, please, might we soon quit this atrocious affray?"
But there was more to observe of this nauseating nightmare.
The gracious livers were ungraciously being force-fed foie gras on *beignets!*

"Maître, is it truly wrong to have lusted for *vins extraordinaires?*
These poor souls' zin was to covet the chic wines of *garagistes.*
Might their insatiable *Weinlust* have just been a sort of imperfect prayer?"

Noblet: "Tis pity they've become fodder for the *gavagistes.*[122]
Perhaps they will receive at long last their fill.
We must move on. May they have a grace-filled afterlife-style and a modicum of peace."

DE CANTO VII

We then ascended a rather formidable hill
And came to a place that so brightly gleamed
Of stainless steel *machinas,* it was virtual Inoxville.

High-tech gizmos, Doonsday-devices, whiz-bang machines.
Ornamented with digital readouts, gauges, dials.
Whine, at last controlled to the nth power (or so it seemed)!

"These are the impedimenta of the 'international style,'
Said Noblet, "and while they are still as shiny as can be,
Note how they languish and sit unceremoniously idle.

"They were the tools designed to set whinemakers free
From the vagaries of vintage (Great Bacchus forfend!),
Available to any 'whinery of substance' for a nontrivial fee.

"Thus, one might a whine's 'deficits' amend,
Rendering it standard, clean, and vacuously perky,
Soulless, soil-less, precipitating Great *Terroir's* end.

"They would banish those *wines* that might be called quirky
Outliers, within a narrowly defined, stylistically acceptable range,
Too weird, too different, ergo, nonviable turkeys.

"'Progress' insures the disappearance of the strange,
The unexpected (*No one expects the Spanish Vinquisition!*),
And we end up with safe, oaky, sterile fruit *bombas* in exchange."

122. French for "one who stuffs geese."

Clearly, the new paradigm had no Red Truck with tradition.
A sense of place was something to be shunned at all cost.
All whine roads led to "Rhône"(-style)[123]—or perhaps to perdition?

Something vital and precious had been unceremoniously tossed.
*Vini*pulation was the great hubristic leap— (not Frog's nor Roo's)
Forward: fruit appeared as if on cue but what *sols* were lost?

Noblet: "They aimed to turn *vins ordinaires* into *grands crus*
Through the magic of *vin*substantiation, and Mother Nature to outwit."
He intoned: *"In Nomine Pétrus, Filhot et Sangiovese Spiritus.*

"Take this Ultra Red,[124] all of you, and drink from it.
This is the cup of blood-red color intensity, which promises a brand's salvation,
In service of the new and everlasting covenant

" 'Tween megawholesalers and megabrands in aggregation.
It will be an intense red for you so that zins may be forgiven.
Do this in memory of return on shareholder equity and upside aspiration."

I then understood how some whinemakers were driven
To do anything for high scores, requiring no coercion.
Market "realities" were perceived as intractable "givens."

We saw the abandoned *machinas*—a device for osmotic inversion,
Flash-détente apparati, must concentrators, spinning cones.
These all, in the wrong hands, instruments of gross perversion.

This then was how upcoming *cavistes* now made their Beaunes,
'Twas just like vinous Viagra, a boost to their mercantile mojo.
Just then I heard a mournful sigh and a piteously doleful groan.

It was my *cher ami* the Madiran producer Patrick Ducourneau,
Inventor of *microbullage,* or oxygenation with tiny bubbles.
Evidemment, his presence here bespoke a recent mortal blow,

123. "Rhône-style" may have as much in common with *wines* of the Rhône as "kosher-style" has with kashruth. 124. Ultra Red, derived from the extract of *teinturier* (red-juiced) grapes, is one of several licit whine ameliorants available to New World whinemakers and is routinely used to punch up the color intensity of red whines, often disposing visually biased critics to upgrade their point scores. Inclusion of *teinturier* grapes or extracts is strictly forbidden in virtually all European *wines* or whines.

But his demise was but the beginning of his postdead troubles.
His sunny, ursine countenance had grown to fair despond,
And his famed five o'clock shadow had turned to unkempt stubble.

Imagine a soap bubble a child may blow with a wand.
Patrick was permanently trapped within one, gargantuan,
Turning end over end, bouncing freely, hither and yon.

He had become the perfectly encapsulated *Viti*-truvian Man.
'Twas a real pity, as I had known Patrick to be a splendid guy,
One who had made a real contribution to the betterment of *vin.*

To a mere mortal, the ways of Bacchus were hard to justify,
But I had not a moment the irony to ponder,
Neither one even to wish my friend a proper good-bye

When I beheld another familiar face in the distance yonder.
Merde, alors; it was my dear pal Clark Smith of Vinovation.
If he had a vinfernal address, there was no doubt he was a goner.

When alive, he had hawked high-tech whine amelioration.
I had myself on occasion of his services availed,
But refrained from bringing that up just now, fearing da vine intervention.

When Clark hove into view, he appeared drawn and pale.
His normally bright demeanor was quite suppressed, I made note.
In wordless pantomime he related his unhappy tale.

He opened his mouth and pointed a finger to his throat,
The universal symbol for unpalatability, disgust, and detestation,
Or at least that's what to me it would connote.

But my *maître* was able to offer a more cogent explanation.
"Your friend Clark suffers a perpetual, insatiable thirst
As a result of his earthly interest in unnatural concentration."

I beheld Clark silently grimace as he cursed,
Whilst with the palm of his hand thumping without stop
The bottom of an inverted bottle of Château d'Osmose Inverse,

Which (owing to its stickiness) poured out not a single drop.
Noblet explained, "It is not *wine* but a catsup-goo.
Concentrators on earth never knew when to stop."

We beheld then a pour soul, who seemed to have suffered a *coup*
De glace—one thoroughly chilled-out dude, he was frozen in ice.
"The iceman calmeth," I offered, as an aperçu.

But this was hardly the time to jest or crack wise.
"Maître, who is this poor *glacé* zinner?" I nervously nattered.
"He was a *caviste* who elected to let his whines cold-stabilize."

These words brought to mind a rather delicate matter
And sent a rather profound chill right down my spine.
Like a calving iceberg, my own world began to shatter.

"You see, there is a friend of a friend of mine . . .
Who makes whine from grapes he artificially freezes,
With the aim of *falsch*ining a sort of faux *Eis*whine . . ."[125]

Noblet's withering look just scared the living bejesus
Out of me, and I knew it was time to move on,
Not to linger o'erlong with this angst-laden aesthesis.

DE CANTO VIII

We descended the hill and immediately our attention was drawn
To a group of lab-coated lost souls who were aimlessly wandering.
Noblet: "They *look* harmless but they are truly Sa-*tannic* spawn."

"Maître, we have been through this vinfernal place, meandering,
Yet I still grasp aught; enlighten me, pray, to its protocol."
"We're in the Fourth Circle; these are whine consultants, given to pandering

"To their clients: 'Your whine is perfect, you're a genius, a natural.'
Alternatively: '*Sans moi*, you'll *never* break the 90-point threshold.
Moi and *moi* alone understands the great mysteries of beverage alcohol,

"'Viz., the value of a well-known "name": solid gold.'
The consuming society has become so habituated
To 'branding,' their buying habits are quite easily controlled.

"A whinemaker can make a whine well loved or hated
By 'impartial' critics, but a consultant by his imprimatur
Gives certainty the product will end up superiorly rated.

125. This would happen "naturally" in the poet's vineyards when the Vinferno freezes over.

"Whinery owners thus imagine it a sort of *droit du seigneur*
To charge a grand price for their *grands-crus*-come-lately,
When in fact they're merely the hottie mulled-over *vin du jour*.

"The consultants who needed to be needed greatly
Are now helpless themselves—feckless, drooling, incontinent,
Their 'value add' nil as they slink around disgracèdly.

"Their 'finish' has been as abrupt as their rapid descent
But I am beginning to chatter now and to run on.
Voilà, he approaches, the Great Fallen Star of the *ferm*-ament."

Noblet was of course referring to M. Michel Rolland,
Who had in the film *Mondovino* been recently portrayed
As oleaginous and sly and, *en bref,* a flaming *con*.

I never knew him on earth, only his whines, which were said
To be *très charmants* when consumed early, but unable to age,
Soft, supple young things, but tragically destined to fade.

Noblet: "It comes down perhaps to the simple matter of pH.
His whines are rich but flabby (thus insuring a high score),
More like *porto* than Bordeaux, if recent vintages are any gauge."

Rolland's arrival was announced by a *vin*imated stentor,
A loose-limbed Jacques-a-napes whose voice like a trumpet blew:
"Four! Four! *Attention!* Coming through! Four! Four!"[126]

"Qu'est-ce qui se passe, mec? Donne-moi quatre virgule deux!"[127]
Noblet thus greeted Rolland and referred to the logarithmic scale,
Wherein Fat Bastard whines had made Michel quite well-to-do.

"It was his plush, overstuffed style that seemed to prevail,
At least among the rather textural-minded critics,
Who did not seem to notice the wet-dog wagging its tail."[128]

126. The editor apologizes for the willful obscurantism of the poet. Whines low in acid are as a rule often high in pH (negative inverse log of H⁺ concentration), though there are other determining factors at work, most notably how much the whine is buffered by K⁺ and other cations. A pH of four or above (where Rolland's whines often languorously repose) is classically thought of as a sort of mortal abyss for whine—there is generally no turning back. Clearly, Rolland's punishment is to be eternally reminded of his numerical and analytical peccadillo.   127. French for "Gimme four point two!"   128. Apart from the lack of acidity that gives the whine its soft mouthfeel, high pH wines are notoriously prone to *Brettanomyces* contamination, a phenomenon resulting in such piquant descriptors as "sweaty saddle," *"pet de cheval,"* "wet dog," and so on.

We espied Leo McCloskey of a firm called Enologix®,[129]
Or Leo-ville, as it is called, known for its shrewd advice
On how to score big with an *oen*vil bag o' tricks.

It was not really such a great surprise
To observe a large contingency of "flying whinemakers"
Who, on earth, fabricated clean, *sol*-less whines at rock-bottom prices.

Noblet: "These men controlled grapes grown on millions of acres
But never left their lab, except to dash for a plane.
Counter-*terroirists* you might call them, these *vinti*-risk-takers.

"For old customs and *terroir* they had nothing but disdain.
Their sense of place was an airport lounge," Noblet expounded;
"But we are mercifully quit of their Mega Purple reign."

These highfliers were now quite literally grounded.
They were now made to eat dirt and to chew rocks.
A greater appreciation of soil characteristics to them thus redounded.

As we made to go, we experienced one further shock.
A *gruppo* of Italian *enologhi* known for fast cars and snappy attire
Approached, clad in mismatched clothes and tattered smocks.

They were pushing a dented-up heap with two flat tires.
"*Ciao, ciao,* Ricardo, Alberto, Franco, Roberto.
You were hot stuff on earth, but nothing like hellfire."

DE CANTO IX

Noblet was particularly proud of that delicious bon mot,
But our work now was to continue our descent and to meet
Ever more grievous zinners—those on the real way doon low.

We walked briskly along, and *tout de suite*
The light began to dim and we lost all definition
Of figure and ground; at least that was my conceit.

129. The poet does not specify Leo's punishment; it may be posited that he is permitted to drink but one
whine for all eternity, inasmuch as his work on earth conduced to that consequence.

The *vinscape* itself seemed to be in the process of transition,
As it had been recently on earth with such great convulsion,
When all good *sols* then seemed doomed to utter perdition.

"Maître, what is this place, and why does it induce such revulsion?
'Tis as if all light's been extracted, spirit's taken flight.
Cher Maître, whence arises this thanatic compulsion?"

"Deathstar light, deathstar bright, what Constellation shines upon us tonight?"
Noblet's words were enigmatic, elliptical, and imprecise.
"Maître, I implore you to speak plainly, not to be impolite."

"We are in the Vinferno's Fifth Circle—*vino greedio,* avarice.
The desire to have it all, that is, whine world domination,
The market locked up as tight as a *capsule à vis.*"

He gestured, "Behold all of the stars in the Constellation.
Their light is trapped, unable to escape,
Like a vinous black hole, drawing dark matter[130] into unnatural concentration.

"Unbridled growth for its own sake is an affront to the grape.
In brighter times, proper *wines* these once were.
Now they're but 'brands,' whose erstwhile *vintegrity* they jape.

"'Tis to the advantage of some a real distinction to blur
'Twixt an industrial product and a *vin artisanal.*
The sands seem to be running out for 'real *wine,*' as 'twere.[131]

"The temptation to go to the dark side must seductively call
All struggling *vignerons* who daily with cash-flow issues deal
And can the once-joyous days of whines and *rosés* recall.

"The upside-doon modern world of whine does seem quite surreal,
And may soon come a day when all the whines on a shelf we see
Come but from a single source, their true origins concealed.

130. The poet had previously mentioned the late obsession on earth with optically opaque whines; their rampant proliferation has led to increased population density in the Vinferno.   131. With "the sands," the poet is perhaps making an oblique reference to Richard and Robert Sands, operating officers of Constellation Wines, the world's largest whine conglomerate (and, coincidentally, producers of Mega Purple and Ultra Red).

"True diversity is crucial for *wine*'s continued life, we'd all agree,
But agglomerators, in heat, create the ultimate whine reduction,
Where originality is lost and whine is 'made' by corporate committee."

"And those responsible for eclecticism's destruction?"
Noblet pointed to some *gris*-flanneled shades and shrugged in a Gallic way
As he offered the following words of *vin*struction:

"Those whose great thirst for 'brand' acquisition did play
A role in diversity's loss, with a corporate mind-set so *farouche*
As to leave naught but *chard* earth, a *goût d'ashtray,*

"Shall for all eternity retain a bad taste, a *mauvaise bouche.*"
"*Moi,* I had little sympathy for those 'suits' so corrupted.
I tended, myself, to regard them simply as corporate *douche*—"

"Bags of money were simply all they wanted," Noblet interrupted,
And signaled that it was time for us to soon leave,
Before this Circle froze over or great magma erupted.

We pressed on and on, as my lungs began to heave.
Our journey was not halfway doon; my brain had grown foggy.
"Remain alert!" Noblet commanded. "Stay on the *qui vive!*"

We slogged on through land become increasingly boggy.
Swamp gas choked us; we were dazzled by fata morgana.
Our soles, our souls, had themselves become indescribably soggy.

It was an unpleasant surprise to come again upon that prima doona,
Char-on; worse yet, another horrendous barge voyage to recap,
"Are we not yet done with him, Maître, this denizen of Vinfernia?"

"I'm sorry, we must beg him again for passage, this odious chap,
To ferry us now across the treacherous River Chypz.
The geography is confusing, might I draw you a map?"

With this damned place I had not yet come to grips
And I had no thought but to forthwith skedaddle.
There was no reassurance forthcoming from Maître's lips:

"We are '*here,*'" he gestured, "that is to say, up Chypz Creek *sans* paddle."
He had produced a brilliant map of the Vinferno, which he then unfurled.
Of it I could not make heads nor tails, my own wits quite addled.

The ride across was like nothing I had experienced in this world.
The entire voyage I held on tightly to my dear Maître.
As Char-on paddled in blackness, fearsome eddies around us swirled.

Clinging to Noblet had come almost as second nature.
I was not, of course, of my cowardly behavior proud.
Char-on declared as we debarked, "I'll be back," à la Ah-nold, the *Ferminator*.

As the ferryman left, we heard then a sound incredibly loud,
As if from a hive of angry wasps or bees.
It seemed to be the buzzing hum of an agitated crowd.

A congregation of tortured souls had gathered around to see
Displayed upon a great Wall, what appeared to be a numerical rebus.
I inched closer and was elbowed by the boisterous Bacchae.

"Maître, can you tell me, please, what is the meaning of this?"
I observed random clusters of numbers, all sixty or below.
Noblet: "Voilà, the Great Wall of the Dissed."

I was astonished by the crowd's fearsome need to know
Who was to be embraced, who to be rigorously avoided,
Who was "hot" (in the Vinfernal sense), who a hero, who a zero.

Noblet: "This phenomenon might be called *Chardonfreude,*
Or the joy derived at seeing the shameful scores another has received
From an important whine journo, with a reputation now destroyed.

"'Tis important to recall these ratings are merely make-believe,
Or imaginary numbers, as the mathematicians would say."
"Maître, I've heard tell that it is sometimes a matter of a pet peeve.

"A certain journalist who is obsessively hung up on TCA,
Will rate a *wine* quite poorly and so deal it a lethal blow,
(The 'flaw' detectible only by a gas chromatographic assay).

"A strange human need to raise some up, only to bring them doon low.
There were certain venerable *wineries* whose only real zin
Was to somehow have been *vin*sensate to a tacit quid pro quo."

Noblet intoned: "Yea, it is for all *oen*ternity *vin*scribed, or *geschriven,*
In the Doonsday Book, *vin*finity, whine without end, amen."
I strained my ears but could not hear my *maître* above the raucous din.

DE CANTO XI

It was certainly far beyond my ken
To know which zins were *vin*ial, which ones cardinal, in Bacchus's eye.
Sols were so easily remaindered in the vast Vinfernal bargain bin.

Noblet: "Perhaps you may someday understand the whys
And wherefores of the Vinfernal bureaucracy,
How the severity of zinners' zins are properly classified.

"But by now you should know what are considered key
Criteria for *oen*ternal damnation and substantial punition,
'Tis the reckless endangerment of *wine*'s sacred *vin*tegrity.

"It would stand to reason, almost by definition,
That whosoever threatens *wine*'s purest expression
Should be made to suffer in perpetuity corrective disposition.

"I speak in the plainest terms of a most grievous transgression:
To wit, the inappropriate means of obtaining whine closure.
I can't put the matter any clearer with greater discretion.

"It still amazes me and makes me lose my composure
To realize how many *wines* or whines o'er the years were tainted, nay,
Outright trashed by closures fobbed off by unprincipled hosers.

"You say a whine is 'corked,' we say it is *bouchonné.*
It is the same word we use for a traffic jam or constipation.
At issue is the noxious substance, trichloroanisole, or simply, TCA.

"An *oen*vil molecule (even in ppb!) that yields in gustation
A suggestion of damp newsprint or moldy underwear.
En bref, an efficient cause of a whine's partial or utter ruination.

"A bad closure can turn a great *wine* into *vin ordinaire.*
Terroir? Absent. Fruit? Poof. Gone with the *vin.* We,
As consumers, never knew we'd been had, sadly left unawares."

I found it remarkable, indeed downright uncanny,
That Noblet's views so closely mirrored my own.
I felt smug to be so right—on earth this had been my modus operandi.

The trek through Whine Hell had been some very tough going,
But I believed I was gradually growing slightly inured
To the piteous sounds of the *vin*-damned, their desperate moans.

But I now found it almost impossible to endure
The stench of the Sixth Circle—the reek of mildew and mold
More piercingly pungent than the foulest ordure.

Choking, wheezing, through this miasmic pong, I did then behold
François Sabaté, former CEO of the firm Sabaté SA,[132]
Speechless for once, his mouth sealed up, bungholed.

"At last an appropriate use for his corks," quipped Noblet.
The assessment seemed a bit harsh, at least so to me,
But it foreshadowed a procession that was bizarre, if not outré.

Overhead wafted the Iberian contingency.
Like hot-air balloons the Spanish and Portuguese cork makers floated,
Fully stoppered-up, *bouchonné,* they drifted free.

Their faces, indeed their whole bodies, bloated,
It would take a *vin*ti-aircraft missile to bring them down to earth.
Noblet and I exchanged glances and *vin*wardly gloated.

(2006)

⌒ Writing this section was a bit uncomfortable for me, as I was consigning some of my good friends straight to Wine Hell—and by what authority? But I was beginning to hit my stride in the conceit of the parallel worlds of whine and *wine.* Those who follow the path of vinous righteousness—the glorification of *terroir*—are privileged to enjoy a sort of heaven on earth. The adulterators, manipulators, and purveyors of a confected, *wine*-like product—that is, "whine"—live in a hell that arises from their separation from this boundless, nurturing well of crystalline order and beauty that is *terroir.*

Part III

DE CANTO XII

"The god Bacchus suffered dismemberment, death, and rebirth.
And despite the *oen*vil that whinemen do, which is well observed,
His spirit, the grape pip, emerges triumphant to prove its worth."

In colloquy, Noblet had touched upon a poignant nerve
Anent the regenerative nature of the fruit of the vine.
Might he, the Grape One, return to find hea*vin* on earth preserved?

132. Sabaté SA is the largest producer of corks in the world and responsible for the Altec closure, a stopper made from ground-up cork "flour." Sabaté has been the respondent in a number of lawsuits regarding whines severely compromised by the effect of their closures.

We had come through circles so unequivocally malign,
I wondered what *malo*factor, what Rhône Estranger, we might next meet.
Grateful I was for these uplifting words, these pearls before Cline.[133]

Noblet and I meandered a bit, and *tout de suite*
We found ourselves ankle deep in a bright red, slimy muck.
Oddly enough, the oozy *rouge* appeared to be treacly sweet.

"Maître, my low karmic point score, or perhaps our bad luck,
Has caught up with us at last, and we remain bloody well mired,
Arrested, as a stressed-out ferment; how might we come unstuck?"

"No worries, old son; my own 'sell-by' date has long since expired.
I am but a pale shade of myself, barely an *éminence gris de gris*.
But, mark, we shall not here perish, after all that's transpired.

"You travel under the aegis of Mme. Lalou; greatly feared is she
By the *vin*fernal minions, demijohn demiurges,
Rutherford dust-devils, *vin*cubi, yeastieboys & other *malo*-evolent *oen*tities.

"These fearsome, blisteringly heavy-toast scourges
Are in truth but *vin*potent bureaucratic *Naparatchiks*,
Ultimate *vin*sider traitors, fearful themselves of nitrogen purges."

While fascinating was Noblet's discourse on *vin*ternal politics,
I remained creeped and creeked out by this slog-fest, this grueling mire-a-thon.
Where in hell were we, sinking doon & soaking up to high Brix?

Noblet: "We are in the marshy trenches of the River Phenolgethon,
A stream that flows a concentrated *teinturier* red."
"But, whence, Maître, this syrupy stream, this rubescent Rubicon?"

"This singular Whine River exists, as it is said.
To float the boats of sacchrophiliacs, a *malo*-practice I deplore."
I had heard on earth a catchphrase that had stuck in my head:

"Twenty-eight is the new twenty-four."[134]
"The mania for *surmaturité* is a case of abnormal psychophenology,
Overripeness is all, for now and seemingly forevermore.

133. It is believed that the poet here may be telegraphing, as it were, a mention of dealings with Fred Cline,
with respect to the sale of Mourvèdre grapes at some point in the distant past.   134. This most certainly
refers to the Brix scale, a measurement of the percentage of soluble solids (essentially sugar) by weight that

"Whinemakers are drawn to the *Cab*-alah, a mystical numerology.
Viz., numbers beginning with a *9* open the celestial gates,
And those nonically impaired portend *vine*-ancial catastrophe."[135]

This was a topic 'pon which Noblet would oft dilate.
But we were then distracted by the sudden appearance
Of a strange whineman-beast whose visage seemed to adumbrate

My growing sense of horror at our present circumstance.
'Twas the monstrous *Vino*taur, rigged up in an outlandish outfit,
Half man, half Red Bull, shooting fiery arrows,[136] clad in toreador pants!

This was no damned publicity stunt for Archerony Summit,
Seeking Vinfernal distribution for its new brand, "Flaming Arrow."
But, mirabile dictu, we became unmired and made a good run for it.

DE CANTO XIII

I quivered still from our escape, which had been incredibly narrow.
To be piercèd by a *Vino*taur-dart or by *la maladie de Pierce*:[137]
Either prospect horrified me doon to my deepest marrow.

My *maître* essayed to distract me from my obsessive fears,
And to divert me from recurring thoughts of our parlous scrape,
By providing a running Vinfernalogue of our present sphere:

"We are in the Seventh Circle—the *vine*-olent against the grape."[138]
I beheld the zinners who had been given to drip irrigation.
Their lips were dry; their tongues hung out, mouths agape.

whinemakers at a given historical moment find represents the movable target of "ripeness" in their grapes at harvest. In the 1970s, for red grapes, 23° Brix was considered desirable and meet; in the 1980s, it moved up to 24° (with a bullet). The 1990s saw the crossing over of the 25° Brix threshold, and the twenty-first century has seen 26° Brix become essentially normative. Mo' better, of course, would be 27° or 28°. Needless to say, there are comparatively few "superpremium" red whines being made these days in Napa Valley, Earth, that are naturally under 14 percent alcohol. Typically, either the high sugar content is diluted with H_2O at the crusher or ethanol is physically removed after fermentation through the process of reverse osmosis or by the "spinning cone," as referenced in De Canto VII. **135.** The poet's disposition to neologism is here further evidenced. "Nonically impaired" would likely signify a point score that is absent a nine in the first position. **136.** No problem to set the arrows aflame, owing to the elevated ethanol level, and hence flammable nature, of the River Phenolgethon, somewhat evocative of the Cuyahoga, in Cleveland, in the late 1960s. **137.** The poet's beloved vineyard in the Santa Cruz Mountains was terminally afflicted by Pierce's disease. **138.** The punishments are far more *oe*nerous for the truly *malo*-volent, who have committed zins of *vine*-olence and are dooned to the farthest circles. In comparison, the punishments meted out to those whose zins were of mere *vin*continence are considered to be more or less *vin*ial.

"To the great Bacchus it is an alarming aberration
To countenance the wretched *goutte-à-goutte*.
'Tis like growing vines *en* flowerpot,[139] a fruit abomination.

"The plants are dumbed doon, lacking gravitas and adequate roots.
They never become themselves; they remain an exquisite fake.
Notions of *terroir* and sense of place are left forever moot."

The irritated irrigators were punished for their mortal mistake
By the drip-drops contrived to fall just past their tongues.
They were to *oe*ternally endure a thirst ne'er to be slaked.

We continued a ways and found that our eyes were stung
By a powerful, acrid aroma that all around us fumed.
We beheld a vast plain with large hillocks of dung.

To my horror I observed that men were therein inhumed.
"Maître, who might these unfortunates be, to be given such a fate?
How came they here, to end up so bonny well doomed?"

"These are the N_2 fertilizers—deployers of urea and nitrate,
Contract growers who cared only for agronomic considerations
And thought captive whineries their obscene yields would tolerate."

I am ashamed to have beheld these zinners with such exultation,
But I gladly shoveled more clods of cow manure on their pates,
High-fived Noblet, and enjoyed a brief moment of *vin*dication.

The fertilizers and overcroppers embodied greed *vin*carnate,
And the justice of their *oe*ternal punition was just sublime,
So smugly certain had they been on earth and so unregenerate.

We then observed four gnarly "Doctor Dick"-head-trained vines[140]
Who suddenly began to speak, which gave me a start.
"What sort of vine-men are these who so glibly spout lines

139. When plants are watered by a drip system frequently in more or less the same area, they lose interest in growing roots outside that area, with numerous untoward consequences, including but not limited to inability to tolerate heat stress and a grossly compromised ability to absorb minerals from the entire soil profile. The real point is, they are incapable of truly expressing a sense of place.   140. The poet may be referring to Drs. Richard Smart, Peterson, and Vine, well-known consultants who do not lack for opinions on all matters vini- and viticultural.

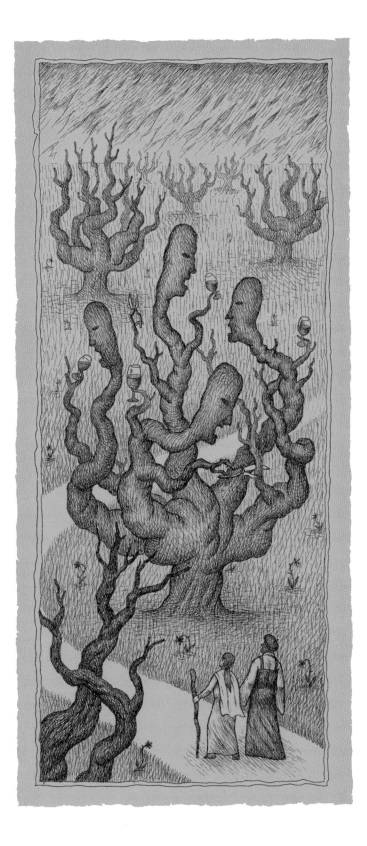

Anent canopy architecture, pruning weight ratios, with pie graphs and charts?"
"They are the Talking Head Vines and can not cease their chatter,
Needful they are of hard arcane-pruning, less gray matter, more heart.

"Great *wine* is mysterious and deep, neither formulaic nor meant to flatter.
Technical mastery may be useful but can itself be a trap.
One must look *vin*wardly to get at the real art of the matter."

I had myself made whines that, while "correct," were still utter crap,
That is to say *vin*onymous, like fathering a child without a name
That is not a place as well—how else to put *terroir* on the map?

These brooding thoughts evoked in me a great sense of shame,
But were quickly dispelled by the sounds of whining and moans.
I saw a queue of scolding harridans—each and every one the same!

Said Noblet, "Somebody must have sent in the crones.
To punish the clonal selectors, there is no better retribution
Than hearing the same grape gripe again and again for aeons.

"Vinfernal logic is thus deployed to provide the *vine*-al solution.
'Tis utterly fair, despite the appearance of a Grand Guigal."
Noblet's words carried great authority, spoken as it were, in the *vrai mamaloshen*.[141]

We then came upon a vast *vin*trepôt, or warehouse of *sols*,
Far from the madeirizing crowd (so we thought),[142] but, opening the door a crack,
We were overcome by the pungent reek of furfural.[143]

More startling was the array of gripe-growers tightly packed,
Les pieds sur la tête; I thought at once of Bloom and Molly,
And Champagne bottles, *en latte,*[144] neatly nestled front to back.

For anyone who was *oeny*body, this was a rather bizarre finale.
I asked about these poor *sols* and how they had gone so astray.
"These are misguided growers from the San Joaquin Valley

141. Yiddish for "exceptionally candid speech," literally, "the mother tongue." 142. To madeirize a whine is to oxidize it by subjecting it to elevated temperatures, as in the case of Madeira. Madera, California, unlike its namesake, *is* truly Vinfernal. 143. Hydroxymethylfurfural is the strongly raisinated or prunish component associated with vastly overripe, or "cooked," grapes. 144. The technical term for the densely packed nested rows of Champagne bottles stored *en tirage*.

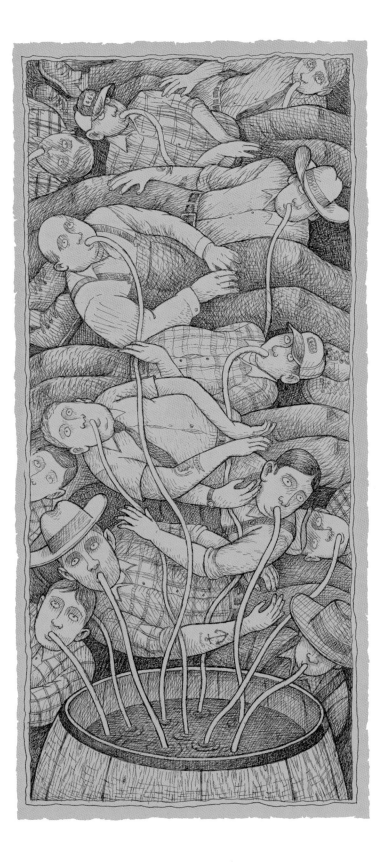

"Who, upon the release of the popular film *Sideways*,
Grafted vast acreages to the well-known Burgundian *cépage*.
The results you can smell yourself—note that particular bouquet."

These late Burgunders[145] were compelled to take *bon courage*
As they straw-sipped sideways from new heavy-toast *tonneaux*
Their penal *noir* and pondered the prospects of *oent*ernal coprophage.

They were to drink from ne'er ullaging casks of Big Valley Pinot.
Myself, I could not feature a torture more meet
For those who had planted this shy, sensitive grape in Fresno.

DE CANTO XIV

We gained some relief from the Vinfernal heat
As we quit that place where *sols* were Pinot-boarded.
My own feelings about the grape remained bittersweet.

This was a *cépage* I had once ardently courted.
But when I had dispassionately considered my "realistic" prospects,
I'd lost my will and quit, dispirited, doon-hearted.

Truth told, it took no great skill to critique the obvious defects
Of whines produced from such a fussy grape, hence easy to malign.
Another matter to find a personal *terroir*, a Grahm Cru, in effect.

"Easier said than doon," Noblet pronounced, reading my mind.
"But essential nevertheless if you are to save your own *oent*ernal *sol*.
La Route du Vrai Vin stands before you, as you have well *divined*."

It had lately become my idée fixe, my most heartfelt goal,
To discover a place where both grape and I belonged,
Truly married to each other, making one another whole.

But would it be Pinot, Fer Servadou, Gros or Petit Manseng
On granite, limestone, slate, or righteously good schist?
A few permutations are *vitting* and right, a billion likely wrong.

145. *Spätburgunder*, or "late Burgundy," is the German term for Pinot noir. The Fresnians are clearly *Zuspät-burgunders* in several senses of the word.

The patent complexity of the proposition was just this:
Finding a new Great Growth, absent twelve centuries of iteration,
Was like finding a Côtes de Nuits-dle in a haystack, essentially *vit*-or-miss.

I brooded on this *vin*tractable poser with ever-increasing frustration,
'Til Maître reminded me our work was still quite far from doon.
There were more zinful *sols* to witness in the Vinfernal appellation.

Noblet led me deeper into the unearthly gloom.
We came to a spot, eerily glowing, emanating a raucous noise.
A portal appeared and we stepped inside a blindingly white room.

"'Tis the 'marketing space,' conceived by the B-school girls and boys,
Naked capitalists, doing what they do best, these devious cohorts,
*Vin*forming/deforming our world with the dark arts they employ."

A cacophony of names of imaginary idyllic venues issued forth:
"Napa Ridge, Brook Hollow, Forest Glen . . ."—the banal litany of *oenvil* was read.
"Counter-*terroirists* they are," sniffed Noblet, "spume and froth.

"There is no *there* there in these sani-*vin*tasized brands; they are 'white bread.'
Sans gravitas, blighted red-and-whited sepulchers.
This wretched domain of *blagueurs* is all, alas, Jest Red.[146]

"Behold before you the fraudulent denominators, the *poseurs,*
Those *vine*-olent to the consumer, and as such meriting *vitu*peration.
On earth they were averred to be but gifted entrepreneurs.[147]

"There is a long old-school tradition of the wholesale appropriation
Of protected *wine* names, a sort of proto-identity theft,
À la 'Chablis' or 'Champagne,' which trade 'pon the reputation

"Of real appellations, with marketing legerdemain quite deft."
We observed then a solitary *vin*dividual cursed to a desolate fate.
In chiaroscuro, he appeared to be of redoubtable heft.

146. *Blagueurs* is French for "jokers," though it has a slightly different meaning in Piemontese dialect, where the word (in the singular) signifies someone who exposes himself. The poet cannot help but feel personally chagrined and deeply embarrassed by his own role in the recent phenomenon of the ubiquity of wine label schtick.   **147.** The poet is undoubtedly referring to the lawsuit brought by the Napa Valley Grape Growers Association against Fred Franzia of the Bronco Whine Company in Ceres, California, in regard to his alleged misleading appropriation of the name *Napa* in his Napa Creek marque, a whine produced from a nontrivial percentage of grapes grown far from the world-famous, brand-name viticultural signifier.

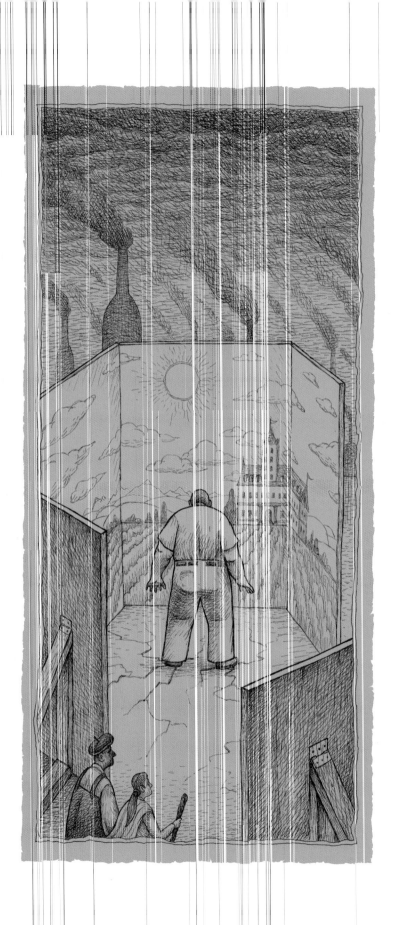

"On earth, this man occupied a vast chunk of real estate;
As a counter-*terroirist,* he now has no ground upon which to tread."
And as he stepped, the earth gave way, due to his formidable weight.

"Maître, how is such a wide swath of the domain of the dead
Taken up by just one whine-man?" I was truly in awe.
"*That* is Mr. Franzia, son, known to his close fiends as 'Fred.'

"His presence here is twice insured by provision of Vinfernal law.
Remember that he is also the mind behind
'Two Buck Chuck,' more properly yclept Charles Shaw.

"Vinfernal justice is, once again, well doon and condign
To spewers of *vin*dustrial waste intent on making a killing,
To overpricers of overboozy, overoaked, overwrought whines.

"To Merlot mongers, peddlers of Pinots e-*grigio*-us, Chardo-nay-sayers, shilling
Their *vin*onymous whines to poor Fat Bastards, true believers in Santa . . .
Margherita and Yellow Tail—a Coalition of the Swilling!"

Noblet was het up, on an antijammy-jelly roll, and quite the ranter.
"Fruit bombs away! *Ich bin ein* Jelly Doughnut! Pardon, *Berliner.*"
This was a far cry from the genteel critiques proffered in *Decanter.*

"Maître, what is to become of those miserable zinners
Who promoted their *vins ordinaires* as the Nectar of Bacchus?"
We then were given to witness the ultimate whinemaker dinner

From hell, and my question was answered in the unholy fracas
That unfolded before us—a *grande bouffe de gourmandises,*
Giving me the feeling of *déjà bu,* or bad tartaric acid flashbacks.

I had myself assisted in more than my share of these
Exercises in gluttonous *maximus,* the Wild Kingdom deep-fried.
Eighteen courses in all, with whines, five desserts plus cheese,

Nary a green veggie or legume on a platter espied.
But the worst was not the food—narcolepsy-inducing, I'll admit—
But the droning whine of the whinemaker who tried

To enlighten the unlettered public on vinous arcana: to wit,
Percentages of new versus one-year-old oak and degrees of toast,
Alliers, Nevers, or Tronçais forest? Quarter-sawn or hand split?

And whether the malo was full or partial, the host
Would take pains to excruciatingly elucidate.
Phenological parameters were also addressed, which for most

Was the part exquisitely designed to stultify, with inarticulate
Ramblings anent Brixes, VAs, pHs, and total acidities.
The whinemaker 'pon these matters would endlessly pontificate

And explore other banal *vinutiae* with single-minded avidity.
If I were to hear the term *physiological ripeness* ever again . . .[148]
I would fain lie doon and die of *oennui* (see *Oennals of Morbidity*).

Clichéd *oeno-babble* filled the dining hall, like purple prosodic rain.
"Maître," I nudged Noblet, his eyes now distant and glazed,
"I suggest we leave at once ere we are (fruit-)driven *vinsane*."

DE CANTO XV

We missed the Tower of Scrapple dessert, *avec crème anglaise,*
But were quite relieved to be quit of that lethal venue.
We then came to a beastly place I'll remember to the end of my days.

It seemed to be a conservatory park, perhaps some sort of zoo.
Please don't feed the marketers, an officious sign bade.
In the *Marketiergarten,*[149] they swarmed in a filthy, caged milieu.

"*C'est très animal,*"[150] Noblet could not help but add.
He was certainly correct in regard to the pungent bouquet
That attended the perpetrators of this particularly execrable fad.

"From my vintage vantage," began Noblet,
"I am alarmed by 'critter whines,' or, as we say, *vins des bêtes,*[151] a
Vinous transgression that is here routinely appraised

"As grievously as that which mortifies the zoophiles of PETA.
We have descended into the Eighth Circle—the Vale of Market-teers,
Where Bambi meets Rexzilla in a grudge-match *vindetta*.

176

Poesy

148. The term *hang-time* might also be applicable to the swift justice due perpetrators of endless vinous cant and jargon. 149. *Tiergarten* is German for "zoo." 150. "It is very gamey"—an expression typically reserved for whines afflicted with *Brettanomyces* infections or certain sorts of reduction aromas. 151. *Vins bêtes* would of course be "stupid whines."

"Their punishment's term is measured out in dog years.
Multiply (or is it divide?) forever by seven, and still you are screwed
By an oeternity spent under the aegis of Three Blind Mooseketeers,

"Scores of Smoking Loons, Mad & Blue Fish, Fat Cats and Emus,
Roaming Goats, Goliath Roosters, Grizzly Bears, and Rheas,
Lizards, Leaping Stags and Frogs and Yellow-tailed Kangaroos.

"A cute, fuzzy, critter whine had become the à la mode idea.
California label-fauna might here safely graze, floor-stacked to the woof they'd climb,
Muzzle by jowl with their beastly brethren of Antipodea."

It appeared we had arrived at the marketeers' feeding time.
The *plat du jour* was announced by the little penguin maitre d'.
"*Tartare de bicycletteur rouge paillardé par un grand camion rouge*,"[152] he pantomimed.

It was an offal sight to behold: Proffered by a dapper wallaby,
Jeroboams of Road Kill Red were poured from a *very* recent year,
And the toasted-head waiter wished us all a hearty "Bon appétit."

"The animals are running this show, or so it would appear,"
I remarked, as an overly familiar seal nosed Noblet most rudely.
Startled, he yelped, "Get the *phoque*[153] outta here!"

I don't know whence arose this beastly craze, but, to put it crudely,
It was the critters now that kept the bestial *vetiquetters*.[154]
The Vinferno, ever just, had designed its punishments shrewdly.

DE CANTO XVI

You would think that we would have known better
Than to linger any longer in this den of *viniquity*.
Suddenly, at our heels was Cerberus, a right wrongo dongo triple-header.

"Nice doggies, good doggies," I ventured with some timidity.
The triune beast just snarled and slavered.
I cursed Jorge Ordóñez and his brand's great ubiquity.[155]

152. Raw thin slices of red bicyclist flattened by a big red truck. **153.** French for "seal." Phoque Blanc Chardonnay is in fact an actual whine, and not the product of the poet's sometimes overactive imagination. **154.** A neologism that perhaps signifies an unleashed "producer of animal labels." **155.** Wrongo Dongo Monastrell from Jumilla, España.

Noblet and I had no time for any further palaver,
As we continued our descent into the marketing space
And found that we had soon come to a spot that I'd rather

Not dwell on in the finest detail, as it was the case
That some very private issues at this time arose,
Which made it for me a most *vin*hospitable place.

"This is the most abject corner of the Eighth Circle, I suppose,"
Said Noblet, as we beheld the hateful vinous hypocrites
Consigned to one of the Vinferno's rottenest boroughs

The mournfulness of their dirge was heartbreaking, I'll admit.
"Who are these *sols* who now seem so remorseful?"
"These are the whinemen, given to excessive cleverness and wit,

"Who, despite their prodigious gifts, were less than resourceful
And squandered the vast reservoir of good will and largesse
That was once showered 'pon them, and are now, of course, full

"Of excuses as to why their whines no longer incandesce.
They became diverted from the vine's true, righteous aim.
These whiners, who once a deep love of devine professed,

"Became distracted by that which to them easiest came.
Far more amusing to plot a brilliant public relations coup de grâce,
Witty labels, screwcap videos, or other foolishness one might name."

I then beheld among the zinners a most familiar face.
It was hard for me to stomach it, without beginning to feel sick,
But I now observed my own keening self, the paradigm of disgrace.

What sort of illusion was it, or perhaps a parlor trick,
That I had myself been to Vinfernal depths consigned,
When I was (at least 'pon recent inspection) still sentient and quick?

I'd always imagined that there would be ample, nay, infinite time
To get around to the work of becoming an original creator.
Enfin, I was but a mere whinemaker with a clever product line.

Poesy

"We may wish it so, but there is in fact no such thing as 'later.'
You are always in Whine Hell if you are forever deferring
Your vinous longings; you become the ultimate whine spectator."

DE CANTO XVII

To Noblet's words there was indeed no demurring.
I was damned as a blatant zinner, most wretched,
And felt the searing shame inside me, *cab*-burn, baby, burning.

I have, dear reader, neither shown self-pity nor kvetched
Anent my own discomfort, in this true and faithful account
Of my *sub-rosé* journey, these *tableaux mourants* I have sketched.

For I was to find myself once again totally busted and caught out,
In mortal humiliation, we're talking *pantalones abajos* here.
The embarrassing incident occurred at just about

The time we had quit the place of hypocrites and marketeers
And walked down a road littered with broken flangèd bottle
Tops and "cigar band" neckers indicating the vintage year.

To my *maître,* I admitted that I had always wished to throttle
The imitative packagers, who themselves had seemed to lack
An original idea in their toasted heads. "Were you not flattered a little,"

Queried Noblet, "by these hopelessly derivative hacks,
Who only sought a little pizzazz, some *vín*imation for their brand?"
But I digress from the incident and will now presently backtrack.

Among the rubble and debris in that blasted land,
Amid the discarded corkscrews and broken glass,
We came upon a lovely terrace and a beautiful stand

Of stately old, *gobelet*-trained vines, and at last
I felt the old stirrings that had once in my breast reposed
When near the real work of a *víticulteur,* a genu-*víne* enthusiast.

"I see you're ready to return to your métier, so I propose
To furnish you with the requisite tools and apparati
To do the job properly. Come then, let us stroll the vine rows."

Poesy

181

He handed me an unfamiliar gizmo I could not at first identify.
"Maître, what matter of strange implement is this?"
"'Tis a pair of pruning shears," he rather brusquely replied.

I felt as if I had just tumbled into a vertiginous abyss
And been inextricably bound over to an *oeno*-da-fé.
Noblet, my *maître*, seemed to morph into a *vinquisitor*, a *Vinfernal catechist!

"Son, what sort of grapes might these be, pray?
Their traits are too obvious for aught but a fool to miss.
Be they Roussanne? Picpoul? Or maybe just Viognier?"[156]

This last *cépage* he pronounced with a scornful hiss.
I felt dispraised and contused and found no relief
In the certain knowledge that I was being mortally dissed.

"That you cannot distinguish 'tween an entire or lobèd leaf,
Or note the open petiolar sinus, glabrous surface, or striated wood
Of these well-known varieties, simply beggars belief."

I walked on in shame, shoulders stooped and head bowed.
It was barely the smallest consolation to observe
A dead zeppelin crashed and smoldering by the side of the road.[157]

DE CANTO XVIII

At this point in the journey, I confess, I nearly lost my nerve,
Having a glimpse of my irrevocable fate been shown
And, for the onerousness of my zins, meted a punishment deserved.

While Noblet could not my *vindiscretions* entirely condone,
He was conciliatory now, advising me not to abandon hope.
There was still time to mend the error of my ways & cuvées and atone.

But it was becoming ever more difficult just to cope
With the vicissitudes of the journey and the piercing psychic pain.
What had begun as a great escarp had defaulted to a slippery slope.

156. The poet is alluding to a senseless and bitter lawsuit (see "Revenge") that he had been caught up in some
years previously and that ultimately devolved to the question of how much ampelographic expertise a grape
grower might reasonably be expected to possess   157. There was a whine on earth called Red Zeppelin,
which was an unabashed appropriation of Le Cigare Volant.

These thoughts I had not but a moment to entertain,
As we began to mount a steep defile that was quite precarious.
Impossible now it was to return to the spot from whence we came,

Caught in a rock-hard place 'tween silex and calcareous.[158]
We were surely dooned; I prepared to bid my *maître* adieu & good-bye.
I knew we'd presently meet up with something lethally nefarious.

Noblet then shouted to me, and bade me cover my eyes.
"We are about to encounter the dreaded Gorgon, Dagueneau,[159]
The guardian of the Ninth Circle, whose steely gaze is sure to petrify!"[160]

The Gorgon spoke thusly: "An extreme makeover is certainly à propos
For those whose whines are jammy or 'fruit-driven.'"
(I did not, of course, see Didier but heard his hog's fortissimo.)

"That a real *wine* must express minerality is a given.
And yet the New World whinemakers this verity ignored
At their own peril—their zins remain irrevocably unshriven."

I heard Dagueneau zoom off and his big bike's deafening roar.
"It is safe for you now to open your eyes," Maître informed me.
Yet I could not grasp what I beheld, and remained just utterly floored.

We observed in the valley below us a tableau of whine luminaries,
Makers of high-scoring whines of no provenance, no guardianship.
Napasonomendacious's finest had all been turned into cold stone statuary!

"Glad to see that Caltrans is back on the job," Noblet quipped.
Sol-less whines—I never grasped what consumers got from them.
"Maître, why do we abide these fakeries, these overpriced gyps?"

Noblet: "Frankly, even for *moi,* it's a real conundrum.
But our time now is short, and but one task remains, which
Is to return to earth from the depths we have plumbed.

---

158. Siliceous and limestone-based soils, respectively. **159.** Didier Dagueneau, the late iconoclastic *wine*-maker of the Loire, was known for his steely, mineral-intensive *wines,* if not also for his dreadlocked hair and predilection for dogsled racing and large motorcycles. **160.** Not exactly the "mineralizing process," as it is classically understood by soil scientists.

"There is only one minor, just slightly complicating hitch."
Noblet paused for effect and his words left little doubt:
"We must pass directly through Sa-*tannin's* own unholy niche."

"The only way through is the way *w-a-y* doon and out,
Smack o'er the back of MepHisto, the Father of Lees and Untruths."
Candidly, I thought we might entertain taking a less scenic route.

My instinct was to turn yellow-tail and run like hell, in sooth.
But I had placed myself in the able hands of my *maître,* Noblet.
As they say, the course of true Pinot NV never runs smooth.

We then descended down a rough-hewn, dark passageway.
In vaporous silence, we prepared to meet the beast.
Fetid fumes reeked & swirled as we lurched toward Doonsday.

To say I was scared spitless is to say quite the least.
Then, whoosh, all at once we plunged down a great sinkhole drain.
We were there, then, in the lair, in the dark heart of the *vino caviste.*

We smelled him before we saw him, Auld Pétomane.[161]
How he conducted a proper tasting in this state is hard to convey.
But there he sat, at a vast *table d'*hate that was blood- and whine-stained,

With tens of thousands of whine glasses around him arrayed,
This immense iridescent, wingèd beast, his great maw crammed
With Messrs. Parker and Shanken,[162] their eyeballs serving as a tasty entrée,

An amused *bouche,* as the French might say. P. and S. were damned
Put out by this double-blind tasting conducted by this *oenographivore.*
Old Mel-nick, the *Teufelweintrinker,* was just getting slammed,[163]

As he busily made tasting notes, looking for the greatest rapport
'Tween texture and flavor of whine scrivener and whine,
The fiendish felicity of which he would award his numerical score.

161. Joseph Pujol, "Le Pétomane" (which roughly translates to "Fartiste"), was born in Marseilles, France, in 1857 and, owing to his singular talent, became one of the most well known and highly paid entertainers in all of France.   162. The editor suggests that it may seem late in the game and perhaps more than a little disingenuous on the part of the poet to express contrition to the aggrieved parties about this particularly disturbing image, but empathizes with his seemingly uncontrollable impulse to make a pun about a "double-blind tasting."   163. Melnik, unknown to most whine drinkers in these parts, is the most successful grape variety in Bulgaria. *Teufelweintrinker* is German for "the devil-whine drinker," a pun on *Tafelwein,* or "table whine." The joke also works in French, with *vin de diable* and *vin de table.*

"Astonishingly full-bodied, with good, firm backbone and spine."
"Rather fleshy 'round the middle, with a huge and complete nose."
"Great legs . . . a long and excruciatingly dramatic finish, I find."

As his Sa-*tannic* Majesty his brilliant whine pairings composed,
We scampered o'er his shoulders and across his leathery back,
Made for daylight, and bid the Vinferno a warm adios.

I returned to terra firma with body and *sol* intact,
And found that I had traversed diametrically through
To the other side of the world (ironically enough),**164** in fact.

I had traveled in the worst Circles with Noblet as my *passe-partout*
And survived to tell all about it in this cautionary tale I relay,
But would I take the deep lessons to heart and my great passion renew?

I blinked in the bright antipodean light as I found my way.
I had been transformed—a new life, a new man.
Ecco Domani; the doon of a new day.

(2006)

I cannot begin to describe how immensely fulfilling it was to work on the Vinferno. Not only was it literally more ambitious than anything I had previously attempted, but in the writing I simultaneously worked out parallel issues of my own life-opera. As it turned out, while the Vinferno was in the process of being published, negotiations for the sale of Bonny Doon Vineyard or some portion thereof were also taking place. Some degree of discretion with respect to the sensitive business negotiation was clearly required, and this had to be balanced with my overwhelming desire to tell all. The last installment of the Vinferno was released simultaneously with the announcement of the major restructuring of the company.

While there has been no shortage of kvetching in the newsletters and speeches for as long as I have been writing them—Why do the grapes and wines in California lack soul? (or some variant whinge *du jour*)—there has always been a gap between what I aspire to and the seemingly intractable Given, with no apparent way to bridge this chasm. Writing this piece helped me bridge that gap, to begin to make my actions more congruent with my beliefs and values. One never knows for sure which levers impel change, but I credit the recent attainment of one-half century of terrestrial residence; the birth of my first child, Amélie (occurring in the same year); and a serious health crisis that ensued the year after. For these reasons, it was absolutely clear that I could no longer continue my hypocritical ways—espousing the value of *terroir* publicly while failing to make any significant changes in my own entrenched modus operandi. And there was (and still is) that small matter of an overpowering personal need, like that of salmon swimming upriver to spawn, to produce a truly soulful Pinot Noir[165] before shuffling off this Merlot coil.

Writing the Vinferno allowed me to clear the slate

---

164. The irony is presumably the poet's extreme aversion to most (though not all) Australian whines.
165. Also excellent to serve with aforesaid salmon.

vendetta-wise, as it did for Dante, though I got a little carried away at times, strafing both friend and foe indiscriminately. The larger point is that many of us in the wine business live in some sort of Wine Hell of our own devising. I wanted to make a clean breast of my own zins, most notably the failure to follow my own heart, having gotten far too caught up in elements extraneous to wine's essence. Writing the piece allowed me to clear space within myself and begin to make the changes my soul had been demanding for quite some time.

TAKING IT DOON-TUNE

Don Giovese in Bakersfield
An Opera Giacosa

Il Cast

Don Giovese, an iconoclastic young winemaker
Lebrunello, assistant winemaker to Don Giovese
Donna Fiana, a beautiful young grower of Chardonnay grapes, contracted to Don Vinodatavola
Don Vinodatavola, a competing winemaker, specializing in the production of Chardonnay wine
Donna Almeria, a grower of Pinot noir grapes, abandoned by Don Giovese
Il Consigliere di Poderi della Università di California

Act One, Scene 1

(Lebrunello, in rubber boots and wine-soaked jeans, enters from right carrying a tank light.)

LEBRUNELLO *(aria)*   Slaving night and day in this cave is

Not what I imagined when I was *immatricolato* at UC Davis.

I'd expected something far more stellar

Than the rodentian life in this damp cellar.

He's always on his way to some winemaker dinner. I just don't get it.

I do all the real work. He gets all the credit.

I'd like to live the life of a *viticoltore*

And do cellar work no more.

Bottling is for the birds and topping is a dreadful bore.

Still now, I hear the buzz of a chainsaw out in the sticks;

My boss must be up and about, plying his tricks.

I had best return to my stultifying chores. *(He withdraws.)*

(Don Giovese is seen attempting to remedially prune the top of a grapevine in a neighboring vineyard with a chainsaw, despite the imprecations of Donna Fiana.)

FIANA   *Sei pazzo?* Radical grafting as you propose cannot be undone,

And this year Chardonnay is going for sixteen hundred dollars a ton.[166]

(She attempts to wrestle the chainsaw away from Don Giovese.)

---

166. A creditable price at the time this piece was written.

GIOVESE   Sweet vineyardist, this emergency grafting is for your own good.
Where there once was Chardonnay, let there be Syrah wood.

FIANA   Your impassioned rhetoric does nothing to inflame me.
Those varieties you call nonstandard, I call cockamamie.

GIOVESE   Stand aside, foolish girl, the *guanto*'s been hurled.
Prepare to enter the post-Chardonnay world.

(*Restarts chainsaw.*)

FIANA (*distraught*)   Someone stop this madman before he destroys my productive,
reasonable, sane, and perfectly hygienic vineyard!

CONSIGLIERE (*officiously brandishing pruning shears at Don Giovese*)
Young man, while I think Petite Sirah is a superlative grape,
What you are attempting here is hardly a jape.
Such unbridled viticultural *passione* I cannot abide.
Sirrah, is that bud wood certified?
Make no attempt now to *evadere*, that is, to cheese it.
Hand over the wood directly, or we'll seize it.

GIOVESE (*aside*)   The *vecchio* can't differentiate Sirah petite
From the noble Syrah, not such an onerous feat.
What sort of fool does he take me for? Good grief.
Does he think I intend to bud over to Durif?

(*Don Giovese and the consigliere face off, air-pruning and lunging menacingly.*)

CONSIGLIERE (*crying out*)   I have inadvertently pruned myself to the quick.
It is your fault, Giovese. Please help me. I'm not feeling too slick.

(*He collapses.*)

FIANA (*turning to Don Giovese*)   You can see what your radicalism leads to.
Now our dear Consigliere di Poderi's been wounded, *ferito*.

VINODATAVOLA (*entering from left, self-righteously*)
The injury inflicted on our *caro consigliere* leaves me shocked and dismayed.
This man is dangerous and should be locked up, better strung up and flayed.
Now, my dear, are you ready to sign the long-term *contratto*?
We'll make beautiful Chardonnay together, with lots of skin *contatto*.

FIANA AND VINODATAVOLA (*duet*)   There's nothing wrong with Chardonnay.
Everyone should drink at least a glass a day.
It's a wine that complements *tutti piatti*,
Be it Thai food or chicken potpie food, and that says a lot, e
Further, you won't embarrass your friends or yourself
If you reach for that name-brand Chard on the shelf.

We're so *contenti* with Chardonnay.

It just blows the lesser grapes away.

Home is where the Chard is.

GIOVESE *(disgusted)*   They are interested only in an effortless sell.

Bah, I've been Chard to a fare-thee-well.

(Gestures expressively and exits.)

Scene 2

(Lebrunello and Don Giovese are walking along a vineyard lane.)

LEBRUNELLO   Boss, may I speak to you in utter candor?

GIOVESE   *Certo.* You could speak to me in utter Mongolian. *(leers and twirls cigar)*

LEBRUNELLO   At the risk of being too bold,

I've remarked a *tendenza* in you, and I don't mean to scold.

I filosofi might call it a tragic flaw.

You don't like just any grape; you seem to love them all.

At least for a season or two, until they no longer enthuse you,

But by then you've found a new vitaceous *musa* to amuse you.

Your grape *incostanza* just makes my head spin.

The last one you've seen enchants you, and it's *amore* again.

Your passion for new varietals leads you down the Faustian route,

Dottore, and it's not Maculan I'm talking about.[167]

GIOVESE *(distracted)*   Lebrunello, your point is extremely well taken,

But look here at these remarkable vines, Grignolino, if I'm not mistaken.

I think these grapes would work well in a program I foresee

Calling "*Vitis vinifera*'s Greatest Hits"—advertise it on late night TV.

Their remarkable scent has already started me swooning.

Let's inquire of that vineyardist over there, she who is pruning.

Yoo-hoo!

ALMERIA *(glaring up from her vines)*

You, who would go on at great length about my pellucid skins

And told me you'd crush my grapes again and again.

All your talk of a wine with voluptuous body, great legs, and elegance

Was only a come-on; please don't insult my intelligence.

O perfidy, O deception—you really handed me a barge

When you told me that my Pinot Nero was erotically charged.

---

167. Fausto Maculan is a diabolically clever winemaker in the Veneto.

Not a single one of your promises turned out to be true,
Viz, wanting to contract to the year 2102.
I believed that together you and I would produce a great *vino*,
An exquisite Bianco di Nero from my *bello giardino*.
GIOVESE (*blushing*)   I never promised you a *rosé* garden.
LEBRUNELLO   If it makes you feel any better, he says that to all his growers.
GIOVESE   I think at this juncture I've heard quite enough.
I'll retire to a good bottle of claret. Lafites, do your stuff. (*exits*)
ALMERIA   The cowardly villain has unceremoniously flown.
What to do now with all the *pazzi* varieties I have grown?
For, after abandoning Pinot Nero, he convinced me to graft
Eighty-five additional acres to Rkatsiteli on his behalf.
LEBRUNELLO (*aria*)   My dear little lady, there might still be
Some consolation in that your grapes neither are, nor will be,
The first or last ones he's toyed with and then *abbandonato*.
Look at this volume of cellar records I have here *compilato*.
It's full of the names of all the varietals he has tried.
Grapes from every part of the world he once loved, then shunted aside.
Take a look, read it with me.
From Germany, two hundred and fifty!
One hundred and sixty Romanian,
Eighty-nine Spanish, thirty-three Albanian.
But from Italia, already one thousand and three.
For a long time he would only drink *francese*.
He was enamored with the *bourgognese*,
Until he discovered the discreet charms of the *bordolese*.
His fickleness just drives me crazy.
One moment he's keen on Nebbiolo,
Then it's Mammolo or Cannaiolo.
He is taken with the scores of Moscati
Till he's served a fresh glass of Frascati.
I've forgotten to mention Dolcetto.
There's Freisa, Ciliegiolo, and Brachetto.
He adores Malvasia, be it Bianca, Nera, or Rosa.
Perhaps he's suffering from anorexia nervosa.
Frizzante and still, red, white, and blush.
He never met a grape he didn't want to crush.

Doon-Tune

There are epiphanous moments in psychotherapy when one suddenly grasps an obvious but previously elusive truth about oneself. Being a hopeless, romantic fool for Pinot noir, I did realize one day that, as truly devoted to Pinot as I imagined myself to be, I was, at heart, at least viticulturally, an inveterate polygamist. Monogamy, or perhaps I should say monovity, was simply an unnatural state for someone of my proclivities. Certainly, if one is really serious about Pinot noir, one must be thoroughly devoted, true to one's *cépage*. I have gotten myself in trouble more than once with a wandering eye for new vineyards and new grape varieties, which are always more attractive in the gauzy, soft-focus mist of young-vine lust. While I believe myself to be a reformed viticultural philanderer—that is, I am now highly focused and 100 percent committed to my primary viticultural relationships—I could imagine an unexpected, accidental indiscretion or three, should the right Sagrantino, Teroldego Rotaliano, or Timorasso catch my eye.

Born to Rhône

Selections from a Rock (and Gravel) Opera

Born to Rhône was a "rock opera" performed at Teatro ZinZanni in San Francisco on January 12, 2004. The lyrics, set to the tunes of various rock songs, treated some of the traditional Doonian themes—the greatness of misunderstood *cépages,* the perils of corks (and the concomitant brilliance of screwcaps), the inappropriateness of *pointillisme.* I've included what I think are the cleverest lyrics and the ones that also give a sense (some minor interpolation required) of the plot line, which follows a fairly traditional dramatic arc. Our hero, Don Quijones, believed to have come "not from around here," is "deposited" by a mysterious flying object in front of the Beverly Hills home of Mr. and Mrs. Quijones on or about April 4, 1953, and the Quijones raise the foundling as their own son. Young Quijones evinces a natural proclivity for chemistry, enrolls at the University of Davis *[sic],* and ultimately secures an entry-level position at Bonny Doon Vineyard, with the primary responsibility of assisting at winemaker dinners. He develops a natural interest in *vins de terroir,* and, owing to some typographical ambiguity, his name shows up on a governmental list of "international *terroiristes.*" He falls victim to the Ashcroft Inquisition, and is remanded to Soledad Correctional Training Facility, where his rehabilitation takes the form of teaching wine appreciation courses to his fellow inmates. Quijones escapes from the Soledad prison, ends up crashing a lifestyle seminar at Copia, the Napa Valley educational institution, and progresses to the town of Oakville, where he is abducted by aliens. He meets his alien sweetheart aboard a "flying cigar" and returns triumphantly to transmit the aliens' important message regarding *terroir* to the planet Earth.

196

SUNG TO: LITTLE DEUCE COUPE *(THE BEACH BOYS)*

———

Little *soucoupe*. You don't know what I got
Little *soucoupe*. You don't know what I got
Well, I'm not braggin' babe so don't put me down
But I've got the bitchinest starship in town
When there's an alien cruiser in my sector he don't
   even try
'Cause if he chooses me off he knows his planet will fry
She's my little *soucoupe*
You don't know what I got
(Chorus: My little *soucoupe*. You don't know what I got)
Just a little *soucoupe* equipped with an anal probe drill
She'll dust a Romulan star-fighter like it's standin' still
She's trans-ported and relieved, and she's stroked and
   she's bored
She'll do warp six point three and take you out of this
   world
She's my little *soucoupe*
You don't know what I got
(My little *soucoupe*. You don't know what I got)

She's got an antimatter fuel cell with four pseudopods
   on the floor
And she purrs like a Qxytlibrolivian kitten till the
   tailpipes roar
And if that ain't enough to make you flip your lid
There's one more thing, I got a tractor beam, daddy
Her invisibility shield makes my ET buds look pretty
   green
She'll blast Tralfamadorians outta the sky like you
   never seen
I get morphed out of shape and it's hard to steer
When I'm channeling the life-form of say,
   a Britney Spears
She's my little *soucoupe*. You don't know what I got
(My little *soucoupe*. You don't know what I got)
She's my little *soucoupe*. You don't know what I got
(My little *soucoupe*. You don't know what I got)
She's my little *soucoupe*. You don't know what I got

TUNE: Monster Grenache

SUNG TO: THE MONSTER MASH *(BOBBY "BORIS" PICKETT)*

———

I was working in the wine lab late one night
When I tasted a grape I thought might be a little
   bit light
But the wine was monstrous, and from the glass
   it did rise
Suddenly to my surprise
Billowed forth intense aromas from a wine of
   great size

It was a monster Grenache
We had monster Grenache
(Chorus: It was Grenache)
It was a vineyard smash
(It was Grenache)
It went great with goulash
(It was Grenache)
It was monster Grenache

168. The French draw a distinction between *soucoupes volantes* (flying saucers) and *cigares volants* (cigar-shaped flying objects).

To my wine laboratory down in Santa Cruz
From Aureole restaurant where all the great chefs
   schmooze
The sommeliers all came, these good ole boys
To catch a little sip of my Clos de Gilroy[169]

(They drank Grenache)
They drank monster Grenache
(They drank Grenache)
It was a culinary smash
(They drank Grenache)
It could be served with panache
(They drank Grenache)
They drank monster Grenache

The tasting party was wild, as befits a brand
   new release
The guests included Henri Bonne-eau, Michel
   Cryptoutier, Marcel Gui-ghoul and his fils[170]
The wine was really killer, a fragrant, full-bodied red
Some older vintages were exhumed and
   pronounced very much undead
The Dead Leaf Bottlers (Feuille Morticians)
   were about to arrive.[171]
With their vocal group, the Rayas-Kickoff Five
(They drank Grenache)
They sipped the monster Grenache
(They sipped Grenache)
It was a vineyard smash
(They sipped Grenache)
It caught on in a flash
(They swirled Grenache)
They swirled their monster Grenache

From deep, deep cold storage Vlad the Impeller's[172]
   voice did ring
Seems he was troubled by just one thing
He opened the screwcap, shook his fist, and what
   did he say?
"Whatever happened to the old Le Gaucher?"[173]
(It's now Grenache)
It's now monster Grenache
(It's now Grenache)
And it's a vineyard smash
(It's now Grenache)
It caught on in a flash
(It's now Grenache)
It's now monster Grenache

Now everything's cool
Vlad's down with the brand
And the monster Grenache is the hit of the Land
For you, who are grateful for red, this Grenache was
   meant too
When you get to the wineshop tell them
The Rhône Ranger sent you
(It is Grenache)
It is monster Grenache
(It is Grenache)
It was a Graves-yard smash
(It is Grenache)
It has caught on in a flash
(Vive le Grenache!)
Long live monster Grenache!

---

169. Clos de Gilroy was a Grenache-based wine made by Bonny Doon Vineyard for many years. 170. Henri Bonneau, Michel Chapoutier, and Marcel Guigal. 171. "Dead leaf," or *feuille morte*, is a typical color for Burgundy bottles. 172. Apologies for this dreadfully inside joke: an impeller is the moving part of certain types of pumps used in winery operations. 173. Le Gaucher was a blend of Barbera and Mourvèdre, produced but twice, with spotty commercial success.

TUNE: It's Only Zinfandel

SUNG TO: IT'S ONLY ROCK 'N ROLL *(THE ROLLING STONES)*

———

If I could stick my thief in the vat
And extract wine as dark as a Grange
Would it satisfy ya, would it slide on by ya
Would you think the boy's deranged? Ain't he strange?
If I could draw ya, if I could pour ya
A red Zin so divine
Would it be enough proof of the winemaker's art
To make you break doon and buy? Really buy-
   uy-uy?
I said, I know it's only Zinfandel, but I like it
I know it's only Zinfandel, but I like it, like it, yes,
   I do
Oh, well, I like it. I like it. I like it
I said, Can't you see that these old vines taste Rhônely?

If I could make a red wine that was good for your heart
A spicy wine worthy of age
Would it be enough for your point-scoring lust?
Would it help to ease the pain? Make a stain?
If I could produce a fruit bomb that was not too tart

If I got a 96 on Parker's scoring card
Gobs of hedonistic fruit flooding all over the page
Would it satisfy ya, would it slide on by ya
Would ya think the boy's *vin*sane?
He's *vin*sane

I said, I know it's only Zinfandel, but I like it
I said, I know it's only Zinfandel, but I like it, like it,
   yes, I do
Oh, well, I like it. I like it. I like it
I said, Can't you see that these old vines taste Rhônely?
And do ya think that you're the only one who swirls
   around?
I bet you think that you're the only connoisseur in town

I said, I know it's only Zinfandel, but I like it
I said, I know it's only Zinfandel, but I like it
I said, I know it's only Zinfandel, but I like it, like it,
   yes, I do
Oh, well. I like, I like it, I like it . . .

TUNE: That Old-Time Pomerol

SUNG TO: THAT OLD-TIME ROCK AND ROLL *(BOB SEGER)*

———

Just take those old bottles off the shelf
I'll sit and drink 'em all by myself
Today's vino ain't got the same soul
I like that old-time Pomerol
Don't give me any of that Napa Merlot
I'll be spitting it right out on the flo'
There's no way I'll be asking for mo'
Not like that old-time Pomerol

I dig Clos Vougeot or some funky Cinsault
That soft texture that just soothes the soul
I reminisce about the wines of old
Like that old-time Pomerol
I won't go to a tasting of Teroldego
I'd rather sip on L'Evangile or some
   Domaine de l'Enclos

There's only one sure way to get me to go
Start cracking open some old-time Pomerol
Call them relics, call them what you will
Say they're old-fashioned, say they're over the hill
Today's vino ain't got the same soul

I like that old-time Pomerol
Still like that old-time Pomerol
That kind of vino that's got a pH of 6'
I reminisce about the wines of old
With that old-time Pomerol

○~

TUNE: Cover of *Le Voyeur du Vin*

SUNG TO: COVER OF THE *ROLLING STONE* (DR. HOOK)

(Chorus, speaking: *Hey Harvey, hey Marvin, tell them who we are!*)

Well, we're big-time winemakers, we got lotsa acres
The wines are loved everywhere they go
   (*That sounds like us*)
We make stuff like Charbono and faux Côtes du
   Rhône-oh
That sell for about fifteen bucks a throw (*Right*)
We make all kinds of swill that gives all kind of thrills
But the thrill that's in our plan, is the thrill that'll getcha
When you get your picture on the cover of *Le Voyeur du Vin*

(*Voyeur du Vin*) Wanna see my picture on the cover
(*Voyeur du Vin*) Wanna buy five thousand copies for my
   mother (*Yeah!*)
(*Voyeur du Vin*) Wanna see my smilin' face on the cover
   of *Le Voyeur du Vin*

(*That's a very very vine idea.*)

We got freaky weird-ass stuff from the brilliant Bascove
Designin' labels worthy of a 100-pt. score
We got my poor ol' red-haired mama schleppin' wine to
   the package stores

Now a "Cellar Selection" is designed to produce
   an erection[14]
For each and every true fan
But abundant new wood just ain't no good 'less you get
   your picture
On the cover of *Le Voyeur du Vin*

(*Voyeur du Vin . . .*) Wanna see our pictures on
   the cover
(*Vin . . .*) Wanna buy five thousand copies for our
   mothers . . . (*Yeah!*)
(*Vin . . .*) Wanna see my smiling face
On the cover of *Le Voyeur du Vin . . .*

Hey, I know how . . . ROCKS AND GRAVEL!

(*Awww, that's beautiful.*)
We got a lot of high-tech DEWNies who'll buy
   anything we say
We got a genu-wine biodynamic guru, who's teachin' us
   a better way
We got all the grapes that money can buy, lotsa
   Marsanne and lotsa Roussanne (*Really, this time*)
And we keep gettin' richer but we can't get our picture
   on the cover of *Le Voyeur du Vin*

---

114. The "Cellar Selection" is a feature of the *Wine Spectator* buying guide.

Le Voyeur du Vin, wanna see my picture on the cover

Wanna buy five thousand copies for my mother
  (*I want one!*)

Wanna see my smilin' face on the cover the cover
  of *Le Voyeur du Vin*

On the cover of *Le Voyeur du Vin*

Wanna see my picture on the cover (*I don't know why we
  ain't on the cover, baby.*)

Gonna buy five thousand copies for my mother
  (*We'd look beautiful in polyester.*)

Wanna see my smiling face (*I ain't kiddin' ya.*)

On the cover the cover of *Le Voyeur du Vin*
  (*Ah, we would make a beautiful cover.*)

(*The first shot, right up front, man, maybe dressed up in a funny
costume with a horse . . . I can see it now . . . on the front, a smilin'
man, with maybe some little bottles in his holster. Who was that
masked man?*)

TUNE: Have a Cigare

SUNG TO: HAVE A CIGAR (*PINK FLOYD*)

Come in here, dear boy, have a Cigare

It's gonna go far, fly high

The marque is never gonna die, they're gonna drink it
  if you try; they're gonna love it

Well, I've always had a deep respect, and I mean that
  most Sancerrely

The brand is just fantastic, that is really what I think

Oh, by the way, which wine's the Pink?

And did we tell you the name of the game, boy?

We call it pimping the discount chains[175]

The Stelvin closure is just a knock out

We heard the wine is sold out

You gotta get your allocations out

You're screwing the whole world, but in a good way

Everyone else's "Big Red" is just Vin Gris, or just
  another Chard

It's a helluva start, it could be made into a fruit-bomb
  monster

If we all pull together to go mainstream

And did we tell you the name of the game, boy?

We call it pimping the discount chains

175. Focusing one's sales efforts on discount chains is an excellent way to increase sales volume, but often at the expense of the wine brand's prestige.

[Spoken]

Is he really marketing wines with screwcaps?

Well, there he is. Let's ask him

Nick, is that a Stelvin closure you're promoting?

Mm-hmm

Gee, it must be great doing his marketing

Is he picking you up after the wine tasting today?

Uh-uh

By the way, where'd you meet him?

I met him at a Beverages and More

But he turned around and smiled at me

You get the picture? (Chorus: Yes, we see.)

That's when I fell for . . . (the leader of the Pac . . . Rim)

The wine critics were always putting him down (Down, down.)

They said his tannins weren't sufficiently round, round

(Whatcha mean when ya say that his tannins weren't round?)

They told me his market research was bad

And were sure that Stelvins were only a fad

That's why I fell for . . . (the leader of the Pac . . . Rim)

One day my V.P. said, "I'm tired of always rolling out something new." (New new)

"You have to tell him ix-nay on bottles with a screw."

(Whatcha mean consumers won't accept a bottle getting screwed?)

Quijones stood there and asked me why

But all I could do was cry

I'm sorry I hurt you . . . (the leader of the Pac . . . Rim)

[Spoken]

He sort of smiled and said, "You Tucker me out."[176]

The tears were beginning to show

As he drove his Citroën away on that rainy night

I begged him to go slow (maybe introduce to a single market)

But whether he heard me, I'll never know

Look out! Look out! Look out! Look out!

(You're losing traction on depletions!)

I felt so helpless, what could I do?

Remembering all the things we'd been through

In business school they all stop and stare

I can't hide the tears, but I don't care

I'll never forget him (the leader of the Pac . . . Rim)

The leader of the Pac . . . Rim—now he's gone

The leader of the Pac . . . Rim—now he's gone

The leader of the Pac . . . Rim—now he's gone

The leader of the Pac . . . Rim—now he's gone

---

176 Nick Tucker, former director of marketing for Bonny Doon Vineyard.

TUNE: Your Wine

SUNG TO: YOUR SONG (*ELTON JOHN*)

It's a little bit funny, the contents inside
It's not one made from grapes that are frozen
    or are dried
It doesn't cost much money, but boy if it did
I'd build a big winery where I'd indulge my id

If I were Georges Vernay, no, make that
    Alain Graillot[177]
Or a rich *vigneron* who had *beaucoup de tonneaux*
I know the wine's quite sweet, but it's the best
    I can do
The grape is Viognier, and this one is *doux*

And you can tell everybody how cool is this wine
It may be a little simple, but it's not too mainline
I hope you don't mind

I hope you don't mind that certain *je ne sais quoi*
Or how great it pairs with a slab of *foie gras*

The grapes sat on the vine, nearly gathering moss
A few of the funkier bunches we just had to toss
But the sun was quite warm, with the grapes
    getting ripe
It's for *becs fins* like you, who enjoy wines of this type

So excuse me forgetting, but these things I do
You see I've forgotten if the leaves are lobed or entire
What's in a name anyway? What I really mean
This is the sweetest wine from this vinifier

TUNE: Uva di Troia

SUNG TO: DESTROYER (*THE KINKS*)

Bought a wine called Violetta, and I took it back
    to my place[178]
Feelin' guilty, feelin' scared, freaky tattoos everywhere
Stop! Hold on. Stay in control

Violetta, I want to taste you with charcuterie
But the wine temperature's not as cool as I'd like
    it to be
'Cause there's a big red that I'm told is ill-bred
And there's a *Wine Advocate* in my head

And there's a wine snob inside of me
That keeps stoppin' me swillin' ya, spillin' ya, refillin' ya

Uva di Troia will destroy ya
Tannins of Troia may destroy ya

Well, I poured a glass, and it smelled kinda queer
The perfume filled the room, and it seemed kinda weird
Violetta seemed to say, There's nothing really wrong
    with it

---

177. Georges Vernay is the leading producer of Condrieu; Alain Graillot is a great producer in Crozes-Hermitage.
178. Bonny Doon Vineyard imported a lovely Uva di Troia from Puglia, given the sobriquet "La Violetta" because of the scent of violets the wine was said to possess.

Just a freaky perfume of violets
The tannin's hard, then it's soft; they'll work
   themselves out
Puglia's got a warm climate going, but the fruit's
   not at all burned out

It's not swilly wine, this Uva di Troia
It's not swilly wine, no palate destroyer
Swilly wine I ain't got much use for
There's so much vino out there, so much to explore
Discounters blow "best buys" out, those palate
   destroyers
Exploiting palates so insecure, they're cellar destroyers

And it goes like this, here it goes: The tannins
   of Troia will not destroy ya
Here it goes again: Uva di Troia will not gag or cloy ya

Wine Dr., help me please, I know you'll understand
There's a wine geek inside of me; I'm a *Wine Spectatin'*
   man
'Cause there's a big red I fear is ill-bred
And there's a *Wine Advocate* in my head
And it said if it's not 90 points, it's just gotta be bad
'Cause there's hard tannin in ya, gnawin' ya, clawin' ya,
   flawin' ya

Swilly Troia, ya score-destroyer, Uva di Troia, they
   will destroy ya
Eclectic-enjoyer, here's to your health
Enjoy strange wines, enjoy yourself
The wine media's device of snobbish elitism
Limited releases, fetishism; it's just mysticism

Yeah, it goes like this, here it goes: Uva di Troia,
   they can't destroy ya
Here's to Troia. Troia, they can't destroy ya
Hey hey, here it goes: Uva di Troia, they won't
   destroy ya
And it goes like this: Uva di Troia, they won't
   destroy ya.
And it goes like this . . .

The warden threw a wine-tasting party in the
　　Soledad jail
The prison band was there, and they began to wail
The band was jumpin', and the joint was awhirl
You should've seen those federal prisoners sip and swirl
Get rock, everybody, get rock
Everybody in the whole cell block
Was getting *terroir* from the Big House Rock

Spider Mite Murphy detected a lot of estery tones
Little St. Joseph scented the spicy nose of a
　　Côtes du Rhône
The leader of the Crips got a lot of *goût de terroir*
They ain't got this sorta limestone down in Chualar[179]
Get rock, everybody, get rock
Everybody in the whole cell block
Dug the structure of the Big House Rock

Prisoner number four hundred and two began
　　to jive
"I'd give this juice about a 95."
Number ninety-six said, "Let's settle this score
　　and pass the raw-milk Brie;
Come on and do the Big House Rock with me."
Get rock, everybody, get rock
Everybody in the whole cell block
Wanted a piece of the Big House Rock

Now, yadda, yadda, yadda, Warden
Hey, what do you say?

This rocked-out wine has got real *minéralité*
Father Flotsky told Dutch, "This is some righteous
　　brew.
And this Stelvin cap ain't no dirty screw."
Get rock, everybody, get rock
Everybody in the whole cell block
Was getting earth tones from the Big House Rock

The autodidact wine snob was reading an article by
　　Larry Stone[180]
Wondering, "Tonight, shall it be a Côtes de Nuits or
　　a Côtes de Beaune?"
The warden said, "Hey, buddy, don't you be no square
You can partner Big House with ribs or a *gigot d'agneau
　　forestière."*
Let's rock, everybody, let's rock
Everybody in the whole cell block
Was sippin' on the Big House Rock

Monsieur Henri said to Mealy Bugs, "For heaven's sake
No one's lookin', now's our chance to make a break."
Bugsy turned to Henri, and he said, "Let's wait for
　　higher Brix,
I wanna stick around awhile and see what gets into
　　the mix."
Got rock, everybody, got rock
Everybody in the whole cell block
Was rocking with the Big House Rock

179. Very small town in the Salinas Valley of California, located approximately ten miles north of Soledad.
180. Larry Stone, M.S., at the time of this writing was acknowledged as the country's top sommelier.

On a wine country highway, warm wind in my hair
Warm smell of baguettes and goat cheese, rising up
    through the air
Up ahead in the distance was a cute grocery
We were low on basil-infused oil
And I had to stop for a pee

The server was quick to pour me
The taste of hard tannins and a hard sell
And I was thinking to myself
"This could be tourist heaven, this could be
    Ch. Potelle."
Then she pointed out the tour guide
Who said she'd show me the way
There were voices at the cellar door
I thought I heard them say . . .

Welcome to Oakville, California
Such a lovely place
May we ship you a case of Grace?
There's plenty of Cab in Oakville, California
Any time of year, you can find wine here

Their minds are Taransaud-twisted, they got the
    Mercier bends[181]
They got a lot of bretty, bretty notes in their
    premium blends
How they smell of the barnyard, sweet scent of
    horse sweat
Some are wines to remember, some are wines to forget

The nose brought up notes of mercaptan
"Please bring me neither Cab nor Merlot wine."
She said, "We haven't had that sort of spirit
    here since nineteen eighty nine."
And still those voices are calling from far away
Break your concentration in the middle
    of a flight
Just to hear them say . . .

Welcome to Oakville, California
Such a lovely place
In the Golden State of Grace
They're livin' it up in Oakville, California
What a nice surprise
To find here the wines of Jean- Michel Deiss[182]

The lifestyle so appealing
The Domaine Chandon on ice
And she said, "We're just looking for some
    tourists here, who'll pay full retail price."
And the winemaker's dinner
They gathered for the big feast
They pair it with their steely Chards
But it can't compete with roast beast

Last thing I remember
My trunk was loaded up with dear wine
I had to find the side road back
Onto Highway Twenty Nine
I was told, "Relax, it's good shite, man."
You are programmed to believe
You can write a check any time you want
But Amex cards you can never leave

181. Taransaud and Mercier are two leading French cooperages.   182. Great winemaker from Alsace who makes
profound *terroir*-intensive wines.

———

In the day we sweat in the cellar with a Rhône-away
    eclectic crew
At night we sit through winemaker dinners with
    suicidal menus
Spring rolls from fusion cafés out on Highway 9[183]
Taiwanese vinegar, umami-injected
And steppin' out all over the wine
Pairing wine with honey-glazed ribs is a knack
It's a food/wine pairing trap, it's vinous suicide,
    a hoisin veggie wrap[184]
We gotta stop trying to pair egg foo yong
'Cause in *champs* like ours, baby we were born to Rhône

Laube,[185] let me in, I wanna be your friend
I want to shape your dreams and visions
Just wrap your palate 'round some Pacific Rim
And bear with me for my constant derision
Together we'll join a bacchante, dare to decant
We'll taste Rhônes till we drop, baby, we'll
    never recant
Will you walk with me out to the Télégraphe wire
'Cause, Laube, I'm just a scared and lonely
    Cigare flyer
But I gotta find out how it feels
I want to know if the rootstock is wild
Dude, I want to know if *terroir* is real

Thanks to Kermit and Alice, stemmy Côtes du
    Rhônes are served at Le Boulevard
Claude Kolm and Tanzer are rearguard reviewers
And the sommeliers push young Cabs so hard
The *amuse-gueule* course rises in my gorge
Kids are muddled over bongs drinking Arbor Mist
I wanna drink "real" wine with you, Laube, some
    '64 Lafite tonight
In an everlasting dis[186]

The wine biz is jammed with Paso Syrah on
    a last chance power drive
Everybody's jumping on the Rhône bandwagon
But there's no way a hack wine can survive
Together, Laube, we'll uncover the badness
I'll share with you all the madness of my protocol
Someday, dude, I don't know when
We're gonna make a Cigare that really expresses *terroir*
And we'll weightlessly walk on moonstones
But till then, in *champs* like ours
Baby we were born to Rhône

(2004)

Doon-Tune

207

---

183. Local highway running up through the San Lorenzo Valley in the Santa Cruz Mountains.   **184.** It is particularly challenging to pair red wines with foods containing any discernible level of sweetness, as sweetness accentuates the perception of tannin, or astringency, in the wine.   **185.** James Laube is the senior editor at the *Wine Spectator,* with the primary responsibility of reviewing California wines.   **186.** Serving the '64 Lafite (an atrocious wine) to anyone would be an everlasting dis. The lyricist, while proclaiming his desire to show Mr. Laube what is truly going on both with the "Rhône Ranger" movement in California and with his own wines in particular, clearly is exhibiting some ambivalence.

I have spoken a bit about the sort of marketing mania or fever that gripped the company and me in the years before the divestiture and downsizing. I can describe it generously as a period of unfettered manic creativity, almost like a self-administered dose of an extremely strong stimulant. Less charitably, it seems to have been the playing out of an obsessive itch for recognition and approbation (especially in light of the tepid reviews Parker and the *Spectator* were giving us at the time). I would date the onset of the more florid symptoms from the moment I was given a taste of media attention in our highly successful screwcap campaign. We had mounted the very public Funeral for the Cork in 2001, as essentially a Doon or Die situation—we had to create acceptance for this technology, or else we were quite literally screwed—and discovered that if one were truly outrageous enough, the world would sit up and take notice. The *Born to Rhône* performance was intended to stimulate our jaded wholesalers and to garner some local and national press, and it did, though it did not particularly help our relationship with some of the thinner-skinned editorial staffers of the *Spectator*. I've always had a slight sense of uncertainty about how loud one should blow one's own horn. Too loud, and one is perceived as a vulgar, loutish cacophonist. Not loud enough, and one figuratively sits in the subway tunnel, shivering in the cold. In recent times, this question has become even more difficult to resolve, as there is now so much competition in the industry that one must play even louder to be heard above the din.

The *Born to Rhône* lyrics don't always stand up to great scrutiny—I have tried in some instances to get as close as possible to the cadence and language of the original tunes. Thus "rearview windows" in the tune "Born to Run" turns into "rearguard reviewers," a sentiment that in no way reflects the true esteem I hold for Messrs. Tanzer and Kolm. Neither should one believe that Kermit Lynch and Alice Waters bear any responsibility for the proliferation of anything less than optimally ripe Côtes du Rhône wines in California Bay Area restaurants.

Doon-Tune

ENOUGH ROPE

EXTRACTS FROM THE NOOSELETTER

Manichean Rules,
or The Continental Divide

I went to Australia to attend a conference on Rhône grape varieties, and this became a good occasion for me to think about these grapes in a more formal manner. My first observation, not entirely obvious, was that the northern and southern Rhône, while fraternally proximal, represent two wildly divergent styles that cut to the geographical and geocultural quick. As human beings, we are always drawing distinctions, inscribing lines in the sand. This part of the universe concerns me (a little bit or a lot), this one does not; this is me, this is not. Yea, the Rhône is cleft by the forty-fifth parallel round about Valence, dividing north from south, and despite the obvious geographical contiguity, there are, shall we say, differences, ones so deep as to be almost metaphysical. Lest the point be obscured, it is not just the northern and southern Rhône that are divided, but the whole world, nay, *the entire universe,* the whole *magilla* we're talking about here—the collected works, the complete oeuvre, the toy store and all its toys, the Borgesian cosmos in all its multiplicities, sports, variants, and alternate endings— that is bifurcated by this wondrous and imaginary line. Northernness and southernness are ultimately much more states of mind than "real" geographical parameters. Rather than simply state the obvious,[187] I would like to offer for your consideration, gentle reader, a brief primer on the more subtle differences one finds as one considers these regions through the salient anthropo-gastronomico-matrices—or are these limned axes more psycho-eno-socio-? No matter. Voilà:

CONTINENTAL	MEDITERRANEAN
Cary Grant	*Anthony Quinn*
Intellect	*Emotion*
Butter	*Olive oil*
Urbanity	*Herbes de Provence*
Monocépage	*Tutti frutti*
Septentrional	*Meridional*
Barriques	*Foudres*
Föhn	*Mistral*
Grêle[188]	*Granita*

187. The southern Rhône is significantly warmer, dryer, and somewhat windier.
188. The French word for "hail."

CONTINENTAL	MEDITERRANEAN
Partly cloudy with a chance of . . .	*Sunshine*
Calvinist work ethic	*Mañana*
Power lunch	*Siesta*
Syrah	*Mourvèdre*
Côte Rôtie	*Châteauneuf-du-Pape*
Claret	*Clairette*
Porto	*Portofino*
Hollandaise	*Aïoli*
Salt and pepper	*Garlic*
Transylvanian peerage	*Garlic*
Oral antisepsis	*Garlic*
Kierkegaard	*Nietzsche (Hon.)*
Bergman	*Fellini*
Fanny and Alexander	*Marius, Fanny, and César*
Apollo	*Dionysus*
Canada	*Mexico*
Ile de Paris	*Il Posto*
Emile Peyraud	*Lucien Peyraud*
Marcel Proust	*Marcel Pagnol*
Diet of Worms	*Vermicelli*
Normans	*Romans*
Brioche	*Focaccia*
Oliver North	*Terry Southern*
Avalon	*Avignon*
Walnuts	*Pine nuts*
Basil Rathbone	*Basil pesto*
Presto	*Largo*
Oysters	*Mussels*
Herring	*Anchovies*
Fortepiano	*Concertina*
Henri Jayer	*Henri Brunier*

Beluga caviar	*Eggplant caviar*
Cognac	*Marc de Provence*
La vie en rose	*Bandol rosé*
Les Fleurs du Mal	*Peter Mayle*
Camembert	*Chèvre*
Cricket	*Bocce*
Thrombosis	*Cirrhosis*
Bretagne	*Brettanomyces*
Jeanne d'Arc	*St. Elmo*
Ratiocination	*Ratatouille*
Balaclava	*Baklava*
Grands crus	*Crudités*
Tomahtoes	*Tomatoes*
Spätzle	*Gnocchi*
Dover sole	*Bouillabaisse*
Bourbon roses	*Wild lavender*
Coco Chanel	*Laura Chenel*
Minuet	*Tarantella*
Savoir-faire	*Savoir-vivre*
Snot-green, scrotum-tightening sea	*Vast, wine-dark sea*

(FALL 1994)

⌒ This is a fun intellectual game—dichotomizing the entire universe into these two eternal, essentially archetypical divisions. The relationship between these two categories is not precisely reciprocal, much like the relationship between, say, Los Angeles and San Francisco. Angelenos are utterly enamored of Frisco, as are the residents of the City themselves. Lenny Bruce, and more recently Jackie Mason, has commented on the Jewish/Gentile dichotomy (rye bread versus white bread, throwing the new car away if it is slightly broken versus fixing it, and so on). The culture of wine is slightly anomalous in that there is a strong, virtual unanimity of interest in being continental (smooth, suave, and Cary Grant–like) versus embodying the earthier, more emotive Zorba, but I believe this is essentially an artifact of the significant price differential between a bottle of Pinot Noir and one of Carignane and, therefore, may be more of a fiscal calculation than a true cultural preference.

Podea,
or Unhand the Maiden, Sirrah!

I am deeply passionate about Syrah and have been toasted head over heels for the grape and the wine for quite some time now. But with the anxiety of any lover comes the fear that I may, *we* may, soon be losing her to a bigger, stronger rival, in this case a gang of stalwart and bold Antipodean stylists[189]—rugbyers to a man, who talk loudly, ameliorate liberally, and carry a big schtick.[190] In fact, *she* (*la* Syrah is unique in being one of the very few named *vinifera* grape varieties that take the feminine article in French, in contrast to *le* virile Petit Verdot or *le* manly Mourvèdre) is really not mine to lose. I do find that she is lately changing in ways that I don't really understand. She has taken on a different style, one that is brash, saucy, and frankly a little over-the-top. She's changed her perfume and is wearing way too much makeup. I can barely recognize the elegant lady; tarted up (better living through acid-base chemistry), the lady is a tramp. And while she may be unchaste, I see when observing the proliferation of floor stacks of brightly colored labels, with their all too piquant nomenclature, that she is certainly not unchased.

Let's put the fancy romantic palaver aside and talk about the lady in red herself, that is to say, *la* Syrah. There has been a lot of discussion lately of Syrah becoming "the next Merlot," and, frankly, that prospect fills me with significant dread. I believe Syrah has great potential for California, but I am equally persuaded that, as with Merlot indeed with virtually all the vinous *nouvelles vagues* that have swept our trend-conscious state, given half an opportunity to muck it up we inevitably will.[191] How will the New World stuff up Syrah? How could a grape variety that has a history of two thousand years in a single location, and that was praised by Pliny for its unique fragrance of violets, be in clear and present danger? Cue the Antipodeans.

Syrah, proper Syrah, is a remarkably complex, seductive wine that harmonizes superbly with modern fusion cuisine. But I worry that too few American palates will now ever bother to

---

189. Not too long after I began my efforts with Rhône grapes in the New World, there formed a rather loose association of California producers with similar interests, the so-called Rhône Rangers. The roster of wineries in Cali (as the Aussies call it) now producing wines from Rhône grapes has increased perhaps fiftyfold since then, but the dominant style is now so deeply deformed by Antipodean sensibility (perhaps via Oz-mosis?) and the market segment now so competitive for market share, that the group might more accurately be called the "Testosterhône Rangers." **190.** Their ameliorations include the whole kitchen sink of technical winemaking tools—acidulation, must concentrators, reverse osmosis, wood chips, you name it. By *schtick* I am referring to their goofy labels and piquant habits of wine naming, but this is certainly the pot calling the *bouilloire noire.* **191.** There actually is an Australian Shiraz called Duck Muck with a cult following.

learn what real Syrah actually tastes like. The Australian stylistic paradigm of Syrah—"Shiraz" as it is so piquantly called in Antipodea—has quietly become the dominant one. Why? First guess is that American critics tend to reward ultraripe wines that taste like *bombas de fruta.* In fact, I have a pet theory, utterly unproved, that we, as primates, heck, even as mammals, likely are genetically predisposed to prefer the flavors of ultraripe fruit, whether a banana, a mango, or a grape. And in the case of wine, it is not necessarily a matter of the degree of sweetness of the grapes, though the very intense fruity esters are generally associated with grapes that attain *surmaturité;* rather, it may have more to do with the perception of softer tannins that one finds in seeds given more time to ripen. The fact that the wine smells like Mom's kitchen after she has put up some raspberry jam doesn't hurt either. California winemakers have even taken to calling their Syrah Shiraz. Can bright yellow or orange labels be too far behind?[192] On very grumpy days, I conceive of Shiraz as a pernicious weed crowding out the strange, rare, and beautiful Syrah specimens found in such corners as the rock-walled terraces of Côte Rôtie.

They seem so disarmingly benign with their "G'days" and "No worries, mates." But beneath their apparently artless geniality and bonhomie, the Aussies are very cool and calculating customers indeed. They have been waging a hugely successful war for the hearts, minds, palates, and wallets of the Anglo-Saxon consumer with their Shiraz, so-called, a wine made from a grape that is genetically identical to Syrah but has little to do with the sublime Old World exemplars. They have clearly shown that nurture wins out over nature, at least at the cash register, and have been fiendishly efficient in producing a wine with a taste and texture profile that somehow greatly resonates with the Anglo-Saxon palate. Or maybe it's the cute mammals and the orange labels.

So, in the interest of really understanding what we are up against, and in order to outline a course correction for the broken-guardrail, seriously-off-road, into-the-bushes, errant walk-about into which we are heading, I have prepared a little primer outlining the salient differences between Shiraz from Antipodea and proper Syrah from what I call Podea, which is to say, anti-Antipodea. Doris Day once sang "Que Syrah, será," but we cannot afford to be so laissez-faire.

PS = Proper (Podean) Syrah   AS = Antipodean Shiraz

PS: Nomenclature of wine is usually determined by the geographical situation of the vineyard.

AS: Nomenclature of wine is determined by the following formula: Cute or piquant animal name + geographical feature[193] (for example, Wallaby Ridge, Roo's Leap, Madfish Bay, Wombat Gorge, and so on).

---

192. Bonny Doon Vineyard produces an impeccable Central Coast Syrah, Le Pousseur, with a rather bright shiny yellow label.   193. If this formula is not employed, then a reference to an obscure World War I cavalry regiment or to an equally obscure vine pathology will also suffice. There is an Australian Shiraz with the rather macabre name of Dead Arm.

PS: Fundamental expression of the wine is elegant, feminine, and stylistically allied with Burgundy.

AS: Stylistically allied with raspberry motor oil.

PS: Primary growing area is rich in cultural history dating back to Roman times.

AS: Region was settled primarily by an ex-convict population.

PS: Grape variety: *la* Syrah, sometimes called Petite Syrah or Serine in Côte Rôtie, though no relation (of course) to Petite Sirah in California.

AS: Grape variety: Shiraz, mate. And assigning a gender to a bloody grape? Sounds a bit left-handed, if you ask me. I don't have to worry about you pitching for the other side now, do I, mate?

PS: The greatest Syrah vineyards are located in close proximity to Lyons, the locus of French gastronomy.

AS: Throw another roadkill emu on the barbie.

PS: Alcohol is typically 12.0–12.5 percent.

AS: Do not open bottle in presence of open flame.

PS: Eminently sippable and drinkable.

AS: Typically gulped, but truth be told, one glass'll do you, mate.

PS: Capable of expressing *terroir* for a French person.

AS: Capable of instilling terror in a French person.

PS: Seduces with its elegant perfume.

AS: Rapes and pillages the palate.

PS: Detectable presence of minerality, and, in the extreme case of Cornas, the sensation of being taken for granite.

AS: Marked lack of minerality, substituted by palpable presence of big tits, sorry, that would be big chips.[194]

AS: *Parfum de chêne.*

PS: *Parfum de chien.*

AS: Parker friendly.

PS: *Par coeur* friendly.

PS: *Brettanomyces* science fair experiment coupled with reductive style—bring in da funk.

AS: "International" style—*frewt*-driven, accessible.

PS: Firm, sometimes slightly green tannins.

AS: Generally soft, or "melted," tannins.

PS: Cynical sugar additions

AS: Cynical tannin and acid additions.

194. It is common practice in the "crafting" of confectionary Shiraz to add oak chips (as well as God knows what else) to the wine.

PS: Primary flavors: white pepper, anise, smoked meat, bacon fat, and licorice.

AS: Primary flavors: blackberry sundae and American oak.

PS: Complex, shifting flavors and breathtaking aromatic development.

AS: No dramas, mate.

PS: Appellation is difficult to pronounce and impossible to remember. Labeling requirements: dull gray or matte color, obscure or cluttered Gothic typography.

AS: Name of wine is related to a cute mammal. Color of label: bright orange or yellow, information readily readable, though appearing often on a diagonal axis.

PS: The wine celebrates the unique characteristics of the vintage.

AS: The wine is usually palatable every single goddamn year.

PS: Commercially iffy. Who can pronounce the names of the appellations, much less remember which years are the "good" ones, which ones the dicey ones?

AS: Commercially successful. Who can resist charming marsupials and/or brightly colored labels?

(FALL 2002)

It is a pity that people in this country are mystified about what proper Syrah should taste like.[195] There is, at least for me, such a radically different quality to these two antipodal, as it were, styles of Syrah that it's almost as if appreciation of them takes place in different parts of the brain.[196] I often wonder what the truly significant barrier to the appreciation of Old World wines is, whether it is really some element of the wine itself—"harder" or "greener" tannins[197]—or whether consumers have already made up their minds not to enjoy the wines before tasting them, in the way that children may be psychologically ill-disposed to the genus *Greenus* and species *vegetabilis*. I suspect the way the wine is framed for consumers creates certain expectations, and the French effort to exalt *terroir* in their marketing efforts may have the unintended consequence of turning off American consumers who anticipate that the wine will be "unfriendly" and too challenging. *Terroir* may well mean to some: "Here is your broccoli; it's good for you."

195. It is my somewhat improvable hypothesis that far too much blowsy, overblown Syrah has entered the American market, turning off Americans to a perfectly wonderful grape variety before they have had the chance to really get to know it. I have recently heard the latest variation of a very old joke: "What's the difference between a case of Syrah and a case of the clap?" "Eventually the clap will go away." **196.** This may not be utterly far-fetched, as many complex cognitive tasks occur simultaneously in multiple areas of the brain. It is not immediately obvious which sets of aromas (fruity esters versus earthier, more mineral-like aromas) fire in precisely which sectors, but I would put my money on any claim that the olfactory product of the Aussie efforts lands squarely in the brain stem, the old reptilian brain. Perhaps the more complex, earthier smells trigger there as well as in other sectors—the amygdala and hippocampus, parts of the limbic system associated with emotion and memory. For me, there is an elusive, unnamable emotion, just below the surface of rationalization, that systematically arises when I taste a *vin de terroir*. **197.** Certainly European wines are "earthier," which is a code word for funkier—replete with aromas generally associated with country matters—and therefore a bit discomfiting to the prissy or squeamish. I imagine that appreciating "earthy" wines is a little bit like delving into the unconscious. Some people are absolutely fascinated with the process of excavation, and others are very happy just not to go there.

Reductio ad Sulfatum,
or A Penny for Your Thoughts[198]

I schlepped (albeit not languidly, Doc) through southern France and northern Spain, essaying to follow the route of the Rosenkreuz (alas, with no Guildenstern for comedic surcease). In France, the object of my *inquiriendo*, the purport of my perquisition, the quintessence of my olfaction quest, I'm talkin' 'bout My Grail, was Syrah. In Spain, however, it was Tempranillo, that tawny temptress, the dusky doxologist who played my Souzão-p[?]ote. Yes, I was a virtual Crusader, rabid for redolence, a fanatic for fragrance, a stalker of the sublimely savory. I was odd for the odiferous, a pervert for perfume. *I was an ester molester, Doc,* in full aromatic arousal, desperately seeking safe scents. I let my nose lead the way, thus always staying a bit ahead of myself. I knew my route was righteous, if convoluted in the extreme, for I was perennially dogged (and a wet dog it was) by a mephitic mist—something reductive if not outright sulfurous, with a little horse blanket thrown in for the kibitz.[199]

SOME GOOD SCHIST. Tasting Syrah in parts of the Côtes du Roussillon, I found that these sorts of aromas were put down (by neighboring growers) as contributions from the soil—the *terroir* was rich in schist, but its proponents maintained that it was good schist. While I never got around to nailing my Senior Thesis to the wall (though I did finish all of the curricular requirements), I was certain that I now traveled within the sphere of influence of Old Scratch and Briff, sometimes erroneously referred to as the Prince of Lees.[200] At Vinexpo, I had sniffed as much Syrah as one man could; my meditation had been on the nature of reductive aromas—sulfides and their permutations.[201] How did they manifest themselves, and was their presence expressed through the absence of other elements, fruit most notably? Traveling through the south of France, I became undone with Pynchonian parancia. Was this intrigue to eliminate the varietal expressiveness of Syrah—the exotic black raspberry and white pepperiness for which

198. A copper penny inserted in a glass of wine is a quick and dirty method for treating reductive "issues." 199. The problem appeared to be multifactorial—sulfides and the ubiquitous *Brettanomyces* the spoilage organism found in a 2 Live Cru. 200. Lees, primarily composed of the spent yeast bodies that settle to the bottom of a tank or barrel, have been given an especially bum rap, public-relations-wise. They have been held responsible for the rotten egg (hydrogen sulfide) odors sometimes found in wine and believed by some to be indirectly accountable for World Wars I and II, world hunger, nuclear proliferation, and the intractable conflict in the Middle East. 201. The reductive quality of these wines is certainly linked to their high degree of minerality (itself a good thing—see the longer explanatory note farther on)—generally boding for long ageability. But in a perfect world, the sulfide complex of aromas should not be grossly evident in the wine after it leaves the cellar, or at least in the time frame in which the wine is intended to be consumed.

we live—a comparatively recent phenomenon, or was the plot line traceable along the Crusader's route, a relic of the highly conspiratorial Knights Templars? Had the alchemists used up all the *cuivre* in southern France for their transmutation lab trials?

NEVER A COPPER AROUND WHEN YOU NEED ONE.[202] I followed the bouncing *oeuf dur*[203] down into Spain, where clearly an inventory reduction, a red sale, if you will, was still in progress—everything must go. *¡Mira!* Tempranillo is a grape variety that, like Syrah, is tragically beset by a tendency to form reductive aromas. The Riojanders are often flummoxed by this problem (not having made the acquaintance of Ducourneau, the Bubble Man) and their solution has been to adopt a *bordelais* protocol—aerating the heck (and the fruit) out of the wine through multiple rackings, off the lees we go, *oop-la,* and rather sanguinely burying the whole bloody business, Jimmy Hoffa–like, under the goal posts—sorry, that's in *barriques* made of American oak. I was prepared to bid *hasta la vista,* baby, to the whole schmear, until I met a very serious wine guy, Juan Carlos López de la Calle, proprietor of Bodegas Artadi in the Rioja Alavesa, with whom I spent several delightful days.

MY TEMPRANILLO'S RISING; I NEED A SHOT OF RIOJA Y BLUESAS. Juan Carlos was red-hot on the trail of Tempranillo; both his enthusiasm and the excitement of the chase were highly contagious. He was uncommonly open (an Iberian anomaly) to new ideas and to admitting his own bafflement with this *bicho raro* grape variety. Juan Carlos, longtime *amante* of Tempranillo, had lately been feeling disoriented as to whom or what he had gotten into bed with. (I am continually typing the name of the grape as *Temptranillo.*) Juan Carlos and I found we shared the same fantasy of one day producing a Temptranillo that was Burgundianly seductive, rich and ample, soft and fragrant, yet still possessed of certain basic wholesome family values. How might one express in the language of Cervantes and Salvador Dalí this sense of fecund viniflorabundance, this plenary perfection of gustatory pulchritude?

There is a unique Spanish locution that sounds odd to our puritanical, polyachromatophobic,[204] blue-nosed ears. If something is truly first-rate, mind-detonatingly glorious, a devout, blasphemous Spaniard will proclaim this entity to be *puta madre*—that is to say, outflippingstanding, great, beyond great, the cat's p.j.s, the kipper's knickers, the bee's knees, *le Bébé Jésus en culottes de velours.* It is the big jackpot, the winning lottery ticket, a round-trip, make that a one-way, ticket to Paris, all expenses paid—the top of the Eiffel Tower with dinner and drinks at La Tour d'Argent thrown in, back when it was *pouf, impeccable,* and you got a duck with your name on it. It is the first wildflowers of spring, the perfect "blood," or Indian, peach of late Indian sum-

202. The use of copper sulfate (the active ingredient in Tidy Bowl) is the most common treatment for persistent reductive aromas in wines. In biodynamic practice, this highly effective treatment is, alas, strictly forbidden.   203. "Reductive" wines will typically have a (generally ephemeral) odor of hydrogen sulfide, or "rotten egg."   204. Fearful of shades of gray.

mer. It is Seattle with great weather or New York City with exemplary garbage collection, Zappa and Mehta at the Hollywood Bowl, or half-court seats behind the press table at the Garden to see the Celtics *and* the Knicks. This *enchilada completa* comes gift-wrapped with a shiny bow, batteries included, no assembly required, and a chorus of seraphim intoning Handel's *Messiah*.

JUAN CARLOS, EL REYO-X. Juan Carlos and I concluded that our mandate was to proceed amain, with no regard for the potential inconvenience or even for our personal safety,[205] heedless of the certainly ruinous expense, indifferent to the inevitable ridicule and mockery, eschewing political correctness, risking even—worst case—permanent banishment from Berkeley's bounds (and we know what *that* means)[206] in order to redline it to the limit and create the ultimate wine, *El Vino Puta Madre*. How then ought one to proceed to create the mother of all 100-pointers? My hypothesis was that, while Tempranillo is a wonderfully seductive grape, there is some integral element missing, *algo que le falta,* that could bring the wine up to a point only a few microns short of Bo Derek– or Mother Teresa–hood, inhibiting it from shining incandescently like a million solar flares in a telephone booth. To put the question another way, what *are* the elements of a truly great wine? What must be brought to Tempranillo to enable its apotheosis? Until now, my thinking has been limited by a Cartesian *Weltanschauung*: in my dichotomous no-mind, wines were either continental or Mediterranean, oxidative or reductive, red or white (an illusory distinction), *barriques* or *foudres,* aromatic or neutral, autochthonous or not from around here.

THREE ON A MATCH. But remember that wine's inmost nature is metaphoric (wine can smell like grapes *and* cigar boxes), that wine's very essence is linked to mutability and to memory. (A truly great wine blows away dualistic thinking as easily as a strong breeze in the Salinas Valley blows away milk cartons.) A great wine is poised and balanced, knowing that it is the center of its own vinoverse, the sun around which the other planets, the lesser growths, revolve, *crusing for a brew-sing*. A great wine is like Borges's "Zahir." You have innocently ordered a glass of *tinto* at the modest, unprepossessing bodega on Calle ——; after you smell and taste the potation, its aromatic impressions are burned into your olfactory bulb, up into your cerebral cortex, and they go on to possess and haunt you displacing all other thoughts and emotions, driving you ultimately to blissful madness. A great wine pushes the limits like a Sid Caesar skit, blowing out the fourth wall, literally coming up out of the glass and grabbing you by the necktie.

A great wine points beyond wine; the imbiber is transformed as much as the imbibed. As a

---

205. When the federal label approval form for El Vino Puta Madre finds its way to the appropriate desk, I can imagine the following telephone call from one small office to another in our nation's capital: "Hello, Janet. The SWAT team is in position, and we've got a clear headshot at the guy. Can't we take him out now, once and for all? I mean, this is the guy with all the fake Italian words on his labels. He gave us Doo tori in zione, f'chrissakes! *Dammit,* Janet, can't we, can't we? *Puhle/ease?*"   206. Having to sneak into the Cheese Board wearing a Groucho Marx–style fake nose and glasses.

prerequisite for greatness, there must be a minimum of three elements in a wine to create suffi-cient oeno-dramatic tension to insure compulsory delight and astonishment. The mysterious third element (spice) is the catalyst that unlocks the other two elements and enables the wine to transcend dualistic oenology—oxidation/reduction, fruit/tannin, slow/fast, push/pull, should I stay or should I go? It is the straw that stirs the 1953 Mouton, the rudder that steers the *George*.[207] This wholly trinity can be conceived in many different ways. For example:

```
        spice                            spirit
        /   \           or               /   \
backbone — body                    will — groundedness
```

Another way of imagining this trinity might be:

```
        Graciano                          Syrah
        /   \            or               /   \
Tempranillo — Garnacha           Mourvèdre — Grenache
```

Still another way might be:

```
        grace                            balance
        /   \            or              /   \
temptation — flesh               reduction — oxidation
```

(FALL 1995)

We collaborated in a slightly Vichy-like sense with Juan Carlos on the production of a wine called Grenache Village, a wonderful red produced in Navarra at a couple of superannuated wineries that had been the glory of the Franco regime, and that had not ex-perienced any major upgrading or renovation in the intervening years. Ralph Steadman designed the la-bel, which was based on a drawing he had done a few years earlier called *A Basque on His Ass on His Own*. We ran into enormous problems with this wine, chiefly from a regulatory standpoint. The wine was produced in Spain, bottled in France, and intended to be sold mainly in England, on behalf of an American com-pany. What could possibly go wrong? In essence, what we proposed was an impossibility from a European-customs-apparatchik point of view, and we came perilously close to seeing the destruction of three containers of wine, winning a last-minute reprieve from a gray bureaucrat somewhere, presumably in Brussels.

This essay evinces a certain misapprehension I held at the time about the nature of "reduction" in wine—

---

207. Hopeless obscurantism. The *George* was the marginally seaworthy vessel, a raft it must be said, that bore the Grahm Crew on its picaresque adventures. (See "The Rimeshot of the Ancient Marsanner.")

that its presence in the bottle or even in the cellar often represents a vinous tragic flaw. I confess that, when I used to visit cellars in Burgundy and Rhône (north and south) in the winter after the vintage, I often secretly judged the winemakers as lacking in skill, incapable of handling a matter as seemingly straightforward as the presence of off sulfidelike aromas in the wine, either in the cellar or sometimes just after the vintage in the bottle.[208] I did not properly understand the complexity of redox chemistry, the phenomenon of "surfing the reductive wave," or the fact that the winemaker might actually intend to keep his wine in this slightly funky state during its *élevage*,

the better to protect the fruit of the wine and engender greater complexity in the developing wine. This exposure to the phenomenon of "reductive winemaking," though I didn't quite understand it at the time, prefigured my interest in the reductive conservation of wines, something I would revisit years later with screwcaps. A brief commentary on the salient redox chemistry of wines, especially with regard to the phenomenon of the allegedly sinister reappearance of reductive aromas in screwcaps postbottling, is treated in the long, somewhat technical footnote appended to this commentary.

---

208. *Oxidation* and *reduction* are terms used to talk about the relative tendency of a particular molecule to lose electrons (oxidation) or gain electrons (reduction); the redox or voltage potential is the strength of a solution to withstand the oxidizing effect of, you guessed it, oxygen. Redox chemistry is a extremely arcane subject; it involves the tracking of electron movements between chemicals and is especially complex when there is a mixture of substances that can both receive or donate electrons. When one molecule gets reduced, another becomes oxidized in a very long chain of reactions; without the presence of inputs from outside the system, the reactions run in the direction of greater to lesser organization of the system. Ultimately, everything rusts, one way or another.

The Chinese have the notion of *qi*, or the life force of an organism. When a being comes into the world, it can be said to have a certain genetic or karmic potential, and it is up to that individual to maximize that potential for a long and happy life. When a being is young, it needs to share its qi freely with the environment—via lots of deep breathing, exercise, and regular tai chi practice—and as it gets older it needs to husband or protect its qi. The qi, or life force, of a wine is its ability to tolerate oxygen. When a wine is young it will, depending on its varietal composition and provenance, generally need a relatively large volume of oxygen; if it does not receive enough, it will actually, counterintuitively, be more prone to oxidation later in its life. Oxygen is needed in the process of polymerization and condensation of red wine tannins, and when the tannins are fully "melted," no more oxygen is required, and further oxygen uptake will tend to create "dry" tannins.

Conservation in a barrel or puncheon generally affords approximately the right amount of oxygen exchange for big red wines such as Cabernet Sauvignon, whereas the softer, more "oxidative" varieties, such as Grenache, do better in larger vessels, exposed to less oxygen. So, "reductive" winemaking does not necessarily mean the wine is receiving no oxygen; rather there is a conscious effort to keep the force of electrons, or redox potential, within a certain carefully defined range, at least during the wine's *élevage*, to favor the formation of some interesting flavor components.

If a winemaker is reasonably attentive, he or she should observe the relatively distinct *momento de verdad* when the tannins have appreciably softened, at least as much as they are going to before drying out, and consider bottling the wine at that point. But this doesn't mean the wine has stopped evolving. The development of "bottle bouquet," the maturation and complexity achieved postbottling, occurs through the recombination of esters and alcohols (transesterification) and has been shown to be a thoroughly anaerobic process, occurring both in corked and screwcapped bottles.

Here is where it gets weird: Wines whose reductive potential has not yet been thoroughly "broken"—you can think of them as willful, wild, bucking broncos (with high electron potential), or even as being vaguely autistic, in that they still maintain a certain tendency to close themselves up—or wines subjected to an environment that is incrementally more oxygen exclusionary, as is created by a screwcap closure (at least compared to cork), sometimes appear to "devolve" shortly after bottling. Their development is obscured by the untoward appearance of a so-called "reduced" character postbottling, sort of like the vinous equivalent of *The Picture of Dorian Gray*. This "problem" can take on many forms—a slightly metallic character (not to be confused with the appearance of *Brettanomyces*), a diminution of fruit (not to be confused with corkiness), a stony or mineral character (not to be confused with the expression of *terroir*), or the presence of some specific pleasant or unpleasant characters, which I will discuss in a moment.

When we talk about the "reductive" character of a wine, it is not reduction we are experiencing directly but rather a reductive proxy—sulfides. You can think of these as the canary in the coal mine, in that the presence of sulfides hints at the reductive character. But here is where it gets complex: sulfides that may have been created during the fermentation process (which itself creates a highly reductive environment) and that have undergone further transformation through combination with other molecules themselves become either oxidized or reduced at various stages of the maturation process and can ultimately be regarded either as a flaw in the wine or as a complexing element, depending on their final concentration in the wine and perhaps on the differential sensitivity of the taster.

Sulfides are formed due to the presence of elemental sulfur on the grapes (used to control powdery mildew in the vineyard), the absence of sufficient available nitrogen in the must (the yeast, afflicted with an intractable case of the fungal "munchies," begins breaking down the sulfur-containing amino acids in the juice, liberating the elemental sulfur), the presence of too much available nitrogen (I don't personally understand this mechanism), metabolic stress on the yeast due to cold, to heat, and to God knows how many other factors. Unless one has a particularly egregious problem with sulfides in the cellar, the "issue" generally tends to be a nonissue by the time the wine is bottled in cork (with the exception of a few unregenerate, highly reductive grape varieties, such as Dolcetto, which is a cellarperson's nightmare). But screwcaps are another story.

When you aerate the wine in the cellar through racking, the smelly compounds tend to disappear, but this does not necessarily mean they are not there; they may be sinisterly lurking in the underbrush, as it were, in the form of disulfides, an oxidized form of hydrogen sulfide (not so easily detected), which, when reduced back to thiol or mercaptan, is detectable at much lower concentrations—one-twentieth to one-fortieth—compared to disulfide, I have read. When wine is bottled, its redox state changes—that is, it is now in a more reductive environment as compared to, say, a barrel. The wine itself has a certain reductive power, which derives partially from its phenolics (primarily seed tannin and anthocyanins from the skins) and may be related to its mineral content (though this is not at all well understood); this is augmented or amplified by the level of sulfur dioxide added. In some instances, what appears to be happening with screwcaps is that, because the closure is more airtight than a cork, the free sulfur dioxide tends to stick around longer than with a cork closure. Acting in concert with the inherent reductive potential of the wine, the free sulfur dioxide causes the wine to achieve a lower net redox potential (more reductive) and re-creates thiols from disulfides.

There is no unanimity of opinion as to how this mechanism works, nor is there a good predictive protocol for knowing whether a particular wine will be subject to the gradual or sudden untoward appearance of reduced character postbottling and, if it is, for knowing when those aromatic characteristics might disappear, though my experience suggests that the time frame is months rather than decades. The factors that appear to be at play are: the starting levels of thiols and disulfides in the wine, the levels of sulfur dioxide and pH in the wine, the rate of oxygen ingress through the closure, and perhaps the antioxidative potential of the wine itself, though this last item is at some issue.

It can certainly be argued that many of these characters are not necessarily bad in and of themselves—the issue is really one of the concentration and/or balance of these elements. Indeed, what we think of as typicity of style for many wines—that is to say, proper French Chablis, red and white Burgundy, New Zealand Sauvignon blanc, proper Syrah from the Rhône, and of course Barolo and Barbaresco aged in large *botti*—is in fact a function of "reductive winemaking" in the cellar: retention of lees and minimal racking, which allow, indeed encourage, the formation of a discreet amount of "reductive" character at certain stages of the maturation process. In Syrah, for example, a reductive winemaking protocol will help to engender some of the "typical" complex flavor components—smoked meat or bacon fat, in particular—that we have grown to love.

Corks may be interesting (their other tragic issues excepted) because they seem to provide approximately the correct amount of oxygen ingress to keep the "reductive problem" in check, at least when the wine is young and being consumed on corporate expense accounts at the finest tables. But I'd like to reverse the argument and ask, "What reductive problem?" This "problem" may be a bit like the so-called "drug problem" where I come from, which may or may not exist providing there are enough drugs. I am being a bit facetious but for me the reduction problem likely does not exist, providing there is enough reduction. What is actually most interesting about screwcaps is their ability to create something like slightly reductive conditions, as a sort of echolalic recapitulation of the cellar reduction; this may be a very clever mechanism to give wines a far greater lifespan.

When wines *en screwcap* are young, they definitely take on a slightly different character—they're wound up tighter. They're steelier or harder-edged, kind of like a resident of the East Village. That "reduced" character can wander perhaps over the edge of what we think of as "polite," but the same thing can certainly be said of some French cheeses or some French people, *n'est-ce pas?* The question is really in knowing where the edge is and how close you can get to it without offending polite company. In my experience, unless the reduction "problem" is severe—that is, the problem would still be a problem were the wine to be sealed in cork—a vigorous aeration in a decanter will generally set the matter right. Certainly over time, the redox conditions in the bottle change—you've got thermodynamics on your side here—and the offending molecules are gradually oxidized back to their nonevil twins.

Allow me a rather crass analogy. The presence of so-called "reduction" aromas in wine can be compared to a mild case of satyriasis in guys—a bit problematic under certain circumstances, but generally an indication that the organism is working well and doing what it is supposed to be doing. If the satyriasis develops into arrant priapism, then, as is advised in the Viagra commercials, some prompt medical attention may be required. (Copper sulfate as saltpeter?)

The Almost Pleasanton Years,
<u>or</u> In the Belly of the Republikaner Beast

I am writing this to you on my laptop, ensconced in an embarrassingly sumptuous hotel room in an unnamed Midwestern city.[209] I am on the excruciatingly gradual diminuendo of an interminable, verging on mythic, road trip, having just returned from the Continent and feeling Europamüde to my very bones—the Rhôneliness of the wrong-distance Rhôner . . . But for now, it's just you and me in this hotel room and a whole lot of random available memory. It is nearly spring, though not by the looks of it in this chilly burg—there has been a substantial accumulation of flaky white stuff on the street, and there has been some snow as well. I am set to give a seminar at the M—— Wine Festival in just a few minutes, and through some technical or perhaps cosmic glitch, my topic assignment appears to be "Big Cabernets and Big Steaks"— two rustically rubine elements of the universe I regard with precisely the same degree of interest. I'll pour them the Cabernet Volant.

SO, WHAT'S TANNAT LIKE? The luncheon was not a complete bust, though I did manage to consume my centennial ration of red meat in a single go. I began by proffering an apologia for my not especially à la mode stylistic predilections, commenting that as a company we esteem fragrance and elegant grace above brute power, weight, and optical density. (Darkness at Doon?) The assembled group of astringophiles grew momentarily jittery as I began to riff on how Santa Cruzans are exceptionally in touch with their gentle, feminine, nurturing sides (some titters) and as a result feel no particular compulsion to bring an additional titer of tannic testosterone toxicity to the fragile ecosystem that is our planet, sorry, palate (very deathly silence). Yet, *d'autre part,* I allowed that we bleeding Rhônely heart types had sensibilities that perhaps had become a tad too delicate, if you know what I mean (more titters—this was a bit gratuitous on my part), and it might well be useful for us to get in touch with our more assertive, chromosomally heterogeneous XY side (nervous laughter). This could be accomplished, I proposed, either through thirty-six consecutive hours of team drumming or through very thoughtful but assertive tannin management. It seems I had momentarily forgotten my new mantra: "I will fear no tannin."[210] We Californians are so incredibly blessed with ripe tannins—derived from grape seeds that have been allowed to ripen to proper physiological maturity—that

---

209. Minneapolis.   210. In the cosmology of Patrick Ducourneau, the maven of microoxygenation, the tannic universe is divided into green, hard, soft, and dry tannins. Tannins can be transformed from one category to another as they are exposed to oxygen. One tries to optimize the percentage of soft tannins at bottling, if possible, while making certain that one does not overdo things and push these soft tannins into the realm of dry tannins, a point, alas, of no return.

we may literally go, maceration-wise, where others with more modest phenological endowments fear to tread.

SIGHS MATTER. For the number of column inches devoted in this organ to the progress of our once and future winery in Pleasanton, one might well conclude that the site is presently a pulsing and throbbing nerve-center of architectonic gravitas; a burgeoning hive; all bloom and Doon; aswarm with activity; abuzz with animation; a plenum of land planners, planers, and prime movers; a conclave of construction workers; an ensemble of erectors; and that the joint is jumpin', everybody in the pool, hail hail the gang's all here to fashion and fabricate this inchoate Vinopolis, this bright and shiny city on the swill. One imagines the landscape limned with weighty dirt-shifting machinery, vast earth engines poised and primed to do their inexorable CAT™-scratch two-step 'pon the pliant Pleasanton-series gravelly loam. I see I-beams, glue-lams, struts and studs, battens and balks, and ties and trusses in the complicated calculus of tensile-town tectonics. The girders are girded, the cement is ready to flow like molten Turley Zinfandel in its brief moment of liquidity before it is medusaed into eternally rock-solid, petroglyphic (barring the Big One) permanence. The architects are all aloft in their airy ateliers, abstracted in profoundly pensive Grappa d' Moscato –induced reveries, sweet dears, their sketchpads smudged with vivid pastel renderings of wine- and vinescape. The engineers—their madras cotton shirts covered by a breastwork of Kevlar-clad pocket-protection, their brains inflamed with the cabalistic arcana of statutory building codes and codicils—have all crunched their codes and gone home, secure in the knowledge that *unser retaining Wall ist ein fester Burg*. Sigh. The landscape lies stone-still for the moment, no action at all but for the blur of the occasional jackrabbit and for the specifically formulated Jack and the Beanstalk–like cover-crop mix, a mélange of barley, bur clover, and bell beans that has gone frankly postal, what with the atypically prodigious precipitation that has this year soaked the gravelly Pleasanton-series loam to its very bones.

LET ME BE PERFECTLY FRANK. I hate to name-drop. It is demeaning to all parties and, let's face it, evinces some pretty serious personal insecurity. But permit me to take you behind the scenes for just one moment as we pierce the veil of the corporate Doonolith. From the outside, it may well appear that we have it totally together and are effortlessly making all the right moves: maintaining appropriate levels of molecular SO_2—with a precision of two sig figs—in the wines at all times, 4-ethyl phenol levels digitally monitored and punctually auto-forwarded by modem to a voice simulator.[211] "Mr. Grahm, please take careful note of the most recent assay of Tank 23," a cool, calm, disembodied, vaguely Oxonian-accented voice instructs me at thirty thousand feet when I retrieve my e-mail[212]— tannin management done with a flick of a switch.

211. Note that 4-ethyl phenol is the marker for *Brettanomyces* infection, and I am exaggerating our level of analytic vigilance by several orders of magnitude. We analyze for 4-ethyl phenol quarterly, which seems to keep the problem under control. 212. Another shameless exaggeration. I am still a relatively low-tech, hopeless "Mac"-ed man, a largely word-processing, e-mail-centric kind of guy.

Then there are the new vineyards just about to come on line, planted to wondrously arcane varieties, biodynamically turbocharged with no less than the energy of the universe. Our worthy competitors are absolutely sick with envy at the cleverness of our labels and contrive to lure Chuck House away, far away, making him a stranger in his own House or at least in the House of Doon. They have made him wildly unrealistic promises they could never possibly honor even were their Puligny-Montrachet/Woodbridge Chard collaboration project to go double platinum.

This is the Walter Mitty moment; the real truth is that lately my most significant success has been in driving myself absolutely crazy, as well as in propelling the rest of my staff down the road to Miltown in my effort to find the right architect for this *verkakte* Ruby Hill winery project in Pleasanton. I have still not been able to settle on the right guy or gal. Another Saturday night, and I find myself out on yet another architect date.[213] I have convinced myself that there is maybe one human being Out There who can bend his or her mind around the Bonny Dooniverse with the appropriate topological congruity to create a building seriously warped enough (but structurally sound) in exactly the right places. I feel like Kafka's surveyor, who glimpses the castle but can never attain it, or Borges's messenger, who never penetrates to the interior chamber of the emperor. In conversation with anyone who will listen, I always say that I am looking for an architectural style that is poetic, sculptural, and witty, something, y'know, along the lines of Frank Gehry.

Talking recently with a builder friend of mine, I found out that he knows someone who knows someone who actually knows Gehry. My friend says, "Well, why don't you just ask Frank himself if he wants the job?" This is a bit like a Talmudic scholar, bogged down in a particularly difficult exegesis, receiving word that God himself will shortly be offering his clarifying pronouncement on an especially thorny patch of scripture. I wrote a letter to Mr. Gehry, sent him some pictures of the site and a bunch of wine for his delectation, and received a note back that said he was indeed interested in having a meeting. I went down to see him in L.A. and was given the nickel tour of the office. Words truly fail me in describing the sublimity of his digs. I might say that it is *Man from UNCLE*-like—a very plain exterior, not exactly a Chinese laundry, but neither the Taj Mahal. Inside, however, it is Geppetto's workshop, and Gehry is the Toymaker, clearly the Supreme Master of his Domain.

Each room was a "war room," or perhaps a "situation room," loaded to the nines with young architectural acolytes hunched over their turbocomputers powered by some ultrapotent, do-not-

213. My friend Topher suggested I am really embarking on the wrong project. What I should be doing instead of trying to design a winery is making a documentary about designing a winery, perhaps called *The Architect* (or maybe better, *Arkitekt,* in faux Swedish). The viewer, who would effectively go out with me on all my architect dates, wouldn't actually see me, but would hear me saying, "Uh huh," "Right," and so on in response to the stream-of-architectural-consciousness with which I am barraged. Have you ever sat next to a couple on their first date? It is absolutely impossible not to eavesdrop. The guy will feed the girl some remarkable lines, and she will listen and feign rapt attention. *Arkitekt* will have the same feel to it.

attempt-this-at-home beta design software.[214] One room was Köln, one Prague, or maybe it was Venice, and one the Jimi Hendrix museum in Seattle. Frank ("Please call me Frank") had a bad cold, which he had been nursing for several weeks, and he had been taking some major antibiotics. "You really shouldn't be taking those antibiotics, Frank," I heard myself telling Mr. Gehry, to whom I'd just been introduced, giving my chute from a state of Gehrian Grace some initial propulsion. "Hmm?" he responded. Careening recklessly forward, I added, "What you really want to be taking are some Chinese herbal preparations, which really work much, much better, and I would be happy to . . ." "My wife also goes to see a quack doctor," he informed me rather curtly.[215]

I am frankly not sure if this was the beginning of the end of my interview with Frank Gehry, but when I told him about the energetic center we had identified on the property that was to function as a funnel for cosmic forces, I noticed that he began to act more than a little fidgety. "I don't think we are quite the right firm for your job, young man," he pronounced at the end of the interview, with some finality. "We *could* do it, of course" (my heart leaped up) *"but"* (my heart sank down again) "I think that our resources here"[216] (indicating with a seigniorial wave his battery of technological armaments) "might be a sort of overkill for the scope of your project."[217] He was, of course, allowing me to save face, gentleman that he was, no doubt suspecting in his heart of hearts that it was a fairly marginal character, a tortured, slightly faded flower child who was asking him to perform an essentially modest exercise in arts and crafts.[218]

IL FAUT THUFFRIR. We recently took a meeting with our bankers (an awfully nice bunch of guys coping well with their congenital *tetany manus*) to explain to them our vision for the development of Ruby Hill. We composed a sort of warm and fuzzy tone poem, sketching out for them our tender hopes and dreams for the project and precisely what the tariff, tally, tab, *summum malum,* total sticker price, frontal, and collateral damage was going to amount to. We presented these poor guys with *l'addition,* a *cuenta* they weren't counting on, the mother of all reckonings. "That should cover it." Josh Wesson might say, throwing a napkin over the thoroughly abhorrent addition and disappearing with preternatural celerity to the Gents.

We talked about our plans to install the new vineyard, hoping to, through deft elision, skim over that greatly misunderstood term *dry-farmed,* that is to say, low-yielding, that is to say, economically dubious. "Well, what varieties are you going to plant?" they queried in all innocence. "Merlot, perhaps?" "Nn-o-oh," I ventured cautiously. "I had thought that we might go with a few that are maybe a teensy bit less mainstream," I heard myself saying with studied calm, in no way, I hoped, telegraphing my ultra-top-secret plan to plant the vineyard in a geometric procession of obscure *cépages,* the Mediterranean Basin's Most Willfully Recondite Hits, one

214. I am betraying my ignorance about the computational world, but these machines looked bigger and badder than any I had ever seen.　**215.** This isn't really true. He really was incredibly nice and helpful.　**216.** Which would be appropriate for the reconstruction of Western civilization, if it ever came to that.　**217.** Read: very, very expensive.　**218.** He didn't really say it this way. He may have said *fine* arts and crafts.

variety per row in a seemingly endless series. Nor did I allude to the fact that we were seeking *the* poorest, the most huddled and unwashed *cépages*, the ones that were always on the outside looking in, their little grape faces pressed, like Popeye Doyle in *The French Connection*, to the ultraluxe Merlotpane. I also suppressed my impulse to blurt out the name of the revenge-of-the-nerd-grape varietal blend under consideration, its working title, Succotash.[219]

"What about row orientation? Were you planning to go north-south so as to avoid the afternoon heat or east-west to take better advantage of the contours of the property?" This innocuous question had come from the extremely quiet guy who had been introduced rather fleetingly and who had up until now not uttered a word. Answering posed a dilemma: an absolutely truthful answer to his straightforward question was apt to cause grave consternation (at least among those who observed proper mental hygiene), and there was some risk that candor might just *quercus* the deal. I began to panic. It was clear that they must have brought in a ringer, a consultant, no doubt, who actually *knew* something about grapes and vineyards, and there was only so much spin, equivocation, sophistry, or pseudology I could weave into a garment that would cover the gapingly immodest lacunae of logic, practicability, and perhaps even semblance of sanity of my modest little proposal. No room to retreat, so it was forward into the breach. My general manager, Patrice Boyle, began wondering how she might discreetly disappear into a conveniently proximal sinkhole as I explained that "the vine-rows were not going to be laid out in straight lines exactly, more like in a helical pattern that would derive from the energetic center of the property," which we had, for the record (or not, if it actually came to a sanity hearing), divined by means of a dowsing rod after gazing at a photograph of the subject property that had been inserted into an unusual electronic device which was sensitive to . . .

I noticed that the bankers had suddenly become very quiet. They were clearly in the Zone, but the question was which Zone? Perhaps I had strained their credulity to the breaking point, or I may have just put them to sleep. "Would you mind explaining again precisely why you are planting the vineyard in this seemingly inefficient, apparently crazy configuration?" the senior banker broke in. "I hadn't actually said," I replied, "but since you asked, we're doing it this way to more efficiently capture the cosmic energy." Fortunately for me, my interlocutor was not actually listening to my answer but had become lost in his own internal woolgathering. "You know," he said, drawing closer, "I think your property is on the direct flight path of the planes coming into SFO, and I'm sure that the helix would be visible from the air. This could be a great opportunity for you to really brand your marque and would probably lead to your tasting room becoming a significant profit center, and that's all full boat, no discounting to the

---

219. I'm referring to the terminally eclectic Heinz 57 varieties that we will plant in concentric helices upon consultation with the *I Ching*. There is nothing that would give me more satisfaction than observing the acute cognitive dissonance engendered in the most uptight, conservative diner at the fanciest, fussiest, clinchèd-sphincter, fine dining establishment as he tries to reconcile the terminally goofy name with the astronomical price tag on the wine list, and strives with every fiber of his being to avoid a vinous faux pas.

wholesalers, instant cash on the barrelhead, but I don't need to remind you of that (wink, wink). We like your project very much." Someone is definitely watching over me. I try my best to *épater* bourgeois capitalist sensibilities and end up being proclaimed a brilliant strategic running dog. This revolution will not be televised, nor will it go better with Merlot. (SPRING 1998)

I still adore the notion of a helical vineyard, of a wildly eclectic field-blend, and the name Succotash for this cuvée. The site in Pleasanton was ultimately replanted to vineyard (by someone else), and we did in fact have the opportunity to purchase some Sangiovese grapes from the vineyard. Alas, the grapes appeared to be nothing to write home about, though that could certainly have been for any number of reasons, including the age of the vines and God knows what else. Discerning the hidden genius of a particular site is as complicated and demanding as making an accurate confirmation of the reincarnation of the Dalai Lama. As early as ten years ago, I was mulling over the idea of a geometric configuration of the vines that potentially would reinforce the order or congruence of the site itself. The "Succotash" notion (since refined a bit) is that one began with an essentially random planting of vines and with observing how they performed on the site. Based on observation, the overall *encépagement* would gradually be perfected, never through the removal of vines (God forbid), but through the continual addition of new and balancing elements. This theme was taken up again in my recent essay "In Search of a Great Growth in the New World," which explores how the idea of generations of iteration and observation might be condensed into a single lifetime.

Up the Yin / Yang without a Paddle

I have been afflicted with a world-class case of writer's block. Nothing to worry about, you say. Happens all the time to the best of them, you say. Every author from the ineffectual, scrivening hack to the true and sublimely tortured genius *littérateur* encounters a dark night of the word processor, pixels unscintillated and thoroughly unaMused. He wonders, is his affliction due to a spiritual malaise, or might it merely be a structural problem that can be rectified by the deployment of a stiffer-backed chair? But my case of writer's block presents a more complicated symptomatology—it seems to have already metastasized into winemaker's block as well.

In the middle of my life, I have found myself suddenly in a dark and unfamiliar wood.[220] The shining path of vinous virtue, once so brightly lit, is now cloaked in shadow, those oenological dreams and viticultural schemes that, in the past, gratified and sustained me so completely do not resonate on any currently familiar frequency. I have told myself stories in an effort to sort out what seems to be the problem, Doctor, but these fictive gests are long on exposition and do little to advance the familial plot. I have fair convinced myself that making soft, lus-

220. I've got about a decade on Sig. Alighieri, but, considering modern life spans (and correcting for excessive winemaker-dinner attendance), the time frame just about works out. Dante was already in my consciousness in 1998, and this found its ultimate expression with "Da Vino Commedia: The Vinferno" (2005). This also goes to show my extreme aversion to ever wasting a worthwhile literary trope.

cious, drinkable, albeit *terroir*-free, wines that typically reek of primary fruit aromas is wrong, all terribly wrong, and transforms me into the oenological equivalent of Stephen King or John Grisham, and that what I need to be doing is making wines of greater seriousness by an order of magnitude.[221] But when I look around and observe the culture of *soi-disant serious* winemakers and *serious* winemaking, I am reminded less of Münchberg and more of Edvard Munch. I want to recapture the original vision of Bonny Doon, which was an imperfectly understood but essentially sound idea—to grow exceptional grapes that one might ultimately transform into exceptional wine—but for once I am at a loss as to how to most adroitly proceed.

REIGN OF *TERROIR*. How does one refind the groove? I periodically delude myself into thinking that my principle frustrations stem from the fact that we work with grapes that are, for all intents and purposes, 100 percent *terroir*-free—that is, they ain't got no soil and, hence, presumably no soul. "If only I had great grapes . . ." I tell the relevant grape gods, the vinous Vishnus, the ramate Ramas. "OK, OK, let them be just a tad less funky," I grouse petulantly. But might this just be a guy (read: hormonal) thing that fuels my compulsive desire to produce a wine of universally acknowledged greatness? To roundly smite mine enemies, ravish their livestock, and slaughter their women? Shouldn't I rather take solace in the fact that any swinging Doctor Peterson can make great wine from great grapes, and that it takes rare talent and imagination to make interesting wine from snips and snails?

IN THE LABYRINTH. I do identify, perhaps to an unhealthy degree, with my alter egos, Quixote and Quijones. I rail or rage with fury about this or that manifest imbecility or injustice; inwardly I wonder if I truly have the quijones to go *mano a mano* with a universe not nearly as perfect as the luminously resplendent alternative one I can propose. It is just so goshdoon easy to retreat to the land of imagination, where Cabs are daily beat into plowshares (or regrafted at least). But man doth not live by fantasy alone, and my plight is like that of a breatherian—there is not enough nutriment in the strictly notional, too few kcals in chimerical contemplation. As seductively otherworldly as they may be, I can no longer dine out on Cigare dreams. I seem to need now the crunch of real engagement, a joust, and a lasting piece of prime vineyard real estate.[222] Perhaps it is time to take a lesson from my masters. What makes Quixote or Quijones into more than simply dyspeptic kvetches is that they actually (in relative terms of course) sally forth and essay to make the world conform to their deluded perceptions, with the painfully inevitable outcome of sustaining bruised everythings.

Speaking for myself, I have jested at Chards that have ne'er felt a wound. We moderns per-

221. One doesn't just go out and add serious yeast to the wine or put the wine in serious barrels instead of in the frivolous barrels that one had formerly used.   222. Although I was kvetching about this oeno-existential crisis as early as 1998, it somehow took me until 2006, with the sale of the Big House and Cardinal Zin brands, to really make a significant change. Needless to say, those eight years of living so incongruently with my deepest values were vinfernal.

ceive the transparently figurative quality of the Don Quixote character—he really is not much more than a straw man—but he creeps into our souls more subtly and completely than we might ever expect or imagine. The *Quixote* is unquestionably our greatest novel, because it is a sublime mirror of the most exquisite clarity and depth. In this way, it is strangely not unlike a great wine, absolutely simple and straightforward on the surface, but once you plunge in, you discover a trove of infinite depth and complexity. *Don Quixote* ultimately is about faith and the transformation that occurs when heroic folly is pushed to the limit and miraculously grows into wisdom. This theme evokes the religious mysteries, alchemical transformation, and—no great surprise here—the creation of wine itself. I am certainly neither the first nor the last to have become obsessed with *Quixote.*

There is a strange Borges story, "Pierre Ménard, Author of the *Quixote,*" in which Borges's "fictional" author "rewrites" the immortal novel.[223] The author, Ménard, has completely immersed himself in the project of re-creating the novel, *Don Quixote,* by subjecting himself to carefully controlled influences, saturating himself in the language and literature that had informed Cervantes's sensibilities, even attempting to re-create the traumatic developmental stresses that shaped Cervantes's psyche. With exacting and excruciating concentration, Ménard then proceeds to rewrite *Don Quixote* or some fragment of it, literally word for word. Borges prints a fragment of each of the two identical versions side by side and, with his characteristically vertiginous sanguinity, remarks on how much richer and resonant the latter-day version appears alongside the original.[224] This remark has its fully intended effect—that is, it sends spooky shivers to all the relevant ganglia. The figure of Don Quixote, his idealistic stance, and the book's inevitably tragically triumphant resolution exist as immortal archetypes within all of us. We have a genetic predisposition to fling some part of ourselves at a mystical and constantly changing notion of ideality and cannot help but continue to rewrite *Don Quixote* with our lives.

THE WU WAY. When we last shared some quality time, I left you with a leisurely, languorous long shot of a copious cover crop rustling in the *bürgerliche* breeze on the site of our once and future Grahm Cru, an eerie, deafening silence descending o'er the Republicanly replete Pleasantonian plane. The plan for the new winery, once a bright and shiny idea of great eidetic clarity, has become shrouded in a vague, recondite mist, a bit like Brigadoon. The potentiating moment seems to stand captured, stock-still, in amber. But time and the Livermore Valley Land Trust wait for no one,[225] and it had been suggested to us in the most genteel tones,

---

223. Like any good postmodernist, Borges creates fictional characters that somehow leave artifacts of their presence in the "real" world. Borges (who was a librarian) created the most exquisitely detailed utterly fabricated bibliographies. You feel that you have suddenly found yourself in hell's lending library.   224. One can't help but imagine the vinous analogy—that is, choosing precisely the same great Pinot noir grapes grown in Chambertin and growing them in, say, the Santa Lucia Highlands, with the intent of producing a "Chambertin." How breathtaking an achievement is the Santa Lucia knockoff!   225. The land trust is the agency charged with the implementation of the Livermore Valley General Plan as it pertains to the maintenance of certain lands dedicated to permanent agriculture.

of course, that we must either plant some vines or get off the plot. As things would have it, we had experienced an unrelenting series of karmic impediments—the gods were either thoroughly unamused or utterly beside themselves with amusement—to the forward momentum of the project, and I was feeling at sixes and sevens about the whole deal, as far as bringing the project to some sort of happily-ever-after-like conclusion. There was, therefore, little recourse but to bring in the heavy artillery, due-diligence-wise.

All rise for Dr. Baolin Wu, feng shui master from the world-renowned, five-thousand-year-old, steeped-in-tradition White Cloud Monastery of Beijing. Dr. Wu came up to the proposed winery and vineyard site in Pleasanton, the runic ruin yclept Ruby Hill, with his entourage of adepts and kibitzers and performed the obligate arcane rituals, *comme il feng*. When he had completed his thaumaturgic toil, I was, of course, anxious to learn how we had fared. The first question I posed to him through his interpreter was about what Dr. Wu thought of the property as a potential vineyard and winery site. It is an ineluctable rule that, when you ask the cosmos for an answer, you must be prepared to take the answer to heart. His interpreter responded, "Dr. Wu says, 'Very good for graveyard . . .'"[226]

HOW CAN YOU MISS US IF WE WON'T GO AWAY? (REDUX). I will spare you, gentle reader, a detailed account of the intervening intracranial pyrotechnics that took place in the last few weeks as I made a rather inept attempt to integrate Dr. Wu's diagnosis with the other, more prosaic terrestrial issues that the property presented. The decision as to what to do about the property was among the most difficult I have ever faced. But there is no time like the fictive present to bring you, profoundly indulgent reader, up to speed on the final disposition of this business and to share with you a quality moment or two in putatively real time. In the discrete ellipsis between this paragraph and the last, so much has changed. Just last week, after some do-it-yourself thoracic surgery, I decided after all, with not inconsiderable fear and trembling, to pull the plug on the purchase of the Pleasanton property.

I wrote a very embarrassed letter to the Wentes, certainly confirming every suspicion they may have harbored that they were dealing with a world-class flake. I told them I just couldn't go through with the deal. My reasons for not consummating the purchase were diverse and personal—it certainly wasn't strictly Dr. Wu's pronouncement. For now, I am still feeling a strong sense of disappointment and loss. And I was doing such a good job of learning how to talk to Republicans! People are always asking me, "So, Randall, what is the next thing?"[227] "Don't even ask," I tell them, or alternatively, "How much time do you have?" But for now, this eternally recurring call and response does not elicit much of a response.

226. I have spoken to a number of people who had worked at the old Stony Ridge Winery that had formerly (prior to its spontaneous immolation) existed on this site, and they all reported the presence of profoundly disturbing, inexplicable auditory phenomena.   227. Actually, just wine geeks ask me. I'm not sure that we even want to get into the philosophical problems relative to the fact that the next thing (which of course does not yet exist) seems to be more highly charged with meaning than the current thing—which of course *is* real and therefore generally unworthy of serious consideration, at least according to my slightly warped sensibility.

So whither Bonny Doon? I can't really say that I know. We think we are pretty close to the purchase of a good-sized building in Santa Cruz, where we might dig in for the long haul. We still need a wonderful new promiscuously cultured vineyard somewhere, planted to obscure, long-shot, crazy-ass varieties, with grapes growing up olive trees . . . I fear that I may have been done in by my eternal archnemesis: that old commitment thing. I hear the strains of strangely familiar music. It is as if one has invited all of one's globally dispersed friends to the blessed but unspeakable event and, amazingly, they have all shown up! All the aunts and uncles, all the first and second cousins from the Other Coast are in attendance. Vaguely familiar casual acquaintances, business associates, and a substantial number of unrecognizable schnorrers swell the ranks. In the interest of amicable compromise, a bright and personable Unitarian minister has been located to perform the nondenominational service. To everyone's chagrin, the groom is nowhere to be found and the bride is visibly distraught. There is nothing to do but eat the catered food, dance, and drink up the booze   *(FALL 1998)*

⌣⎯ I was genuinely saddened at the time that my plans for the Pleasanton vineyard and winery did not come to fruition, though in retrospect it might have been a blessing that they did not. (For one thing, it is not certain that we had the money at the time to pull this off, and moving forward might well have been the undoing of the company.) The yearning to find a home, to have a large canvas on which to imagine or create a vineyard in the form of a mandala has become one of the organizing themes of my psyche, and a theme that crops up, as it were, again and again in this book. I wonder sometimes whether it is my fate to become a professional dreamer about marvelous vineyards, rather than a planter of them.

Ca' del Solo, or Home Alone

MEET THE WINEMAKER. Perhaps some sincere apologies are in order for that last breathless Nooseletter, a rather thinly disguised plea for Tibouren and sympathy. It was a genuine *cri,* if not exactly straight from the *coeur,* then at least from some part of the limbic brain, but a real Bonny Downer nonetheless, *n'est-ce pas?* I hope no one took this perfectly pitched *Geschrei,* a sliding sinker doon and away, so much to heart as to emulate Young Randall and fling his or her pale and trembling self into the Rhine, Rhône, or any large swiftly flowing body of extremely cold water, or to seek impalement on a splintery grape stake, or to prune off any vital bit with a *sécateur,* or to consume a potentially lethal dose of Big Valley Merlot and, in the final throes of mortally green poivritude, top it off with a herbicide chaser.[228] (*That* really would be the Last Roundup™.) I know that any such rash and misguided act would be done with the very best of sympathetic in-

---

228. This will be the very last snide or "climatist" reference to the Big Valley that you will ever see in a Bonny Doon newsletter. I have just returned from a visit to the other Deep South (Italia), and I am here to tell you that absolutely exceptional wines can be created under some thermically challenging conditions.

tentions, and I do thank you in advance for any rash or misguided deed you might still be contemplating. I did receive a number of letters from people who were concerned about my current state of no-mind.[229] It's just a midwife—no, they must mean *midlife*—crisis, I was counseled. "Perfectly normal, you'll soon get over it," I was solemnly assured.

NAVEL MANEUVERS. "Get over it," my colleague Ted (in sales) advises me. "People assume that Bonny is doon for the count, that you have at last done what people have long been predicting, that is, flown too close to the Sungrantino, *crachèd* and Cab-burn, baby, burned, melted doon, gone off the rails, stripped your gears, conked, or freaked out. The smart money says that you have gone seriously *da solo,* repaired to a mountaintop in Central Asia, where you are living the life of a recluse, an anchorite, completely cloistered and secluded, *ermitagé,*[230] home or om alone, if you will, up at the crack of doon to milk the yaks, or, alternatively, that you currently repose, having been secreted away at an undisclosed location,[231] in a twilight, semivegetative state—inert, moribund, cataleptic (let's take a quick peek at those fingernails, chief), comatose, lifeless, dead in the wat . . ." "I take your point with glowing, almost luminescent clarity, Ted," I tell him. My colleague, it must be said, is nothing if not relentless.[232] "You see, the customers would like the teensiest evidence of a more, shall we say, *positive* attitude," says Ted. "If you can't think of something nice to say . . ." But I haven't wanted to get completely over it, truth be told, and that surprises me. Why should this *verkakte* swath of sward, this redoubtable relic of Republican real property,[233] be seemingly so charged with inherent meaning (even to a post-postmodernist such as myself)? I have told myself (and anyone else who would listen) that Pleasanton represented a sort of newfound maturity, the putting away of childish toys.[234] I imagined myself at long last prepared to quit the role of the trickster Quixote, of the slippery and oleaginous willie. At last, to be able to stand, center stage (Doon in front!), and loudly and proudly declaim the "C" word—though commitment to another sort of institution might appear to the casual *osservatore* to be the more efficacious way to go.

PARK OF MONSTERS. Perhaps the issue is as simple as the little boy in me, fabricator of an amazingly intricate and complex Dooniverse, wanting only that every single sentient being on the planet take a good long, admiring look at the prodigious wonder of his creation and marvel: My, how fiendishly clever, and who would have thought that you could hermetically seal barrels with

---

229. Three, but one was from my mother.   230. In the nineteenth century, Bordeaux wines were occasionally *hermitaged,* which is to say, a generous dollop of strong Rhône Syrah was added to put some starch in their otherwise limp, effete collars.   231. Coalinga or, alternatively, Parkfield, California.   232. I *did* mention that he was in sales.   233. Before John Locke left for India, he asked me if I had any words of advice for him. "Make wines to please yourself, John, not the critics, don't use too much SO_2, and always go with the alliteration," I told him as he stepped out onto the tarmac.   234. The compulsion to snipe safely from the sidelines at the congenital *connerie* of my confrères, for one, and the tragically compulsive Don Giovese complex I seem to possess, for another—an unslakable lust for new, fresh grape skin. Ferment 'em and leave 'em seems to have been my byword.

Provençal beeswax and float them in an œno-amniotic solution fifty meters below the surface of the earth in a temperature-, density-, and pH-calibrated secret underground glycol river, using the earth's magnetic field and specially fabricated stirring bars to effect automatic and perpetual *bâtonnage,* with the resultant resuspension of yeast lees?[235] I recently traveled in Italy and passed not far from the fabulous statuary Park of Monsters in Viterbo, where I had visited last summer with Enric Miralles, the elusive architect of my dreams. This immediately brought back the poignant feeling of how alive and aflame I had felt in the planning and dreaming phase of the Pleasanton project. Maybe planning and dreaming are what I do best. I thought of the great sculptural monster head that was intended to be the entrance to the Pleasanton facility. If one were to construct a winery in the belly of the Republican beast, what better means of ingress?

CRUZING FOR A BRUIZING. So the Pleasanton deal is, in the manner of Generalissimo Franco, still utterly and completely dead. We recently purchased a building on the West Side of Santa Cruz on Ingalls Street, yclept Marx/Ingallsstrasse. This fairly momentous item I relate perhaps a little too offhandedly. I can only say that the deal came together with breathtaking rapidity, and I am still areel anent its deeper implications. I feel a bit like one who greets the rosé-fingered doon the morning after the night before, having (at least this was the account of reliable witnesses) gotten heavily toasted—medium +++ char—and, in a totally manic episode (undoubtedly under the malefic influence of Le Canard Froid), with @≠Ω&¥¶§◊∂∆ only knows what sort of volitational assistance, having ended up, crazed and *vin*fused, in Vegas, with one of those gold doohickeys on one's left ring finger. Now maybe (or maybe not) the outcome of the midnight flight to Vegas was in fact salutary,[236] but the point is that you are still in a complete state of shock that you have actually gone and done it. The joint is a real fixer-upper I can say with no fear of contradiction. The decision to shack up at our Nearly Completed World Headquarters, with its rather gritty, workaday façade and its proudly Châteauneuf-du-Populist pedigree[237]—it was formerly a granola-manufacturing plant (what could be more quintessentially Santa Cruz?)—really does feel like a practical marriage of sorts, something not unlike an arranged affair, a ménage of convenience. I feature that the only items missing are the golden retriever, the station wagon, and the kid's soccer practice schedule tacked on the fridge with a Big House Red magnet. So one's dedicated bachelor self (as went the euphemistic parlance) did not end up with Isabella Rossellini, but rather with the plain but sweet-natured girl next door—in our case, it is literally next door to our current winemaking facility at Ingallsstrasse in the industrial sector of downtown Cruz.

INGALLSSTRASSE. So, it is still rather hard for me to grok the fact that I am in some sense settling Doon. Who wants to settle for anything? But it has been Rhônely (and exhausting) at the top, making wine at these multiple and far-flung venues. The consolidation and rational-

235. The end result being vinous immortality, but (yawn) we have already discussed that in previous newsletters.　236. No post-op complications from the "surgery."　237. Rayas on! All Power to the Picpoul!

ization of our winemaking program should, in principle, greatly ameliorate the quality of this whinemaker's life. We still lack a crucial piece of the puzzle—an extraordinary Grahm Cru vineyard located somewhere to the East of Mount Eden; its palpable absence is like the raw socket of a missing molar. One is perfectly capable of operating with slightly deficient doontition, but a plenary complement would truly be most helpful in sinking one's teeth into the next quixotic *vinjaune* quest. I *am* perfectly prepared to settle Doon quote and unquote one of these days, to give my entire heart and Ca' del Solo to the matter. It is just a matter of finding the right . . . er, *terroir.* **(SPRING 1999)**

Dr. Wu, the selfsame feng shui master who had pronounced on the Pleasanton property, also visited our site at Ingalls Street just before the purchase. I picked him up at the San Jose airport on an extremely dreary rainy day, and it drizzled continuously on our trip over Highway 17. When we at last visited the property, it had just stopped raining but was still very overcast. Dr. Wu strolled around the perimeter of the property and then walked across the street, the better to observe the frontal aspect of the building. "Randall, look up in the sky," he said, pointing upward. "When I do a feng shui consultation, I wake up early in the morning and pray for a sign to make an accurate reading. This is the sign I was praying for." I immediately looked up. If one had drawn two imaginary vertical lines extending from the edges of the building up into the sky, one would have observed that, in the sky, the visual fields directly to the left of the building and to the right of the building were entirely gray. The field directly over the building, however, was bright, solid, celestial, etheric blue, the blue of nothing but blue skies, and this, of course, provoked one of those Rod Serlingish moments. "You should buy the property," said Dr. Wu, very succinctly, and I did.

Revenge

Revenge is a dish best served cold. —NINETEENTH-CENTURY SICILIAN PROVERB

For this hunt, my malady becomes my most desired health. —CAPTAIN AHAB IN *MOBY-DICK*

When preparing to extract revenge, one does well to dig two graves. —CHINESE PROVERB

Nothing on earth consumes a man more quickly than the passion of resentment. —NIETZSCHE, *ECCE HOMO*

Hell is other Picpoul. —R. GRAHM

Nothing like this has ever happened to me before, and as such it has been a dislocation. Not that I've ever felt completely infallible or bulletproof, but perhaps something like that. I have been neck deep for the last year or so in the Big Muddy of a thoroughly senseless, staggeringly expensive, and utterly gratuitous lawsuit. I have recently given my adversary a slug of money and promised that I would cease my Cuvée Samsonite ways—don't ask how that managed to come into it—so that he might simply go away and cease his relentless, Javert–like pursuit and persecution. I am certain that I would prevail in the lawsuit were it to go to trial— maybe this is my dangerous and unrealistic sense of untouchability. His whole claim is laughable, absurd. The catch is that it would cost me far more to defend myself than to settle the suit. I am angry with this man and with the American judicial system, which allows deep-pocketed litigious individuals to more or less do their worst and outspend their adversaries into capitulation.[238]

I have been blocked on the "creative writing" part of the newsletter. Nothing new. I generally follow more or less the same ritual, some ambulating around Bookshop Santa Cruz in a sort of semitrance, looking at the titles of the books, trying to relax my mind, and hoping that the Muse will give me a very significant hickey. I wander into the fiction section of the bookstore. It occurs to me that my life has taken on an absurdist cast of late—perhaps something sort of existential might work. How about *Crime and Punishment?* Now, that cuts a little too close to the Beaune. *The Idiot?*—that sounds about right, though I'm not sure precisely who would be the title character. I look at Beckett. *Waiting for Godot? Godot, Guigal, Garganega*—I'm rolling the sounds around in my brain. *Estragon* becomes *Herbacé.* The two bums represent . . . what? Or should I say, whom? Think, man, think. Wait, they are the California wine industry, and they're waiting for a new white grape variety that will supplant Chardonnay. They're waiting for . . . Godello! The problem, of course, is that only two people in the entire world have ever heard of Godello, and they are both Northern California wine importers.

OK, Beckett is out. How about Camus then? Sounds like a name that has become familiar to me of late. I remember that *The Stranger* features a character called Meursault; that should give me a running start. Maybe if I set the scene in the dry, sun-flecked, windy Salinas Valley and call the piece "Le Vin Etranger"—that's what the French call our wine, by the way. At the beginning of the book, the protagonist—I'll call him Puligny—receives a crumpled-up Old Telegram. Something has happened to his mother: she suffered a terrible accident at a wine tasting in Aspen when a well-heeled but deranged patron, enraged by the parsimony of the *very* discreet tasting sample she poured (she does in fact count the molecules in each pour)[239] leapt over the table and did her grievous damage . . . Cut to Puligny back in the Salinas Valley, who is in some sort of senseless set-to with the *cholos* of Chualar. Somebody flashes a corkscrew, or is it a Swiss Army knife? He overreacts, and this leads to his eventual shame, undoing, and disinvitation to the New York Wine Experience. This might work . . . , but I continue walking the aisles, and suddenly come across Sartre. *No Exit, bien sûr. Huis Clos* will become *Huis Clos Vougeot;* this is much better, a no-brainer, in fact. But whom am I going to send to hell?

Well, obviously I must consign myself to the netherworld—it seems that I'm already most of the way there.

The opportunity to pillory, to ridicule, to mock, to unfairly malign my mortal nemesis, late of the legal action, feeds my fantasy of revenge just a little too well. I'll call him C. Veganaire.

238. If I were to dare to characterize my nemesis as litigious, would he take umbrage and sue me for defamation and, in so doing, undermine his own case?   239. This is actually an accurate biographical detail of my own mother, God bless her.

We need a third person, of course, to create the perfect infernal triangle, thus maximizing the dramatic tension. But who can that be? I'm afraid the best my febrile brain can come up with is the publisher of an influential national wine magazine.

I've been working on the story for a few weeks and find myself in San Francisco, eating lunch at the Tadich Grill, typing away on my laptop. Whom do I see walk in the door but the afore-mentioned publisher of the aforesaid influential national wine magazine. This must be a sign, and a spooky one at that. I tell him what a remarkable coincidence it is to bump into him, as I've literally just been working on a story in which he plays a prominent role. "It's an *hommage,* see," I explain, not very convincingly. He gives me an extremely pained look.

So the story clunks along. I honestly can't figure out if it is funny or not, but I'm beginning to suspect it is rather not. There are a couple of humorous bits, but they are largely situational. Hell turns out to be a smoke-free, scent-free, hypoallergenic establishment. (The publisher, disoriented, imagines that he's in West Hollywood.) The only wines served in hell are ones that scored between 80 and 86 in the aforesaid wine organ. We learn that Jesus is partial to soft, velvety Merlots, especially Pétrus. (Go figure.) "A gentle lamb of a wine," says he. The bit I like best is when each character tells how he came to die. My nemesis reluctantly allows that he ended up inadvertently poisoning himself with some unpasteurized chèvre he had smuggled in from France that had sat too long in his suitcase during a layover at O'Hare. ("Really should have paid more attention to those USDA guidelines, chief.") I meet my own demise by drowning in a large fermenting tank late one night while making systematic but unauthorized additions of raspberry extract to each and every tank of red wine in the house.

Frankly, the best thing about the story is the cast of characters:

Dramatis personae:
M. Shanquin
C. Veganaire
R. Grammaux
Various farm animals

The story I have written is just not that funny. It is frankly mean-spirited and scandalously obscene, and I have a sinking feeling that the whole thing might get me dragged back into court were I to publish it. Further, I am risking infuriating that influential publisher, who has never done me any harm.[240] To what end? It occurs to me that a side of me really likes dancing close to the edge, and if I fall over, well, too bad.[241] But the jokes just do not seem to be funny enough: they feel forced, tinny, and as gapingly toroidal as the midpalate of an overcropped Salinas Valley Cabernet. I prefer my humor a little on the edgy side, if you haven't already noticed, but I

---

240. Apart from disinviting me to the Wine Experience (see the essay "Are You Experienced?" *infra*).   241. It is an absolutely sacred tenet that I share with Penn and Teller that one should be staunchly prepared to risk death and dismemberment if the punch line is funny enough.

am beginning to think that real humor, as outrageous as it might be, must come from a certain special sacred place. How can I characterize this place? The best jokes can be risqué or nearly libelous, but they come from a place of purity and, as counterintuitive as this may sound, from a sort of humility. When I have been blessed enough to complete some really good comedic writing, the work seems, in retrospect, to have been more or less effortless, as if I had channeled the spirits of the Great Shpritzers who had gone before; I am merely a willing conduit.

One can certainly work from anger—there is perhaps no better motive force—but anger is quite different from the thirst for revenge. Anger is mutable, fluid, almost magical. The thirst for revenge is more like a compulsive behavior; it is a private and closed system, a grim inside joke. In any event, it seems to possess a fatal impurity: it is not universalizable; does not work on the large screen. When you experience the dislocation that I have described, you imagine that you have suddenly been cut off from the world (actually, from your concept of the world). The desire for revenge is a primitive, reactive urge to put things to rights, to return the world to the "fair" and organized state one imagined it to be in predislocation. But seeking revenge has the real effect of cutting oneself off from the world rather than reconnecting to it. For Sartre, hell may be other people, but for me hell is not being able to let go of the overwhelming desire to inflict psychic harm on someone, with the knowledge that one immolates oneself in the process.

I am not going to publish the story; I will instead burn it. I really do wish to put this terrible business behind me. My job now is to concentrate on my work and do the very best I can do. Let my nemesis go and find his own thoroughly benighted toper, Spiegelau stemware.

But one cannot thoroughly rule out the possibility of an upcoming release of Ignoramus Special Select. *(SPRING 2001)*

The lawsuit really did come as a major shock to me, and it dealt the final blow to my persistent willful naïveté. Certainly, my decision to downsize the company was based largely on deeply held values and a desire to bring more meaning to my life, but perhaps the psychic (and economic) vulnerability I felt in being the owner of a larger company subconsciously entered my thinking as well. During the lawsuit, I imagined that I resided in the farthest reaches of Wine Hell, and this may have also given some inspiration to my composition of "The Vinferno."

CONNERIE

SCHTICK

Preface to Unwritten Book

When you first start drinking wine, you have, like it or not, entered into a new culture. And, like any Marvin-come-lately to the neighborhood, you do your best to fit in. You listen to the pronouncements of the viterati. You attempt to properly hold by its fragile stem your Riedel crystal glass. You essay to make the correct, thoughtfully discreet slurping sounds at wine tastings, punctuating your sips with observations like, "Nice wine, though it could have stood a tad more (or less) lees contact" or "It really is a pity that M. Ygrec continues to believe in the innocuous nature of pad filtration." You buy *en primeur* when your impeccable sources assure you that the *régisseur* of that currently undervalued fourth growth had the wit to harvest Before the Rain. You learn how to identify 2,4,6-trichloroanisole, finding that, with the mere utterance of this shibboleth to the highly officious but ultimately papier-mâché wine steward, the suspect bottle of Ducru magically vanishes with no further argument. You petition for and finally attain admission to the Williams Selyem mailing list. Life is good, very good. You begin to fancy yourself a Master of the Wine Universe, and this benign universe seems complete. No, more than complete: it is replete and overflowing.[242] Every Monday and Doonerstag, the *Wine Spectator* profiles a brilliant new Cab. But the producers you have come to know, love, and trust have lately begun to divide and clone themselves like so many protozoa, spawning a frightening array of secondary, tertiary, and quaternary labels. The *millésimes* march on relentlessly, and your cellar begins to fill up. Star winemakers, like famous chefs, leave the safety of the nest, that winery you could always count on, to strike out on their own. There is so much to keep straight. "Did it rain that year in the Médoc, and was Saint-Emilion spared, or was it the other way round?"

The universe of wine ultimately seems so bewilderingly large and unfathomable that to taste one's way through it is a bit like attempting to eat at every Chinese restaurant in lower Manhattan. *Mesdames et messieurs,* I bring you very disturbing news. What you imagined as the metes and bounds of your broad and far-reaching oeniverse is, in fact, merely the local precinct. Your

---

242. The universe of wine is seemingly so inexhaustible and chock-full that one cannot help but think of Passover and the intonation of "Dayenu." If the Lord, our God, Creator of the vine, had given us the Vitaceae family but not all of the diverse genera of *Vitis,* it would have been sufficient. Had he given us *Vitis vinifera* but not *labrusca, aestivalis,* or *rotundifolia,* it would have been sufficient. Had he given us the entire Pinot family, and seen fit to delete Pinot blanc or Pinot Meunier, it would have been sufficient. Had he, in his infinite wisdom, fashioned the great Central Valley but not furnished it with adequate irrigation water to support the luxuriant growth of the Thompson seedless grape, it would have been sufficient. Had he given us the Chardonnay grape but not given us full-blown malolactics, it would have been sufficient. Had he contrived western Sonoma County, but not created Helen Turley, it would have been sufficient. Had he created Helen Turley and not likewise fashioned her brother, Larry, it would have been sufficient.

infinitely vast cosmos is but a drop of sand. In the same way that non-Eskimos have rather a dearth of snow-related vocabulary, the culture of American wine drinkers is arbitrarily and artificially bounded and is a small neighborhood. So, if you have become a wine drinker recently, likely as not you are an imbiber of Merlot or Chardonnay or Cab or Zin, not because they are the divinely revealed *cépages* of destiny, but because they are the fashionable *cépages du jour*. We focus on these grape varieties because to do otherwise would be to admit the existence of the barbaric hordes of the strange-sounding Rkatsiteli tribe. A Manhattanite imagines that he has everything within his grasp—the most carefully selected foodstuffs, clothing, art, and music. Why would he dream of ever leaving the island? Fasten your seatbelts, ladies and gentlemen. We're going to vitaceous New Jersey. *(2001)*

I might well have written this book had I not compiled the present one. This preface reflects my deep concern with the need to preserve and encourage a diversity of wine styles and rare and unusual grape varieties. I'm not sure exactly where the book would have gone—I got only as far as the preface—but it might have focused on wine's capacity to delight and astonish us, to neutralize our tendency to become jaded and cynical, which is a profound gift.

There is always a danger in criticism (or appreciation, for that matter) of any art, of killing or maiming the object of inquiry. Wine criticism, despite its best intention, often seems to verge on trivializing the splendor of its subject matter—maybe due to the utter inadequacy of language to capture wine's unique character—and often seems to tire one out, rather than energize or inspire.[243]

Why French Wine No Longer Matters, or How I Stopped Worrying and Learned to Love Long-Chain Tannins

I must state at the outset that I am a not-so-closet Francophile. When it is running, I drive a French car. I have been known to read French books,[244] collect French wine, travel extensively in France, and actually attempt to speak French every now and again. I have nothing but respect for my French winegrowing colleagues and their unique vinous sensibility. Indeed, the French, with their patrimonial intellectual rigor coupled with a profoundly innate sensuality, are biologically overdetermined to be fanatical perfectionists in the technologies of their pleasure-taking. When one speaks at any length with a great French winemaker (someone like Gérard Chave, the great producer of Hermitage, for example) and observes the remarkable

243. At least, it tires me out. After reviewing pages of compendious tasting notes, especially notes on particularly high-octane wines, I would fain lie down.   244. Actually, mostly French comic books. My life (maybe it's the French car) often feels like something out of the comic book adventures of Asterix and Obelix.

affinity he has for his métier, the intimate conversancy he has with each and every *terroir* and exposition of his vineyard, and with the nuanced wines that emerge therefrom, one feels every bit like a callow schoolboy consulting his sage and august professor.

OK, so what's the problem? Is there trouble in *paradis*? *Franchement* and *entre nous,* the answer is *oui.* The dirty little secret is that, while great French wines are incontrovertibly great full stop, and genius French producers remain genius producers who create fabulously interesting wines even in those highly problematic vintages that would send every single yuppified New World winemaker scurrying, shrieking, from his snug Napa Valley aerie directly back to Stanford B-school, the reality is that, in less than brilliant vintages and when made by winemakers who are themselves less than absolutely brilliant, French wines very often lack what might bluntly be called charm.[245] Yes, they are often "complex" and indeed often present an interesting aromatic profile. But, alas, I fear that, often as not, they are not all that much fun to drink. The wines I reference might be thought of as too acidic or austere—they are typically produced from grapes that have attained somewhat less than perfect "physiological maturity." This situation obtains when there is inadequate "hang-time" for the grape acids to diminuendo to mellowness and the seed tannins to properly ripen to a dulcet and *soyeuse* texture. In any event, these wines tend to be sort of mercilessly green and mean, and even the most sincere *apologia pro vino suo,* every pious protestation like "It's a great food wine" or "It just really needs more time,"[246] seems like so much fatuous rationalization.

That Bordeaux wines are absolutely sound but boring, predictable, and wildly expensive has been said again and again and does not bear repeating.

What to me is remarkable is that there really have been lots of blind tastings in which California wines routinely and thoroughly humiliate their Gallic counterparts—and these tastings are often conducted with experienced European tasters. What the heck is going on here? Confession time. For as long as I can recall, I have been an inveterate French wine snob who would look down his not inconsiderable nose at any philistine who would favor a California Cab over, say, a fourth-ish-growth Bordeaux, a Zin over a Gigondas. What could these people possibly be tasting in these wines? Could 50 million Frenchmen possibly be wrong or—more unlikely—200 million Americans possibly be right? Well, *peut-être.* I have come to believe that well-made California wines actually do seem to hit on more hedonic cylinders more consistently than wines produced by our *beaux amis* on the other side of the Atlantique—with the caveat that there is still nothing close to the sublime perfection of the *grands vins français,* and that there are still killer deals to be had on some of the inexpensive models from southern France with names like Fitou, Pic Saint Loup, and Faugères. And yes, there can be a sort of stylistic clunkiness in

---

245. I have posited the existence of what I call the *anticharmeur* device, a bit of machinery that conveniently plugs into one's bottling line, extracting every molecule of primary fruit and soft tannin as the wine goes to bottle. **246.** This argument actually does have some merit, and the fact is, you have bought the wine and you're taking it home *that* evening.

a lot of the California stuff, especially at the lower end, but, withal, after one has reached cruising altitude of, say, over ten dollars, it is hard to go terribly wrong in California, and the wines are quite satisfying.

Is it because we are so remarkably clever? Ah, . . . no. *Pourquoi, alors?* I think it really is nothing more than the incredibly benign climate with which we are blessed. California enjoys a climatic regime during its growing season for which most French growers would either kill or seriously maim. We have dry and generally temperate weather in the summer and very often perfect ripening weather in the fall. Coupled with the fact that we possess the *droit d'arrosage*[247] and can create an idealized hydrologic milieu for our precious and sensitive vitaceous *bébés*, it is really no great surprise that the wines seem so well balanced and hedonically satisfying. It's the tannins, *mes enfants.* They're ripe.

Is France played out? I don't think so. I do, however, believe that the genius of its Appellation d'Origine Contrôlée[248] system, which was intended to assure wine quality and typicity through a stringent set of viticultural and oenological guidelines, has been also a gross impediment to change and innovation. One is simply not permitted to grow the grapes of one's choosing where and how one chooses in Old Europe, or to vinify them as one pleases. Perhaps if French growers were permitted greater latitude, they could produce truly innovative and exciting *vins de table*[249]—with the express understanding that their freedom would most likely preclude an EEC-subsidized safety net to catch them if they fall. If my *fantaisie* of a sensualist but bureaucratically liberated France someday becomes a substantive reality, I'm so there.   (1998)

I was asked to write this piece for *Food & Wine* magazine in an issue that sought to generate some controversy by asking if French wines still mattered. Alas, Kermit Lynch was selected to write the brief for French wines, a position I felt more comfortable defending. I shaded my argument on behalf of the New World wines carefully, artfully disguising my true sentiments. If I could take back my comment about how lucky we are in the New World to enjoy the right to irrigate, I would. I fear that this particular freedom, while perhaps responsible for the breathtaking stylistic consistency of New World wines, has been gained at a great price—the loss of individuality and distinctiveness in our wines. It has allowed the New World to grow grapes virtually anywhere, and their "anywhereness" is certainly one of their most salient features.

247. The right to irrigate.   248. Growers are further constrained by various EEC regulations that govern planting practices. Suffice it to say that if this correspondent were an EEC resident and somehow imagined that he might ply his current *métier* over *there*, he would not currently be the carefree *flâneur*, at liberty and leisure.   249. Analogous to the superb *vini da tavola* of Italy, which generally carry no pejorative associations.

Connerie

~~~
 ᴑ᷈
~~~

Totally Screwed
Three (3x) Top Ten Lists

How did I come to forgo corks in favor of the not-yet-particularly-à-la-mode screwcaps? To paraphrase Tolstoy, every happy winemaker is alike; every unhappy one is unhappy in his own way, and in the 1990s I was particularly unhappy about corks for reasons I have publicly kvetched about ad nauseum.

At the end of the last century, because of the severity of my "issues" with corks, I flirted somewhat disastrously with synthetic closures for a couple of years and, unfortunately, ended up greatly compromising the quality and longevity of a few wines that were quite important to us—a real pity. One must remember that the initiative we took to bottle our entire production of 2000 Big House Red *en screwcap* was a doon-or-die proposition, and therefore we had to pull out all marketing stops, however crass, to insure its success.[250] I have not detected at my back a thundering herd of vintners seeking a new form of closure, but *Decanter* magazine recently proclaimed Stelvin screwcaps as superior to corks as a wine closure for virtually every

---

250. We staged a mock funeral procession and wake for M. Thierry Bouchon at the Campbell Apartment in Grand Central Station in New York, enlisting Jancis Robinson as one of the coconspirators. (She delivered the eulogy.) The wake was conducted as part of a "Black Dinner," following the literary example of Joris-Karl Huysmans in *A rebours,* in which all the dishes served were "black"—tapenade, caviar, black pudding, pumpernickel, black cod, chocolate and licorice desserts, and so on. Despite our desire for total transparency, we did not include the Huysmanian touch of totally unclad black servers.

An interesting behind-the-scenes view anent the decision to proceed with the screwcap campaign: My colleagues in sales, marketing, and finance were more than a little concerned about releasing the entire production of Big House Red *en screwcap,* which was almost fifty thousand cases at the time and represented a significant amount of the company's income. They argued for caution and prudence—two words not generally found in my lexicon—and favored a limited "test" release, perhaps in a single market, like Ohio, before rolling out the campaign nationally. It was obvious to me that every large winery had likely already conducted its own focus group studies, and the glaring absence of screwcaps found on premium brands was presumptive evidence of their cool reception, at least by focus groups. While at the time consumers might have harbored some prejudice against screwcaps—the putatively appropriate closure for a wine (or any other intoxicant ready to hand) consumed by the railroad tracks when down on one's luck—I noted that both wine writers and sommeliers were consistently weighing in on the issue of "corkiness" in wine, almost to the point of obsession; they could therefore likely be enlisted as natural allies in a campaign to make wine safe from cork taint. It struck me further that there was a nontrivial public relations opportunity for the first company to take an extremely strong stance in favor of screwcaps, or indeed, in favor of any truly first-rate alternative to cork closure—Plumpjack had released 150 cases of very expensive Cabernet with screwcaps a year or two earlier, causing quite a ruckus, but their story was clearly in the novelty and incongruity of a very expensive wine *en screwcap.* We had the extraordinary opportunity to actually change long-held perceptions in a fairly good-sized population. I lament that I will likely go down in wine history as a brilliant marketer *tout court* (and therefore may have screwed myself in the bargain), but am in fact proud of the brilliant marketing campaign we conducted to bring screwcaps in from the back alleyway to the bourgeois tableside.

application.[251] Being particularly interested in enhancing wine's ageability (a positive feature of screwcaps that is not intuitive, but you'll have to take my word for this),[252] I remain thoroughly delighted with the product's technical performance, consumer acceptance, and the fact that the number of skeptics does appear to be dwindling. But not that long ago, we felt the need to resort to silly lists like these:

Top Ten Reasons to Use Screwcaps

1. Never pay corkage fees again.
2. When celebrating significant occasions (parole, commutation of sentence, etc.) with one's colleagues, it is often difficult to locate a corkscrew.
3. Reverse chic is just so in.
4. You can use as a conversational gambit with waitresses the line "Would you, er, unscrew my bottle?"
5. Screwcapped beverages are perfect for clothing optional events.
6. You will never fall for the old "left-handed" corkscrew gag again.
7. It's hard to find corkscrews down by the railroad tracks.
8. The proper usage of cork oak will rectify the acute worldwide shortage of trivets.
9. You can no longer be accused of being a cork sniffer.
10. You will never again experience the heartbreak of 2,4,6-TCAoriasis.

Ten More Compelling Reasons to Use Screwcaps

1. Have a great laugh as Martha Stewart tries to glue her collection of screwcaps into a wooden frame.
2. You will never hear the phrase "Put a cork in it!" again. Ever.
3. The very silly macho Italian pastime of cork-length comparison will also cease forever. Concavity will reign supreme, and a soft, vaguely pastel, feminine, glowing aura will cover the world, leading to millennia of world peace and amity between all men, women, and those of indeterminate gender.
4. You will never have to confront the sommelier at the poshest restaurant in town with the tragic news that his last bottle of Le Pin is slightly "off."
5. You will never again hear a joke with the punch line "Every Ah-So has one."
6. Colleagues in your tasting group will stop addressing you by the sobriquet "Corky."

251. There is near unanimity (at least among the people who know what they're talking about) that screwcaps generally do enhance a wine's ageability, but there are still some semiunanswered questions (see my very long footnote about this in "*Reductio ad Sulfatum*") about the tortuous path a wine might travel to get to that endpoint. Certainly in light of the mild retardation (of flavor development) associated with screwcaps, corks may well be the more appropriate choice for closure for some wines consumed in the short- to midterm.   252. Or read the exceptionally comprehensive footnote, mentioned in the previous note.

7. The expression "I've been totally screwed!" will take on a new and slightly gentler meaning.

8. Pechiney Corp., manufacturer of the Stelvin closure, a mega-huge French corporation, can now show profitability without resorting to "creative" accounting.

9. Residents of County Cork, Ireland, will finally be given relief from allegations of 2,4,6-TCA-tainted linen and shamrocks.

10. Aspiring histrions who are moonlighting as restaurant servers will be given the opportunity to make the *pop* sound when the screwcap is unscrewed, thus leading to their potential "discovery" and ultimately lucrative careers in film and television.

Ten Reasons Why You Should Discard Your Corkscrew

1. Playing Russian roulette is appropriate in old Akim Tamiroff films, not when opening premium bottles of wine.

2. The glut of used and new corkscrews currently offered on eBay has rendered yours virtually worthless.

3. We will send you an unspeakably fashionable "2,4,6-TCA! How many wines did you taint today?" T-shirt.[253]

4. You could easily put out an eye.

5. The airlines will confiscate them anyway.

6. Your drawers will seem cleaner, neater, and safer.

7. In so doing, you are eloquently stating that, with the wines you personally serve, it just taint so.

8. The still thoroughly dead Thierry Bouchon should be permitted to rest in peace.

9. Corkscrews are still considered in some areas (at least around Santa Cruz) to be primitive phallocentric symbols of male aggression.[254]

10. Requiring a corkscrew to open a fine bottle of wine is now as compulsory as the need for a crank to start one's engine.

(2001, 2002)

David Letterman has culturally appropriated the top ten lists; their irreverent, hip/ironic attitude is perfectly well suited as a propagandist's tool in the culture wars between cork sniffer (old fart) and Stelvinist whippersnapper. In our introduction of Stelvins, the most remarkable thing we found was that, for our customers at least, the type of closure presented was absolutely irrelevant. Bonny Doon customers, not all of whom are young or particularly hip, do seem to be enormously open-minded and have no particular negative baggage pertaining to corks and their cultural significance.

253. Another instance of the inexorable shift of focus from progressive politics to progressive tasting menus, and of the obsession with fine dining among members of the Baby Boomer generation, at least those inhabiting the Bay Area.   254. Wielded by pale patriarchal Pinot people.

The Heartbreak of Wine Geekdom
Ten Ways You Know You've Met a Real Wine Geek[255]

1. If you hear one or more of the following terms, you may be in big trouble and should consider making an immediate and careful study of all possible routes of egress: (a) Brix, Balling,[256] Baumé, or (steady now) Oechsle, (b) *cépage* or, even worse, *encépagement,* (c) *inox,* (d) hectoliter, (e) cap or tannin "management" (f) *pigeage,*[257] (g) skin contact, (h) calcareous, (i) *barrique,* (j) maceration, *macération,* or (heaven help you) "extended" maceration, (k) cold soak,[258] (l) polyphenol, (m) potential alcohol, (n) titratable acidity, (o) *rendement,* (p) autochthonous, (q) *Brett* (or *Brettanomyces*),[259] (r) "500,"[260] (s) physiological maturity, (t) facultative aerobe, or (u) *lieu-dit.*

2. He has brought his test questions from the Master of Wine, or Master Sommelier, exam to dinner.[261]

3. He has brought his own Impitoyable tasting glasses to the restaurant.[262]

4. He actually uses the Impitoyable glasses to drink out of—guaranteeing that he will have red wine running down his chin and onto his shirt.

5. He has brought his own food to the restaurant.[263]

6. He will stun you with a dizzying display of serial name-dropping[264], a sycophantic litany so shameless in its exhaustive inclusiveness that you will be left aerobically challenged—

Connerie

255. This was first published in the Bonny Doon newsletter *It Takes a (Grenache) Village* (Special Wine Geek Issue), no. 4 (April 1999), a bit of ephemera occasioned by the somewhat sluggish sales of the wine Grenache Village. The theory was that, if I continued to inundate our customers with a monthly progress report on the glass-by-glass depletion rate of Grenache Village, eventually either the customers' interest would be piqued or an untapped reservoir of compassion or pity would be discovered. **256.** Ugh, gag me, the worst. There is no discernible difference in meaning between the words *Brix* and *Balling,* except the latter is obscurantist to the extreme. **257.** Just moments ago I googled the word *pigeage* to determine the correct spelling and was immediately directed to the Website www.winegeeks.com. I'm telling ya, I know what I'm talking about. **258.** *Macération à froid.* **259.** This may in fact be forgivable, as *Brett* can be a very real problem, and if one detects it well, why not speak up? But what is totally beyond the pale is to refer to the spoilage yeast as *Dekkera,* which is the ascosporogenous, or sexual, form of *Brett.* Obviously, if a discussion of this particular point of distinction were to ensue, or if the wine geek under discussion were to use the term *sporogenous* or *sporulating,* immediate escape from the premises would be absolutely compulsory; possibly blowing up the house might also be indicated. **260.** Not the Indy racecar event (these are wine geeks we're talking about after all), but the biodynamic preparation of cow manure that resides all winter in a buried cow horn. Obviously the potential likelihood for the wine geek to trot out arcane knowledge anent the Steinerian oeuvre remains a clear and present danger. **261.** This seems absolutely unbelievable, but I was once present when this occurred. **262.** Let's forgo political correctness. We all know that besides Serena Sutcliff and Jancis, all wine geeks are guys. **263.** He has brought his own wine to the restaurant as well, and this is suggestive, but not a priori evidence, of wine geekiness. **264.** This factor should be used in conjunction with the first item in the list to triangulate with complete certainty the proximal presence of a wine geek. In other words, let's just sorry, that's gasping for oxygen. If you hear two or more of the following proper names in a single conversation, you must put down your knife and fork and make a clean break for it: André, Lalou, Aubert, Dom, Angelo, Fausto, Marco, Egon, Helen,[265] Paul, Josh, Gérard, Jim,[266] Marvin,[267] Randy, Jancis, Hugh, Ricardo, Michel,[268] Manfred.

7. He will *spontaneously* recite all thirteen permitted *cépages* (oops) of Châteauneuf-du-Pape, as if a world-historical blending decision hangs in the balance.

8. He will break the awkward conversational ice with the topic sentence "Is the 1855 Bordeaux Classification still valid?[269] Please discuss."[270]

9. He has intimated that he would like to "date" Jancis.

10. He believes that a recitation of the conversion of the Oechsle scale of must density into Brix at table is an appropriate conversational gambit.

(1999)

It takes a geek to know a geek, and I know whereof I speak. Wine geekiness is an affliction that never really disappears; like any chronic condition, it has to be appropriately managed. It is certainly due to the grace of God that I have managed, just barely, to not be considered a complete geek myself, though it is merely a matter of time before I am outed.

---

imagine—this is highly unlikely, by the way—that the geek actually has a friend named André who is *not* in the wine business. You should be especially vigilant for sentences that go something like, "I was just asking my good friend André the other day what he thought about extended maceration." Bingo. You're so outta there.   **265.** This is a reference to Helen Turley, and you now know that not only is this guy a geek but he is also a total fraud. True wine insiders know that Helen Turley does not actually exist, and that Robert Parker invented her.   **266.** It could only be Clendenen. If he means Fetzer or Concannon, he really does need to get a life.   **267.** Run, not walk, away from the table.   **268.** Could be Rolland, though possibly Chapoutier; in any event, woe is you.   **269.** Virtually all conversation apart from comparisons of vintage years and discussion of exceedingly arcane wine miscellanea is essentially impossible for the true wine geek.   **270.** At this point you have no choice but to stab him with the small knife provided with most sommelier-style corkscrews, known as the "waiter's friend," and not without good reason. Then run for it.

Good Morning, Swedes

April 4, 2005

Good Morning, Swedes:

I have been asked to write a few words about the April 4 release of the 2003 Ca' del Solo Big House Red,[271] available from the Systembolaget.[272] I have consulted *All These Women* in my office to try to come up with a significant connection between Big House and Sweden, and I was met with only *Silence*. I mean, you would have to be some sort of *Magician* to come up with such an association. Let me, however, assume the *Persona* of a proper Swede and give it a try: you are in *Prison,* suffering from great *Thirst*.[273] Imagine opening six bottles of wine sealed with corks, and what do you know? They're all afflicted with TCA. But the *Seventh,* sealed with a Stelvin closure (easily opened with just a *Touch*) and poured out into a *Magic Flute*,[274] is bright, fruity, vividly exuberant, and certain to provoke *Cries and Whispers* of delight. A perfect wine to sip in a *Pleasure Garden,* and certain to provoke great *Joy* and *Smiles of a Summer Night*. One scents the fragrance of opulent fruit, particularly *Wild Strawberries,* in the nose, and the color is deep enough to view *Through a Glass Darkly*. It would be a *Shame* if you did not immediately go out and buy many bottles.   *(2005)*

Connerie

—— This was just a little airy *divertimento,* but indicative of possibly the only real talent I possess— that of bricolage, or the ability to cobble together disparate elements into a semicoherent whole. Certainly the winemaking up until now has benefited from that skill—namely, the composition of Le Cigare Volant, an eclectic blend from diverse climats and *terroirs*— and perhaps the art direction for the label design has as well. It does beg the question as to whether this odd gift might ever actually be harnessed for great good.

---

271. This day is in fact my birthday (my fifty-second), and I would appreciate it if you could all gather round Sweden and sing a couple of verses of "Happy Birthday" or, failing that, "For He's a Jolly Good Fellow." 272. The Swedish alcohol monopoly, created with the mandate to, in their own words "minimize alcohol-related problems by selling alcohol in a responsible way, without a profit motive." Systembolaget is the world's largest single customer of wines and spirits.   273. I know that *This Can't Happen Here*—that is, prisoners are generally not allowed to either drink alcoholic beverages or possess sharp objects like corkscrews—but this is progressive Sweden.   274. You may personally prefer a standard INAO all-purpose tasting glass

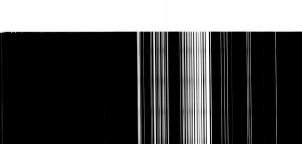

Le Cigare of the Future

What will the Cigare of the future taste like? Connoisseurs will think back on the legendary 1984. The elements were already apparent, albeit in a somewhat nascent form—the spiciness, herbal, berry, wild mushroom, mud-soaked primitive quality, but it had not yet shed its cordial civility. The '84 could still be taken to a dinner party without fear of scandal. The '84 was a little risqué, but the Cigare (of the future) is *shameless*. It even smells vaguely seditious. Crushed junipers, mulberries, *fraises des bois,* wild plums, dried cherries, anise root, and raw meat. It is a wine for the urban hunter-gatherer. But what is it really like? It is like living to be two hundred years of age. It is a bouquet of ultraviolets. It is the sun pouring through one's sievelike body. It is the taste of the colors mauve, nutmeg, and rosemary, the muted moan of violaceous velvet. It is all the virtues and more vices than are dreamt of in Miami. It is one's self, that hollow shell, being stuffed with veal and pork, heavily infused with cloves of garlic, anchovies, capers, parsley, tomato, and rosemary. It is being ready to eat or be eaten. It is more than that. Very limited, but then so are our days.   *(FALL 1995)*

We've never quite succeeded in making a wine that tastes like the one I've described here, but the aspirational language still obtains. Definitely a little over the top as far as purple wine prose goes, but the thought here was to imagine a wine made in the New World that surpassed our language to describe it. Great wine may move one to poetry, but might as easily provoke an inspired silence.

Making the List at Elka's

I have a new gig. Not that my old gig is no longer tenable. It's just that my friend Elka has asked me to help with the wine list for her new restaurant. Composing a wine list is, in fact, something I have wished to do for many years. Part of that desire is fiercely ideological. (I am rabidly opposed to the uncontrolled and rampant proliferation of the hegemonic grape varieties, a phenomenon I have elsewhere termed *Merlotnoma*. The other part, I am somewhat chagrined to admit, is my still thoroughly adolescent, self-indulgent craving to spank a certain genre of Chard-swilling yuppie scum. What could possibly be more fun (and utterly infuriating to the aforementioned yupsters, to boot) than to create within the restaurant an effectively Chardonnay-free zone? My fantasy is to maintain under the "Chardonnay" heading a page completely blank, the null set, nada, (Far) *niente, bupkiss,* unconditional *Chardlosigkeit,* the nuclear winter of our dissed content. Customers will turn the page over and there will be nothing, back again, still nothing.

No Ferrari-Carrano to drive away the demons of oenological uncertainty, no Sonoma-Cutrer to cut their fear of social embarrassment down to size, no Acacia to assuage their oenological anomie. Chalone *aleichem,* and *There Goes* Mr. Jordan! Sorry, pal, no Chards for you!

While I'm on this puerile rant, what I really hate about so many wine lists is their absolutely predictable sameness. More shocking is to find *not a single, solitary bottle* (raving italics mine) that actually complements the cuisine of the restaurant. I am determined that my wine list will not denominate commonly, but rather will incrementally elevate palate-consciousness. This list will be about diversity and taking chances. With some gentle encouragement, the customer will be going places he or she has never been before. I am resolved to make the world safe for Scheurebe, Sagrantino, and Schioppettino. The quirky, oddball, ugly-duckling grape varieties of the world will soon be given their day. Elka and her partner, Constance, God help them, have invested me with full charge to create whatever wine list I think would work best with Elka's intensely vibrant, Bamboo-Meets-Godzilla style of cooking. Like any rebellious adolescent, I am desperately seeking boundaries and limits.

I called my friend Hiram for advice. "Hiram, I really want to Make a Statement with this wine list. What do you think about a list that is All Riesling, All the Time?"

"Absolutely brilliant, Randall. You'll put the restaurant out of business within two weeks."[275]

"Right."

I made calls to virtually all of the Northern California suppliers just to get a sense of who the players are, schmooze them a bit, and find out who's got the righteous juice.

I have not worked the buying side of the fence for many years. So much has changed. I used to purchase wines for a wine store in Los Angeles more than twenty years ago. Many of the salesmen who used to call on the store were what we called "retreads"—old liquor guys who had been taken in for reconditioning and a modicum of reeducation and refinement. But old habits die hard, and their selling point ultimately would devolve on the question of price. "We've got this [pronunciation unintelligible] Château on special this month. How many cases do you think you need?"

"What's the wine like?"

"Don't worry. If you don't like it, we'll take it back."

The people who work in the wholesale wine business in Northern California appear to be an entirely different breed. They actually know something about wine—in fact, they take your breath away by the depth of their product knowledge. They have clearly been to the mountain; they will throw out terms like *minerality* and *hectos per hectare.* They speak authoritatively about hours of "skin-contact" time and the exposition and soil typologies of subsections of various vineyards. They are what you might call wine geeks.

I admit it. I have been looking forward to basking in the regal power, smugly confident that

---

275. It actually took slightly longer than two weeks.

I possess the requisite wit to penetrate any wine salesman's unctuous spiel, avoiding the embarrassment of an inadvertent ten-case drop of borax. I will discern any and all potential wine defects *way* before these bottles find their way to the tables of our fastidious customers. But this state of hyperalert *qui vivosity* is actually proving to be an enormous hindrance. I have no difficulty in identifying the clunkers, or even in apprehending the well-made wines that are somehow missing that extra spark of originality. What I am finding, however, is that I am being hoisted by my own petard, strange-brew-wise. My self-imposed mandate has been to find wondrously idiosyncratic, original wines. But what is to be done when, if presented with these wacky wines, even I am unable to discern their virtues in view of their extremely edgy strangeness?

The quality of discrimination that enables us to differentiate relative degrees of quality among wines turns on us like a rabid . . . er, sommelier, when we confront a taste that is well beyond all familiar reference points. A connoisseur friend of mine recently bade me to taste a very rare and odd Vin Jaune[276] made from the fairly esoteric Roussanne grape, thinking that it would be right up my alley. It pained me to tell him that I just couldn't get it.

How do we learn to transcend our seemingly immutable paradigms and find the qualities in wines—heck, in anything or anyone—that do not possess "quality" by our own definition? How do we admit into our lives the strange and unusual? Terry Theise, brilliant iconoclastic importer of German wines, has written simply, "Let love in." It seems that one gains entry to strange new worlds through one of two routes—by benign and gradual acclimation or, if favored by the Gods, in a magical lightning instant when the switch is suddenly, unexpectedly turned on. But just like with falling in love, one has to learn to leap.

From Elka's Wine List

Imagine that you have been afforded the opportunity to enter an alternative universe where the sky is often an attractive mauve color, life-forms are not carbon-based (perhaps silicon?), and, let us say, Cabernet Sauvignon, Merlot, and Chardonnay do not exist at all, except as speculative fictions. The highly evolved life-forms that have lived all their lives in this alternative reality do not miss Chardonnay any more than we have regrets about not having green blood or functionally opposable basal appendages. Imagine on every wine list in this alternative universe a vast range of wine styles, flavors, and textural impressions, reflective of the abundance of life's extraordinary possibilities. Imagine an alternative reality where we feel safe enough to surrender unconditionally to our deepest yearnings for balance and harmony, eschewing the bright, safe shore of the all too familiar for the unknown, buoyant, wine dark sea. Congratulations, you are already there. *(2001, 2002)*

---

276. An extremely stylized and concentrated wine produced in the Jura, through the effects of flor yeast, and possessing certain flavor characteristics associated with wine spoilage or, more intentionally, with sherry.

Elka Gilmore is an extraordinarily talented chef and a friend of mine. For reasons known only to her, she imagined that I might make a reasonable wine buyer and sommelier at her restaurant. I was not a particularly gifted sommelier—that is, someone who has enough empathy and insight into human beings to actually intuit what might be within a customer's comfort and interest zone, so that choosing a bottle of wine would be no more traumatic than it had to be. I certainly tortured those poor customers—for their own good, of course.[277] At the end of the day, it is enormously satisfying to share with someone the magical experience of a particularly felicitous food and wine pairing, whether he or she is ready for it or not. The concerns of this piece are echoed in the essay "Six Feet Under." How do we learn to love (or even understand) that which we mostly don't? In its expansion, the universe of wine, like our own universe, appears to be approaching something like a steady state. At a certain point, virtually anyone, despite his or her avowed esteem of open-mindedness and diversity, will reach the critical saturation point, and precious little new information will trickle in. And yet, sometimes one can still be surprised at the most unlikely moments.

Preface to WINES OF ITALY

I attended the prestigious University of California at Santa Cruz in the very early seventies—we called it Uncle Charlie's Summer Camp back then. There were no letter grades offered to the students, rather something called "narrative evaluations." As a result of this unorthodox arrangement, and perhaps owing as well to the zeitgeist, the university found itself with a certain genre of matriculating student. One might characterize this student in many ways, but the words that come immediately to mind are: brilliant, sensitive, socially challenged, and lazier than shit—your classic late-blooming, nerdy underachiever. I maintain that it was this experience in the company of other ugly ducklings that has given me an acute sensitivity to the putative underachieving, "secondary" grape varieties of the world, the misunderstood, under-esteemed, vitaceous ugly ducklings, if you will.

My credentials established, let us fast-forward thirty years. Fast-forward is right; *avanti* is the byword of Modern Life. We are currently bombarded with information and confronted by a dizzying array of personal choices in virtually every arena of our lives. As wine drinkers, we find that the names of wineries, appellations, and grape varieties flicker past us like subway stops on the high-speed uptown express. Against this backdrop, unifying, simplistic solutions have grown increasingly more attractive to some, and none is more simplistic and straightforward than the "international style" or New Wood Order, as I prefer to call it:

277. One customer greatly resisted my suggestion of a pairing of Maximin Grünhäuser Auslese with lamb carpaccio prepared with lemongrass and yuzu. In a battle of wills, I ultimately prevailed, and the customer was so knocked out by the pairing, he literally fell out of his chair.

"soft" tannins, lotsa alcohol, lotsa oak, and deeply saturated color. The sad fact is that we seem to be losing distinctiveness of character in our wines worldwide as this juggernaut gathers momentum.

Y'know, we never ever really completely graduate from high school, and the same *agon* between the popular "in" crowd and the nerdy, pocket-protected outsiders gets replayed over and over for the rest of our lives and in very unlikely fora. The new international style is the cool jock quarterback of the football team. Almost everyone wants to like him and to be like him. Even, it pains me to admit, some extremely distinguished Italian winemakers.

How does any of this relate to the subject matter of this book? Italian grape varieties, especially the oddball ones, are among the most misunderstood in the world. In the cliquey, fraternal world of wine, they are definitely in with the out crowd: they require study, patience, and understanding.[278] There is no quick way to apprehend their subtlety and unique qualities. In many of the reds, the quality of the tannins is not particularly warm and fuzzy. But every high-quality Italian wine is made with a particular intention, and each fits snugly into a fully realized aesthetic context.

I can speak only about my part of the anglophonic world. Despite our protestations to the contrary, in America we don't properly appreciate diversity, strangeness, and specificity—certainly not in our wines. We tend to go for the one-size-fits-all approach. Italian grapes and wines—so remarkably diverse and heterodox, reflective of the vaguely anarchic fabric of Italy itself—are about nothing if not particularity. They can be fussy, unreconstructed; most of them don't want to go along to get along. They have an attitude, an edge.

Often in discussions about food and wine pairings, there is an egalitarian sentiment voiced

278. The strange magic of wine, especially of a true *vin de terroir,* possessed of a life force—that is, the ability to tolerate oxidative challenge—is that it can be enormously moody and mutable, virtually bipolar, you might say, constantly changing and evolving, a true vinous kaleidoscope. Wines made from certain varieties—namely, from Nebbiolo, Pinot noir, and Grenache—do not have the obvious structure of wines made from Cabernet or Merlot, and while in fact they are enormously strong (well-made Burgundies notoriously can live much longer than first-growth Bordeaux), they may sometimes appear to be weak if one is not paying sufficient attention. Natural, unmanipulated wines of a place seem to be more sensitive to the physical and etheric fields that surround them—to the vagaries of room temperature, to atmospheric pressure, to the phases of the moon, and to the astronomical calendar, not to mention the physiology, mood, and psychology of the taster himself or herself. As happens to members of certain indigenous tribes, the soul of these wines is stolen when we take a snapshot view of them. Subtle, more delicate wines may appear to be utterly "closed" upon initial impression, and one may have to wait and wait, decant and recant, before the shy and shrinking violet suddenly emerges from her shell and graces one with the two-thousand-watt smile, a cactus flower blooming in the desert; if you blink, you've missed it. Tasting wine rapidly and coming to a judgment about its intrinsic qualities is fraught with danger—rather like the vinous equivalent of speed-dating. To really know and appreciate wine, you have to move toward it, to learn to accept it on its own terms. As one does when risking falling in love or attempting to make a great Pinot Noir in the New World, one must be willing to appear very foolish. The reluctance to appear foolish is a common human trait but greatly weakens modern wine criticism, as I argue in the essay "'Great' Wine in the Postmodernist World."

about how one should simply drink the wines that one likes with the food that one likes. On the face of it, this makes perfect sense. Yet the genius of Italian wines is their particular affinity with certain foods and, sometimes, their odd specificity. Certain wines are made particularly to accompany *salumi*, wines that have become so ritualized that they are consumed only at particular times, on particular holidays. Food and wine pairing is an art, an obsession in Italy. You cannot even begin to understand the meaning of *fastidious* and *fanatical* until you have observed a *dottore del vino* agonize over the most felicitous application of his wine to comestible fare. Yes, it is often fussy, but the aim is to provide the maximum potential pleasure that a human being can possibly stand.

It is terribly important that we preserve these heterodox grape varieties and *molto particolare* wine styles—not in a museum, not on these pages, but in our experience. Italian wines in their profusion of styles and textures speak to the abundant exuberance of Italian life itself, its zest and its beauty. You don't get it by reading about it. Italian wines are meant to be experienced.

If the rest of the world doesn't understand Italian wines, it matters not a whit to Italian winemakers. They know who they are and know the wines they love and why they love them. If you were to suggest to them that they were on the outside looking in, they would have no idea what you were talking about. From their perspective, it is a personal tragedy for anyone who does not have the fortune to be born Italian and to consume Italian wine on a daily basis. Call it the revenge of the Nerdolinos. *(2005)*

A friend of mine asked me to write a preface to her book on the subject of Italian grape varieties, a topic that immediately brings up thoughts of what's on for lunch and for dinner today and for the near-term gastro-temporal horizon. In the footnote, I've made mention of the absolutely obdurate, strange, and mysterious character of wine—its ability to retreat, to disguise itself. Unconsciously, I made a connection in this essay between wine's magic and Prospero's enchanted isle, which can only be Italy itself. My friend's book has finally come to press, but my preface inexplicably seems to have ended up on the editor's floor. My friend never explained to me what happened, but presumably the language was a little too informal for her very sober, serious book.

~O~

Are You Experienced?

We have recently been informed by the *Wine Spectator* in a tear-stained form-epistle that we are not being invited to participate in the 2001 New York Wine Experience, despite our attendance for the last twelve seasons. It seems that their selection policy has recently changed in the direction of a more rigorous reliance on numerical ratings, and our wines have in the last year failed to match the stratospheric, rarified altitude of some of our high-flying colleagues. Our Department of Sales Prevention and Anti-Marketing leaped immediately into action and generated the following missive, which, although proving to be futile in creating the desired result, provided a lot of mirth in its conception. I've tweaked it a little, but this delectable morsel of joy can be laid squarely at the feet of Mr. John Locke.

April 1, 2001

Dear *Marvin* ,

Friends, Tuscans, ladies and gentlemen of the Jory, lend me your ear; I come to praise Screaming Eagle, not to fricassee it.[279]

We were very recently informed that we would not be invited to participate in the 2001 *New York Wine Experience* , due to the rather modest numerical altitude attained by some of our *petites soucoupes,* cigarillos, if you will, in recent reviews in your august journal. While I am generally not in the habit of corresponding with industry periodicals such as *The Wine Spectator* , I feel perhaps that Bonny Doon has not done a brilliant job of late in communicating the relative merits of our humble institution and the ever-expanding legion of estimable products and syllables that constitute its output. Indulge me in a few well-turned phrases to rectify this sorry state of affairs.

For most of our tenure in this business, Bonny Doon and *The Wine Spectator* have enjoyed what we believe to be a mutually gratifying relationship. We have over the years sent you a dizzying array of wines to review and to assimilate; one could easily come to believe us to be incorrigible generalists and obscurantists. Further, you can hardly be taken to task for viewing the many Bonny Doon wines recently reviewed in your publication as representative of our total output. It must be said, however, that the recent "underachievers" constitute a rather diminutive, microtome-sized wedge of our offerings and, dare I say, of our achievement. Le Cigare Volant, Old Telegram, Muscat Vin de Glacière and some of our other starship offerings have acquitted themselves admirably by any metric for many years now, though of late

---

279. Though it does make for some mighty tasty eatin'.

they have not been evaluated with the same frequency in your venerable periodical as when our vinous portfolio could be counted on but one hominid's hands and feet. It is these products, this winemaker humbly submits, that should be judged to determine if our elegant dirigible should occupy the same lofty airspace as our altitudinally achieving avian confrères.

Bonny Doon has over the years produced wines widely viewed as paradigmatic examples of their type. In fact, we have pioneered many of the wine styles now hailed as necessary alternatives to the hegemonic domination of the prevailing Ch . . . well, you've heard that rant once or twice before now, haven't you? I must also confess that I have always enjoyed _New York_ in _October_.

I will resist the temptation to promise, cross-my-heart-and-hope-to-be-a-Bordelais, that we'll release a 97-point Le Cigare Volant next year (even though we most assuredly will). We have been working late at night in the laboratory to construct a new 50–115-point scale to accommodate its elegant sublimity.

Lastly, I should just come out and admit that we would very much like to attend the prestigious _New York Wine Experience_, and most humbly request that you reconsider your earlier decision and let us come out and play.

Most Sancerrely,

(2001)

The note, as was to be expected, was received by the *Wine Spec* with a certain stony silence. Being dismissed from the in-group summoned up memories of painful rejections experienced in elementary and junior high school; one never quite knew the reason for the sudden ouster from the state of okayness. In retrospect, we were faltering a bit. The most brilliant vintages of Cigare, 1997 and 1998, were unfortunately bottled with synthetic closures, and the wines did not age gracefully. And, as referenced in the letter, we were producing so many different wines, the case could be made that we were not keeping our eye on the ball. We still have not been invited back.[280]

Doon to Earth

In 2009, two years after the sale of the Big House and Cardinal Zin brands, there is still considerable confusion about what precisely has been sold and exactly who or what constitutes Bonny Doon in its current incarnation. Most disturbingly, it now appears to be karmic payback time after many years of pushing the envelope, marketing- and promotion-wise. The wines we are now producing are much better and more "serious"—if by that we mean as winegrow-

280. This is likely an apocalyptic omen, correlative to the Mayan calendar, but mirabile dictu, we were invited back for the 2008 Wine Experience.

ers we are more focused and attentive—but I fear my reputation as a jocular marketeer may forever doom (or doon) my chances of the world ever taking the wines themselves seriously.[281] Our distributor in New York somewhat facetiously suggested that I consider taking out an advertisement in the *Wine Spectator* to dispel the confusion within the industry about the company, with the ancillary benefit of improving diplomatic relations with the *Spectator*. I was nervous about taking out the ad for a number of reasons—it was quite dear for a winery our size, and the received wisdom suggested that if you were a small winery that advertised, what you seemed to be advertising was that you were in trouble.

The piece was revised numerous times. When I first wrote it, I attempted to channel the spirit of Robert Crumb (in the vague and unrealistic hope that I might persuade him to draw the strip). The early versions were perhaps a bit too raw, self-deprecating, and self-revelatory.[282] Maybe a little too self-consciously, I ended up toning it down more than I should have. I had tried to make the case that my company was really all about transparency, and it seemed that a little brutal honesty would likely be well appreciated. Or not.

Crumb was, not surprisingly, unavailable, but we were fortunate to find a wonderful cartoonist in Ed Piskor. Ed was infinitely patient with my unending requests for revisions, and in the end the strip, shown in the following spread, turned out great, with a lot of fine detail. The strip ran, and the *Wine Spectator* loved it. We turned it into a lovely poster, and many customers called us to obtain a copy. But it did not seem to drive sales a whit, one very important metric of how one's brand is valued. Maybe there is more karma to be worked out. Alternative explanation: people are now too absorbed in their own problems to pay much attention to almost anything that does not hit them squarely over the head.   *(FALL 2008)*

---

281. I expect that on my deathbed, as I gather my last breath, my protestation that "this time I'm serious" will be perfunctorily dismissed as a mere attention-getting device.   **282.** There was a great panel in an early version that had me sitting at a table in a restaurant, dishes piled high in front of me, gesturing to the server that I was stuffed to the gills. The caption read: "Lately, wherever I go, people are incredibly nice to me, but sometimes I feel they regard me as an interesting historical artifact, unaware that we're making the best wines we've ever made." The footnote to the panel read, in the best Crumbian confessional style, "I love getting free food at restaurants." Well, of course I do; everyone does. I now feel bad that I suppressed this panel; my friends, who were only trying to help, had advised me that, in such a public venue, I should try not to appear to be overly venal, nor convey my insecurities about how I am now perceived in the wine marketplace. And yet I feel that I have missed a great opportunity to connect with our customers by not sharing these vulnerabilities.

HI, I'M RANDALL GRAHM, OWNER AND WINEMAKER OF BONNY DOON VINEYARD IN SANTA CRUZ. YOU'VE PROBABLY TASTED OUR WINES OR HEARD OF US FROM SOME OF THE WACKY MARKETING INITIATIVES WE'VE DONE OVER THE YEARS.[1]

1. THE "DEATH OF THE CORK" FUNERAL PROCESSION AT GRAND CENTRAL STATION WAS PRETTY OUTRAGEOUS AND SOMEHOW I PERSUADED JANCIS TO DELIVER THE EULOGY FOR "THIERRY BOUCHON."

IT IS PRETTY IRONIC TO BE TELLING MY STORY IN THE WINE SPECTATOR.

"THEY HAVEN'T ALWAYS GROKKED OUR STYLE."

SPECTATOR POINT SCORES

THERE HAVE BEEN SOME EPIC CHANGES AT THE WINERY IN THE LAST TWO YEARS, AND A LOT OF PEOPLE ARE STILL CONFUSED ABOUT WHAT'S GOING ON.

BIG HOUSE

"WE SOLD OFF THE BIG HOUSE AND CARDINAL ZIN BRANDS TO THE WINE GROUP IN SEPTEMBER, 2006. IT WAS A BIG LOAD OFF MY SHOULDERS."

"WE'VE GREATLY TRIMMED OUR PRODUCT PORTFOLIO STILL OWN PACIFIC RIM. IT'S DOING GREAT, AND BEING RUN INDEPENDENTLY, UP UP IN WASHINGTON."

WHY DID I SELL THE BIG BRANDS AND CHANGE EVERYTHING AROUND? BONNY DOON HAD GROWN INTO A FAIRLY LARGE WINERY...

"WHILE IT WAS DEFINITELY A VERY CREATIVE TIME — I CERTAINLY LEARNED A LOT — AND HANGING OUT WITH THE LIKES OF RALPH STEADMAN WAS A GAS..."

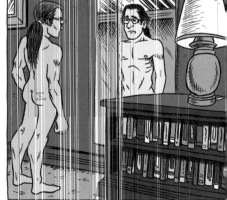

"I JUST HAD THE FEELING I WASN'T BEING TOTAL TRUE TO MYSELF AND REALLY EMBRACING THAT WHICH WAS TRULY IMPORTANT TO ME."

DRAWN BY ED PISKOR

"BONNY DOON HAS ALWAYS BEEN AN INNOVATOR AND ALWAYS PUSHED THE ENVELOPE. I THINK BACK ON ALL THAT WE HAVE AS A COMPANY ACCOMPLISHED..."

CRYOEXTRACTION

MICROOXYGENATION

YOU GIVE ME RIESLING TO LIVE!

LEE'S HOTELS

SCREWCAPS

"IT DOONED ON ME THAT WHAT I NEEDED TO DO NOW WAS HARNESS ALL OF THAT GREAT INNOVATIVE AND EXPERIMENTAL ZEAL THAT IS THE COMPANY'S FORTE... AND CHANNEL IT INTO A CLEAR, PRECISE DIRECTION..."

" DISTILLING ALL OF OUR PRIOR LEARNING AND EXPERIENCE TO ATTEMPT THE MOST AUDACIOUS NEW PROJECT OF ALL — THE DISCOVERY / CREATION OF TRUE VINS DE TERROIR, WINES EXPRESSIVE OF A SENSE OF PLACE."

"IT'S STILL VERY EARLY GOING, BUT WE ARE IN CONTRACT TO PURCHASE PROPERTY IN SAN JUAN BAUTISTA, NOT TOO FAR FROM SANTA CRUZ, WHERE WE HOPE TO ESTABLISH A HIGHLY ORIGINAL ESTATE PROPERTY — A PROPER, INTEGRATED BIODYNAMIC FARM."[2]

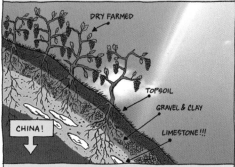

DRY FARMED

TOPSOIL

GRAVEL & CLAY

LIMESTONE!!!

CHINA!

2. MY BANKER AND G.M. WOULD BOTH KILL ME FOR SAYING THIS, BUT IN A CERTAIN SENSE, IT DOESN'T REALLY MATTER IF THE PROJECT "SUCCEEDS." THE SUCCESS IS TRULY IN THE EFFORT.

"BUT WHAT ABOUT NOW? THE WINERY IS MUCH SMALLER - JUST 35,000 CASES (AND SHRINKING). WE'RE MAKING FEWER KINDS OF WINE AND WE'RE HIGHLY FOCUSED. IT'S A LOT MORE REWARDING AND FEELS A LOT MORE REAL."

QUARTZ-IMPREGNATED, CEMENT-LINED TANKS

"THE WINES WE'RE MAKING NOW ARE VIBRANT, SOULFUL. THAT'S THE ONLY WAY I CAN DESCRIBE THEM. THE CIGARE VOLANT IN RECENT VINTAGES HAS BEEN AWESOME — CONCENTRATED AND ELEGANT, AND MOST SIGNIFICANTLY, AGE-WORTHY."[3]

3. PARTIALLY DUE TO BEING BOTTLED IN SCREWCAPS, BUT CERTAINLY DUE TO MUCH MORE RIGOROUS VINEYARD WORK AND MORE ATTENTION PAID TO DETAIL IN THE WINERY.

"WE'RE INTO SOME PRETTY COOL, ESOTERIC STUFF, AS WE FOCUS ON THE HOLISTIC HEALTH OF THE VINEYARD, TRY TO UNDERSTAND THE DEEPER ORGANIZATION OF THE WINE AND ENCOURAGE ITS FULLEST EXPRESSION IN OUR GROWING AND WINEMAKING PRACTICES.[4] OUR OWN CA' DEL SOLO ESTATE VINEYARD WAS RECENTLY DEMETER® CERTIFIED BIODYNAMIC®."

SENSITIVE CRYSTALLIZATION LABEL!

4. PRODUCING SOME INCREDIBLY MINERAL-INTENSIVE WINES.

"WE'RE PROUD THAT WE'RE ABLE TO MAKE WINES IN A MORE HANDS-OFF, NATURAL MANNER[5] — UTILIZING INDIGENOUS YEAST AND FEWER ADDITIONS. AND EVERYTHING THAT TOUCHES OUR WINE IS LISTED RIGHT ON THE LABEL."

CA' DEL SOLO

2007 Albariño

CA' DEL SOLO VINEYARD, MONTEREY COUNTY

INGREDIENTS: BIODYNAMIC® ALBARIÑO GRAPES (76%), OTHER BIODYNAMIC® WHITE GRAPES GRAPES (24%), SULFUR DIOXIDE
OTHER INGREDIENTS USED IN PROCESSING: INDIGENOUS YEAST, BENTONITE

PRODUCED & BOTTLED BY BONNY DOON VINEYARD
SANTA CRUZ, CA USA ~ CONTAINS 30 SITES
750ML ~ ALC. 12.5% BY VOLUME
www.bonnydoonvineyard.com

GOVERNMENT WARNING:
(1) ACCORDING TO THE SURGEON GENERAL, WOMEN SHOULD NOT DRINK ALCOHOLIC BEVERAGES DURING PREGNANCY BECAUSE OF THE RISKS OF BIRTH DEFECTS. (2) CONSUMPTION OF ALCOHOLIC BEVERAGES IMPAIRS YOUR ABILITY TO DRIVE A GOLF CART OR OPERATE SAILBOATS, AND MAY CAUSE HEALTH BENEFITS.

"BARE BONES, UNADORNED WINEMAKING"

SANS MAQUILLAGE (WITHOUT MAKEUP), AS THE FRENCH WOULD SAY.

"WE'RE WORKING TO GREATLY ENHANCE THE QUALITY OF OUR FRUIT - MORE RIGOROUS FRUIT SELECTION, LOWER YIELDS, AND TO PUT ALL OUR GROWERS ON THE PATH TO BIODYNAMIC® OR ORGANIC CERTIFICATION. WE HELP THEM IN THIS PROCESS, MAKING COMPOST FOR THEM OR SPRAYING THE BIODYNAMIC PREPS."

"OUR WORK IS A GREAT ADVENTURE — WHO KNOWS WHERE IT WILL LEAD? COME VISIT US AT: WWW.BONNYDOONVINEYARD.COM/DOONTOEARTH TO LEARN MORE ABOUT OUR DISTINCTIVE ESOTERIC WINE NETWORK WINE CLUB AND DISCOVER SOME LIMITED RELEASE WINES THAT ARE OUT OF THIS WORLD."

YEE HAW!

ESTABLISHED IN 1983

UNFILTERED

LE CIGARE VOLANT

Restored & Bottled by BONNY DOON VINEYARD Santa Cruz, USA

RED WINE OF THE EARTH

EARNEST SPEECHES AND SOBER ESSAYS

Sustainability

Good morning. I have been asked to say a few words to you today about sustainability in matters vinous, vitaceous, and otherwise. This is, of course, utterly ironic, as I am perhaps the least qualified person in the universe to talk about sustainability. If you are looking for an expert on burning the candle at both ends, on creating vinous ziggurats of architectonic wonder and complexity that teeter and wobble and are about to collapse from their own weight, then perhaps I'm your man. I should also mention that my subspecialty is thoroughly and terminally pissing off highly influential wine writers so they will write about my wines never, ever again. So the caveat must be issued: Do as I say, not as I do.

I am hardly a maven on sustainable viticulture. By all rights, my own vineyard in the Salinas Valley should not exist qua vineyard. It is a frankly miserable place for a vineyard: there is not enough rainfall to sustain grapes, and the soils do not have a particularly brilliant moisture-holding capacity for storing the little rain that does fall. The water with which we irrigate is slightly saline. There are about two and a half picoseconds per day when the grapes are actually photosynthesizing.

I will talk to you instead in the most general and also personal terms about sustainability as it relates to metawinemaking and grape-growing issues and leave the heavy lifting to the people who actually know what they are talking about.

When we talk about sustainability, there are various ways to look at it, but ultimately the question is ecological: Is the system in balance or is it unstable? In the agricultural example, are we engaging in farming practices that will require ever-increasing inputs to remain viable? Put another way: What are the hidden costs of agrichemical codependency? Is the land that we are farming growing more or less arable? In the little microcosmos that is our winery or vineyard or life, are we continuing to turn over fresh soil, nurturing our customers and ourselves ever more deeply, or are we simply plowing the same old hardpan? Is our farm or vineyard or winery advancing the way of life and the values—the virtues of stewardship and community and the therapeutic value of the work itself—that we esteem?

We certainly can't work out all these issues this morning. But if we can insinuate the notion of sustainability into our thick cranial armor so that it is always with us, sort of like a politically correct *I Dream of Jeannie* or a Socratic daemon, a conscience, an advisor, we will be very well served. Sustainability is simply about having the imagination to envisage the future, to understand that what we do has a consequence.

Sustainability in the business end of the wine business is the ability to create a product that the market continues to purchase. Since the market, by definition, grows continually more competitive, one must have a clear vision of whether one is continuing to evolve and improve the quality of one's product. (The other question is whether the ongoing work is continuing to feed and nourish the winegrower himself or herself.) Is one cultivating an arable field?

There is an essential difference between making wine in the New World and in the Old World which I'm sure has not eluded the vast majority of those here today. Essentially, we in the New World are making it up as we go along. We do not have the benefit of centuries of experience to inform us about the appropriate choice of grape varieties in a particular location, or about the optimal cultural practice to bring to these grapes. We follow our instincts, hoping to learn and to do our best to extrapolate from the successes and failures of our forebears.

In Europe, history and practice have instructed *vignerons* as to where they might grow grapes in generally noncatastrophic areas, and where they might actually ripen their grapes most years out of ten. Further, *vignerons* have learned on which particular sites a grower might expect to find small and distinctive variations that differentiate the wine made from that site from that made from an adjacent one. These small qualitative differences, which express the uniqueness of a site, the French call *terroir*. Whether or not he is explicitly conscious of the fact, the serious European vintner knows that the sustainability of his enterprise is inextricably linked to his ability to express the *terroir* of his site. He may be a simple farmer who has never taken a graduate course in marketing, and the term *brand differentiation* would not trip easily from his lips, either in French or in English, but he knows intuitively that ultimately his *terroir* is his brand. He knows or suspects that any potential great lover of wine will come around to seriously obsessing about Pinot and will, finances permitting, seek a greater and more subtle expression of this, the noblest red grape of them all. If you are sitting on real estate in Clos Vougeot or Chambertin, you have been given a very small franchise to create and sell a product that a nontrivial number of human beings simply cannot live without. The path to sustainability in the Old World is meditative, inward. An Old World grower can think of his vineyard the way a sculptor considers a piece of marble—and can attempt to find the essence that inheres; for an artist or *vigneron*, one's work is that of discovery or maybe excavation. One is looking for that which is already contained within; the vineyard itself becomes a sort of mantra or prayer wheel and successive vintages are our reincarnations.

One way I conceive of the difference between Old World and New World grape growers and winemakers is by analogy to the New and Old Testaments. In the Old World, they have been given the Good News: they know they are already saved. They must simply follow the guidelines set out by the Appellation d'Origine Contrôlée (though their mileage may vary). We New Worlders, on the other hand, are like the ancient Hebrews wandering the desert, hoping for a sign, a burning bush, a 90-plus-point review indicating that we are perhaps on the track of vinaceous righteousness.

When I taste my own wines and compare them to their Old World counterparts, I become slightly nauseous. My wines strike me as simple, puerile. Yes, they have tons of fruit and soft tannins and they're easy to like, but they are puppy-dog wines. I ask myself every day, "When will the world wise up, figure out that my wines and I are a total sham and take their business elsewhere?" I don't know that I will be able to discover *terroir* in this lifetime. What I do know is that, if I want to continue what I am doing, I must learn to create far more complexity and flavor interest in my wines. I must also create more depth and subtlety in my practice as a winemaker.

I recently read the most wonderful book, which I recommend to all of you, *The Heart Aroused,* by David Whyte. In it he talks about what we can do to nourish our souls while operating in the challenging, read soul-deadening, corporate arena. Among the many things he touches on is learning how to maintain a proper balance between innocence and experience; to nourish the soul, one must cultivate both. It appears that we learn to improve at what we do as we continue to acquire experience. As winemakers we experiment with such things as wild yeasts and *bâtonnage* and the techniques we learn from our winemaking colleagues and from our travels and studies. But experience alone is not enough to sustain us, to render our efforts sustainable.

We can manage the outward trappings of mastery, the exoteric signifiers of competency and skill—but anyone can make wine by the numbers, can buy Taransaud barrels, plant the sexy clones du jour, and thin rigorously to three tons per acre, or forty-five hectos per hectare, if you are of the Continental persuasion. What is required above and beyond experience is, in fact, the cultivation of inspired innocence, the wellspring of our creativity. Its hallmarks are the qualities of openness, curiosity, passion, and imagination. These qualities might enable us some day to make a thoroughly unusual, strange, necessary, and compelling wine. This wine will be so particular and resonant that it will take us years to figure out exactly what it is we've done.

As it turns out, our alleged curse—our lack of tradition and lore—is in fact our saving grace. We are so incredibly fortunate to be relatively unencumbered by rules, regulations, and the onerous weight of history. Our customers themselves are generally open, amazingly open, to the new and startling experiences we can provide them. For our enterprise to be sustainable, we ourselves must be sustained. Our work must be linked to our souls, and when it is not, we are just making wine by the numbers—and this is doomed to failure. The work of the winegrower can be metaphorically so rich. Seeking to craft complexity in our wines can be a way of touching our own inner depths of complexity. We must allow ourselves to find an opening, a communicating passage to our own creative daemon, the one that counsels us to plant, say, Albariño on the north-facing slope where we can't ripen our Pinot noir.

What we are doing in the New World is audacious, outrageous, without precedent. If we truly comprehended how utterly impossible it is to do what we seem to be doing, we would become fatally paralyzed. As Blake put it—and this was communicated to me directly by none other than the sagacious and semimythical Norman O. Brown himself when I was a thoroughly confused sophomore at UC Santa Cruz—"If the sun or moon should doubt, they'd immediately go out."[283]   *(MAY 2001)*

283. This speech was delivered at the International Pinot Noir Celebration, McMinnville, Oregon.

Delivering this speech was a sweet moment for me. I hadn't been back to the Pinot Noir Celebration since its inception twenty years earlier, when it was still a home-grown, small-time event. As you can see, I am continuing to gnaw at the Beaune of the oeno-existential dilemma: How does one create real meaning out of essentially nothingness? Is it enough for a wine to simply provide naïve pleasure, or must it make an eloquent "statement"? At the time of the speech, I was feeling slightly less confident than I am now about mustering the will to pursue *terroir* in the New World despite the enormous difficulty of the proposition. I don't now believe the path is any easier or *terroir* any more findable, but feel that its pursuit is the only course that makes any sense.[284]

I was struck by the irony that I, not a Pinot Noir producer, was chosen to speak to this august group of Pinot producers and Pinotphiles. There is a kind of ontological abyss that separates those who talk from those who do, and I was certainly on the lee side of this vast chasm. My younger self might have wished to share with them his formulations about how one *might* produce a great Pinot Noir on the Left Coast but mercifully I spared these good folks. I was, at least for a moment, with my people, my tribe, albeit standing on the sidelines. As cordial as that reflective moment was, there was (and remains) no question that ultimately I must soon get back in the game.[285]

Bungle in the Jungle

How Does a Wine "Mean"? *or* A Season in Wine Hell

How does a wine or wine package communicate subtle and hidden cultural messages? Where do great wine successes come from? What do our wines and wine packaging tell the world about who we are? We will look at how a wine's packaging both hides and reveals what lies beneath. Since in *vino* there is theoretically a good measure of *veritas,* let's then throw off the veils.

I am afraid that most of the news I bring you today is not particularly inspiring; it is, in fact, downright depressing, and I have subtitled this speech "A Season in Wine Hell" for reasons that will soon be apparent. I must also at the outset personally apologize for the historical overemphasis in my own wines, on form over content, style over substance, wine "buzz" over the inherent quality of the wine itself. I am deeply chagrined about my own role in the current proliferation of terminally cute wine labels, a phenomenon that has in recent years morphed into the ubiquity of what are called "critter wines"—furry or naughty creatures who signify God only knows what; perhaps it is the disinhibitory power of wine that reunites us

284. Perhaps I have become the viticultural Samuel Beckett: "I can't make wine, I'll make wine." 285. Emphatically not the game of who can produce the sexiest, most acclaimed Pinot Noir, but rather the game that one plays alone, seeking to find a way of authentically being present with one's land in the discovery of the expression of its *terroir.*

with primal, totemic spirits. Despite my sincere personal remorse and contrition, I am certain that I am doomed, or dooned, to Wine Hell.

The good news, I suppose, is that certain individuals have become extraordinarily adept at introducing new wines and growing these brands at impressive, even exponential, rates. The bad news is that in general the success of these winelike beverages has had little to do with the inherent quality and uniqueness of the products themselves, and more to do with the ability of certain producers to deliver their product at a compelling price point, which, to be fair, is in itself a nontrivial accomplishment. The formula for success seems to be to present a package that is visually arresting, catchy, or edgy, a wine with an "attitude," and then to orchestrate a highly aggressive sales and marketing campaign, primarily through significant financial "incentivization" of all of the relevant players of the three-tier system.

The reality is, what we might speak of as "innovation" in the sales and marketing end of the wine business is really more a function of (a) marketers becoming efficient at plugging into the limbic systems of their customers through both taste profiling and package presentation, and (b) the application of formidable sales muscle to both extra-large wine distributors and super-sized retail chains—two sides of the same coin. The advent of these new species is essentially a byproduct of the recent extensive consolidation within the distribution channels. This phenomenon of course is not limited to the wine business and is certainly not limited to the United States—there are analogs in virtually every retail business sector around the world.

But this new ecology, or rather the debasement of the older, perhaps healthier ecology—one that supported greater diversity of range in the scale of the players: small, medium, and relatively benign large ones—allows now for the phenomenon of megabrands, wines that have seemingly come out of nowhere (which indeed they have, in the sense that they have no connection to anything resembling a characteristic appellation of origin) and are suddenly ubiquitous. The wines succeed not because they are technically superior but because they are friendly enough, downright "likeable" in fact, and, more significantly, there is an unholy amount of money being spent throughout the distribution system to insure their ubiquity.

I am speaking to you from the front line of the marketing wars, and I tell you it is not pretty. Real wines, that is to say, wines that convey a sense of place, a genuine originality, are still greatly esteemed, perhaps are even all the more diligently sought after, as a result of the sea of banal uniformity and standardization that surrounds them. Perhaps by definition these handmade, artisanal wines must of necessity remain limited in production. A vast ontological chasm lies between the meanings of an artisanal wine—its unique *terroir,* for example—and those of a larger brand that attempts to establish its credibility on essentially the fact that it sells well.

It is interesting that the outrageous success of branded wines may have inhibited the marketing of real *terroir* wines, many of which seem to be frozen in the headlights with respect to the creative expression of their individuality. Most producers of "real" wines prefer to let their wines speak for themselves, and tend to fall back on the earlier signifiers of quality, particularly on appellation of origin. But in the anything-goes, postmodern universe, appellations of origin have been largely drained of meaning. The "meaning" of a wine is now generally assumed to be its ability to command such and such a price, and this correlates positively with another set of signifiers, all too widely observed, which we needn't dwell on here. But it should be said that the presence of a 90-plus-point score in association with a particular wine might be by far the most powerful symbolic association that a wine might carry, at least in the short term.[286]

In the United States there is a cultural predisposition—one that will soon show up elsewhere, if it hasn't already—to reduce one's message to the very lowest common denominator. This is evident in sound-bite political messaging and in the superficiality of television network news broadcasts. For the moment, bright, shiny surfaces and the communication of one simple idea appear to be all that is required to link with the consciousness of the modern consumer, and this is nowhere more evident than in the packaging and presentation of wine. It might be useful to deconstruct some of the most successful wine brands in an effort to understand how they communicate so well to the changing market.

Yellow Tail is a recent "pheenom," having the most rapid sales growth of any wine ever observed in U.S. history. Starting with essentially no base, no history, no connection to a narrowly defined geographical locale—except of course the iconic Australian continent and its own icon, the kangaroo—the wine is now selling slightly fewer than a million cases per month in the United States, scarcely five years since its introduction. No doubt the success of the brand is largely predicated on its highly attractive price point, approximately six dollars on retail shelves, and on its delivery of a lot of "presence" in the mouth—soft tannins for the red wines and a dollop of residual sugar. But its real punch is its unabashed Australian-ness, which in the American fantasy is the antidote to Frenchness.[287] Everything about the French seems to roil the unsophisticated American wine drinker (who seems to suffer from a wood chip on his shoulder)—everything from their uncooperative foreign policy to their uncooperative tannins and challenging nomenclature. The French and their wines are so "old Europe"— feckless, spineless, not at all straightforward—they always exhibit some degree of ambiguity. And those final letter bits at the ends of words—sometimes you pronounce them, sometimes not. Are they not specifically designed to make Americans look foolish?

286. There is a belief among many, myself included, that he who lives by scores, dies by scores. There are many instances of wines that have meteorically arrived on the scene (seemingly from nowhere) with blisteringly high point scores and, to continue the astronomical metaphor, seemingly dropped forever from view and consideration when those scores faded to the cool and solemn darkness of the night sky.   287. More than thirty years ago, Randy Newman wrote a prescient song about American foreign policy titled "Political Science (Let's Drop the Big One)." After nuking virtually all the uncomprehending nations of the world ("Boom goes London, boom Paree, more room for you, more room for me"), the narrator sings, "We'll save Australia. Don't want to hurt no kangaroo. We'll build an All-American amusement park there. They got surfing, too." Australia is the American fantasy of an earlier, carefree, and less complicated Eisenhower-era America which America tragically yearns to return to.

While I am sure that wine marketing scholars will debate the etiology of the phenomenon of "critter wines," it seems all but certain to me that they originated with the appearance of the iconic Australian Paul Hogan, aka Crocodile Dundee. Rassling alligators must be only slightly more challenging than dealing with the hard tannins one encounters in Old World wines; throwing a bit of shrimp on the barbie and sipping a soft, buttery Chard must sound a lot more congenial to the xeno-oenophobic American than attempting to navigate the complexity of a challenging wine list with unpronounceable foreign names and a supercilious sommelier.[288] Someone worked out that Americans have never been very good at remembering geographical names, and that the mnemonic of a cute critter with a bold, iconic visual—the archetypal "primitive" or aboriginal art serves very well in this regard—is absolutely irresistible. This formula has lately been refined to include a comical, echolalic name, making the product even more unforgettable. There is a wine called Wrongo Dongo, a Mourvèdre or, more accurately, a Monastrell, produced in Jumilla, Spain—a very nice wine but successful in large part due to its brilliant presentation. The appellation of the wine, the grape variety, the style, are all utterly obscured; there is only the iconic brand.

Needless to say, if one can find for one's obscure grape variety an officially recognized synonym that carries more positive associations, it will present an interesting stratagem for overcoming consumer ignorance or resistance. There are some folks now seeking to market "Zinfandel" from Puglia, theoretically a name more congenial than "Primitivo." Conversely, certain Californians seek to market their Zinfandel as Primitivo, presumably on the theory that the road to commercial success must be composed of some admixture of the familiar and the strikingly new. American producers of Syrah have lately taken to calling their wine "Shiraz," on the assumption that the name is far "friendlier" and carries less political baggage. A consumer can expect a wine that is fruity and has soft tannins rather than a wine that, God forbid, might actually taste of the earth.

Certainly Yellow Tail would never have been the great success it is without the advent of the "floor stack," an American innovation that has gained prominence in the last ten years with the arrival of discount, warehouselike wine stores and the growing importance of big-box chain stores such as Costco, Target, and Wal-Mart. The intense and iconic yellow ochre field of the Yellow Tail label on boxes, visible from as far as a hundred meters away, set out in floor stacks, was a marriage made in heaven.

Yellow and orange are hot colors; they provoke a call to action. They connote brashness, spontaneity, lightheartedness, and the breaking of stuffy convention. One should have "no worries, mate" about mispronouncing the name of the wine, and in fact one needn't even remember the name of the wine, merely the color of the label, a color that attracts human beings as reliably as it does the genus *Hymenoptera*. The mildly risqué associations with the name Yellow

288. Xeno-oenophobia is the fear of strange, unfamiliar wines.

Tail connote disinhibition; at the very least, one knows that one will not be required to make august pronouncements on the wine's organoleptic profile.

The brilliant Yellow Tail package owes a tremendous intellectual debt to the truly innovative packaging and marketing of Veuve Clicquot, designed more than thirty years ago. Clicquot was clever enough to use the iconic color orange in all of its packaging and communication. It connoted just the right degree of brashness—the brightly colored silk lining of the otherwise sober formal dress jacket—in the oh so serious wine world of a generation ago. I have myself observed that, among wine sales and marketing people, real drinkers of marketing Kool Aid, as it were, Clicquot still retains a certain mystical allure, which is a testament to the enormous power of its brand.

Another wine company that has used highly creative imagery in its communication and vaulted directly to the top of the heap is Ravenswood Winery of Sonoma, which was sold just a few years ago for something on the order of $150 million and has continued to grow in value; it currently produces approximately a million cases annually. Whether by accident or by design, the winery essentially did everything right in order to thrive in our current highly competitive business environment. Early on, it established itself as one of the leaders of a rapidly growing category, high-priced Zinfandel, and produced a limited number of cases of various vineyard-designated wines, along with its substantial production of a more generic Zin.

The whole notion of "product category" seems to be an innovation of the American wholesale wine system, but I think it in fact corresponds vaguely to something we all do, which is to create our own mental map or taxonomy, ordering the known universe into discrete categories. In a happy coincidence for those who are included, the leading Zinfandel producers in the United States *all seem to have names that begin with R*—Ridge, Ravenswood, Renwood, Rosenblum, and Rochioli. It is stupid that this sort of thing would matter, but the New World wine enthusiast is a fetishist, insisting on order and predictability, sort of like a small child who insists on repeating the same game over and over again. There is no question that the singular advantage that the New World enjoys is its incredibly consistent climate and, therefore, predictability. No great vintage variations, no nasty (or extraordinarily pleasant, for that matter) surprises.

Now, Zinfandel is truly the all-American grape, a highly successful immigrant that has been here so long it could have come over on the *Mayflower.* It reflects the American personality and many aspects of modern American culture: it's oversized, loud, blustery, lacking finesse, intent on "making a statement," and therefore impressive in its own way. It is the SUV of grapes, the wine for wine enthusiasts—not connoisseurs, but enthusiasts.

Zinfandel drinkers are a visceral lot—they are feeling types, endomorphs, rather than thinking types. Their wine-drinking pleasure does not derive from the intellectual apprehension of the subtleties of *terroir,* from the delicate play of changing flavor tonalities and the revelation of subtle nuances. They are satyric orgiasts. They want to experience the power, the weight, and most significantly, the alcohol; they need to feel the burn.[289] Zin aficionados gather at a mammoth tasting event held every year in San Francisco, mounted by an organization called ZAP (Zinfandel Advocates and Producers). The ZAP tasting perfectly embodies the state of the wine industry. It is loud, incredibly loud, and many of the producers have unfamiliar labels; most significant, you simply cannot believe that so many people have come out to taste Zin. Virtually all the wines begin at 14 percent alcohol and go up, way up, from there. Joel Peterson, the founder of Ravenswood, is the patron saint of this tasting, this bacchanal; people come here to commune, to feel the power.

The label—it is extraordinary. Designed by David Lance Goines, there is a mythic, almost archetypal power to it. The label hypnotizes and draws the viewer toward it. The symbol, ravens in a tree, is in fact a mandala, or perhaps a swastika. I don't know if they still do this, but at one point Ravenswood handed out stick-on tattoos of their logo when they observed that a significant number of their customers had already tattooed the Ravenswood logo on themselves. Talk about brand loyalty . . . The design is certainly about power and darkness; one enters into a sort of enchantment, like Hansel and Gretel wandering into a dark wood. Joel, who is an exceptionally nice man and one lacking in pretension, has become a wonderful blank canvas onto which consumers can project any character they wish. Wild man? Satyr? Mr. Natural?

Ravenswood came up with the most brilliant bit of marketing ever conceived: "No Wimpy Wines!" The bumper sticker, formerly observed just about everywhere in Northern California, is also available in Spanish (*"No vinos sin huevos"*) and other languages. I cannot begin to express how brilliant this is. It is a credo that enables one's clientele to clearly define themselves: "I'm a guy who is no wimp." I'm not wimpy, and my wines aren't wimpy either. It reduces judgments of wine quality to very simple criteria. The aspiration to nonwimpiness in one's wines is definitely within reach of any winemaker who begins with reasonably ripe grapes that are not overcropped and vigorously punches his wines down many times a day in a thoroughly manly fashion. It goes without saying that a Ravenswood drinker would rather drink poison than "white Zinfandel."

Umberto Eco, the Italian semiologist and novelist, visited the United States in the 1980s in an attempt to understand the American psyche, and for him the most revealing notion was the "bottomless cup of coffee." In Europe, as we know, you order a coffee, and if you want a second one, you order another. But in restaurants in the States, at least in the pre-Starbucks days, you order coffee and the server keeps returning to fill it up, presumably until you float away. Eco also observed the portions of food served at American restaurants, and their gigantinormity defied belief. He concluded that if customers did not receive far more than they could possibly eat, they did not feel they had received quite enough.

289. I have attended more than one tasting where a consumer has come up and asked me if I had any wine that would really "kick his ass." "Does your ass need to be kicked?" was the only response I had the wit to muster.

There is no question that this mentality permeates Americans' view of "wine quality." The United States is an immature wine culture, and Americans continue to equate quality with quantity, whether it be the degree of ripeness, oakiness, optical opacity, or tannin, or just generalized "concentration," and this error is perpetuated by our most influential wine critics. Robert Parker did not create the prevailing aesthetic of the "international style," the soft, ripe, concentrated fruit bomb that can come from just about anywhere. He is, rather, a man of the zeitgeist, really very much the egalitarian. I believe he does not, alas, have overmuch interest in wine's historical, cultural, or aesthetic context; he simply wants it to please him, and for that it must push the limits of what is in fact pleasurable.[290] To this extent, he is a man of our time and our culture.

Yes, size does appear to matter, at least in the minds of wine marketers. In wine marketing, the preoccupation with size takes many shapes, from the Phelps Insignia bottle that weighs just a ton to the nomenclature on a bottle. There is an incredibly successful wine called Rex Goliath, whose "hook" is the fact that it features a forty-seven-pound rooster on the label. Americans are obsessed with objects that are large enough that they are not strictly useful—from our oversized cars to our enormous kitchens. Obesity is epidemic, as we know, and it has spread to our wines. At Bonny Doon, we ourselves somewhat inadvertently hit upon Big House Red,[291] a spoof on old gangster-movie slang for "prison" (our estate vineyard is just a leg-iron's throw from the California Correctional Training Facility), as well as a pun on the fact that it is a "big" house wine. (The label also just happens to have been designed by Chuck House.) Big House appears to have spawned a raft of sincere flatterers: large beasts (Big Moose Red and Three Blind Moose), larger and smaller conveyances (Red Truck, Red Bicyclette), and out-and-out appropriators (Big Red House).

Perhaps it would be useful to revisit the concept of critter wines and try to understand what might be the source of their extraordinary success. Wine writers have said that the rash of animal labels was spawned by the success of Yellow Tail, and that the aim of this genre is to target both women shoppers in supermarkets and younger wine consumers, who are believed to be put off by the seemingly impenetrable language and putatively snooty packaging of classically branded wine labels. Critter brands are said to be fun, unthreatening, and accessible, but this explanation begs the question of their true meaning. I am struck by the fact that on these labels one seldom observes the critter in anything like a natural habitat. It is usually a (mad) fish out of water, in an anomalous context, thrust into human society or at least into human commerce, perhaps against its will, like a dancing bear. It is a freakish anomaly like Rex, or sort of a naughty critter, behaving badly but in a faintly endearing way, like the loveable pet who chews up one's best shoes or pees on the carpet.

290. It is not coincidental that one of the most glowing descriptors Mr. Parker will award a wine is "decadent."
291. A brand that Bonny Doon no longer owns. I, for one, not least as a result of the daunting level of competition in that marketing space, am immensely glad to be thoroughly quit of the "cute" label sector.

About thirty years ago, John Cudahy published an interesting and controversial book called *The Ordeal of Civility*. It dealt with the experience of nineteenth-century Jews from the ghettos of eastern Europe who were essentially attempting to transition from a sort of medieval existence to modern secular life in western Europe. How painful and angst-ridden this transition was for them as they tried to learn "appropriate" behavior, unable to express themselves as they had once done. The host Gentile population was indignant about the rude Jews who talked too loudly, didn't dress right, and didn't mind their manners. It is the author's contention, however, that, out of this cultural clash and, in some sense, rage, emerged the possibility of a fresh, trenchant, outsider's perspective, and out of this psychic conflict emerged such key figures as Freud, Marx, and Lévi-Strauss, turning the whole culture on its head.

The hidden meaning of the critter wines, especially the naughty ones, is that Americans, believe it or not, greatly resent having to learn the rules of appropriate behavior—whether it is mastering vintage charts, pronouncing foreign words correctly, or remembering which are the *grands crus* and which are the village wines. Like Tom Sawyer, they are generally not interesting in becoming "sivilized" *[sic]*, and now that they are off leash, they are reveling in their inherent wildness. The dancing bear of Toasted Head and the Wrongo Dongo are both creatures that would fit in if they could, but they know they can't, so they will just have to be naughty. It is said that our pets become like us, and we become our pets. I suggest that some of us in the wine business have become our wine labels.

I must offer at least a few positive observations on creativity in packaging that successfully differentiates a particular product from its competitors. Didier Dagueneau, for example, has done a wonderful job in communicating the quality of minerality in his wines in the label illustration for his wine Silex. The label is a beautiful and accessible representation of *terroir;* the only thing potentially intimidating about this wine is the price tag. Anne-Claude Leflaive has reproduced a "sensitive crystallization" of her wine on the back label. Sensitive crystallization is a biodynamic methodology that has created a way of visualizing the degree of "organization" a wine might possess, among other elements. Granted, there are only four people in the world who can actually interpret these pictures meaningfully, but it is still a highly pertinent detail that Leflaive provides, and it is, at least theoretically, a means of representing how her wine differs substantially from those of others.

In conclusion, the old signifiers of appellation and historical tradition are now largely drained of their meanings, except among the most knowledgeable segment of wine drinkers, which remains quite small. What is of primary importance is the power of the brand, and this power is generally understood to mean the ability of a wine to "pull"—that is, to more or less sell itself without heroic efforts on the part of the resellers. For a number of reasons—including the impossibly large number of wines currently brought to market, coupled with the fact that our own lives have become impossibly busy—we now depend far more on other people to tell us what we should be consuming. We tend to purchase benignly familiar products because they are seemingly everywhere. The thin veneer of collegiality within the industry that once existed has eroded in these modern, corporately competitive times. In virtually every aspect of the wine business, it has truly become a jungle out there.[292]   *(2006)*

Someone suggested to the mucky-mucks at the OIV that I was clever with marketing, so they asked me to attend their international congress and deliver a speech on the subject of "communication, image, and innovation of viti-vinicultural products" with the aim of developing markets. Frankly, I had no idea what they were talking about, so I decided to interpret this assignment very loosely and talk about what was interesting to me—how does a wine or wine package communicate subtle and hidden cultural messages? I was a philosophy student manqué—never had much rigor in my analytical reasoning, if you haven't noticed—but I still have great fun reading semiologists like Roland Barthes and Umberto Eco, who see covert signs in all our communication. Since theoretically there is an impermeable layer between the inside and outside of a wine package, the consumer of a bottle of wine must limit all his or her sniffing to the scents that arise from the outward presentation of the bottle; this is one reason why packaging is absolutely crucial to the success of a wine brand.

When I delivered this speech, it was not long after the events of 9/11 and the mercifully brief appearance of the term *freedom fries* in our lexicon, a phenomenon that set me to thinking about the great cultural divide between the United States and essentially everywhere else: our aversion to subtlety, nuance, and ambiguity was applicable both to foreign policy and to foreign (or foreign-sounding) wines.[293] I know that my speech, with its reliance on idiom, was exceptionally challenging to the simultaneous interpreters, but I think its delivery was a success. One gentleman approached me after the speech and told me he had never heard anything like this at an OIV conference before. (One might interpret that in several ways.) Another thanked me profusely for his new insight into the American wine-buying psyche. ("I've been in the business for thirty years and up until now could never figure out what Americans wanted.")

As with one's family of origin, one has an innate desire to wish one's country of origin to be smarter, more sophisticated, better behaved in public, and so on. America is still at base not a wine-appreciating country, or at least it tends to appreciate perhaps the least interesting but most obvious virtues a wine might possess—texture and strength—a point that comes up regularly in this volume. And significantly, Americans, like children about to go nighty-night, desperately want to hear a story.

292. Speech delivered to the Organisation Internationale de la Vigne et du Vin (OIV) Congress at Logroño, Spain.   293. Ditto the (mis)understanding that all power need derive from the barrel of a gun, or from the barrel made from oak.

How I Overcame My UC Davis Education

When I was a student at UC Davis, I was a holy terror—or actually a holy *terroir,* come to think about it. I had a million questions, most of them about Pinot noir—what about clonal diversity, what about close spacing, what about skin-juice ratios? And about those limestone soils—why do 50 million French people think limestone is important?[294] Most of my professors, the sainted Dr. Webb notably excepted, were less than keen to answer my barrage of questions. They would get a worried look when they saw me coming down the hall and tended to duck into the nearest janitorial closet.

As a would-be viticultural Francophile, I assumed the role of the defender of the French paradigm—to the extent that I understood this paradigm—which, in retrospect, seems like a bit of a stretch. I had this perverse desire to torture my professors. After class, I would sometimes assemble a very small cadre of tolerant listeners and try to systematically rebut all the points the professor had made in the lecture. I do wince to remember the incredible arrogance I displayed, but I was just a kid, and a rather snotty one at that.

As I said, every single waking moment of every day, and actually many of my dreaming moments, were spent in reverie about Pinot noir. Pinot noir was my mantra, my obsession, my idée fixe. I ended up in the Bonny Doon area of the Santa Cruz Mountains trying to grow the Great American Pinot Noir. I bought some Pinot grapes from Oregon in 1983—this was back when people weren't too sure about Oregon—schlepped them back to Santa Cruz, and found the grapes to be infinitely more interesting than the ones I was growing in Santa Cruz. Bummer. But it did lead me to discover the wonderful grapes of the Rhône, and the Rhône has been berry, berry good to me.

There is an important lesson to be learned here. We New World grape-growing human beings have the illusion that we can control things—we'll simply grow some great grapes, out of sheer will, that's what we'll do. I was incredibly naive. One can be a cowboy, buy a huge parcel of land, and move heaven, but more typically, earth, to plant a great vineyard of the grape variety du jour, but often the smallest amount of patience and observation will yield an infinitely more satisfying result (read: save you millions of dollars). I cannot say it any more simply: "Look before you leap." This may sound odd coming from someone who is sometimes portrayed as a viticultural wild man, the Dr. Gonzo of grapes, one who will try absolutely anything at least once. My suggestions to anyone who will listen to me: Look around. Do some research. Think, meditate, and pray for inspiration. But also call the National Germplasm

---

294. I attempt to at least partially answer this question in "In Search of a Great Growth in the New World," coming right up.

Repository, as well as some of the smaller, more adventurous nurseries and growers, and see if they happen to have some Teroldego or Nero d'Avola or anything else you imagine might flourish on your site. Go through the process of finding some interesting grapes in Europe and figure out how to bring them in, observing the salient regulatory guidelines for importation. Field-bud a couple of vines each of as many different varieties or clones as you can manage, and see how they perform on your site. (Is the acid and pH where you want it, at the appropriate Brix and level of phenological maturity? Do the grapes ripen more or less when you want them to? Do you imagine they could be dry-farmed?) Try a few things—maybe some unusual companion plantings or some unorthodox spacing or trellising regimes. *Then* leap. Look at what your neighbors are doing, and if you want your wines to taste a lot like theirs, follow what they do. If you want them to taste totally different, you will have to engage in a lot of deep thought, meditation, and prayer.

You really do need to open your eyes—to see really where you are on this planet. My great critique of California winemakers and grape growers is that they are willfully naive. They don't truly care to know where they stand in the scheme of things. Some of this naïveté expressed itself as arrogance on the part of some of the Davis faculty years back—the very Old School— when I was a student there. But this attitude also permeated the entire industry—it was almost like a religious fundamentalist's self-satisfaction. We are saved and, regrettably, everyone else is going straight to hell. Here's rude revelation #1: California wines are as good as they are largely as a result of nothing in particular that we are doing. Rather, their "quality" (which in large part is their consistency) is generally a function of the absolutely outstanding weather we enjoy—weather that Europeans would kill or maim for.[295] We have largely, as an industry, grown lazy and complacent; we do not feel any particular impetus to improve or change. I could cite the pitiful amount of money invested in grape and wine research in California— something on the order of one-fifth the amount that Australia invests (and our industry is twice its size). Certainly, no one feels this more acutely than the faculty here at Davis. Why should winegrowers want to change when some of us are, or at least were, selling our wines for sixty or seventy dollars a bottle?

The Greeks have a word for this. *Hubris.* In Yiddish, it is *chutzpah.* California wines sell well in the States for a number of reasons that we can discuss, but they are not particularly competitive on the world market and are becoming less so. Moreover, there are vast vineyard holdings in southern France, southern Italy, Spain, Portugal, and of course Chile and Argentina, all of which have the potential to make absolutely stellar wine on the serious cheap.

So, here's the deal. To succeed, we have to understand where we are and who we are. What are our strengths, and what can we do best? And ultimately, we must try to find some core of

---

295. Climatically speaking, we were born on third base, but many New World winegrowers still persist in the belief that they have hit a triple.

originality, something that sets our work apart. In France, there is the Appellation d'Origine Contrôlée system, which I am wont to ridicule because I generally despise all rules and regimentation. Despite the fact that the appellation system is a bit corrupt and has historically been sensitive to political influence in no small degree, its continued existence remains a valiant attempt to recognize and organize differences that are site specific and, therefore, infinitely precious and more or less immutable—though with the prospect of global warming, perhaps all bets are off. The notion that the wines of the appellation Morey-Saint-Denis in Burgundy, for example, will eternally possess characteristics that set it apart from an adjoining appellation should, in principle, insure their survival because, as human beings, we crave difference. What a French *vigneron* strives for is typicity—to make a wine that transparently is what it is. You should all meditate on this notion.

And where does typicity come from? To thine own *terroir* be true. There is no such thing as typicity without *terroir,* a wine's unique set of taste attributes associated with the physical attributes of a site. For me, a wine that expresses its *terroir* is perhaps the most satisfying wine that one can experience, and a wine that will have true sustainability. But I know this is a minority opinion. New World palates are not tuned in to *terroir*—we want lots of jammy fruit, lashings of fruit, high alcohol, and tons of wood. I don't know how much longer Americans will insist on wines like these. These wines fool our senses in a certain way, in the same way that our primate physiology responds to the sugar and fat in doughnuts and McDonald's burgers. I don't imagine that the craze for these wines—especially the very expensive ones—will last. They are vacuous, bimbo wines, perhaps satisfying to go out with once but murder if one attempts a serious conversation.

My idea is that we should go with our strength—our extraordinary, long, and benign growing season. Often we can grow grapes in areas significantly cooler than where they are traditionally found in the Old World, potentially enabling us to develop wonderful finesse, even if the soil type is not absolutely optimal. Further, we are gifted with the fact that we do not have a tradition that either enlightens or enslaves us. And more important, we have the perspective to learn from a diverse array of traditions and sources. We are utterly free to experiment with a wide range of grapes—not entirely wide enough in my humble estimation—where and how we see fit. This is an amazing gift. And this is why it is so exasperating that, despite all this freedom, so many people are marching lemminglike down the same path. We have the freedom to create our own unique styles—what would Tannat and Dolcetto taste like blended together?

Having said all of that, here are a number of things I wish somebody had taught me when I was at Davis:

1. Wine is not infinitely manipulable. You can add only so much acid, so much bentonite, tannin, Ultra Red, Mega Purple, can take the wine for a spin on the spinning cone or subject it to hypothermia, before the sum of the wine's parts adds up to zero. It's like the old

vaudeville joke, "Doctor I broke my leg in three places. What should I do?" The answer is: Stay out of those places. If you are working with grapes that compel you to make whole-sale manipulations, maybe you should stay out of those places.

2. Filtration often tragically compromises wine, especially if not done carefully. The various particulate bits undoubtedly act as antioxidants, helping to preserve the wine's life force. Take the time to make sure your wine is very filterable before filtering it, since otherwise it can be a traumatic experience for the wine. If you have a raging *Brett* infection in your wine, a careful cross-flow filtration may be a rational thing to do. But make sure there is some life force in your wine—more on this in a moment—because this may allow your wine to survive filtration.

3. Merlot actually does pretty much suck—and it is not particularly "soft."

4. The presence of perfect "numbers" is no assurance that the wine will be any good. Ultimately, people drink wine and not numbers. *Brix* will only tell you how much alcohol you might expect, not whether your grapes are ripe or even possess any flavor. (Hint: look at the maturity of the seeds and taste the grapes.)

5. And on the question of numbers, since when did twenty-eight become the new twenty-four? If the site is well selected, you should in fact be able to harvest grapes at twenty-four degrees[296] Brix and make a perfectly wonderful, intense wine. Darrel Corti should be given a medal for his courageous observation that the overripe emperor has not only no clothes but also no soul.[297]

6. The absence of defect in wine does not necessarily equate to the presence of quality.

7. If you surrender to perceived economic "reality," you have still surrendered.

8. Don't follow leaders, don't be a slave to pH meters, and don't go with the pack. The pack has no idea where it is heading. Think for yourself; develop your own palate. You will be more successful if you make wines to please yourself instead of others. Then, try to figure out how to communicate what it is you've done.

9. Efficient is not always better. I was taught that the sooner one completed malolactic fermentation the better. My experience has taught me the reverse. From a strictly business perspective, it is a tragic truth that, in general, whatever one can do to slow down the development of a wine (and hence its timely drinkability or even presentability)—from minimal racking to the use of screwcaps—will generally redound to an ultimately superior product. Sorry.

296. Yielding a wine of 12.5–13.0 percent alcohol.   **297.** Darrel, the brilliant Sacramento wine merchant (who has clued me in to the true identity of Mataro in California), recently launched an idealistic campaign against the escalating alcohol in "table wines." With the exception of fortified wines and certain others—for example, Amarone, which has existed so long that it has established historical credentials—"table" wines over 14 percent were summarily banned from his store.

10. You absolutely, positively, cannot have it all—high yields *and* high quality. Get over it *now.*

11. Drip irrigation is not the savior of the grape industry. It is the Vintichrist. Drip may be interesting from a water conservation standpoint, but locating the drip irrigation in-row and on the surface is not very clever at all. It encourages weed growth, shallow rooting, and a constricted root zone, and potentially makes the vine far more susceptible to thermic stress. If you are absolutely compelled to irrigate, a much cleverer idea might be to use microsprinklers and irrigate away from the vines or contrive to inject the water at a depth of several feet, as far away from the vine as you can manage. But in the best-case scenario, you find an area that has abundant natural rainfall and adequate water-holding capacity in the soil and dry-farm it.

12. To dry-farm successfully in California, one must look at how things were done a hundred years ago. Think about old-fangled rootstocks such as Saint George, wider spacing, and head-trained vines. Stay away from nursery bench grafts (they're wimps and need to be pampered) and consider planting rootstock, allowing it to establish itself over a period of a few years and then field-budding it. This is a fairly inefficient process, but ultimately it may give you a far more drought resistant vine that is capable of producing for much longer, which ultimately represents a far more sustainable proposition.

13. Big-time changes in the wine's chemistry or physical milieu—whether these be rapid temperature changes, large drafts of oxygen, big doses of sulfur dioxide, tartaric acid, and so on—tend to leave lasting scars. Small, incremental changes (when absolutely necessary) tend to preserve the integrity of the wine. (See my earlier vaudeville joke.)

14. SO_2 also really sucks and should be used with the lightest possible hand, but know that you will have to get a real handle on what is going on microbiologically.

15. A propos of point 14, it is not necessary to burn down the winery in the event of a *Brettanomyces* infection. It does happen in the best of families. I suspect that maybe, just maybe, someday we will begin to think of *Brett* as a tertiary fermentation and inoculate our wines with benign strains of *Brett.* Perhaps *Brett* might also be controlled through the use of temperature changes, electromagnetic or sonic waves, maybe even the New Agey deployment of appropriate crystals. Who knows? Analogously, if a virus is detected in your vineyard, it may not be necessary to napalm it to kingdom come.

16. The belief that your cultured yeast strain is actually fermenting your grapes is truly a matter of faith. I might also add that, as a rule, purchasing cultured yeast is a great waste of money. Indigenous yeast, if used correctly (try a well-supervised *pied de cuve*), will give you a lovely, inefficient (from an alcohol conversion standpoint) fermentation, resulting in more reasonable levels of alcohol in the wine. Also, indigenous yeasts do not generally "stick" any more often than expensive cultured yeast.

17. Punching down is generally more interesting than pumping over. Small lot fermentations are almost always better than large ferments, and if you can figure out how to ferment these small lots in a wooden vessel, so much the better. There are other really cool materials with which to fabricate a fermentation vessel—glass, cement, and clay. Clay amphorae or ovoid cement tanks are particularly cool.[298] Stainless steel does have some things going for it—ease in controlling fermentation temperature being one—but apart from that feature, as well as ease in cleaning, it doesn't do much for me.

18. It is impossible to make great wine on a vast, heroic scale.

19. Oak is not a primary flavor in wine. Those who think so also tend to think of ketchup as a vegetable. Oak barrels these days, by the way, are mostly suspect. Also, no one has yet really figured out how to fabricate oak chips that will add much finesse to a wine after it has fermented. Untoasted chips added at a reasonable rate (2 g per liter) before the onset of fermentation will generally yield a pretty benign result (slightly better structure and more stable color), but will not deform the essential character of the wine in any substantive way.

20. Not all soils and vineyard sites are created equal. There are "smart soils"—ones that are sort of homeostatic in their water-holding and -dispersing characteristics—and there are "dumb soils." The effects of their dumbness can be only slightly mitigated through irrigation (ideally, not drip).

21. The viticultural reality that presently obtains is ephemeral and is largely the result of historical accident. There really is no historical inevitability to the dominance of Cab, Chard, and, God help us, Merlot.

22. The most interesting grape varieties are yet to be planted in California and will come from southern Italy or perhaps Greece.

23. The Central Valley may well be the savior of the California wine industry, at least in its potential ability to grow flavorful grapes at a reasonable cost. But the names of these grapes will most likely end in a vowel.

24. We will enjoy sound, vibrant wines made without SO_2 in our wine-drinking lifetimes.

25. Screwcaps totally rock for a number of reasons, not the least of which is that they enable wines to live longer and allow the winemaker to make stable wines using lower levels of SO_2. They will become increasingly more commonplace in our industry as people come to their senses. The problem of reduction with screwcaps is not that big a deal and will soon be mastered as more people begin to work with screwcaps.[299] Wines generally do not

298. Cement tanks are becoming popular again in Europe among the most switched-on winemakers, but the savoir-faire of their fabrication and maintenance does not appear to have traversed the Atlantic. Everyone I know on this side of the pond (ourselves included) who has tried them has come to some sort of grief, but this does not negate their profound coolness.   299. "Reductive winemaking," which is just another way of saying that one is consciously managing the phenomenon of reduction and attempting to hold the redox po-

need to "breathe" after they are bottled, though they tend to present better in their infancy if bottled with a more porous closure.[300] But certainly for long-term ageing, the less oxygen transmission through the closure the better.

26. There is no such thing as the best grape variety or best clone. A good variety is one well suited to its growing environment. A blend of clones will almost always be superior to one superclone.

27. Old-fangled is sometimes best. For example, we have not yet improved on head-training for grapevines in a warm climate. Pergola trellising systems also seem to be particularly interesting for warmer climates, as they are naturally cooling.

28. We know absolutely nothing about rootstocks. Those who think they know anything are grossly deluded.

29. Go spend some time in Europe before you get too tied down here. It's not that they're smarter or better than we are; they just have a very different perspective on things. And the broader your vision, the more thoughtful a winemaker you will be.

30. Organic farming is wonderful; biodynamic farming is even more interesting and represents a more sustainable model. However, farming biodynamically will still not insure that your wines are marvelous; you still need to be a good grower and, above all, select a brilliant site for grapes.

31. Back to the question of life force in wine: It is a quality that is fairly easily demonstrated—that is, it's the ability of a wine to tolerate an oxidative challenge. If you open a bottle and drink a glass or two from it, then replace the cork (or better, screwcap), the wine should in fact stay fresh for the better part of a week. New World wines are generally dead in the water the following day, whereas Old World wines are not. No one has worked out the details of this mechanism, but I am convinced it is related to minerals in the wine, which in turn derive from the way the grapes are grown—and this entails planting in certain kinds of mineral-rich soils, restricting yields, maybe raising smaller grapevines headed lower to the ground, and, above all, growing deep and wide-ranging root systems (that is, no drip irrigation) and healthy soil microflora.

32. This is probably the most disturbing news of all. I sincerely believe that if you are really serious about creating great wine, you must thoroughly let go of the profit motive. You can think of it as performance art or as a great adventure, but not as a means of making a bun-

285

Speeches and Essays

tential of the wine within a reasonably narrow and defined range, at least during its tenure in the cellar (*élevage*), is a powerful tool for fostering complexity in a wide range of winemaking styles. **300.** The coolest system of all might be a "smart" closure that is relatively porous immediately after bottling, and that gradually tightens up over time to become essentially a perfect seal. The only downside to this system (apart from its challenging technical difficulty) is that it appears to rely overmuch on the ratiocinations of human beings and not enough on the inherent intelligence of the wine itself.

dle. It has always been thus. The monks who toiled anonymously to create the great *crus* of Burgundy did their work with nary a thought of reward in this life. I think the best strategy for a winery owner is to draw a sort of Maginot Line between that which you do commercially and that which is done for pure love, that which is beyond compromise

(SPRING 2008)

Every couple of years, the normally astute staff of the Department of Viticulture and Enology of the University of California, Davis, forgets that I was quite the rabble-rouser as a student, at least as far as viticultural matters, and invites me back to talk to the students of Vit. 199. Big surprise, I do not sugarcoat my remarks to the students but sincerely tell them the things I wish someone had told me. Every time I go

back, I am more impressed with the earnestness and thoughtfulness of the students, especially regarding issues of sustainability. They understand that their world has become a fragile place, and many of them seem to want to make a real, positive difference, not simply grow grapes and make wine because it is a particularly fashionable thing to do, which of course it is.

Six Feet Under

A Meditation on Roots, Minerals, and Vinous Immortality

I am haunted by Josko Gravner in much the same way that sensitive young readers, myself included, were once obsessed with J. D. Salinger.[301, 302] If I could just *meet* him for a short visit, the dim, umbral light that flickers in the *cave* of this Platonist winemaker might suddenly blaze forth with clarity and purpose. The path toward authenticity—let's face it, how can one make wine in the New World without suspecting, nay, *knowing* that one is a complete and utter fraud?[303]—the true and righteous approach to the Holy Grail of *terroir* in the New World, is not, shall we say, completely obvious. I am certain that one is needful of a spiritual advisor or, at a minimum, an avuncular encourager, who will assure one that all of one's febrile imaginings and false starts are an inescapable, vital part of the karmic *route de vin* that he must tread.

I have made no pilgrimage to rural New Hampshire to see the reclusive Salinger but I have,

---

301. This is a rather precise analogy. The alienated, if self-absorbed, young readers felt grossly misunderstood by their peers (all phonies!) and by the relevant authority figures, in my case the latter would be highly influential American wine writers. **302.** While no one has seen Mr. Salinger lately, as in the last fifty years or so, it seems that the two men might also bear some physical resemblance to one another—both are tall, with a large, somewhat "horsy" countenance. Mr. Salinger, likely nonconversant with biodynamics, is reported to have an interest in homeopathy and alternative medicine. **303.** However, there certainly are a great number of New World winemakers who never experience a Dark Night of the Soil and sincerely believe in the profundity of their achievement. Their zin of willful naïveté will be dealt with in the nether reaches of the Vinferno.

in fact, made a real effort to meet Mr. Gravner—on perhaps four or five separate occasions—to no avail. He and I have mutual friends in Friuli, Italy. They call him on my behalf a day or two in advance of a proposed visit; it never seems to work out. He has some tractor work that must be done or a conference that calls him away or wine that must be prepared for bottling tomorrow.[304] I have the sense that, if I were there on behalf of the Swedish Academy to present him with the Nobel Prize for Viticulture, he would have need of an emergency pedicure and beg off. He certainly does not seem to countenance significant distraction.

Josko Gravner is a winemaker in Friuli who for many years made great, if relatively normative, wines that were routinely awarded *tre bicchieri* by *Gambero Rosso,* the supremely influential Italian wine publication. At some point the magazine stopped awarding Gravner any *bicchieri* at all, stopped reviewing his wine, struck him from the record, as it were, and has essentially treated him as a wine nonperson ever since. Gravner is loosely affiliated with a group of Italian winemakers who call themselves Il Gruppo dei Pazzi, or "the crazy guys." He is a practitioner of biodynamic viticulture,[305] a discipline replete with arcane and mysterioso practices, though it is clear that Gravner now operates in perhaps a still more rarified realm. He is said to have modeled his current winemaking practices on ancient techniques, including, but not limited to, extensive maceration of white wine on skins,[306] eschewal of sulfur dioxide, and extended ageing in clay amphorae interred in the cold, wet Friulani earth.

There is a great mystery as to what becomes of us when we die, but there are also great mysteries that attend our lives while we are still above ground, especially when one is a stranger in a foreign land; the nuances of Italian politics and culture are sometimes particularly opaque. It was reputed that *Gambero Rosso* stopped reviewing Gravner when they clashed over politics. The magazine is or was nominally affiliated with the Italian Communist Party; why did it take them twenty-five years to figure out that Josko was not marching shoulder to shoulder with them? Why should Italian leftists be obsessed with gastronomy, anyway? For that matter, how or why is there still a Communist Party in Italy? And how does one shovel grape pomace out of amphorae if they're buried in the ground? How do you know if the wine is in some sense "ready" to bottle if it has presented itself as essentially oxidized for the last, say, three years? These were among my many vexing questions, the answers to which vinquirying minds needed to know.

---

304. It might be argued that the precise timing for the bottling of his style of wine—that is, preoxidized—is less temporally sensitive.   **305.** Biodynamic viticulture is uniquely suited to aiding in the discovery of *terroir;* its practice allows the vine to become more self-regulating and to explore the soil more deeply, the better to extract everything it requires to flourish and express itself. Biodynamic practice also greatly abets the "mineralizing" process by which a healthy soil microbial population exists in symbiotic association with the vine and actively transports minerals into its root system.   **306.** This practice is utterly contrary to modern white "reductive," or oxygen-excluding, winemaking. Grape skins contain astringent substances called phenolics, which are in fact antioxidants, so one might imagine that a healthy concentration of them would *inhibit* oxidation (as is the case with red wine). But in fact, when white wine contains a heavy phenolic load, it turns brown (or perhaps pink or orange) rather sooner than later; this is counterintuitive.

There is a possibly apocryphal story about Gravner, which I adore, whether or not it is factual. I am told that a few years back he summoned his European distributors to the winery to publicly apologize to them for the very successful wines he had been making for the preceding twenty-odd years. "After twenty years, I have finally begun to understand how to make wine," he was alleged to have said. "Henceforth my wines will be much, much better." Even if he never said anything like this, his spirit, or my sense of his spirit, stands by my side every time I am compelled to make a sales presentation to one of my wholesalers.

A few years ago I asked Daniel Thomases, a close associate of Luigi Veronelli, former editor of *Gambero Rosso*, what he thought of Gravner. "He's really gone around the bend," said Thomases. "He's making something that one could theoretically drink, but you can no longer honestly call it wine, as we tend to think of it."

This mystery of putative mental illness—a great wine mind gone off?—fascinates me. Is he really mad, or perhaps tuned in on a sublime level that eludes us plodding left-brain wine drinkers and -makers, who expect our white wine to be fresh, clear, and bright? Might he be a gifted but perhaps attention-seeking provocateur/show-off, somewhat like Dalí, trying to *épater bourgeois* palates? The radically new (and old) generally strikes us as bizarre and outré, but it certainly behooves us to grasp what visitors from another realm are trying to tell us.

You seldom if ever see Gravner's wine here in the States. The last time I saw a bottle was in Milan five or six years ago, when Gravner was still selling wine that we would normally think of as "wine." It was a rather expensive bottle of Ribolla Gialla, and all I really remember about it was that it was highly concentrated and extremely oaky. A few months back I chanced upon a bottle of 1999 Bianco Breg, at Sam's in Chicago; it is said to be a blend of Chardonnay, Sauvignon, and Pinot Grigio. It was brutally expensive (about seventy-five dollars), but I had no choice; this was a wine I had to try.

I assemble a few of my braver colleagues, and we sit down to taste. The wine is a shocking but vividly beautiful shade of amber-orange. There is a nontrivial level of acetaldehyde, or sherry character, present and a slightly elevated volatile acidity. The nose smells a bit apple-y—this is a typical oxidation aroma—with a suggestion of orange blossoms and perhaps a twist of lime. But if one focuses intently on the wine, one picks up an unmistakable earthiness—I call it minerality—that seems to organize the wine about the midpalate and is responsible for the wine's very great persistence. If there is one character that I can definitely identify, it is humus—the smell of organic matter that has been reduced to its most elemental state. The wine tastes very, very old.

I've had the bottle open now for the better part of a week, and I can tell you that it is behaving in a very strange way. There are times when I taste it that it seems short, lifeless *ausgespielt*. But when I taste it again a few hours later, suddenly it seems to have magically grown younger and fresher. The wine seems to be a sort of Rorschach test of my own feeling-state. If I am brutally honest with myself, I have to admit that I really enjoyed the first glass of it, but couldn't fathom consuming the better part of a bottle with a meal. I am certain that all of us currently walking this earth have different conceptions of an afterlife, and some of us will have to reconsider their expectations at some point. I had a different conception of what the Gravner wine was going to taste like before the actual experience. I fully expected it to taste somewhat oxidized and was psychologically prepared for its lurid color. But part of me also wished it to be more recognizable qua wine. I wanted it both ways—young and fresh but also possessing the wisdom of the ages.

This morning, I scanned the Internet for some information on Gravner and learned several important things. According to a recent article by Eric Asimov in the *New York Times,* things did get a little dicey at the cantina during the stylistic transition, and Gravner did lose a number of erstwhile loyal followers. But one reads the article and comes away with the impression of a man who very much knows what he is doing and where he is going.

The amphorae are interesting, especially if they are buried in the ground. It may be that the electrochemistry of the wine is slightly altered by conservation in the earth: perhaps a weak electrical current coming from the earth itself is enough to maintain redox equilibrium in the wine and prevent it from oxidizing profoundly, even in the absence of SO_2. It is my own belief that wines rich in minerals are the only ones truly capable of long-term ageing; the minerals act in some sense like batteries in the redox circuit. Efficient, modern viticulture, with its emphasis on higher yields and reliance on drip irrigation in the New World, essentially ignores the role of minerality, and it is not surprising that most modern wines have greatly foreshortened life spans.

One point I extracted from the article was that Gravner did not fully implement the use of amphorae until the 2001 vintage, so it is conceivable that the wine I tasted was a work in progress. This allows me the fantasy of imagining a wine—perhaps his wine, perhaps someone else's—that is untouchable, one worthy of esoteric Taoist masters who will toast with it on their three hundredth or seven hundredth birthdays. I conceive a wine that has seen it all, perhaps done it all, and remembers everything. If oxidation is the worst thing you can do to me, then bring it on. Wines, like mortals, are creatures of a day; they/we flower briefly and then are gone. We focus on the qualities in a wine that somehow correspond to those we attend to in life. We delight in the play of the senses and fix on the phenomena that are most obvious—the brightest and shiniest baubles. The "fruit" in a wine is terribly pleasing to us; perhaps it reminds us of the succulence of our brief lives. But if all we look for in wines is fruit, then perhaps that is all we will find. SO_2 artificially keeps wines alive in the same way that modern medicine keeps us around, but in relying on SO_2, do we miss out on some vital pieces of the puzzle? We as a society profoundly fear death and decrepitude and generally (if we have the means) wish to maintain the outward trappings of youth and vibrant health. Perhaps there are some valuable life lessons to be learned in wines made by the group of crazies. It is interesting to contemplate both a life and a wine that focus on those mysterious elements that remain resolutely fixed, as hard as granite, immortal.[307]   (2005)

Perhaps this paradox can be addressed by quantum theory, but sometimes it seems impossible to determine whether a rogue, genius vintner is attuned to a celestial music that other mortals are insensible to, or is in fact an utter charlatan. Maybe, as quantum theory might suggest, he is both. It is said that we pass through time the way a fish swims through water—time is a great abstraction that we are largely oblivious to. And yet wine itself is a sort of time machine, a mechanism that lets us slow time down or speed it up. The qualities we generally look for in wine—the fruity bouquet, the soft texture—occur on a temporal horizon that we think of as the "present" (which of course is imaginary). But what I imagine Grauner and others are thinking about are qualities that emerge on a different time scale, over hours perhaps even days, not the fleeting seconds of a wine taster. My guess is that if one could significantly slow one's own internal process down to the gustatory equivalent of the auditory "I buried Paul," there would emerge sensible qualities in the wine that are for us but theoretical constructs.

"Great" Wine in the Postmodernist World

What is great wine? What makes it great? And how might a winemaker who has not had the extraordinary karma to have inherited, married into the relevant family of, or otherwise miraculously come to possess and/or control a *grand cru* vineyard—that is to say, a vineyard site that has a long history of growing extraordinary grapes—have the audacity to imagine how he or she might fashion great and distinctive wine from the produce of a new and untested site, essentially *de novo*?

I confess (and this is a matter of some personal shame) that for a long time I fled from the terrible awareness that, if you were sincere about making great wine, you would have to get very, very serious about growing great grapes. This is an incredibly daunting proposition involving an enormous investment of all the relevant currencies, chief among them time, emotion, and of course great gobs of that other green stuff (not Grüner Veltliner). Everyone knows you can't make great wine without great grapes, but I kind of conveniently forgot this relevant fact for a while, a bit like a trauma victim. I lost a wonderful vineyard in the Santa Cruz Mountains to Pierce's disease in the mid-90s, and the result was like getting thrown off a horse and not wanting to get back on.

It wasn't always such a great vineyard. I had started out trying to grow Pinot noir, blissfully

307 "Six Feet Under" originally appeared in a different form in *Wine Review Online*, November 2005; reprinted by permission of Robert Whitley.

ignorant of how challenging was the Pinot proposition. But I was persistent, like jock itch. I schlepped in heroic amounts of limestone, sheep manure (the sheep manure was, in fact, a very good idea),[308] and risked temporary suspension of personal liberty and perhaps confiscatory fines with my Cuvée Samsonite ways. (This was before the days of Homeland Security.) But despite my Sisyphean efforts to grow Pinot, the wine was really nothing to write home about. I ripped out the Pinot noir grapes and planted Syrah in their place, and field-budded that popular white grape Chardonnay (what had I been thinking?) over to Marsanne and Roussanne (which in fact turned out not to be Roussanne, after all, but that is another story). The Syrah turned out to be accidentally magnificent, and the Roussanne that wasn't Roussanne was absolutely brilliant. We called this wine Le Sophiste.

So, I was and remain shocked by the essentially random contingency of viticultural success—the failure part is a lot more dependable. With my vineyard in Bonny Doon, I seemed to have more or less won the lottery, but a few years later my vineyard suffered the equivalent of getting bonked by an incoming asteroid. For a number of years I put the idea of a great, new original vineyard on hold and told myself I would get around to it perhaps later than later. Maybe I had internalized the dominant winemaker-as-auteur paradigm popularized by some of the more significant American wine publications. But winemakers do get into trouble when they begin to believe their own hype. The grapes might look and taste like total crap, but *no problema,* we'll just fix them with our little bag o' oenological tricks. Perhaps at this juncture I might mention the two divergent explanatory mechanisms, both erroneous because incomplete, that purport to explain why great wine is great:

Explanation #1: Winemaker as genius-auteur. One thinks of Helmut Dönnhoff, Marcel Guigal, Ricardo Cotarella, and perhaps even of Helen Turley. On the face of it, this theory does seem to have some merit. Helmut Dönnhoff appears not to possess the most favored vineyard sites—he's growing grapes in the Nahe, for heaven's sake. And yet he consistently produces some of the most electrifying wines in Germany. He is undoubtedly both a real artist and a complete fanatic, two necessary characteristics for winemaking excellence. Not only are his vineyards absolutely impeccable but also he has a real feeling, call it intuition, about when each discrete section of each parcel is absolutely *à point.* Fanatics don't compromise; they would never release a wine not up to their standards, and they hold all their collaborators to a very high standard, sort of like Charlie Trotter in his kitchen, minus the sharp knives.

On the subject of sharp knives, Philippe Guigal once proffered an interesting mot regarding his father, Marcel, when he was showing me their automated grape reception area. "Before

308. There is a belief in some parts that the single salient reason Old World wines exhibit such a great degree of minerality is that the soils from which they derive were grazed by sheep for millennia. Sheep manure is said to have a particularly mineralizing effect on soils, making certain micronutrients more available to grapevines.

harvest my father takes his heart out and after harvest he puts it back in?" I should mention that Guigal's grape reception apparatus is the ultimate passive-aggressive *apparatus*. Guigal's growers warrant that their grapes have attained a certain degree of sugar, which, despite the appellation's name, is often the salient criterion for quality in the solar-radiation-challenged vineyards of Côte Rôtie. (Other relevant criteria, such as maximum yield per acre, are regulated by law, at least in theory.) The grapes are loaded off the grower's truck onto the Guigal conveyor, where they are instantly analyzed for sugar. If, however, they do not make the cut, the conveyor is simply reversed and the grapes, which the grower has worked all season long to perfect on hillsides sloped at a back-breaking sixty-degree angle, are efficiently conveyed back to the grower's truck with no possibility of further discussion or negotiation. Somehow one imagines that the grower is given an automatic receipt such as the one you receive on the French autoroute. *Merci et au revoir. Bonne route!*

Explanation #2: Location, location, location. According to this notion, great wines come only from great sites, and the sites are essentially responsible for the individual personality of the wine. If the vineyard is managed *comme il faut*—that is to say, with the legally prescribed grape varieties as demanded by the Appellation d'Origine Contrôlée, and strict adherence to AOC guidelines as far as cultural practice—your wine should come out just fine, that is to say, great, if it is a great *cru,* but more important, it will be *typique,* typical, true to its *terroir,* true to itself. The old dray horse knows how to find its way back to the barn; a vineyard in perfect harmony creates grapes that in some sense know how to make themselves into wine. I read that a few years ago Château Haut-Brion hired a very young winemaker, just out of school, with this precise idea in mind. The winemaking, it was believed, was no big deal, really. You follow the prescribed formula; the real work that makes a difference has already been done in the vineyard.

I'd like to propose another lens through which to look at the problem. Imagine creating a great wine as if one were writing a novel. Is the winemaker fashioning something out of nothing or somehow discovering the novel that is somewhere out there in the ether/zeitgeist waiting to be discovered and written down? As winemakers, we build on the discoveries of our predecessors; we don't have to figure out for ourselves, for example, that among the hardwood trees, oak works particularly well for barrels. And yet like novelists or any other artists, we, at least those of us in the New World, are (or at least should be) thoroughly daunted by what has come before. There are, what, five basic story lines that can be told, and how many classic wine styles? The universe of wine may sometimes seem Borgesian in its vastness, but as a practical matter, how might we presume to create an original, nonderivative work? How might a Pinot Noir that we fashion in the New World have the depth, the resonance of association of great Burgundy, which conveys a sense of place and even a whole cultural universe? The Borges story of Ménard, a fictive writer in the modern era who rewrote, word for word, a chapter of *Don Quixote* by creating conditions in his own life that engendered a sort of Cervantes-consciousness, particularly resonates with me and, frankly, is the main thing that keeps me going.

If we carry the literary analogy further, the Old World winemakers still work in a "modernist" style, whereas the New World is thoroughly postmodern. By "modernist," we might mean there are still remnants of the classic form. For example, a modernist novel has discernible characters and a plot that unfolds in something analogous to linear time, and it observes the basic dramatic unities. The novel's excellence, despite being a palpable fiction, lies in its trueness to life and its instantiation of a universal truth. Similarly you "read" an Old World wine, and it coheres in a logical, predictable way. A Chambolle-Musigny will always be made from Pinot noir, and a good one will have characteristics that eloquently bespeak its origins. It is as great as it is true to its genre.

What are the kinds of things that a winemaker does to make a wine true to itself? These are the very, very subtle moves alluded to in my mention of Herr Dönnhoff. The vineyard must be impeccable. And in general, it also needs to be old. For some of the wisdom reposes in the winemaker, but most of it reposes in the vineyard itself, which has been managed by succeeding generations of human beings and has benefited from their accumulated observation and care. Consider "massal selection." When a vine dies or gets blighted by a tractor or whatever and needs to be replaced, the winemaker will walk through the vineyard and identify particularly interesting vines, ones that seem to be especially well adapted to that vineyard. The cumulative effect of massal selection of a vineyard over, say, three or four generations may contribute greatly to the vineyard's unique personality. As does how scrupulous you are in your cultural passes, be it weed or mildew control or shoot thinning to open up the vine to just the right level of light—too much and the grape sunburns, not enough and the grape cluster does not color properly. Fanaticism concerning which cluster to harvest and which cluster to drop in the vineyard may make the difference between good wine and great wine: every cluster should be harvested neither underripe nor overripe, so that it might express the maximum amount of its individual personality. These are in a sense trivial activities—every grape grower should know how to perform them, but few perform them at a level of dedication that transforms good to great.

In the winery what transforms good to great is knowing how to make subtle adjustments in style to accommodate the grapes that nature has given you in a particular year: are the tannins still a little bit green because you had to pick earlier than you wished, owing to the imminence of inclement weather? Therefore you may not be able to sustain as long a *cuvaison,* or time in the fermenter, as you might in a more favorable year. The winemaker's genius in the Old World is having the skill to every year bring the wine back to a sort of Platonic ideal, which is the notion of the Appellation Contrôlée, at least in principle. Superficially, the vintages will appear different—one ripe and powerful, the other more lean and elegant, but always the typicity of the *terroir* will shine through. In the Old World, typicity is all about balance. Not one element obtrudes. As an aside, there was, not too long ago, a juicy cultural conflict between two eminent wine writers, Jancis Robinson and Robert Parker, over a recent vintage of Château Pavie, concerning the very matter of typicity and balance. Robinson thought the wine was utterly bizarre because it was atypical of its appellation—very ripe and powerful, almost bordering on port. Parker, who absolutely loves this style of wine, thought the wine a masterpiece.

Making great wine in the Old World is semistraightforward. You have the good fortune to be the scion of a well-landed family or you have made tons of money and/or you have married well. You begin with a great site, some old vines, and you don't screw them up. But what of the New World? Here is where we find ourselves in a postmodern wilderness. If we try to emulate the Old World models, we tend to end up hopelessly derivative and somewhat banal. At best we make wines that are all sound and screaming eagle shrieks and fury, signifying nothing. Doing what we imagine is everything right—buying the best barrels, selecting the best clones and the best rootstock, limiting our yield, and hiring the cleverest consulting winemaker and viticulturist—gives us a wine that may be technically excellent but still lacks real personality and originality. The problem in a nutshell is that we have (or so it would appear) only one lifetime to work out certain issues. There does not appear to be the opportunity for sufficient observation and iteration that would seem to require many, many generations. How could something in any real sense be typical if you are doing it for the first time? How can it be true to a tradition if there is essentially no tradition? Winemaking in the New World is a very, very different proposition from winemaking in the Old World. Linguistically they look the same, but they are worlds apart.

What you end up with is Robert Parker, and to some extent the *Wine Spectator*, becoming the arbiters of wine taste.[309] They have discovered, very fortunately for themselves, that their

309. There is another aspect to the phenomenon of the ascendancy of the all-powerful wine critic, and it may have to do with several factors. First, in the last twenty years, wine has dramatically appreciated in price relative to virtually everything else. Second, U.S. laws have changed to allow wine to become a more fungible asset. For these reasons, more wine is purchased as a speculative investment than before. (Previously, one bought wine because one liked a particular producer or style, and one expected to drink it oneself or will it to one's worthy or unworthy heirs.) So the market, seeking efficiency, demands an arbiter of Great Authority. (If Robert Parker didn't exist, he would have to be invented.) With the concentration of so much authority in relatively few taste buds, influential critics must, to retain their power, continue to burnish their own brand, partially through a Starbucks-like ubiquity (which contains its own contradictions) by daily tasting far more wines than is perhaps humanly possible, and at the same time trying to establish a certain kind of dependability, reliability, or consistency.

I am not certain whether critics innately *prefer* bigger, brawnier, riper wines. Their predilection for this style may derive partly from the fact that they taste a great number of wines on a daily basis and partly from the typical rapidity of their tasting program: the bigger, more evident wines may be the only ones that actually register at all, and are likely the only ones that can consistently be identified. A more subtle, psychological explanation might also be proffered: The greatest embarrassment facing anyone who states an opinion for the public record is inconsistency or self-contradiction (an essentially normative state of affairs in the universe of wine [see note 278] if one is brutally honest with oneself). If a critic focuses on concentration or optical opacity as the primary criterion for wine quality, this feature will reliably emerge no matter the circumstances of the tasting. The critic remains consistent (like Starbucks) in his or her public utterances but, along the way, unfortunately misses out on a vast universe of wondrous, beautiful wines—wines that are perhaps more sensitive to their surroundings (the virtuous introverts), often those that undergo dramatic changes upon exposure to oxygen. For me, at least, these are the most interesting wines of all.

taste, at least for wine, is to some extent that of Mr. Everypalate. They like feel-good wines—which I think are the vinous equivalent of comfort food—soft, rich, and creamy. Certainly feel-good wines are better than feel-bad wines, but they appeal to a certain altitudinally challenged denominator—maybe they key into our biological predisposition to favor ripe over less-ripe fruit. The principal criticism I have of both Robert Parker and the *Wine Spectator* is that they seem to be largely incurious about the deeper aspects of the fashioning of great wine, its historical and cultural context; they tend to focus simply on whether they themselves like it or don't. Wine as solipsism; it is relevant only to the extent that it can be conceived of by the drinker.[310]

There is a universe of wine out there, Old World and New World wines, and they really are worlds apart. We call them both "wine," but New World wines are made with so much self-consciousness, so much hyperawareness of the economic consequences of "failure"—that is to say, the failure to win 90-plus points—or of the tremendous upside of success, that their art often becomes deformed. They often lose their esprit, their ability to navigate true *terroir*-north with their own aesthetic compass.

It is against this background of formidable economic pressure to produce a wine within the normative range of critical criteria that one imagines a wine really, really out there. If you are truly interested in making great wine in the New World, you must understand one important thing: It can in no way be a for-profit venture; it must be art for art's sake. You must be willing to think about growing grapes and making wines in ways outside the conventional norm.

310. As this book was entering its final revision, I chanced to reflect (just for a moment) on whether this statement is fair and accurate. (Maybe accurate, but not so fair.) But in so doing, I experienced a small glimpse of self-knowledge: my criticism of Robert Parker's "shallow" or "rapid" reading of wines may equally be leveled at myself and at my own epistemological methodology. Like many others, I am a "thin-slicer," in the parlance of Malcolm Gladwell, one who gauges what is really important often very quickly and from a relatively narrow range of experience. I am capable of sometimes making astute judgments based on very limited data, but I am also capable of allowing my likes, dislikes, and prejudices to color my thinking and exclude new information. For example, Château de Beaucastel is a wine that I have tried many times in years past (though not lately). Over time, I learned that its typically (there I go again, thin-slicing or at least extrapolating based on out-of-date experience) barnyardy aromas, artifacts of *Brettanomyces* (this part I know, or imagine that I know, to be true), were not particularly to my liking. I've gotten into the habit of calling the wine *Brettcastel*, perhaps unfairly, and I can never seem to begin to appreciate its other virtues. Château de Beaucastel will likely need to make twenty or so consecutive vintages of microbiologically quiescent wines before I am apt to alter my perception of its product, which is a real pity. It is said that science tends to observe that which it is capable of measuring, and the same thing might be said of wine critics. Robert Parker undoubtedly possesses a sensorium that rivals that of a gas chromatograph, and I would suggest that its brilliance may well be a hindrance to him. Because he is so good at being consistent, at least within a certain range of parameters, there is not a lot of reason for him to venture outside that range. He has certainly managed to thin-slice many aspects of wine quality—indeed to the point where these criteria can be reverse-engineered by the likes of Leo McCloskey of Enologix—but in so doing, has he excluded or ignored something precious: quirkiness, strangeness, originality?

Your postmodernist wine may not look at all like a modern wine. It may or may not convey a sense of place in the way we understand French *terroir*, but it will be thoroughly distinctive. It will have the ability to move us in some way and, therefore, maybe be indispensable.

Whatever big new idea you might attempt in the vineyard has to address the idea of enhancing complexity, as well as allow for intensive observation and iteration for the possibility of new information to emerge without the distraction of too much noise. You may need to think of the actual production vineyard as your laboratory, the production itself as a vast experiment or perhaps even a game. What we tend to forget is that when we are privileged to drink an amazing and original wine, a great Burgundy, say, the wine is not the result of a group of venture capitalists getting together to formulate a massively profitable business plan for the creation or discovery of a *grand cru*. Rather, many years earlier, a group of anonymous monks toiled for generation upon generation, each adding an incremental contribution, until perhaps there was a moment of self-conscious awakening, a recognition that this was some pretty miraculous juice they were fashioning. I propose a toast to *mes semblables, mes frères*. *(2004)*

⌐ This essay is a potpourri covering a range of subjects linked by the theme of "great wine"—a term potentially greatly misunderstood across an oceanic and cultural divide. The essay treats the dilemma of the artist working in, really, any medium. We pretend otherwise, but on some level most, if not all, creative people have an unconscious fantasy that their works— even those as ephemeral as a bottle of wine—will live forever, ultimately be the stuff of legend. We aspire to greatness, but great by what standard or authority? Making a great wine in the Old World means somehow capturing and rendering a Platonic essence; in the New World it means achieving a point score in the mid-90s.[311] It is bizarre that these differing conceptions of greatness have been thoroughly confounded. And it is ironic that perhaps the greatest danger facing the wine business is its recent unprecedented success and the deforming self-consciousness that that has engendered. I am old enough to remember hearing crusty old-timers say things like, "I make wine to please myself [expletive deleted], and if no one wants to drink it, well, I'll drink it myself." (No one says that anymore.) In 2004, Jonathan Nossiter made the film *Mondovino*, which attempted to draw a distinction between small producers making "authentic" wines and large, well-funded companies (whose politics were to the right of Attila the Hun) making cynical, manipulated wines highly favored by the critics. The premise of the film was a bit convoluted, but Nossiter almost got it right. I believe the salient distinction between winemakers is between those who experience their own wine as a first-order, I-Thou encounter with their land and vines and the wine itself, with all the attendant fear and trembling and strange ambiguity, and those who view the meaning of what they do primarily through the eyes of the Other, be it critic or consumer, forever seeking approbation. They are always wondering, "Does the malo make my butt . . . er, . . . my Chard look too big?"

311. Ironically enough, many of the high-scoring "modern" wines offer pleasure for but the briefest instant. They are flowers that bloom and quickly fade.

In Search of a Great Growth in the New World

For the longest time, I supposed myself to be an agnostic on the question of finding *terroir* in the New World. It was not that I was a member of the anti-*terroirist* brigade. Quite the opposite. For me, a wine that conveyed a sense of place was the only wine that was truly "necessary," that incrementally made the world more interesting, beautiful, and more meaningful, in the sense that it created more connection between ourselves and the natural world. And yet there was a plethora of fatal impediments to creating or discovering a true *terroir* wine in the New World; the appearance of something like a New World Great Growth would be nothing less than a miracle.

This is the central paradox, or perhaps the existential dilemma, facing anyone who is "serious" about making great or meaningful wine in the New World. You can try to learn from what others have done successfully or unsuccessfully—which is the logical way to proceed. In the New World we do something very well, maybe diabolically well, but despite our vociferous protestations to the contrary, what we do is, I gently suggest, not about *terroir*. Were one to be serious about producing an authentic *vin de terroir* in these parts, one should be filled with a great and overpowering sense of existential angst, and there should be much gnashing of teeth and rending of garments. The very cornerstone of the proposition to produce great, authentic, and original wine—the identification of an outstanding site and the planting and cultivation of a vineyard thoroughly appropriate to that site—is tenuous; it is the construction of an elaborate edifice on shifty sand, gravel, or perhaps clay loam.

The belief in *terroir* holds that a *vigneron* might produce a wine that exposes both the inherent distinguishing qualities of a particular vineyard site and the unique qualities of the vintage year. The differentiating qualities of the site and ultimately of the wine, its originality, are most certainly linked with the site's ability to solve particular environmental challenges—its ability to drain water in the event of excess precipitation and, conversely, its ability to provide moisture to the plant in a thrifty and measured way in a vintage that is hydrologically challenged, a condition that obtains essentially every year in most places in California where grapes are grown. There are small but telling differences that distinguish the site from neighboring ones, that create the clarionlike distinctiveness of the more favored sites. *Terroir* is about solving environmental challenges, and certainly about solving them *elegantly*. In a warm and challenging environment, a great site allows vines to keep their cool in a suave, Cary Grant–like way.

Put another way, in the Old World, there has evolved a sort of homeostasis, a "learning" between vine and soil under the watchful eye of a human being. Vines have in some sense "taught" soils—through the mediation of their symbiotic microbial demiurges, mycorrhizae, and the like—what their specific needs are. Soils (and microclimates) have in some sense taught vines what they might expect over a growing season. Over many generations a sort of stately, rhythmic dance has emerged. The most interesting wines that arise from this dance are the ones that have captured this distinctive rhythm or waveform, this unmistakable signature, which we call *terroir*. My great dilemma, the dilemma of anyone interested in producing a truly distinctive wine is: How are you going to be so clever or lucky to work out this exquisite balance, this elegant harmonic in the one lamentably brief lifetime that you are given? How can you identify a priori a site capable of expressing *terroir* and real distinction? There is so much to be done and, at the same time, so much not to be done.

All our efforts in the New World to "improve" our vines—whether through the selection of "superior" clones, the use of deficit drip irrigation, or soil amendments—help us produce wines of breathtaking consistency, wines of the "highest quality," but perversely they rob the vines of their originality, soilfulness, and soulfulness. In our aim to improve quality, we obviate the possibility of originality, the essence of a Great Growth. We love our dear friends for their uniqueness, their strange quirks and foibles, their vulnerability, their humanness. In the New World, one finds oneself experiencing wines that are easy to admire but difficult to love.

New World viticulturists tend to live in the culture of control, and this is the single major stumbling block to the discovery of the truly original. It is a non sequitur to talk about the *terroir* of an irrigated vineyard, rather like trying to accurately describe the natural history of an animal by observing its behavior in a zoo. So, if you sincerely seek to produce a wine that expresses *terroir*, where do you begin? The lessons learned from growing clonally selected, virus-free, irrigated grapes of selected popular varietals on modern trellis systems have little applicability to the establishment of a truly original vineyard.

Before talking more about the possibility of discovering a Great Growth in the New World, let me say more about *vins de terroir*. *Terroir* wines do not always appear to be particularly "friendly" in the style of the abundantly fruity, painfully pleasant New World wines. Cheerleader wines, I call the latter, and it is particularly painful for us Californians to imagine that others consider us to be anything less than absolutely and unconditionally friendly. *Terroir* wines are virtually always reserved upon opening and generally require copious amounts of oxygen and time to begin to show themselves. *Terroir* wines are quirky in the sense of being much more sensitive to environmental conditions—temperature, barometric pressure, and lunar and celestial cycles as described in the biodynamic calendar, for example. And *Terroir* wines seem on some level to be (you may imagine me completely crazy for saying this, as if you needed any further evidence) sensitive to the thought and emotions of the individual tasting them. I know this sounds like the pathetic fallacy, but there you are. A *vin de terroir* is a chameleon, changing and evolving in the glass; it is not a wine capable of being captured in a snapshot, as many of our wine critics would like to do. Most important, a true *vin de terroir*—whether or not it is sulfited, rich in tannin, and high in acid—possesses a certain life force, which I believe is linked in some way to its mineral content or to how the minerals in it are held.

The life force of a wine, its qi, is its ability to tolerate oxygen, and this quality is easily demonstrable. A wine with life force can be opened for days at a time, often for as long as a week, without becoming discernibly oxidized; this does not seem to happen much in the New World. *Terroir* wines, apart from their aesthetic harmony, provoke a certain emotional reaction from us, and I think this is linked to the physical, visceral apprehension of the depth of the wine—again, a link to the earth, and something I believe comes only from wines made from deeply rooted vines that have retained an imprint of where they have been. We love that which we sense nourishes us on various levels. Perhaps we love *vins de terroir* because we apprehend that they physically sustain us. Drinking alcohol depletes the body of minerals, and we tend to feel the worse for wear the next morning if we drink wines that do not replace the minerals they deplete. So a *terroir* wine, or at least a mineral wine, is perhaps the poison *and* the antidote in the same bottle.

The question remains: how to find something that is truly authentic, something that truly matters and that makes the world richer and happier for its existence? If you are lucky or skilled enough to find it, how do you know you have found it, especially if its virtues are opaque to the relevant opinion-makers?

I have a friend in the Côtes du Rhône by the name of Philippe Viret who practices something called "cosmoculture," and who may be making some of the most distinctive wines in the world. Philippe uses no fertilizers or other treatments in his vineyard, neither sulfur nor Bordeaux mix nor even compost teas. He employs what are called "cosmic pipes." These are not something to be smoked, but are, essentially, stone menhirs strategically situated throughout his vineyard, the better to balance the energetic field of his domaine. He refers to this practice as "viticultural acupuncture." Philippe's father, Alain, is a "sensitive," a water witch, among other things, who has been able to identify the significant energetic vortices on the site. The winery itself, constructed from massive, formidable limestone blocks, is configured at the confluence of two extremely powerful energetic vectors. The scale and geometry of the winery has been precisely calculated for optimal harmony,[312] and one cannot escape the feeling of having inadvertently wandered into some sort of mystic and powerful Druidic edifice.

---

312. I recently spent a day in New York with my friend Serge Hochar, proprietor of Château Musar, discussing precisely these things. I had last seen Serge a few years ago in Spain, when we had a very long, speculative discussion as to whether the geometric configuration of the vineyard might have an effect on grape quality, possibly the result of solar reception or even on a more subtle energetic level. Serge had read an article claiming that vineyards planted on a heptagonal scheme would be absolutely optimal. (Heptagons are the most mysterious of all polygons and perhaps the deepest as far as spiritual resonance, but they do not generally work and play well—that is to say, array well—with other polygons, at least in two dimensions.) After I returned from Spain to the States, the image of heptagons began to burn in my brain. My desk became littered with heptagons, hexagons, and pentagons in my effort to find some brilliant and elegant way

Philippe uses no sulfur dioxide in his wines at all, either for red, white, or pink, and what is truly remarkable is that the wines can be open for as long as a week and they don't oxidize. I must confess to feeling a strange and disquieting sensation when I visit the Virets. Coming from Santa Cruz, I am no stranger to what one might call New Age methodologies. Maybe it is the fact of being in southern France, historic home of the Gnostics, Cathars, and Kabbalists of all stripes, but when I visit with the Virets I can't help but feel more than a little like the sorcerer's apprentice. I feel unworthy when they seem to be sharing the Secrets of the Universe with the likes of me. They are practicing a sort of alchemy, and I recognize a kind of implicit "Do Not Attempt This at Home at the Risk of Inadvertently Precipitating the Potential Heat Death of the Universe"–like quality in their work.

I am currently working through my own issues—fear of commitment, fear of failure, and so on—in my attempt to identify a great vineyard site here in California. I sincerely doubt that I, unlike Viret *père*, will ever possess the psychic sensitivity required to fully apprehend the subtle energetic potential of a site; I will never see with a sorcerer's eyes. And yet I still feel there is a crucial balance to be struck between the scientific, or "objective," assessment of a site's potential and the more personal emotive, or spiritual, apprehension of its suitability. Those whom the gods favor will find a perfect congruence between the objective factors—wonderfully textured, geologically distinctive limestone soils, for example, with adequate rainfall for dry farming—and the compelling subjective features: a landscape that feels like home, and the feeling of safety or wholeness that one experiences when observing a site that is also a *clos*, an enclosure, a proper *domaine*.[313]

There is an interesting point of divergence between the views of orthodox *terroirists*, who might hold that a great *terroir* is a great *terroir* in a sort of eternal, timeless sense, independent of the

---

to array them with minimal "wasted" ground. I searched the Internet to find the article that Serge had mentioned, but had no luck. I tried several times to reach him at Musar and in London but alas my attempts coincided with a very difficult time in his country, and communication did not seem to be in the cards. So in New York I was very pleased to see Serge well and in good spirits, and after we had talked awhile about this and that, I dumped my bag of paper heptagons out on the table that we shared. We spent a couple of hours moving the strange shapes around until an elegant, indeed seductively beautiful, pattern began to emerge.

[313]. The best strategy for approaching important viticultural decisions is to move slowly, beginning with the most ethereal considerations, maybe a vision of the feeling tone or the "vibe" of the vineyard. How do you imagine you will feel on entering the space? What sensations are created when you visualize the shape of the vines themselves and the other natural features? What features might be created to profoundly link yourself to the site so that it feels like home? For me, it is now time to think explicitly about creating beauty in the vineyard rather than simply conceiving of the vineyard as an efficient machine that churns out raw material for wine. I cannot defend my argument with any kind of rigor but I am certain that a vineyard designed to allow its operator to truly play within it will produce wines with a quality very different from that of wines deriving from a site more soberly conceived. What is the aim of a vineyard after all? I imagine it is there to finish the soul work of the *vigneron*, an external correlative of his inner self screen that might enable him to better understand why he is here and to provide him with something like pure delight.

human beings who exploit it, and the more humanistic view that suggests *terroir* requires not simply the human presence but a specific human presence. Unless a specific human being is capable of resonating with his or her *terroir,* the discussion of *terroir* is moot. I think Viret would hold that an indispensable element of *terroir* is the deep emotional and psychic connection that the grower establishes with the land. A winegrower must absolutely and unconditionally love his or her vineyard. Whether love conquers a potassium deficiency remains an open question.

So, this mystical connection is something I personally aspire to but, owing to my own limitations, perhaps will never find. However, even failing this sort of cosmic affirmation, this impeccable congruence, one may still hope to find, if not create, something like a *grand cru* vineyard in the New World, taking the more humanistic sense of a *vin de terroir.*

A *grand cru* is great because its *terroir* has a unique and sublime organization: the parts—the vines, soil, and human presence—fit together to create a seamless homeostatic feedback loop. Some iterative mechanisms, massal selection being one of them, have been in play for multiple generations for this organized entity to have evolved, for the living, vegetative element to have synchronized with the more static hardscape. So the question is: How can one learn enough in a single lifetime to bring to light a vineyard of great distinction? Or, what can be done to accelerate the process of learning and adaptation?

I have an idea that may be utterly mad but, equally, may be the most inspired, revolutionary, if enormously impractical, viticultural practice ever contemplated: Why not grow grapes from seedlings? That is to say, why not collect the seeds from the fruit one has harvested and then germinate them, selecting for characteristics that one deems appropriate? Bear in mind that there is a reason why 99.99 percent of grapevines on the planet have been planted from vegetative cuttings, not seeds. Apart from the fact that it is easier by many orders of magnitude to propagate from cuttings, the cutting, or daughter plant, remains genetically true to the mother plant. If you like the characteristics of the vine, a cutting will enable you to replicate it. Conversely, taking the seeds from a plant will completely and randomly reassort all the genetic material that is in the vine's DNA but not expressed. So a red grape like Pinot noir will yield mainly red progeny but also white and pink and all colors in between, some with thicker skins, some with thinner, some very productive, some not at all, ad infinitum.

This is a very, very ambitious project, and it rests on a couple of core beliefs, the validity of which is essentially unknowable until the deed is doon. The first is the belief that the wine produced from grapes grown from a large number of genetically distinctive vines, none or few of them possessing "superior" characteristics, will in fact be more interesting and complex than a vineyard planted to relatively few genotypes, all possessing highly favorable characteristics. The second belief is that the rooting characteristics of vines grown from seeds allow one to render a much more amplified and perhaps distinctive expression of *terroir.* This is the more interesting aspect of the project, but why should this be the case? Vines grown from seeds exhibit a much higher degree of geotropism, or the tendency to form a taproot, growing straight down to China. You can observe this in volunteer plants that pop up in the garden, which have germinated from seed. A vine with a more downward rooting habit will go more deeply and possibly exploit a wider range of minerals, and my surmise is that it will make a vastly hardier, more drought-resistant plant. All of this assumes, of course, that one is planting in an area sufficiently isolated and without a history of planting, so that *vinifera* might peaceably grow without fear of imminent phylloxera infestation.

To be rigorous, one would begin with nongrafted vines planted on the site, and with as wide a range of clones and subvarieties as possible. When these vines come into production and the seeds are harvested, approximately half the seedlings will be sterile, being either male or female and thus incapable of pollinating themselves; these would be discarded on the slag heap of viticultural history. The offspring will resemble their parents only slightly, and yet there should be a certain familial resonance and harmony, if one considers this ragtag collection of vines as a unitary entity. This may be an irrational belief, but I imagine there is something transformative in the production of seeds, that the mother plant imparts some words of wisdom to her children. "It doesn't rain in California, at least in the summer," she whispers. "Don't exert yourselves and grow too vigorously, too abundantly in the springtime; it is a long, dry stretch until October."

What I find compelling about this project is the opportunity for a grower to take advantage of the stunning richness, diversity, and adaptability of nature, expressed in the seed's potential, as well as of the experience of a collection of grapevines responding to a particular set of environmental challenges. But what is also interesting is the opportunity for a human being to employ his or her intelligence to make multiple, discriminating, empirical judgments concerning the kind of vines that seem to be most harmonious and congruent for a particular site, and concerning the wine that speaks most personally to him or her. These judgments will certainly change with experience. For example, if I were to essay to produce a red wine from Pinot noir, I would likely begin by selecting only thicker skinned, more deeply colored red grapes for the cuvée. And yet, with time, I might find that including a certain percentage of white or pink-skinned grapes actually produces a wine of greater complexity and interest. There is a lovely open-endedness and scale to the project that perfectly suits my own slightly eclectic and obsessive-compulsive personality. There is also the incidental fact that, if I can pull this off, I will be midwifing at the birth of literally thousands of new grape varieties the world has not seen before; this is a congenial thought to entertain. I love the fact that I do not know where the project will ultimately go, and that the road there will be a very, very slow and meandering one.[314]   *(2006-2007)*

314. This feature first appeared in a different form as a series of articles (part 1: issue 13, 2006; part 2: issue 14, 2006; part 3: issue 15, 2007; part 4: issue 16, 2007; part 5: issue 17, 2007) in *The World of Fine Wine* magazine, www.finewinemag.com.

This is a companion piece to the earlier "'Great' Wine in the Postmodernist World" opus, more deeply thought out and perhaps an attempt to imagine some concrete, quasi-practical solutions to what is essentially an existential question: In making wine or growing grapes, where does true meaning repose? And ultimately, meaning for whom? There are ironies within ironies inherent in this question. Let us consider a hypothetical case: Imagine a tortured New World winemaker who just adores Pinot Noir . . . when it is grown in Burgundy. Would the crafting of a profoundly "Burgundian" Pinot Noir in the Santa Cruz Mountains, say, be truly meaningful even if it never approaches the epic complexity and majestic coherence of a *grand cru* Burgundy? Would it not be a greater contribution to the world to somehow discover an altogether new style of Pinot, one that afforded comparable complexity and pleasurability? (Can he or she learn to imagine a different Pinot-Platonic form?) And yet fashioning a Pinot so radically disparate from the known paradigm calls for an extraordinary exertion of human imagination, thus possibly effacing the distinction between a *vin d'effort* and a *vin de terroir*. In trying to identify the most meaningful thing a winegrower might accomplish in a short lifetime, one confronts essentially the same issues that one might confront on a spiritual quest: How might one use one's self to attain selflessness (one's *effort* to attain *terroir*)? How and where is one to park one's ego in the process? For whose benefit is one performing this work? How can one simultaneously strive and let go? How does one know when one is sufficiently aligned in one's practice that one can let a force greater and wiser than oneself steer the bus?[315] Ultimately, the planting of a great or a humble vineyard is a folly in the Castanedan sense, and its "meaning" undoubtedly reposes in the quality of attention and intention that one brings to its establishment and care, as much as to the commercial éclat that it might enjoy.

Terroir and Going Home

I have for so long defined myself as "the guy who is going to plant a great vineyard someday." I am persuaded that there is absolutely no way to produce great wine (a compelling personal aspiration) apart from planting a vineyard *from scratch* with the intention of expressing the *terroir* of the site. I suspect one must follow a radically nonstandard protocol to even have a chance at attaining this end: dry-farming, field-budding, employing a diversity of planting stock and situating the vines within a thoughtfully conceived polyculture, arraying the plantation to correspond to the template of sacred geometry, energetically balancing the plants with crystals or perhaps "cosmic pipes"—all the sundry criteria that figure in my febrile imaginings. There was a character in Steinbeck's novel *Cannery Row* who was always constructing a new boat, but each time he neared completion of the vessel, he decided the design was all wrong and scrapped it and started over. (It turned out that he was mortally afraid of the water.) I wonder sometimes if I am not the viticultural equivalent of that boat builder.

For me, the vineyard represents my spiritual path, perhaps the only shot I have at bringing

---

315. I think of my five-year-old daughter, Amélie, who is just learning to ride her bike without training wheels. Yes, she has a helmet (and kneepads), but it is nevertheless brutally difficult to let go.

balance into my life and achieving something like contentment. While naturally I will be profoundly disappointed, even—forgive me—crushed, if the wines do not turn out brilliantly from the get-go, I will also consider it an unprecedented lifetime accomplishment to at least temporarily interrupt the clatter and chatter of my recursive conscious mind and return to the meditative silence of the vineyard, at least for a few hours every day. I know that I will never be a particularly gifted or sincere spiritual practitioner. I don't have the *Sitzfleisch*, the patience, perhaps, or the tolerance or empathy. I suspect that, all things being equal, I might do better with plants than with higher animals.

To work in a vineyard, one must above all be present, "grounded." It is like being a parent, with a child who is always reminding you to wake up and pay attention. I am not a naturally gifted agriculturist. When, years ago, I actually spent some time on a tractor, more than a few times I narrowly missed turning it over and barely managed to avoid maiming myself with all manner of agricultural implements. I have always held on to the fantasy that I was a gifted pruner, but in looking at it now from a slightly different angle, I realize I *am* a gifted pruner, but not in the sense of being brilliantly fast and accurate. Rather, the vines have gifted me with a certain amount of magical, meditative, timeless time to be present with them. Pruning is an active meditation: one loses one's sense of self as one is guided automatically through the movements with elegance and economy of motion, cutting here to one bud or two, selecting the strongest, most upright spurs, pulling away the brush, all of it done essentially by reflex, with no conscious deliberation.[316] Would that I could be so effortlessly decisive in "real life" in the cutting away of that which is extraneous and clearing the path to burgeoning growth and the flowering of self-fulfillment.

I, who hope to make a great wine some day, am struck by the fact that winemaking, or more accurately, wine growing, like any artistic process, might be thought of as an extension or projection of the "self" unto the external world. I have the tendency, maybe more than most, to engage in instrumental thinking—one does X in order to attain Y. Clear (less brutal than *cut down*) majestically tall trees and bothersome brush to open up land suitable for planting; plant a great vineyard to get great wine; make great wine to get a great bottle price, and lots of acclaim, adulation, and sycophancy will ensue. And yet, I cling to the idea that this vineyard will enable me to transcend this kind of thinking. What if the only way to find "greatness" in a vine-

316. I love pruning grapevines that have been trained in all sorts of different ways, but the most fulfilling to prune are the head-trained spur-pruned vines called *gobelets* in France or "bush vines" in Australia. They tend to be rather small and squat in Europe and backbreaking to prune, but the American versions that are very old (more than a hundred years old) are approximately as tall as a man or a small bear, vitaceous Mother Kalis. Pruning is a bit like shaking hands; you size up a vine or a person in your initial approach. Whereas a bilateral cordon-trained vine or vertical shoot-positioned cane-pruned vine exists more or less in a single plane with its left and right sides balanced like the assets and debits in a banker's ledger (or the virtues and vices of a human soul presenting itself at Saint Peter's gate), the *gobelet* is a three-dimensional structure, more like a circular mandala, an integral whole, a microcosm of oneself or perhaps the universe. Withal, approaching the vine is an opportunity to locate oneself *somewhere* in a complex, patterned world.

yard were to assume a posture of gratitude and humble reverence to it? What if one were to systematically seek permission from and accord with the spirits of the land for every action taken on it? I am looking to create a wine contained within itself, one that seeks nothing further. It has occurred to me that, unless I find something like that harmony within myself, the wine itself is unlikely to attain the balance and self-sufficiency I seek.

Growing grapes is more like parenting than one might ever conceive. My daughter, Mélie, while absolutely brilliant, often needs encouragement to step outside her comfort zone, to challenge herself and become more independent and self-reliant.[317] And yet, the question every parent asks is: Am I pushing my child too far, too fast? It is equally easy to park a child in front of a video screen or to turn on the drip irrigation when vines are showing signs of stress. The work of a parent or viticulturist is to gently and fearlessly encourage our charges to challenge themselves, to go where they have never been before. I hope I have the requisite skill and patience to let my child and my vineyard gradually show me who and what they truly are. No doubt both vineyard and child will order themselves in ways I have not yet conceived. I hope I have the wisdom and heart to fully celebrate and cherish the unique entities that emerge.[318]

(2008)

As I draw closer to actually planting a new vineyard, most likely the last word/act I will have on the subject, the process itself seems to have become a mirror to my own deep "issues." I now understand that the work outside the vineyard is perhaps more formidable than the work within it. Simply conceiving of a vineyard that will outlive oneself, and that might enrich the patrimony of the world of wine, is a useful spiritual exercise whether or not the resultant wine is ultimately as *terroir*-expressive as one might hope. The vineyard is a microcosm of the human being who plants it; tending one's outward vineyard or garden may create the template for the cultivation of the sweetest, most succulent fruit of the spirit.

317. The other side of this, of course, is that the parent is continually confronted with his or her own weaknesses and insecurities, and children have laser-guided detection systems that pinpoint these with unerring accuracy.   318. This feature first appeared in a different form, as "First Nose: Terroir and Going Home," in issue 19 (2008) of *The World of Fine Wine* magazine, www.finewinemag.com.

A Meditation on Terroir: The Return

The French make a salient distinction between *vins d'effort* and *vins de terroir*—wines that are notably marked by the imprint of human efforts, as opposed to wines whose character primarily reflects their place of origin. Ultimately, *vins d'effort* are wines easy to like—presumably they are constructed with precisely that in mind—but difficult to love, at least in the thoroughly obsessive, *I've just seen a beautiful face and I will go mad if I cannot see it again* kind of way. *Vins d'effort*, especially those of the New World, attempt to hit the stylistic parameters of "great" wine—concentration, check; new wood, check; soft tannins, check. And yet the net result is like a picture of a composite, computer-generated "beautiful" person: it is never as compelling as the picture of an aesthetically "flawed" but unambiguously real person. I believe that some part of us—very likely a part that doesn't function on a conscious level— responds to the deep order of a *vin de terroir* to a level of complexity that derives only from the ordering of Nature itself, not from the order imposed by a human being.

What is this ordering about, and how can we recognize it when we experience it? How can we avoid getting distracted by what I call the more superficial, obvious charms of a *vin d'effort*— new oak and profoundly ripe and somewhat confected fruit being the obvious ones? First, I believe that the deep ordering—which we experience as an unfolding in the taste experience, where layers melt away and reveal deeper layers (somewhat like in *The Matrix*, if I can make that analogy)—provokes a flash of recognition in us, a link to something we apprehend as being vast and unbounded. It may be like our wonder at the night sky. A wine that moves and changes with the gradual removal of the veils—the obscurations of the wine's true essence— speaks eloquently to our innate thirst for order and meaning and beckons us forward.

We are all metaphorical beings—that is to say, not everything we understand is apprehended neutrally or in a vacuum; everything we experience links by association with our personal (or perhaps suprapersonal) history. A rich experience is one that resonates with earlier experiences, and perhaps nothing resonates with us more than "tasting the earth." Maybe it is the ashes-to-ashes, dust-to-dust, knowledge we carry inside us—the knowledge that, in the end, all we are is dust—that stimulates in us a unique sympathy with a *vin de terroir*. There is an aesthetic frisson when we suddenly recognize a certain pattern miraculously coming into focus as a known and loved wine of our experience, the velvet glove of a Chambertin, the peacock-feathered expansiveness of a Musigny, rather like the recognition of the face of a friend.

But it is more than the ability to successfully "read" a wine that gratifies us: it is the intimation of a highly complex and organized world that abuts our own, one that we instantly recognize, but with the knowledge that we comprise but a small part of it. Our perception of a *vin de terroir* is undoubtedly like the perception of a range of ordered resonant frequencies, tones, and overtones sequenced on our palate. The sense of mineral "earthiness"—not quite an explicit taste, like a fruity raspberry ester, but more like the originating conditions for the expression of a taste or its subtext—is perhaps an expression of the lower frequencies, the rumbling bass that we don't so much hear as feel in our solar plexus or in the soles of our feet. Something appears to open within us when we experience a *vin de terroir*—New Agers might suggest it is the first chakra, the energetic center of the body linked with our foundation, our grounding in and connection to the physical plane. The experience of a *vin de terroir* floods us with associations, memories, and emotions linked to something beyond our direct experience—to archetypal forms that seem to antedate our individual short-term tenures on this earth.

Maybe what we experience is the sense of mirrors within mirrors—the knowledge that the golden ratios that obtain in musical scales, in the figures of regular polygons, and in starfish are the same ones that describe the geometry of our bones and our cathedrals and condition our ability to create order out of the seemingly chaotic universe that comprises our world. A *vin de terroir* carries the strong imprint of Nature's greatest ideas—which are undoubtedly particularly felicitous ratios. A great, organized *vin de terroir* might present itself as a recursive spiral, ever-changing, sometimes appearing to "close up," to turn back on itself. Its general movement, however, will always be in the direction of greater depth and complexity, and with each turn will appear yet another resonant note or overtone.

I can't quite put words to why I am profoundly comforted by the fact that a wine can also be a place, that mere fermented grapes can coalesce into a product of such rare beauty and meaning. There is something deeply primal about the whole notion of place or "home"—the idea that everything has a place, that everything (and everyone) has a home. We are moved when we enter a space that is truly habitated.[319] I don't mean simply a place that has kitschy trinkets strewn everywhere, but one that bears the signs that a human has made this a warm and welcoming home.[320] Without a home, a touchstone, there is no place for us to rest, to repose; a *vin de terroir* is like the wayfarer's stopover along the long, windy, and sometimes tedious *route de vin.*

Maybe *terroir* is simply an intimation of the vibrational persistence of phenomena, even if they are not manifestly, palpably present—a knowledge that nothing is ever truly lost, but continues to exist as a signal that we can apprehend, assuming we still have the wit and capacity to tune in. Might this explain its message of comfort and consolation? Earlier I mentioned the

---

319. There is an analogous feeling when one enters a *clos,* an exterior space delimited or enclosed by natural or human-made features. **320.** While *terroir* is a mirror of the natural world, paradoxically it cannot exist without the perception (and participation) of a human being. It is the human being who identifies and names the *terroir* and works to individuate a particular parcel, whether through organic, biodynamic, or other life-force-enhancing practices. The conscious cultivation of biological complexity within the farm ecosystem, whether by the use of biodynamic preparations or by the skillful establishment of an insectary or well-suited companion plants, as well as certain cultural practices—pruning, composting, and crop-thinning—that aim to bring the vine and its environment into balance, work toward the explicit elaboration of *terroir.*

sense of *terroir*'s grandeur, its linkage to earth and, by extension, to Earth (and perhaps the cosmos). In the end, however, it is not its vastness but its intimacy—like a late night telephone conversation with someone living on the other side of the world—that creates the sense of wonder. How am I so privileged that one small, albeit very organized, piece of the world will disclose itself to me so frankly?

Perhaps the sheer wonder of the miracle of wine itself, its unexpected presence in the world, indicates the very real possibility of alchemy, the transformation of the base, humble, and mute into the noble, sublime, and articulate.[321]   *(2008)*

— This is just a brief reflection on the subject of *terroir*, a trope that seems to follow me everywhere I go. Terroir is a metaphor through which we can glimpse nature's order refracted through a wine glass darkly. I am taken with the notion that order exists all around us despite the apparent chaos introduced by the human presence. The spiritual impulse in mankind is to participate in the elucidation of something greater and more beautiful than anything we might conceive in our rational thinking. Planting a vineyard or building a cathedral is something that human beings might accomplish—though not without heroic labor—that might inspire others to observe the wondrous order that imbues all things.

1. This feature first appeared under the same title but in a slightly different form in issue 21 (2008) of *The World of Fine Wine* magazine, www.finewinemag.com.

110 Rupestris du Lot (110R): Grape rootstock of Texas origin, particularly well suited for calcareous conditions.

2,4,6-trichloroanisole (TCA): Odiferous molecule implicated in the phenomenon of cork taint, detectable at extremely low concentrations.

4-ethyl phenol: A pungent molecule that is considered a signifier of a *Brettanomyces* infection in alcoholic beverages.

Acidulation: The addition of an acid (typically tartaric, though sometimes malic or citric) to a wine or a grape must.

Ah-So: Proprietary brand of twin-tined cork extractor.

Ampelography: The science of grapevine identification.

Amphorae: Clay vessels employed for the fermentation and storage of wine since antiquity; possibly the coolest way ever conceived to age wine.

Angel's share: The ethanol that is evaporated in the ageing process of Cognac or Armagnac.

AOC: Appellation d'Origine Contrôlée, the French system that regulates the naming of wines.

Aroma wheel: Invented by Dr. Ann Noble, a professor at UC Davis, this is a visual graphic of the different categories and aroma components found in wine; it does not actually rotate

Assemblaggio: (It.) Cuvée, or assemblage.

Asterix and Obelix: Characters in the exceptionally strange fantasy series of French comic strips set in ancient Gaul. An acquaintance with the strips *Asterix* and *The Adventures of Tintin* is compulsory for an understanding of the French psyche.

Auslese: (Ger.) "Late-harvest," generally indicates a wine with significant residual sugar.

Autochthonous: Originating in the place where found. There are still numerous hotbeds of autochthonous grapes—Friuli, Calabria, and Gascony are places that immediately come to mind.

Autolysis: The postfermentation breakdown of the cell walls of yeast bodies, which adds savoriness to a wine and enhances its texture. The phenomenon is well known in sparkling wines, but its role in still wines is greatly underappreciated.

Balling: A measurement of the dissolved solids (mostly sugar) of a solution; essentially synonymous with Brix, though slightly different due to a temperature compensation adjustment.

Barrique: (Fr.) A 225-liter barrel.

Bâtonnage: (Fr.) Circulation of lees (mostly yeast cells) either through stirring or other mechanical agitation.

The glossary contains a number of technical and foreign-language winemaking and grape-growing terms that the lay reader may not know, as well as the names of significant personages, at least in my wine world. In addition, the reader will, perhaps surprisingly, find a number of Yiddish words, which also appear in the text. I've included them in the glossary at the instigation of my editors, who, bless their academic *goyische kops*, were lexically *farmisht*, if not *farshimmelt*, at the terms' precise meanings. Initially, I found myself resisting the notion of including Yiddish words in the glossary of what is essentially a wine book. I imagined that their presence would be jarring—*verkakte* alongside *vigneron* is a bit much, though there are certainly a fair number of *verkakte vignobles* in this world (one of the subtexts of this book). I looked at my resistance: did it say something about my own ambivalence toward my Jewish identity? I had always been more or less *d'accord* with the brilliant Dr. Jonathan Miller who professed "not to be a Jew exactly" but rather more "Jew-ish." In the end, I found that I liked the Yiddish bits sprinkled into the mix, like pimiento peppers. It is consistent with the essential bricolage nature of the book itself.

Baumé: A standard for the measurement of specific gravity, developed by the French pharmacist Antoine Baumé in 1768.

Bettane, Michel: Influential wine critic, affiliated for many years with *La Revue du Vin de France*.

Biodynamics: The agricultural practice outlined in a series of lectures given by Rudolf Steiner in 1924. Biodynamics seeks to invigorate the life force of a farm through a more intimate connection with the energetic forces of the planetary and celestial spheres.

Biotype B: A particularly aggressive genotype of the glassy-winged sharpshooter insect, the vector for Pierce's disease.

Bize-Leroy, Lalou: Legendary former coproprietor of Domaine de la Romanée-Conti, present owner of Domaine Leroy in Burgundy, and producer of really great and expensive wines.

Bonneau, Henri: Top Châteauneuf-du-Pape producer who creates powerful, traditionally styled wines.

Bordeaux mix: A fungicide composed of copper sulfate and hydrated lime, used primarily for the treatment of downy mildew in grapes; it leaves an eerie blue residue on the leaves and the ground.

Bordolese: (It.) Stylish and heavy high-shouldered claret bottle; the inhabitants of Bordeaux.

Botte: (It.) Large (greater than 500-liter) wooden storage vessel.

Bouchonné: (Fr.) Cork tainted.

Brettanomyces: Wine spoilage yeast, said to impart a "barnyard" or "sweaty saddle" character to wine or other fermented beverages. Sometimes abbreviated as "Brett."

Brix: The most common scale in the United States for the measurement of the soluble solids (sweetness) of a fruit must or juice.

B'rucha: (Yid.) Ritual blessing said over wine.

Calcaire: (Fr.) Limestone, the Holy Grail for Pinot Noir.

Cane pruning (le système Guyot): Style of pruning, consisting of leaving one or two fruiting canes and a corresponding number of renewal spurs.

Capsule à vis: (Fr.) Screwcap.

Carbonic maceration (macération carbonique): Intracellular anaerobic fermentation, a technique typically used for Beaujolais Nouveau, creating a rather particular fruity aromatic profile, sometimes referred to as a "bubblegum" character.

Caviste: (Fr.) Cellar worker, but also "winemaker," depending on the context.

Cépage: (Fr.) Grape variety.

Chais: (Fr.) Ageing cellar.

Chapoutier, Michel: Flamboyant producer of Hermitage and other appellations of the Northern Rhône (and elsewhere).

Chaptalization: The addition of sugar to grape must with the intention of boosting its alcoholic degree (after Jean-Antoine Chaptal, a proponent of the practice).

Char: The degree of "toast" found on the interior of a wine barrel, said to impart particular sensory characteristics.

Chazerei: (Yid.) Junk or junk food; literally, "pig's food."

Chemise: (Fr.) The "shirt"—the tannin-and-protein complex that precipitates on the side of a bottle after long bottle-ageing.

Chêne: (Fr.) Oak.

Chips: Typically, oak fragments added to wine either during or after alcoholic fermentation.

Clape, Auguste: Distinguished producer of Cornas.

Claret: English term for a Bordeaux wine, derived from the French *claret*, meaning a light, clear wine (of Bordeaux).

Clendenen, Jim: Highly loquacious owner of Au Bon Climat Winery.

Climat: (Fr.) Most generally, "climate" but in Burgundy, a specifically defined vineyard area, usually an individual field.

Clone: A genetically distinctive organism descended from and genetically identical to a single common ancestor.

Clos: (Fr.) A walled or otherwise enclosed vineyard.

Cold soak: The maceration (typically of red grapes) at a low temperature prior to the onset of fermentation.

Cold (or tartrate) stabilization: The precipitation of potassium bitartrate in a wine solution, normally effected by chilling the wine to slightly above its freezing point.

Compost tea: A liquid solution or suspension made by steeping compost in water; used as both a fertilizer and a prophylaxis against bacterial and fungal diseases.

Condom: Town in the region of Armagnac.

Connerie: (Fr.) Foolishness (slightly vulgar).

Cordon (bilateral or unilateral) training: Grape-training method commonly used in the New World, owing to the simplicity of its establishment and maintenance.

Cosmic pipe: A modern device based on ancient principles that uses rudimentary electric circuitry for the channeling of cosmic forces to create a positive agronomic outcome.

Cosmoculture: An eclectic agricultural methodology practiced at Domaine Viret in the Côtes du Rhône utilizing such esoteric elements as geobiology, planetary marking, radionics, and the memory of water.

Crème de cassis: (Fr.) Liqueur made from black currants.

Crise de foie: (Fr.) A "crisis of the liver," a term for stomach ailments routinely experienced by

French people but largely unknown outside the francophonic milieu.

Cru: (Fr.) "Growth," or vineyard site.

Cryoextraction: The process by which grapes are frozen; ice crystals remain behind in the grape as the clusters are pressed, thus concentrating the sugar in the expressed juice.

Cultured yeast: A yeast selected for its favorable fermentation kinetics and organoleptic characteristics.

Cuvaison: (Fr.) Duration of time a fermented must is held in the fermentation vessel before pressing.

Cuvée: (Fr.) A particular batch of wine.

Dayenu: (Heb.) "It would be sufficient." This refrain is uttered as part of the Passover seder and is intended to demonstrate the gratitude of the Children of Israel to their God.

Débourbage: (Fr.) The settling of grape solids.

Diatomaceous earth: Filtration aid, composed of the fossilized remains of diatoms, a type of hard shelled algae.

Disulfides: Class of sulfur-containing compounds said to smell like onions, leeks, or garlic.

Dönnhoff, Helmut: Brilliant winemaker in the Nahe region of Germany.

Droits de succession: (Fr.) Rights of inheritance in French law.

Dry-farming: Farming without benefit of irrigation.

Ducournau, Patrick: The inventor of *microbullage*, or microoxygenation, and proprietor of Domaine Mouréou and Chapelle L'Enclos in Madiran.

Eiswein: (Ger.) The sweet wine produced by the freezing of grapes on the vine.

Elevage: (Fr.) The "upbringing" or cellaring of a wine prior to bottling.

Encépagement: (Fr.) Relative percentages of different grape varieties composing a wine blend.

Endcaps: Cases of wine stacked at the ends of aisles in wineshops, liquor stores, or grocery stores.

En primeur: (Fr.) First sales offering of a wine, typically before it is bottled.

En vrac: (Fr.) In bulk.

Ester: An aromatic molecule that results from the combination of a fatty acid and an alcohol; the most common ester found in wine is ethyl acetate.

Etiquette: (Fr.) Label.

Exchangeable cations: Metallic ions (chiefly calcium, magnesium, sodium, and potassium), found in soils with observable clay content, which enhance the water-holding capacity of soils and serve as a source of plant nutrition.

"Family Plan": The discounted wholesale price available across a wide range of products from a given producer.

Fardrai zich dem kop: (Yid.) Drive yourself crazy.

Farmisht: (Yid.) Confused, befuddled.

Farshimmelt: (Yid.) Slightly more confused and mixed up, owing to a moldy mind.

Field-budding: Grafting a scion (fruiting variety) onto the rootstock of a plant already established in the field.

Fining: The introduction into a wine of a substance that ultimately precipitates out, with the aim of either helping clarify or settle the wine or improving its sensory characteristics.

Flash-détente: (Fr.) High-tech system for imploding the cells of grape berries to effect a more complete extraction of tannins and other polyphenols.

Flatteur: (Fr.) Flattering, charming.

Fleishig and **milchig:** (Yid.) In the Jewish practice of *kashrut,* there is an ontological distinction between foods containing milk in any form (*milchig*) and those containing red meat or poultry (*fleishig*), and between the serving utensils designated for each. (There is yet a third category, *pareve,* for foods containing neither.)

Flor: (Sp.) A strain of yeast used in the production of sherry or *vin jaune* that forms a film on the surface of wine in a partially filled barrel.

Foudre: (Fr.) Large oak casks typically oval in shape.

Fruit bomb: A modern wine style, the result of the harvest of exceptionally ripe grapes and, often, the utilization of a fruitiness-enhancing cultured yeast.

"Fruit day": In biodynamics, a day in which the fruit element of a vine or its produce is more fully expressed. Thus, fruit days are optimal for grape harvest or for tasting wine.

Galet: (Fr.) Stone, typically a river rock. Also, the name of a highly respected French ampelographer.

Garagiste: (Fr.) Very small (garage-sized) boutique winemaker.

Geschriven: (Yid.) Written or inscribed.

Gevalt: (Yid.) An expression of anxiety or shock.

Gobelet: (Fr.) System of vine training in the form of a self-supporting head-trained vine, found in older, nonirrigated plantations in California, as well as in many parts of southern France and Spain.

Godello: A very aromatic white grape, native to Galicia, most widely planted in the Valdeorras denomination of origin.

Gondola: Large harvest receptacle, typically of three- or six-ton capacity.

Goutte-à-goutte: (Fr.) Drip irrigation.

Governo: An old winemaking technique used in Tuscany (alas, now mostly in desuetude) involving the partial drying of grapes and their addition to the fermenting vessel at the completion of fermentation. Wines produced in this manner are said to be softer and more approachable than their conventional counterparts.

Grand Cru: (Fr.) Great growth.

Grêle: (Fr.) Hail.

Guigal, Marcel: Highly respected winemaker, located in Ampuis in the Northern Rhône, known primarily for his single-vineyard "La La" wines in the appellation of Côte Rôtie, La Mouline, La Landonne, and La Turque.

Guyot, Dr. Jules: Inventor of the eponymous "cane-pruning" system.

Haut-Médoc: The portion of the Bordeaux wine region of southwestern France that is located on the left bank of the Gironde estuary.

Hectoliters/hectare: The measurement by which tonnage or yield is typically expressed in most parts of western Europe. The numbers themselves carry a certain ideological subtext. In some premium appellations in France, such as Burgundy, low yields are strongly associated with higher quality; this belief has become gospel among certain wine writers who are always seeking explanatory mechanisms for why some wines appear to be "better" than others. In other areas, such as Alto Adige in Italy and some parts of Germany, low yields are sometimes considered unthrifty and vaguely reprehensible.

Herbacé: (Fr.) Herbaceous.

High-toast: Heavy charring of the interior of wine barrels or puncheons.

Hydrogen sulfide: The primary odiferous molecule associated with 'reduction' issues and said to smell like rotten eggs.

Hydroxymethyl pyrazine: The molecule implicated in the strong herbaceous and bell-pepper scent of improperly managed Cabernet Sauvignon and Merlot grapes.

Impitoyable: (Fr.) Literally, "merciless." A large wine-tasting glass used for technical tasting, configured so as to enhance taste and amplify aromas, though effectively impossible to drink out of without having wine dribble down one's chin.

INAO: The Institut National des Appellations d'Origine is the French organization charged with the regulation of controlled place-names.

Inox: (Fr.) Stainless steel.

International style: A modern style of winemaking that emphasizes the use of extremely ripe fruit, soft tannins and a generous percentage of new oak, to the detriment of the expression of the unique characteristics of the grape variety or the site on which the grapes were grown.

Kabinett: (Ger.) Under German wine law, the lowest level of ripeness for a Prädikatswein, lower

than for a *Spätlese*. A *Kabinett* wine is typically crisp, refreshing and semisweet, though it may also be dry if designated *trocken*.

Kvell: (Yid.) To be filled with pride and elation to the point of needing to share this emotion with everyone.

Lees: The spent yeast bodies that fall to the bottom of a fermenting or storage vessel.

Leflaive, Anne-Claude: Very serious biodynamic producer of soulful wines in Burgundy.

Lieu-dit: (Fr.) A subappellation, or part of a named vineyard, sometimes deriving from a colorful or memorable story about that vineyard.

Limousin: Forest in central France, west of the Auvergne Mountains, responsible for relatively loose-grained oak, easily extracted in an alcohol solution. Limousin barrels were fashionable in California in the 1970s for white wine fermentation and ageing but like other fads of that time, they have gone the way of bell-bottom pants. They are now used primarily for the ageing of spirits.

Loureiro: Aromatic white grape of the Iberian Peninsula, used in Vinho Verde and sometimes blended with Albariño.

Macération à froid: (Fr.) The maceration of grapes at low temperature prior to the onset of fermentation.

Macération pelliculaire: (Fr.) *See* Skin contact.

Madeirization: The subjection of a wine to warm storage conditions which brings about its oxidation, either intentionally in the instance of Madeira, or unintentionally in the instance of leaving it in a warm car with the windows rolled up.

Maître de chai: (Fr.) Cellar master.

Malolactic fermentation: A secondary bacterial fermentation occurring in wine; it converts malic acid to lactic acid, softening the wine and giving it added complexity.

Massal selection: Distinguished from clonal selection, it is the selection by the *vigneron* of individual plants for propagation and replanting from a given vineyard, with an eye to their suitability for that particular vineyard.

McCloskey, Leo: Winemaking consultant and owner of Enologix®, known for his ability to prognosticate high-scoring wines well in advance of their commercial release.

Médocain: (Fr.) Of or deriving from the Médoc, the central grape-growing area of Bordeaux.

Mercaptan: A large group of very smelly sulfur-containing compounds (aka thiols). Terms such as *cooked cabbage* and *burnt rubber* are used to describe them.

Meritage: An invented term and certification mark used by California wines for Bordeaux-style red and white blended wines.

Meshuggene: (Yid.) Crazy.

Microoxygenation (*microbullage*): A system, invented by Patrick Ducourneau, for administering small, measured amounts of oxygen to wine, with the aim of managing its tannic structure.

Millésime: (Fr.) Vintage year.

Minerality: The aspect of a wine related to its mineral content—though this is still a somewhat controversial concept. "Minerality" may well mean the presence of a certain (unknown) group of minerals in wine, but may also reflect the oxidation state in which they are held. The presence of sulfur-containing molecules may also be implicated in the phenomenon of the perception of minerality.

Mishpoche: (Yid.) Extended family.

Mondovino (2004): Documentary film produced by Jonathan Nossiter about the problematic impact of globalization on the wine industry.

Monocépage: (Fr.) Single grape varietal wine.

Mycorrhizae: The fungal symbiotes living in association with plant roots, responsible for the active transport of many micronutrients into the root hairs.

Oechsle: The Oechsle scale, used primarily in German-speaking grape-growing areas, is a hydrometer scale measuring the density of grape must, an indication of grape ripeness and sugar content.

Ordóñez, Jorge: Noted importer of Spanish wines, and the mind behind the product Wrongo Dongo.

Organoleptic: Having an effect on one of the organs of sense, such as taste or smell.

Ostertag, André: Innovative winemaker from Alsace.

Paradis: (Fr.) Paradise; also a designation of extremely old Cognac.

Parker, Robert: Extremely influential wine writer and publisher of the *Wine Advocate.*

Pergola: (It.) Overhead trellising system employed in Trento and Alto Adige—often as a means of enhancing yield (these are thrifty Northerners, after all)—and in Puglia, where it is artfully employed to shade the grapes from direct sun and to enhance the humidity under the canopy, providing some measure of evaporative cooling.

Pet de cheval: (Fr.) Horse fart.

Pétillant: (Fr.) Fizzy.

Peynaud, Emile: French oenologist and researcher, credited with revolutionizing modern winemaking.

pH: The inverse log of the hydrogen ion concentration; loosely, the base neutralizing capacity of a solution.

Phenolics: The group of compounds found mainly in the skins, stems, and seeds of grapes, including anthocyanins and tannins, responsible for the astringent and sometimes bitter flavors in wine, as well as for their antioxidant activity.

Phenology: The study of the timing of recurring natural phenomena; in the case of grape vines, it refers to salient events such as bud break, flowering, *véraison* (color change), and maturity.

Pied de cuve: (Fr.) A yeast culture normally derived from the indigenous yeast found on grape skins, initiated a week to ten days in advance of the date of harvest. It serves as an inoculum for the larger lot to be fermented.

Pierce's disease: Serious bacterial disease, believed to originate in the southeastern part of the United States, that attacks grapevines. The disease is transmitted by the blue-green and glassy-winged sharpshooter insects.

Pigeage: (Fr.) Punchdown, or manual submersion, of the mass of skins that form at the top of a fermenting must.

Plotz: (Yid.) To collapse from exhaustion or to be overwhelmed with excitement or embarrassment.

Polyphenol: Any of a large class of organic compounds of plant origin having more than one phenol (ring-shaped) group; they tend to be colorful and to possess antioxidant properties.

Pomme prisonière: (Fr.) Apple brandy bottled with an apple inside the bottle. (This is accomplished by placing the bottles on the trees as the fruit is developing, thus "imprisoning" it.)

Post-off: A published price reduction in a state that requires a public posting (typically monthly) of wholesale wine or liquor prices.

Pruno: High-octane distillate illicitly fabricated in prison from any fermentable source material.

Prunus: An eau-de-vie made of apricot, plum, and cherry, produced by Bonny Doon Vineyard.

Pump over: The process of circulating wine from the bottom of a fermenter to the top, with the intention of wetting the mass of skins (the "cap") to help cool the fermentation and make sure the tannins and anthocyanins are well extracted.

Punch down (v.); punchdown (n.): See *Pigeage*.

Puncheon: Double-sized barrel, typically five hundred liters in volume, well suited for the *élevage* of Rhône-style wines.

Puttony: (Hu.) Basket. In Tokaj, Hungary, the number of *puttonyos* indicated on the label reflects how many baskets of heavily botrytised must (unfermented crushed grapes) have been added to the must of uninfected grapes and, by extension, the level of sweetness in the finished wine.

Quercus: The genus of the oak tree; used in the fabrication of wine barrels and wine "ameliorants."

The species of *Quercus* most widely used for barrels is *alba*.

Racking: The transfer of wine from one vessel to another.

Redox: An abbreviation for "reduction-oxidation," a process in which there is an exchange of electrons between two or more molecules.

Reduction: Chemically, the gaining of an electron by a particular molecule; in wine terms, it is most relevantly the transformation of an element sulfur molecule into the rotten-eggy hydrogen sulfide. The hydrogen sulfide molecule undergoes numerous transformations, and the particular forms we don't enjoy smelling are imprecisely called "reduction aromas."

Régisseur: (Fr.) In its application to the wine business, a vineyard and winery manager.

Rendement: (Fr.) Yield.

Reverse osmosis (l'osmose inverse): A process by which a solvent is separated from its solute by passing it through a semipermeable membrane.

Riedel: Austrian producer of an eclectic array of wine glasses.

Rootstock: That part of the plant in physical contact with the ground, selected for its favorable characteristics—of growth or rooting habit—as well as for its ability to meet specific environmental challenges, such as drought, free lime, and the presence of nematodes or phylloxera.

Sagrantino: Extremely tannic and flavorful red grape grown in Umbria.

Saint George: An exceptionally deep-rooting, vigorous rootstock, now largely out of favor in California but well suited for dry-farming, especially on hillsides.

Schande: (Yid.) Shame or disgrace. Cf. the German *Schade*, an element in the word *schadenfreude*, a wonderful term that I've appropriated as *Chardonfreude* (the pleasure one derives in observing other winemakers *fardrai* their *kops* over the *eppis* grape variety Chardonnay).

Schav: (Yid.) A chilled soup made from sorrel or spinach.

Scheu(rebe): Odd grape variety hybridized by Dr. Georg Scheu in 1916. Long believed by everyone (including me) to be a Riesling × Silvaner cross, yet recent DNA analysis has shown that Riesling was the father, but the mother was an unknown wild vine.

Schmear: (Yid.) A dab, as of cream cheese, and by extension a number of things that go together: an aggregate, as in "the whole *schmear*."

Schnorrer: (Yid.) Freeloader.

Schtarker: (Yid.) Literally "strong man," one who really knows what he is doing, or in the vernacular, a "heavyweight."

Schvitz: (Yid.) To sweat.

Scion: In botany, the shoot that is selected for grafting onto a rootstock and that will ultimately bear the fruiting variety of interest.

Sécateur: (Fr.) Pruning shears.

Selbach, Johannes: Serious Mosel producer in Zeltingen and a great Riesling enthusiast and advocate.

Sensitive crystallization: In biodynamic practice, a methodology used to illuminate the organization and life force of a wine.

Serine: Antique selection of Syrah from Côte Rôtie.

Shanken, Marvin: Publisher of the *Wine Spectator*.

Shpritzer: (Yid.) *Tummeler*.

Skin contact (*macération pelliculaire*): The period of time between the crushing and pressing of white grapes, typically on the order of several hours or none.

Smith, Clark: Brilliant, innovative, and highly opinionated winemaker, often mentioned in connection with ingenious technological solutions to problematic wine issues.

Sol; sous-sol: (Fr.) Soil; subsoil.

Soutirage: (Fr.) *See* Racking.

Spätlese: (Ger.) In German wine law, "late harvest," a wine that has been harvested at a certain minimum must weight, at an intermediate ripeness level between a *Kabinett* and an *Auslese*.

Spinning cone: A high-tech apparatus used in the wine industry for the removal of alcohol.

Spur pruning: The retention of just a few (usually one or two) fruiting buds at a spur (a cane shortened in the previous year's pruning), either in a head-trained vine or in a two-dimensional cordon.

Stagiaire: (Fr.) Apprentice.

Sulfide: Any of several types of chemical compounds containing sulfur in its lowest oxidation number, −2.

Sulfur dioxide: Chemical used for the last hundred years (or so) as an antioxidant and bacteriostat in wine production.

Surmaturité: (Fr.) Overripeness.

TA: *See* Titratable acidity.

Tannin: The class of molecules found primarily in the seeds of grapes, but also in skins and stems, contributing astringency and sometimes bitterness to wine.

Tannin management: The winemaker's practice of working with the tannins in a wine to optimize their presentation on the palate.

Tanzer, Steven: Wine writer and publisher of the *International Wine Cellar*.

Tartrate stabilization. *See* Cold (or tartrate) stabilization.

Tastevin: (Fr.) Tasting cup, sometimes ceremonially worn by sommeliers.

TCA: *See* 2,4,6-trichloroanisole.

Tchelistcheff, André: Famed Russian oenologist and producer of legendary wines, who worked many years for Beaulieu Vineyards in the United States.

Teinturier: (Fr.) Red-juiced grape variety.

Tête de cuvée: (Fr.) Denotes special prestige or deluxe bottling; often applied to Champagne.

Three-tier system: The orderly way in which most wine is sold in the United States. The three tiers consist of the manufacturer (or importer), wholesaler, and retailer.

Tinto: (Sp.) Red wine.

Titratable acidity (TA): A measurement of the total amount of protons available in a juice or wine, expressed as tartaric acid equivalents; the term is often (erroneously) used interchangeably with "total acidity," a measure of the total organic acids present in juice or wine.

Toast: The degree of exposure of the interior of barrels to open flame in the coopering process, resulting in the favorable caramelization of the wood sugars; synonymous with *char*.

Tonneaux: (Fr.) Barrels.

Transesterification: The anaerobic recombination of esters and alcohols in the ageing process resulting in the development of "bottle bouquet."

Trans-resveratrol: The strongly antioxidative molecule believed to be the active agent of the French paradox (the phenomenon of significantly lower than expected incidence of heart disease in a population that consumes copious amounts of foie gras and other fatty foods); it is present in significant concentration in both Pinot noir and Tannat grapes.

Trayf: (Yid.) Unkosher.

Tre bicchieri: (It.) "Three glasses," the highest rating awarded by *Gambero Rosso,* a highly influential Italian wine publication.

Uvaggi: (It.) Grape varieties.

Vay ist mir: (Yid.) Woe is me.

Vendange tardive: (Fr.) Late harvest.

Verkakte: (Yid.) Shitty or messed up.

Vigneron: (Fr.) Winegrower.

Vin de garde: (Fr.) A wine capable of long-term ageing.

Vin de glacière: (Fr.) Wine of the "ice box," not to be confused with *vin de glace* (ice wine)

Vin jaune: (Fr.) Literally, "yellow wine." An unusual, somewhat oxidized wine style typical of the Jura.

Vino da tavola: (It.) Table wine, once a term of opprobrium, but no longer. (It has given progressive winegrowers a path by which to circumvent well-intentioned but stifling Italian wine regulations.)

Viticulteur: (Fr.) Grape grower or viticulturist.

Vitis vinifera: (Lat.) European wine grape species.

Volatile Acidity (VA): A measure of the steam-distillable acids present in wine—primarily acetic acid but also lactic, formic, butyric, and propionic acids, and their conjugate esters. At appropriate levels, a modicum of volatile acidity enlivens a wine; at higher levels, it creates an unpleasant vinegar-like or nail-polish-like aroma.

Weingut: (Ger.) Wine company.

Die Welt als Wille und Vorstellung: (Ger.) *The World as Will and Representation,* Arthur Schopenhauer's dense philosophical tome, propounds the idea that the sole essential reality in the universe is the will, and that all visible phenomena are merely subjective representations of that will.

Zedreht: (Yid.) The terminal state of nervous collapse attained after a sustained period of being thoroughly *fardrait* (mixed up).